CASE CLOSED™

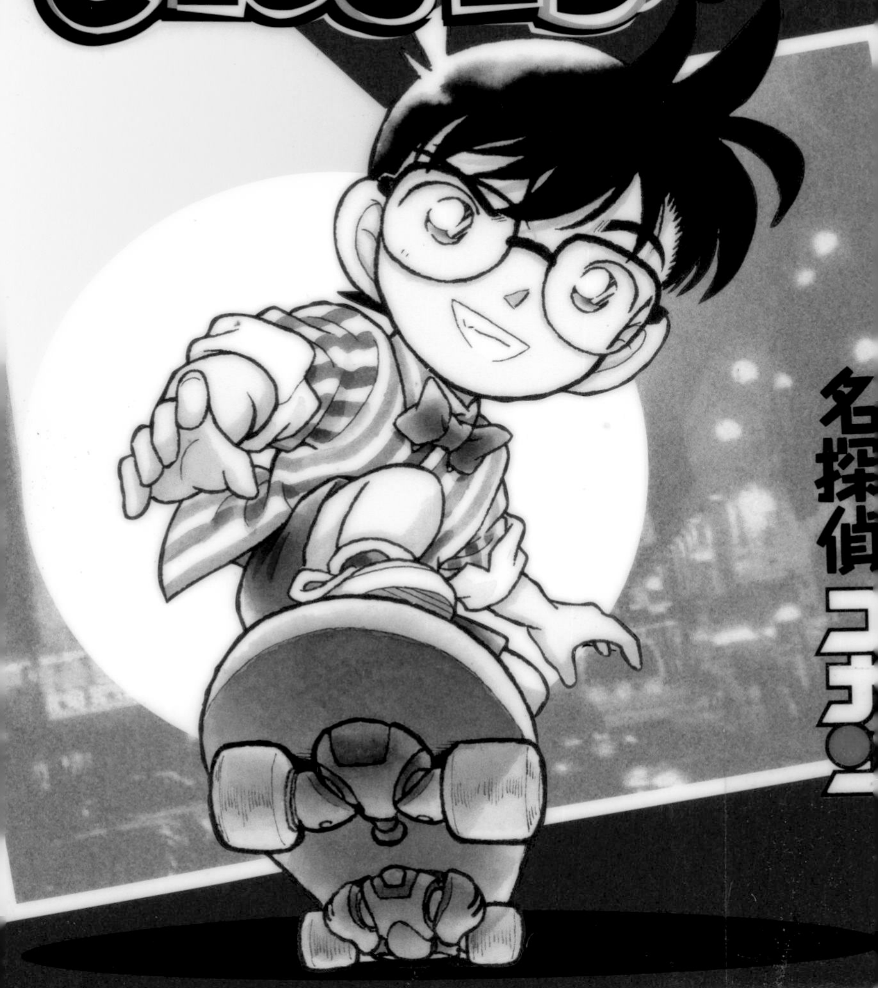

名探偵コナン

Story and art by
Gosho Aoyama

Vol.9

CASE CLOSED™

VOLUME 9

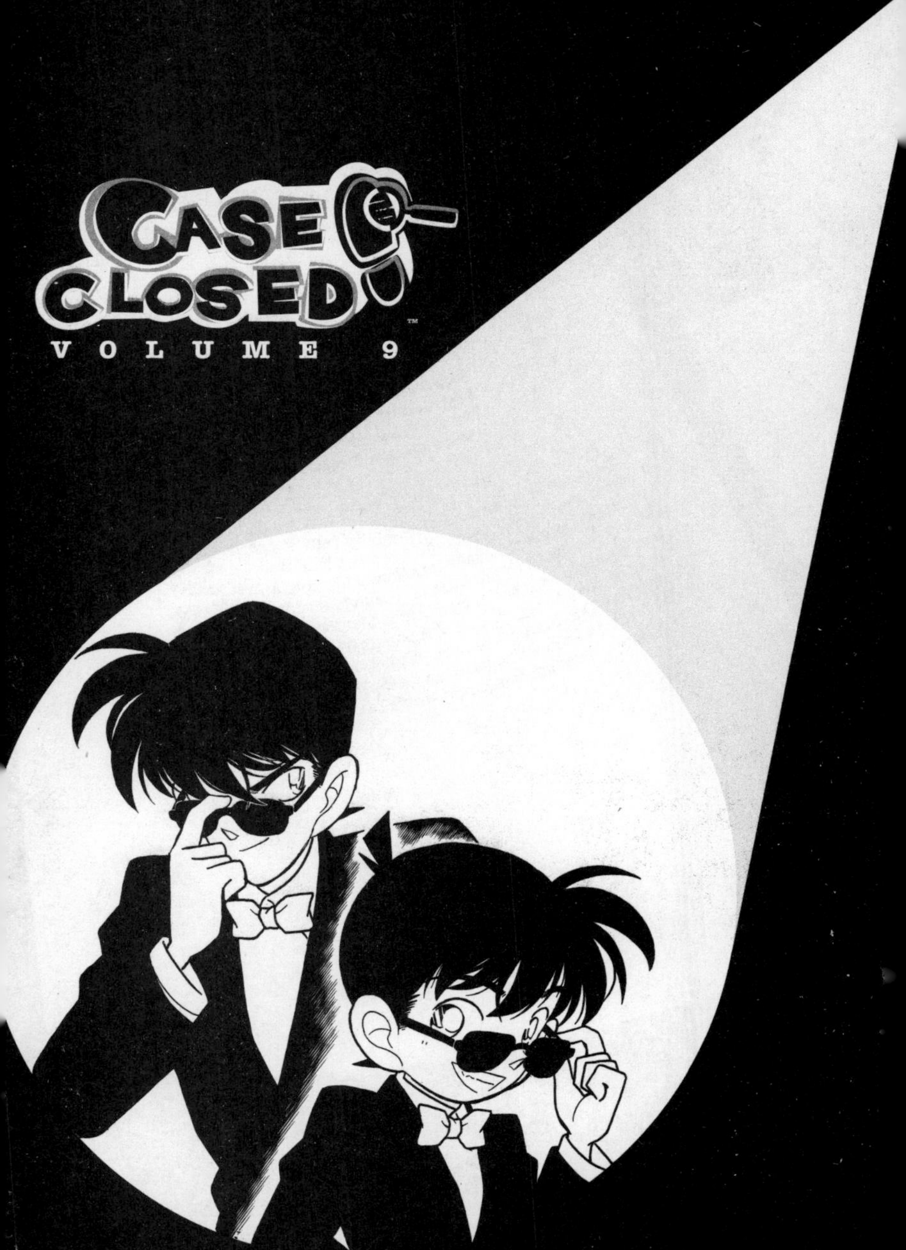

Gosho Aoyama

Case Briefing:

Subject:
Occupation:
Special Skills:
Equipment:

Jimmy Kudo, a.k.a. Conan Edogawa
High School Student/Detective
Analytical thinking and deductive reasoning, Soccer
Bow Tie Voice Transmitter, Super Sneakers,
Homing Glasses, Stretchy Suspenders

The subject is hot on the trail of a pair of suspicious men in black when he is attacked from behind and is administered a strange substance which physically transforms him into a first grader. When the subject confides in the eccentric inventor Dr. Agasa, they decide to keep the subject's true identity a secret for the safety of everyone around him. Assuming the new identity of first-grader Conan Edogawa, the subject continues to assist the police force on their most baffling cases. The only problem is that most crime-solving professionals won't take a little kid's advice!

Table of Contents

CASE CLOSED

Volume 9
Shonen Sunday Edition

Story and Art by GOSHO AOYAMA

MEITANTEI CONAN Vol. 9
by Gosho AOYAMA
© 1994 Gosho AOYAMA
All rights reserved.
Original Japanese edition published by SHOGAKUKAN.
English translation rights in the United States of America, Canada,
the United Kingdom, Ireland, Australia and New Zealand arranged with SHOGAKUKAN.

English Adaptation
Naoko Amemiya

Translation
Joe Yamazaki

Touch-up & Lettering
Walden Wong

Cover & Interior Design
Andrea Rice

Editor
Urian Brown

Printed in the U.S.A.

Published by VIZ Media, LLC
P.O. Box 77010
San Francisco, CA 94107

10 9 8 7 6
First printing, June 2005
Sixth printing, December 2019

FILE 1:
A DANGEROUS GAME OF HIDE AND SEEK

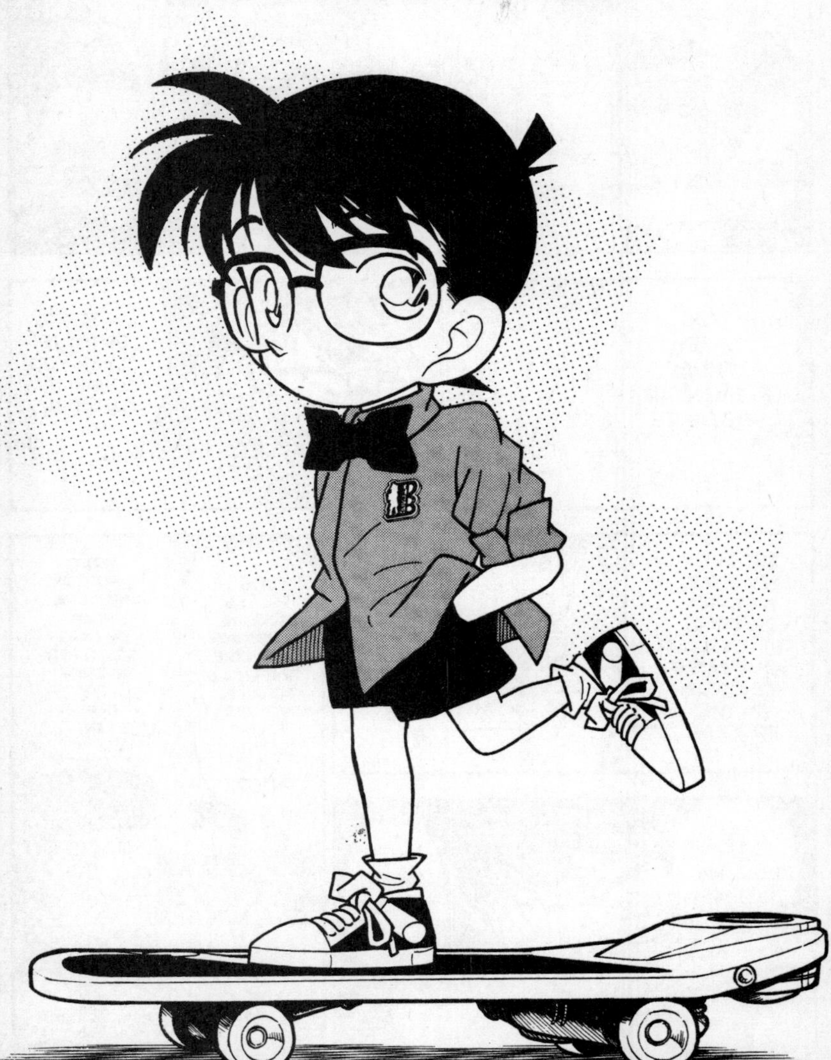

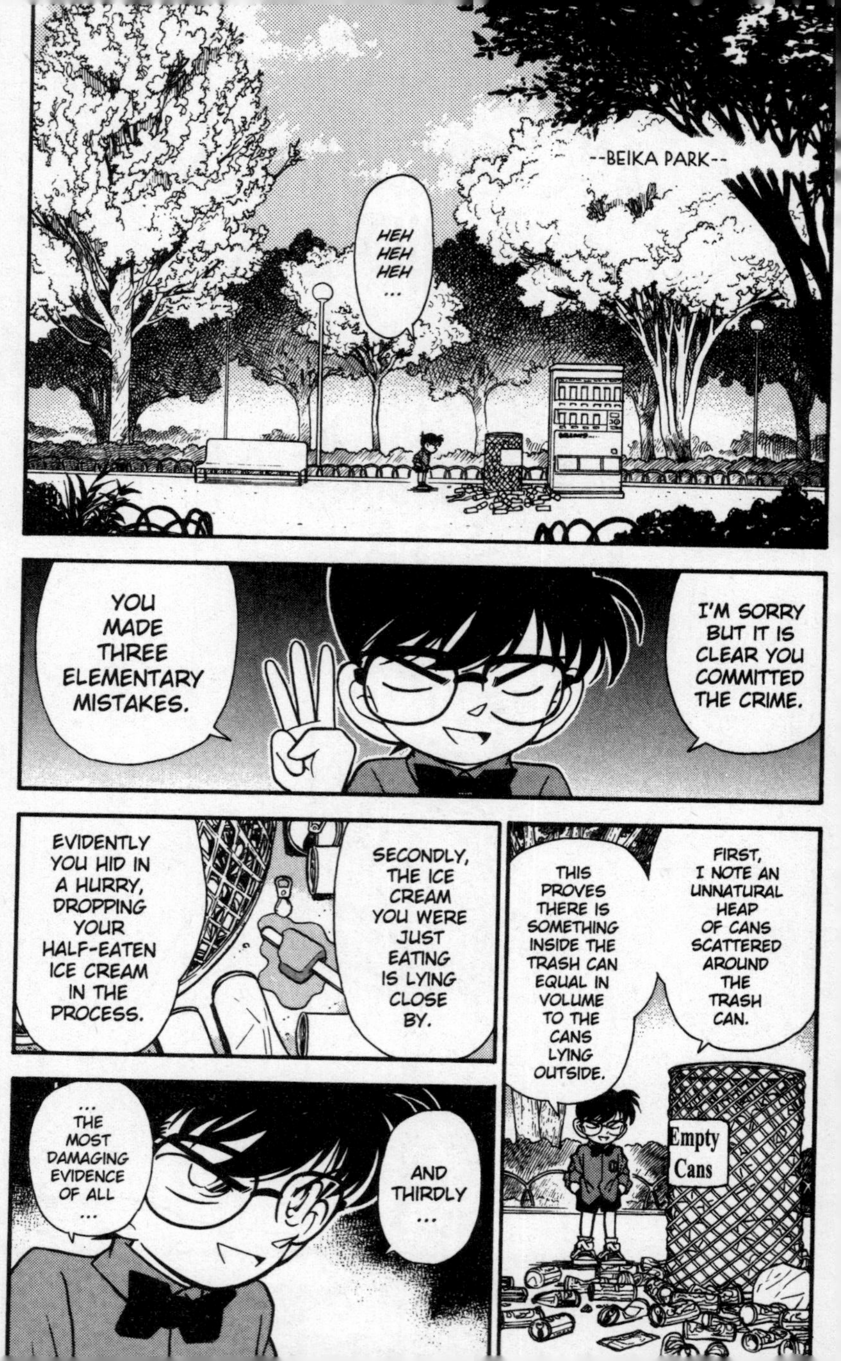
--BEIKA PARK--
HEH HEH HEH ...
I'M SORRY BUT IT IS CLEAR YOU COMMITTED THE CRIME.
YOU MADE THREE ELEMENTARY MISTAKES.
FIRST, I NOTE AN UNNATURAL HEAP OF CANS SCATTERED AROUND THE TRASH CAN.
THIS PROVES THERE IS SOMETHING INSIDE THE TRASH CAN EQUAL IN VOLUME TO THE CANS LYING OUTSIDE.
Empty Cans
SECONDLY, THE ICE CREAM YOU WERE JUST EATING IS LYING CLOSE BY.
EVIDENTLY YOU HID IN A HURRY, DROPPING YOUR HALF-EATEN ICE CREAM IN THE PROCESS.
AND THIRDLY ...
... THE MOST DAMAGING EVIDENCE OF ALL ...

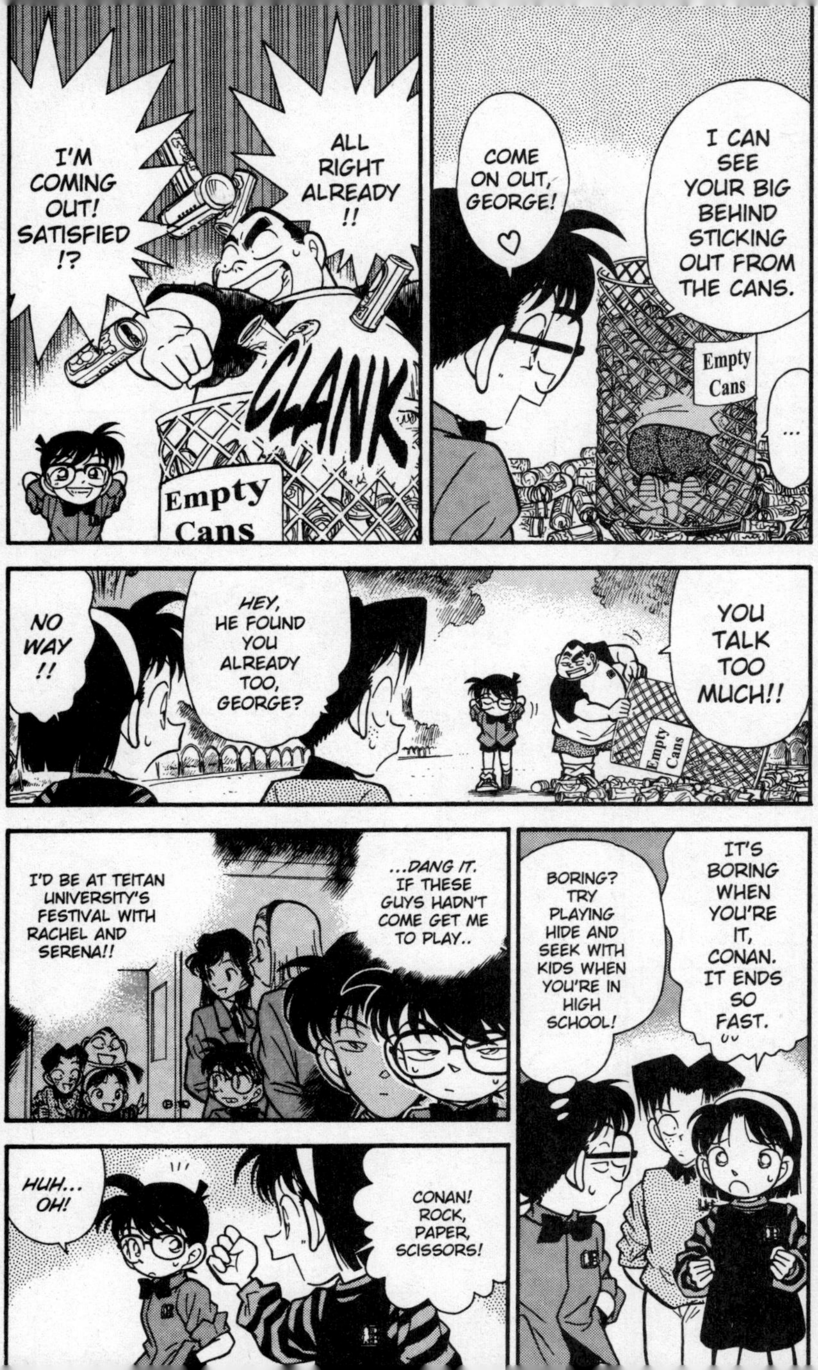
I CAN SEE YOUR BIG BEHIND STICKING OUT FROM THE CANS.
Empty Cans
...
COME ON OUT, GEORGE! ♡
ALL RIGHT ALREADY!!
I'M COMING OUT! SATISFIED!?
CLANK
Empty Cans
YOU TALK TOO MUCH!!
Empty Cans
HEY, HE FOUND YOU ALREADY TOO, GEORGE?
NO WAY!!
IT'S BORING WHEN YOU'RE IT, CONAN. IT ENDS SO FAST.
BORING? TRY PLAYING HIDE AND SEEK WITH KIDS WHEN YOU'RE IN HIGH SCHOOL!
...DANG IT. IF THESE GUYS HADN'T COME GET ME TO PLAY..
I'D BE AT TEITAN UNIVERSITY'S FESTIVAL WITH RACHEL AND SERENA!!
CONAN! ROCK, PAPER, SCISSORS!
HUH... OH!

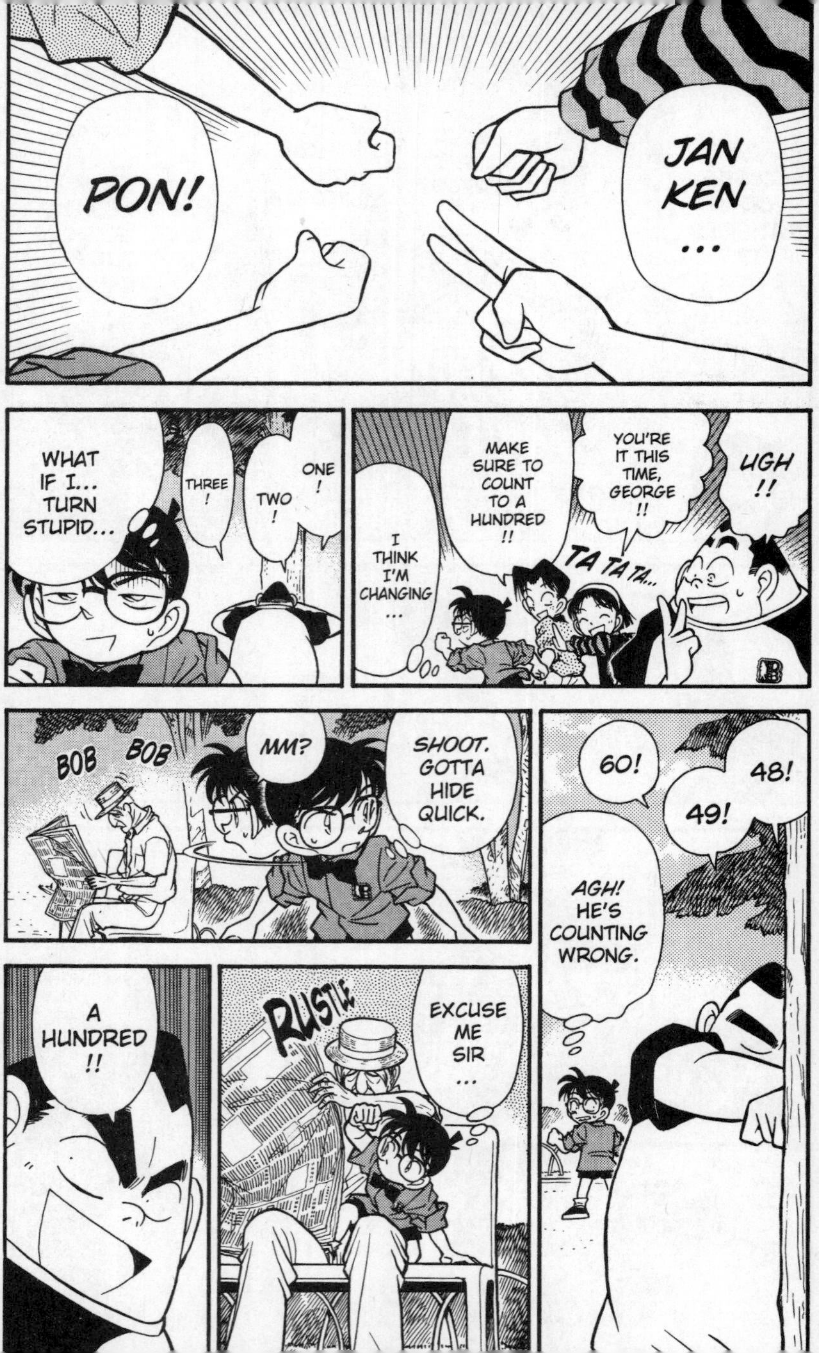
JAN KEN ...
PON!
UGH !!
YOU'RE IT THIS TIME, GEORGE !!
TA TA TA...
MAKE SURE TO COUNT TO A HUNDRED !!
I THINK I'M CHANGING ...
ONE !
TWO !
THREE !
WHAT IF I... TURN STUPID...
48!
49!
60!
AGH! HE'S COUNTING WRONG.
SHOOT. GOTTA HIDE QUICK.
MM?
BOB BOB
EXCUSE ME SIR ...
RUSTLE
A HUNDRED !!

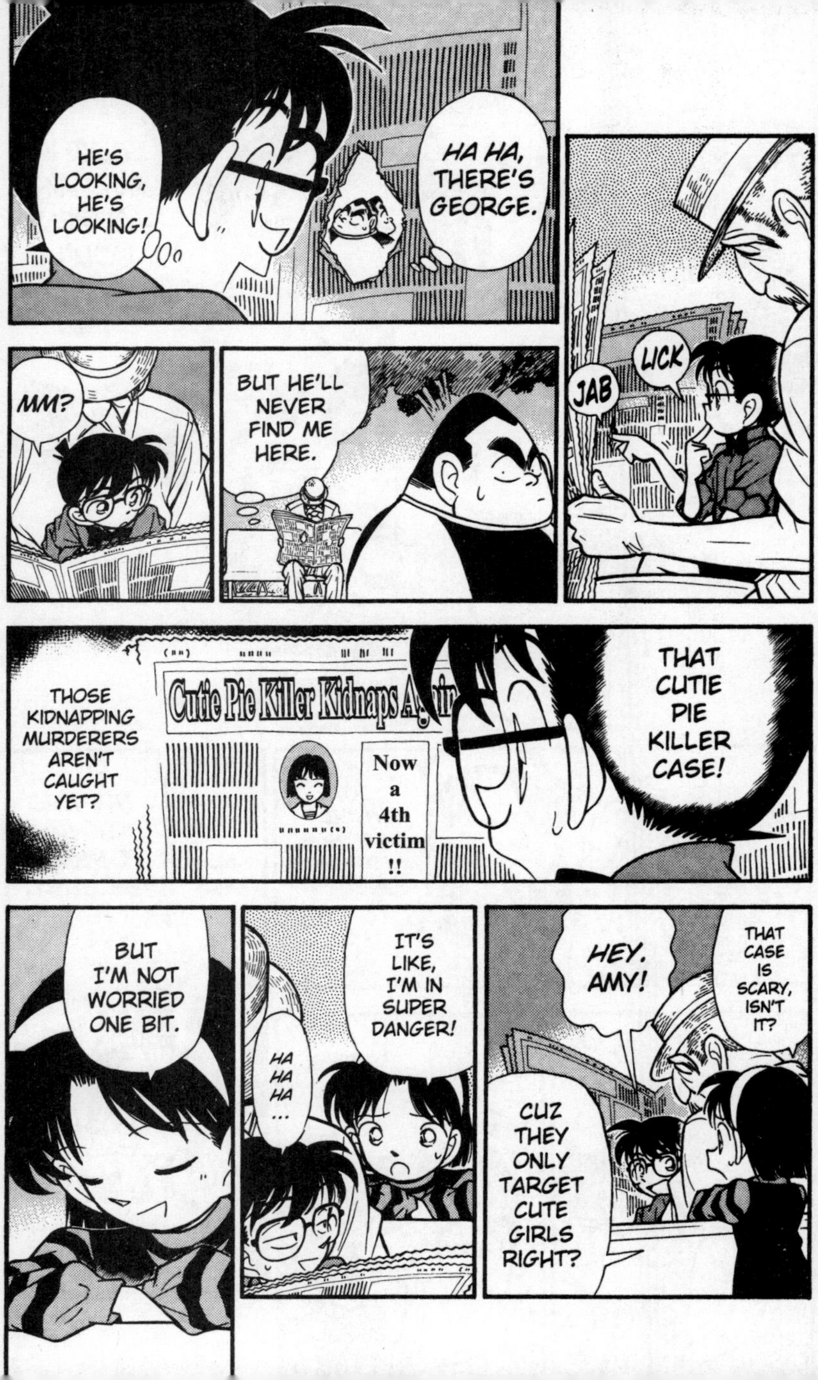
LICK
JAB
HA HA, THERE'S GEORGE.
HE'S LOOKING, HE'S LOOKING!
BUT HE'LL NEVER FIND ME HERE.
MM?
THAT CUTIE PIE KILLER CASE!
Cutie Pie Killer Kidnaps Again
Now a 4th victim !!
THOSE KIDNAPPING MURDERERS AREN'T CAUGHT YET?
THAT CASE IS SCARY, ISN'T IT?
HEY. AMY!
CUZ THEY ONLY TARGET CUTE GIRLS RIGHT?
IT'S LIKE, I'M IN SUPER DANGER!
HA HA HA ...
BUT I'M NOT WORRIED ONE BIT.

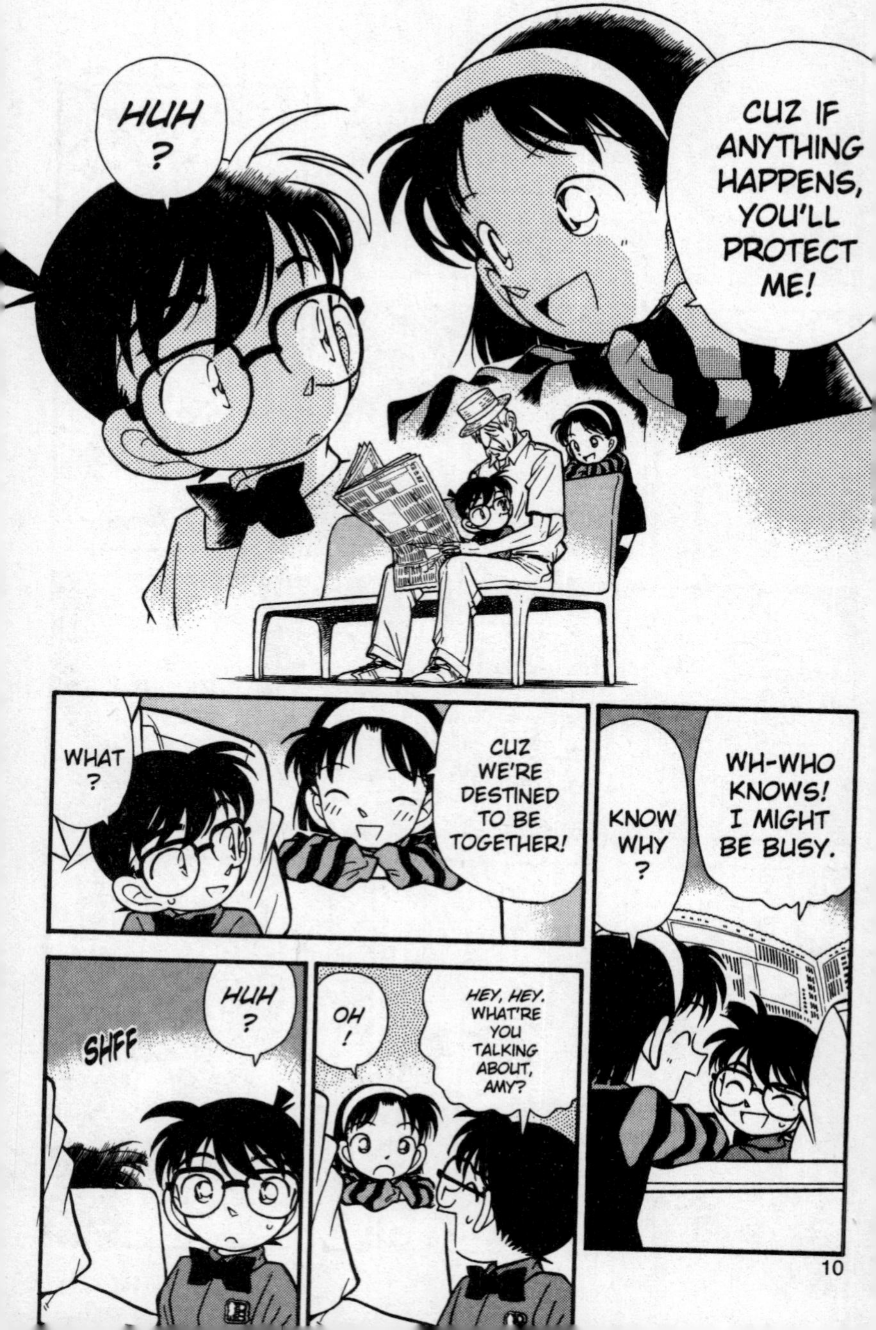
CUZ IF ANYTHING HAPPENS, YOU'LL PROTECT ME!
HUH ?
WH-WHO KNOWS! I MIGHT BE BUSY.
KNOW WHY ?
CUZ WE'RE DESTINED TO BE TOGETHER!
WHAT ?
HEY, HEY. WHAT'RE YOU TALKING ABOUT, AMY?
OH !
HUH ?
SHFF

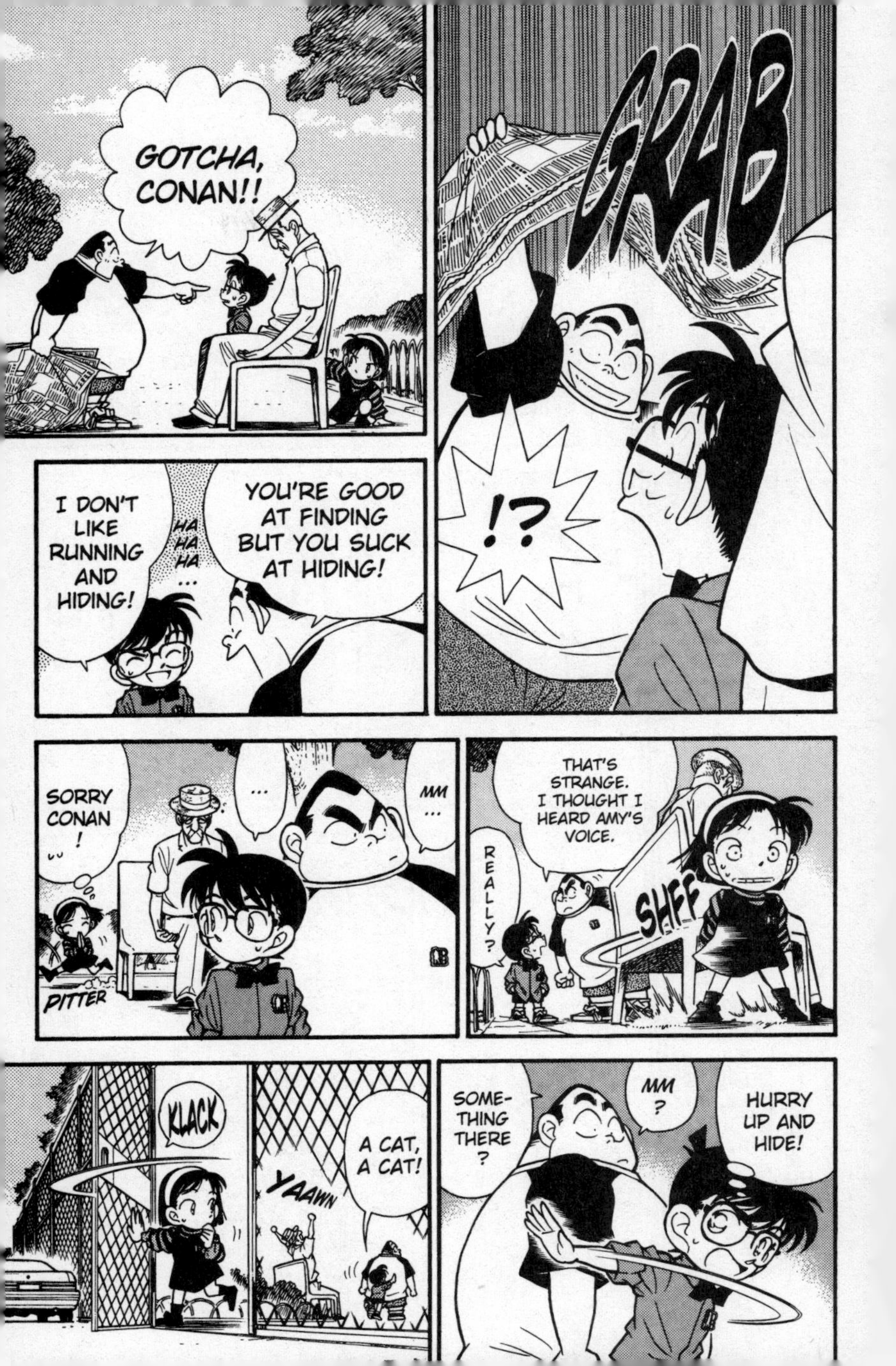
GRAB
!?
GOTCHA, CONAN!!
YOU'RE GOOD AT FINDING BUT YOU SUCK AT HIDING!
HA HA HA ...
I DON'T LIKE RUNNING AND HIDING!
THAT'S STRANGE. I THOUGHT I HEARD AMY'S VOICE.
REALLY?
SHFF
MM ...
...
SORRY CONAN!
PITTER
HURRY UP AND HIDE!
MM ?
SOME-THING THERE ?
A CAT, A CAT!
YAAWN
KLACK

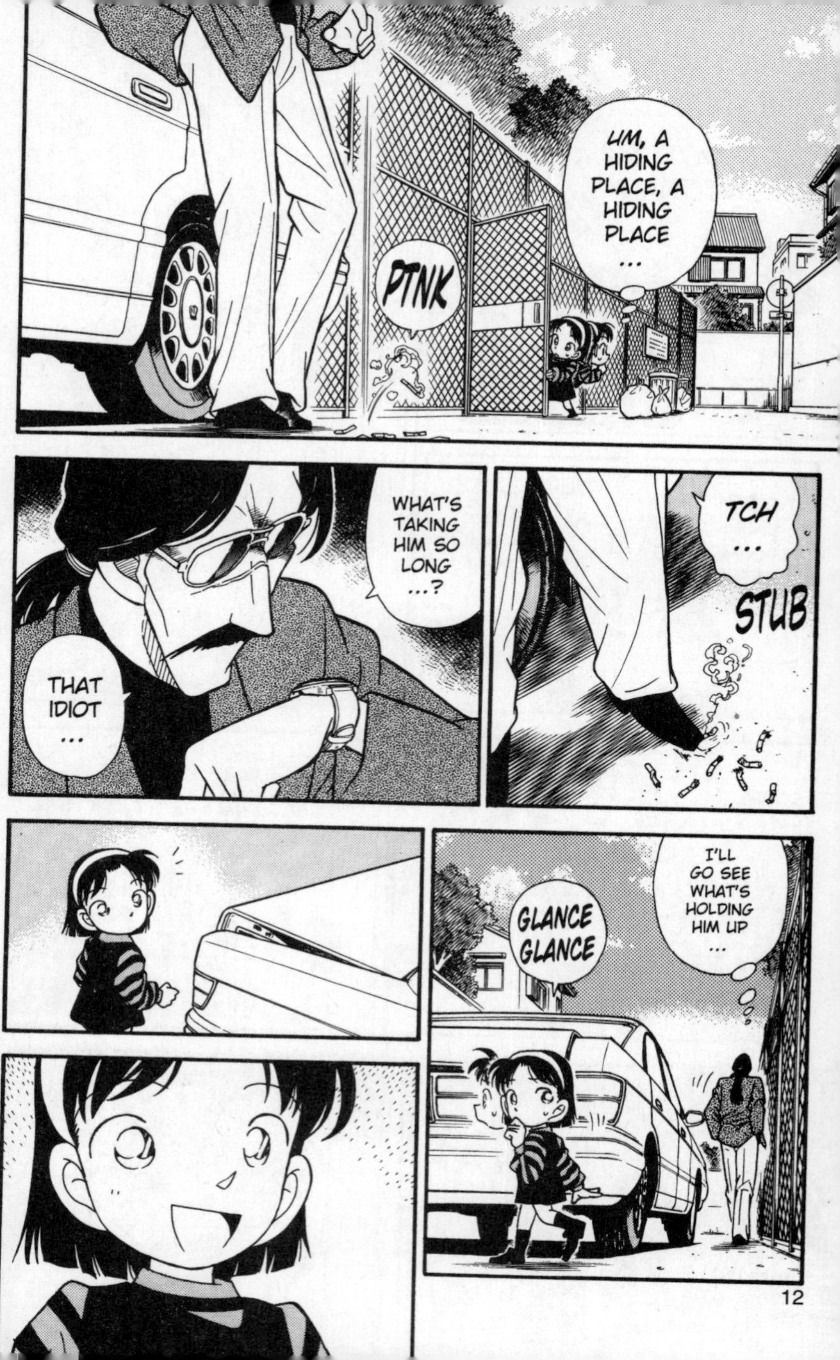
UM, A HIDING PLACE, A HIDING PLACE ...
PTNK
TCH ...
STUB
WHAT'S TAKING HIM SO LONG ...?
THAT IDIOT ...
I'LL GO SEE WHAT'S HOLDING HIM UP ...
GLANCE GLANCE

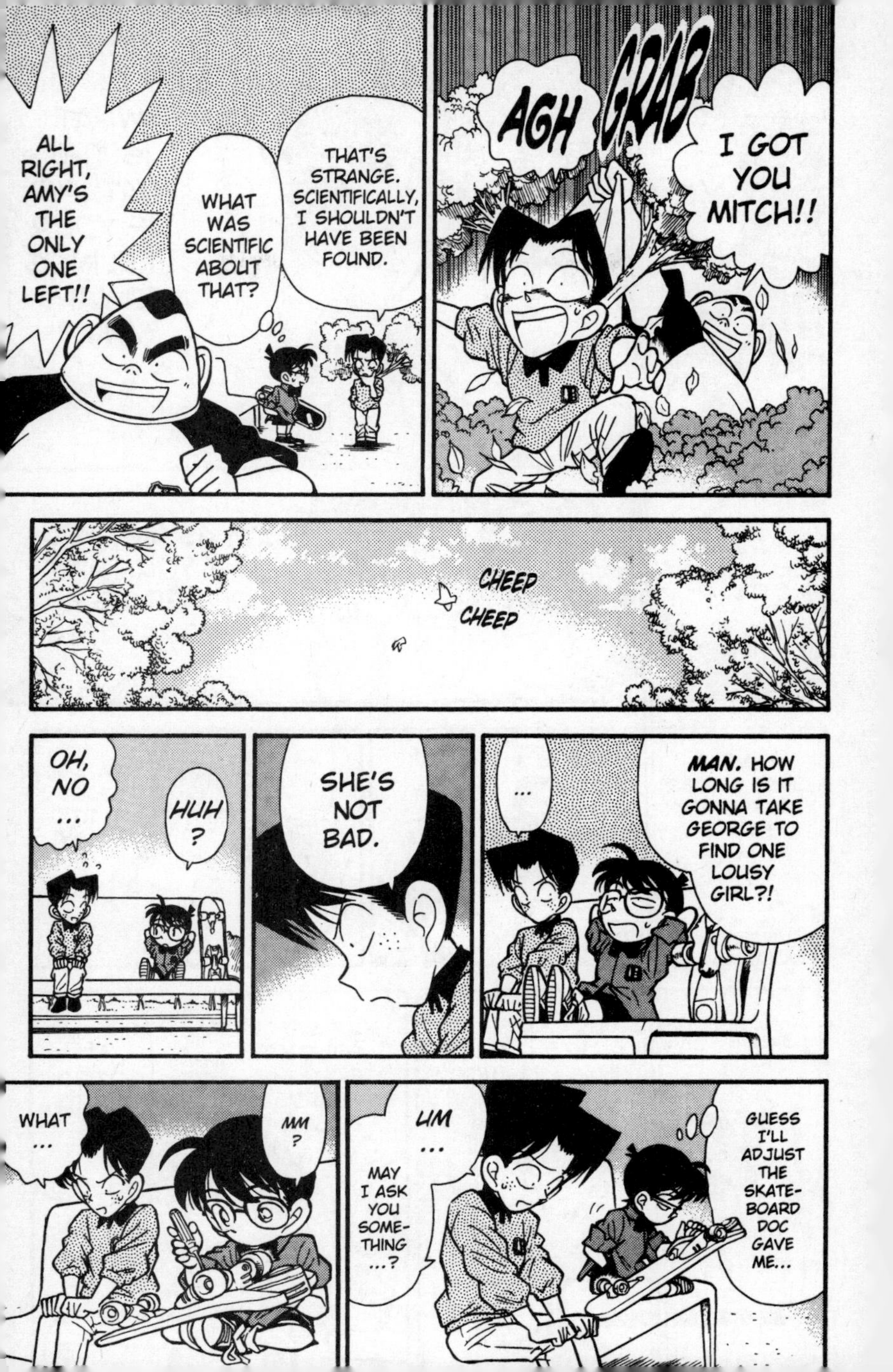
AGH
GRAB
I GOT YOU MITCH!!
THAT'S STRANGE. SCIENTIFICALLY, I SHOULDN'T HAVE BEEN FOUND.
WHAT WAS SCIENTIFIC ABOUT THAT?
ALL RIGHT, AMY'S THE ONLY ONE LEFT!!
CHEEP
CHEEP
MAN. HOW LONG IS IT GONNA TAKE GEORGE TO FIND ONE LOUSY GIRL?!
...
SHE'S NOT BAD.
HUH?
OH, NO ...
GUESS I'LL ADJUST THE SKATE-BOARD DOC GAVE ME...
UM ...
MAY I ASK YOU SOME-THING ...?
MM?
WHAT ...

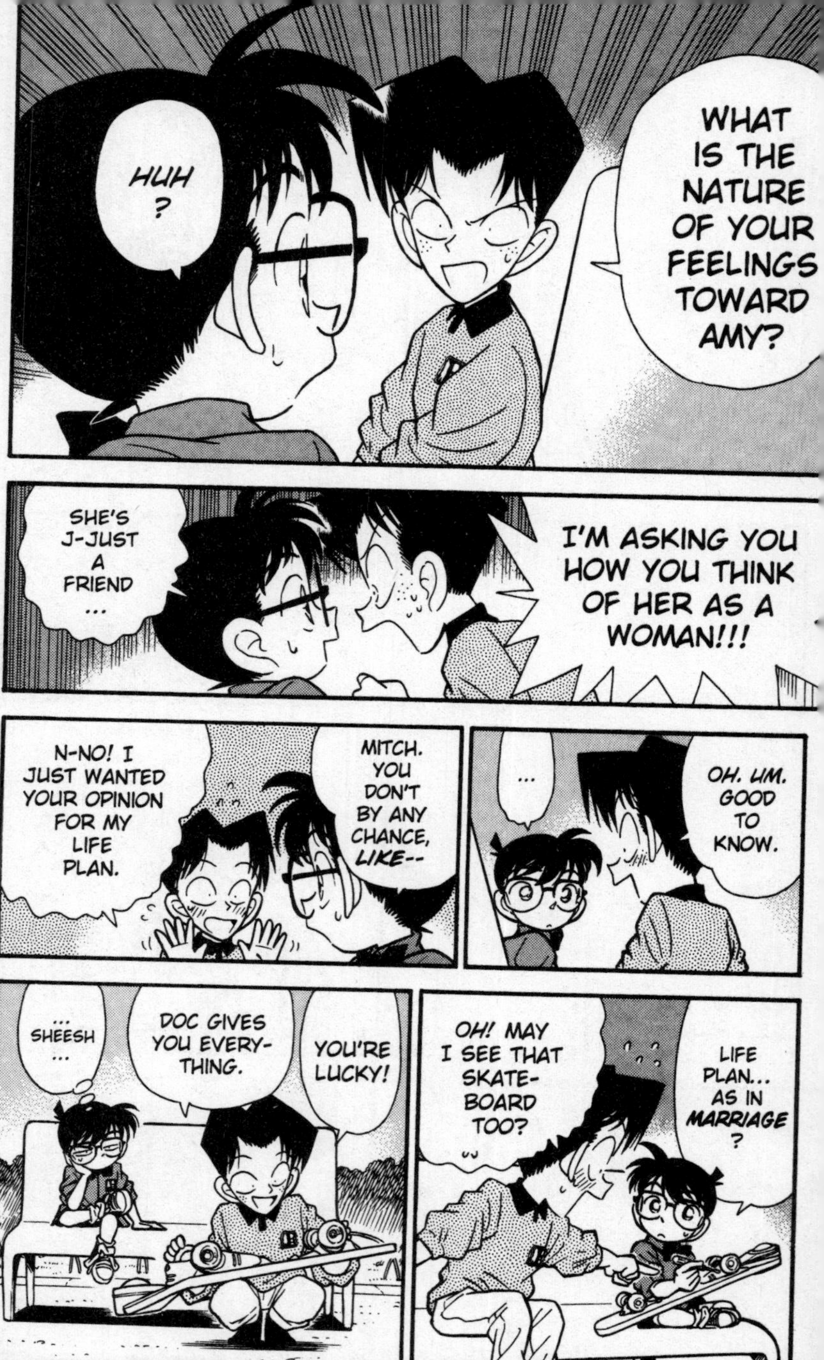
WHAT IS THE NATURE OF YOUR FEELINGS TOWARD AMY?
HUH?
I'M ASKING YOU HOW YOU THINK OF HER AS A WOMAN!!!
SHE'S J-JUST A FRIEND...
OH. UM. GOOD TO KNOW.
...
MITCH. YOU DON'T BY ANY CHANCE, *LIKE*--
N-NO! I JUST WANTED YOUR OPINION FOR MY LIFE PLAN.
LIFE PLAN... AS IN *MARRIAGE*?
OH! MAY I SEE THAT SKATE-BOARD TOO?
YOU'RE LUCKY!
DOC GIVES YOU EVERY-THING.
... SHEESH ...

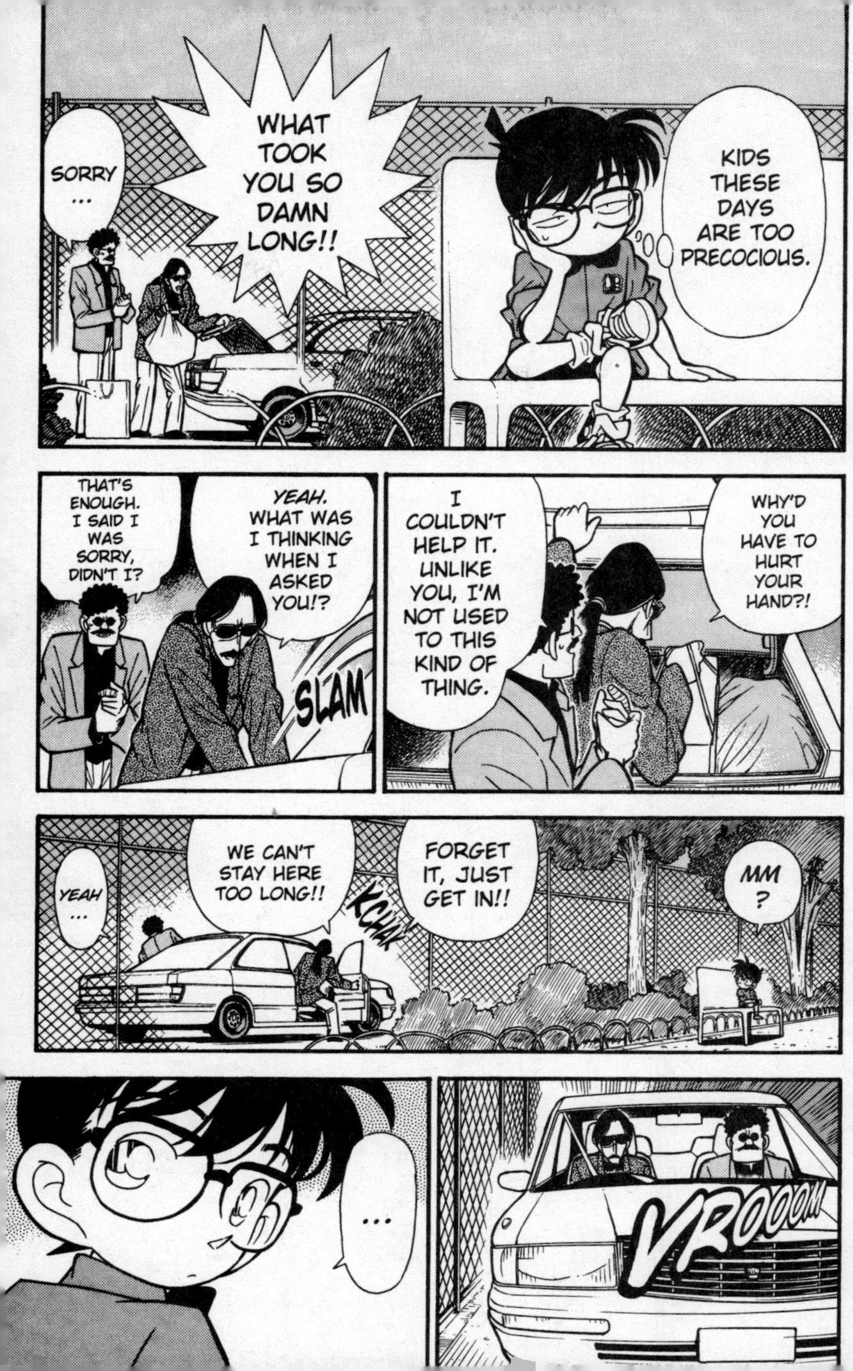

KIDS THESE DAYS ARE TOO PRECOCIOUS.
WHAT TOOK YOU SO DAMN LONG!!
SORRY ...
WHY'D YOU HAVE TO HURT YOUR HAND?!
I COULDN'T HELP IT. UNLIKE YOU, I'M NOT USED TO THIS KIND OF THING.
YEAH. WHAT WAS I THINKING WHEN I ASKED YOU!?
SLAM
THAT'S ENOUGH. I SAID I WAS SORRY, DIDN'T I?
MM ?
FORGET IT, JUST GET IN!!
KCHAK
WE CAN'T STAY HERE TOO LONG!!
YEAH ...
VROOOM
...

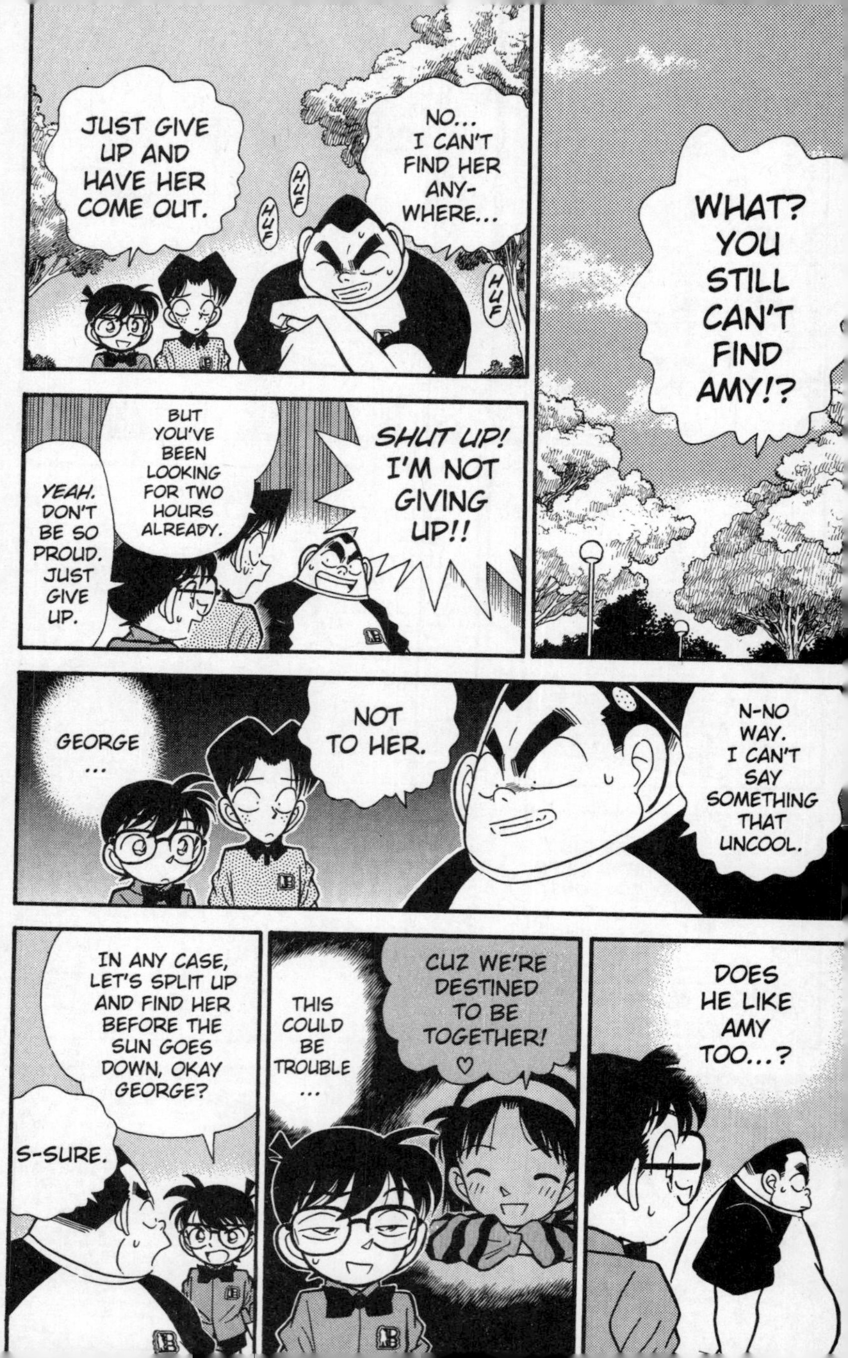
WHAT? YOU STILL CAN'T FIND AMY!?
NO... I CAN'T FIND HER ANY-WHERE...
HUF HUF HUF
JUST GIVE UP AND HAVE HER COME OUT.
SHUT UP! I'M NOT GIVING UP!!
BUT YOU'VE BEEN LOOKING FOR TWO HOURS ALREADY.
YEAH. DON'T BE SO PROUD. JUST GIVE UP.
N-NO WAY. I CAN'T SAY SOMETHING THAT UNCOOL.
NOT TO HER.
GEORGE ...
DOES HE LIKE AMY TOO...?
CUZ WE'RE DESTINED TO BE TOGETHER! ♡
THIS COULD BE TROUBLE ...
IN ANY CASE, LET'S SPLIT UP AND FIND HER BEFORE THE SUN GOES DOWN, OKAY GEORGE?
S-SURE.

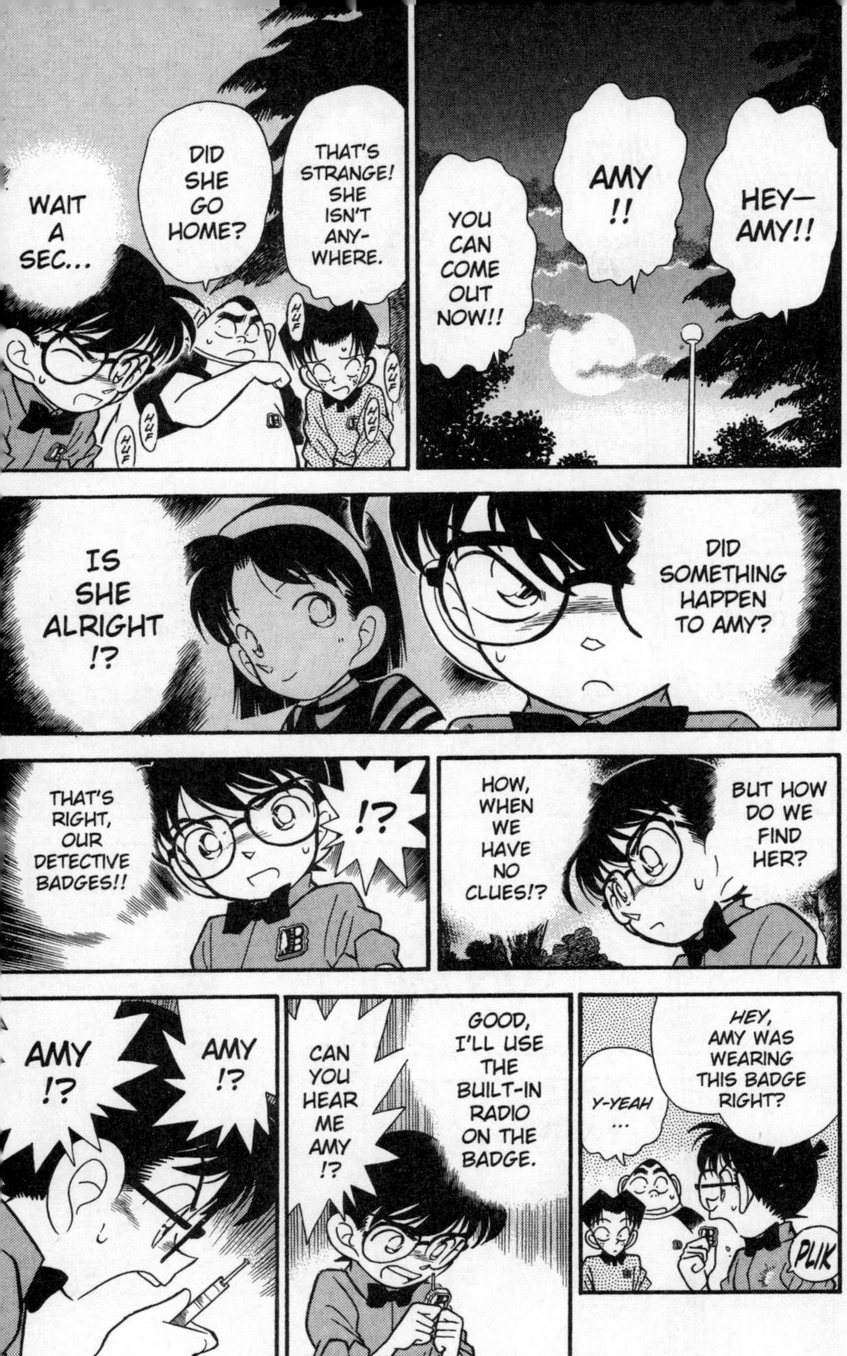
HEY— AMY!!
AMY !!
YOU CAN COME OUT NOW!!
THAT'S STRANGE! SHE ISN'T ANY-WHERE.
DID SHE GO HOME?
WAIT A SEC...
HUF
HUF
HUF
HUF
HUF
DID SOMETHING HAPPEN TO AMY?
IS SHE ALRIGHT !?
BUT HOW DO WE FIND HER?
HOW, WHEN WE HAVE NO CLUES!?
!?
THAT'S RIGHT, OUR DETECTIVE BADGES!!
HEY, AMY WAS WEARING THIS BADGE RIGHT?
Y-YEAH ...
PLIK
GOOD, I'LL USE THE BUILT-IN RADIO ON THE BADGE.
CAN YOU HEAR ME AMY !?
AMY !?
AMY !?

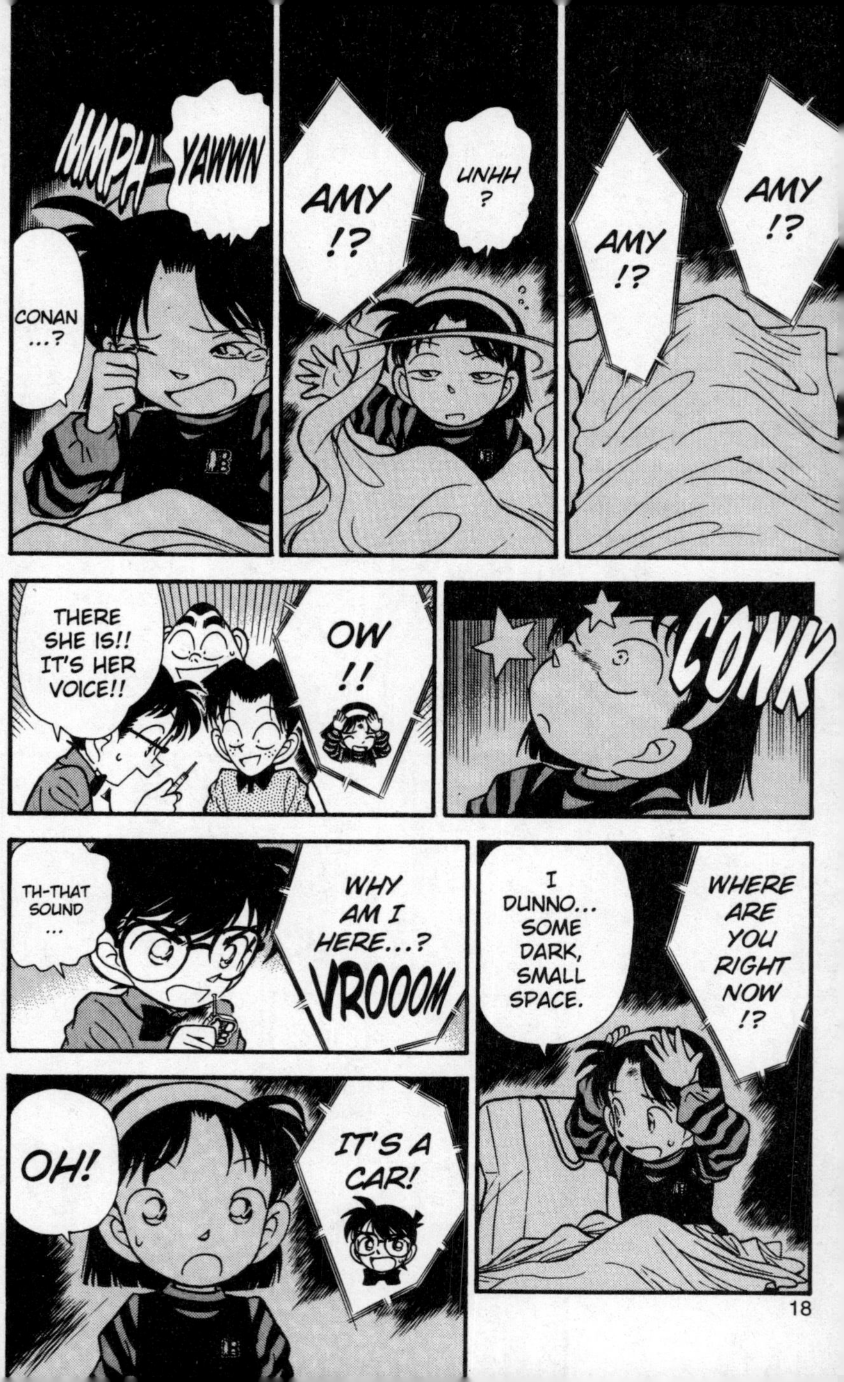
AMY !?
AMY !?
AMY !?
UNHH ?
MMPH—YAWWN
CONAN ...?
CONK
OW !!
THERE SHE IS!! IT'S HER VOICE!!
WHERE ARE YOU RIGHT NOW !?
I DUNNO... SOME DARK, SMALL SPACE.
WHY AM I HERE...?
VROOOM
TH-THAT SOUND ...
IT'S A CAR!
OH!

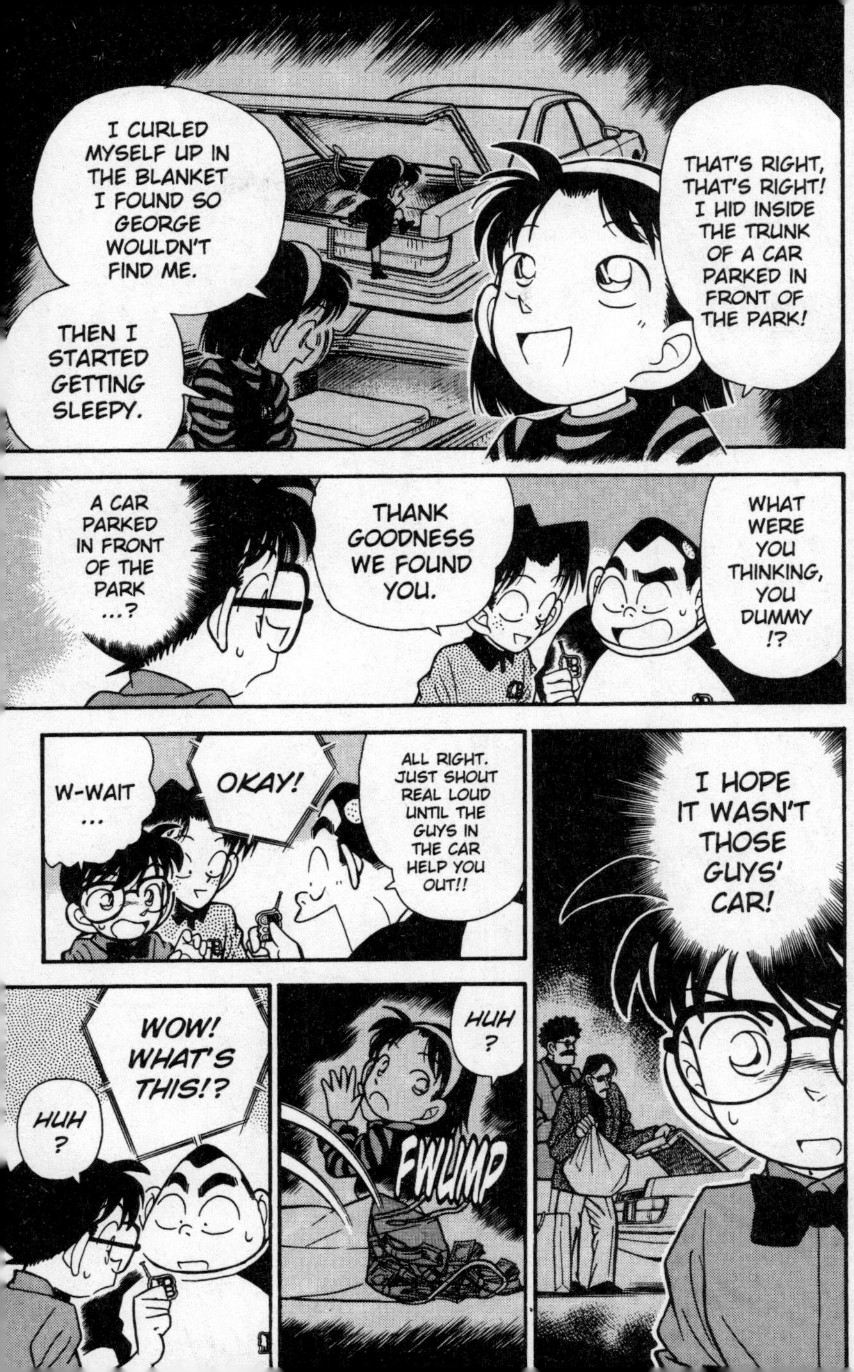
THAT'S RIGHT, THAT'S RIGHT! I HID INSIDE THE TRUNK OF A CAR PARKED IN FRONT OF THE PARK!
I CURLED MYSELF UP IN THE BLANKET I FOUND SO GEORGE WOULDN'T FIND ME.
THEN I STARTED GETTING SLEEPY.
WHAT WERE YOU THINKING, YOU DUMMY!?
THANK GOODNESS WE FOUND YOU.
A CAR PARKED IN FRONT OF THE PARK...?
I HOPE IT WASN'T THOSE GUYS' CAR!
ALL RIGHT. JUST SHOUT REAL LOUD UNTIL THE GUYS IN THE CAR HELP YOU OUT!!
OKAY!
W-WAIT...
HUH?
FWUMP
WOW! WHAT'S THIS!?
HUH?

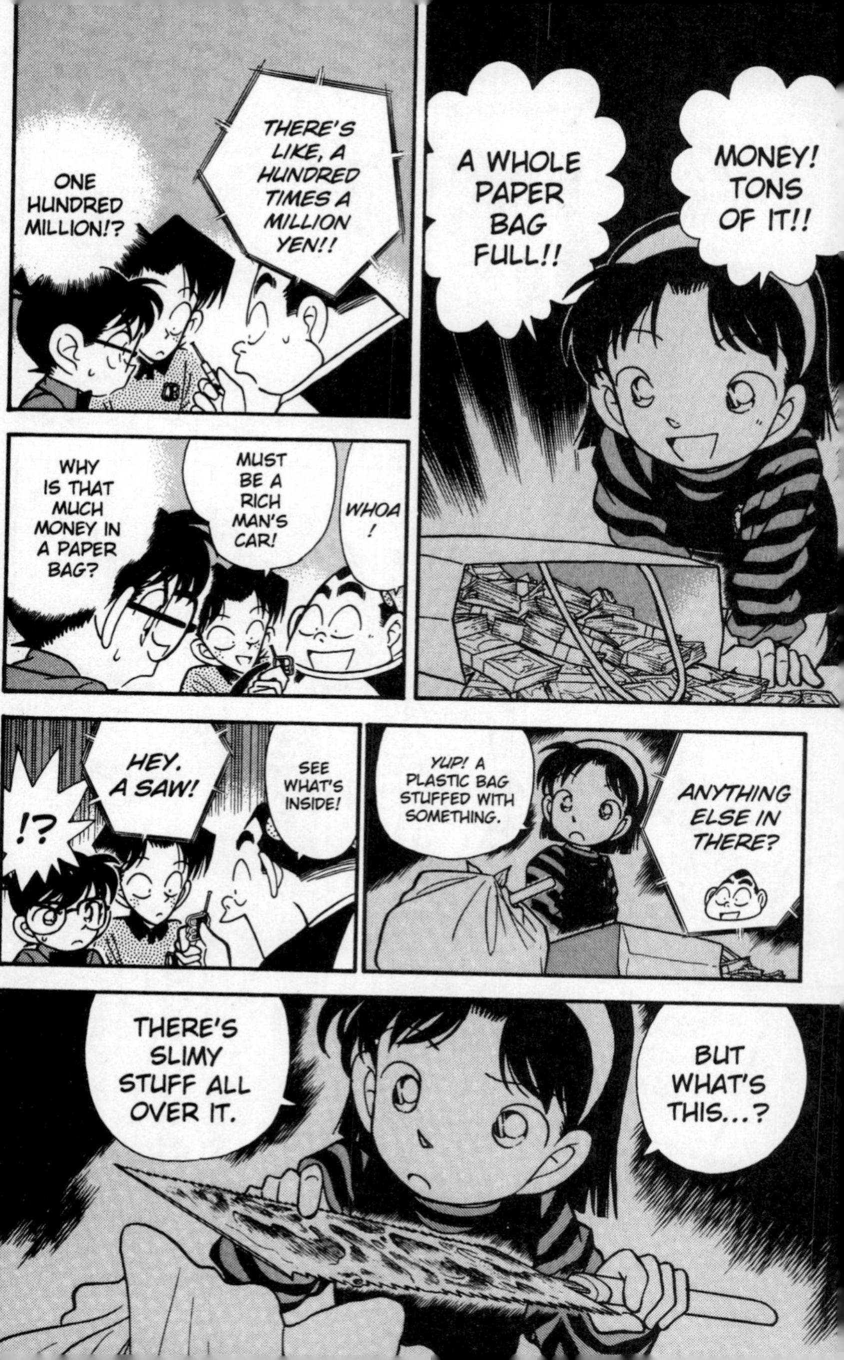
MONEY! TONS OF IT!!
A WHOLE PAPER BAG FULL!!
THERE'S LIKE, A HUNDRED TIMES A MILLION YEN!!
ONE HUNDRED MILLION!?
WHOA!
MUST BE A RICH MAN'S CAR!
WHY IS THAT MUCH MONEY IN A PAPER BAG?
ANYTHING ELSE IN THERE?
YUP! A PLASTIC BAG STUFFED WITH SOMETHING.
SEE WHAT'S INSIDE!
HEY. A SAW!
!?
BUT WHAT'S THIS...?
THERE'S SLIMY STUFF ALL OVER IT.

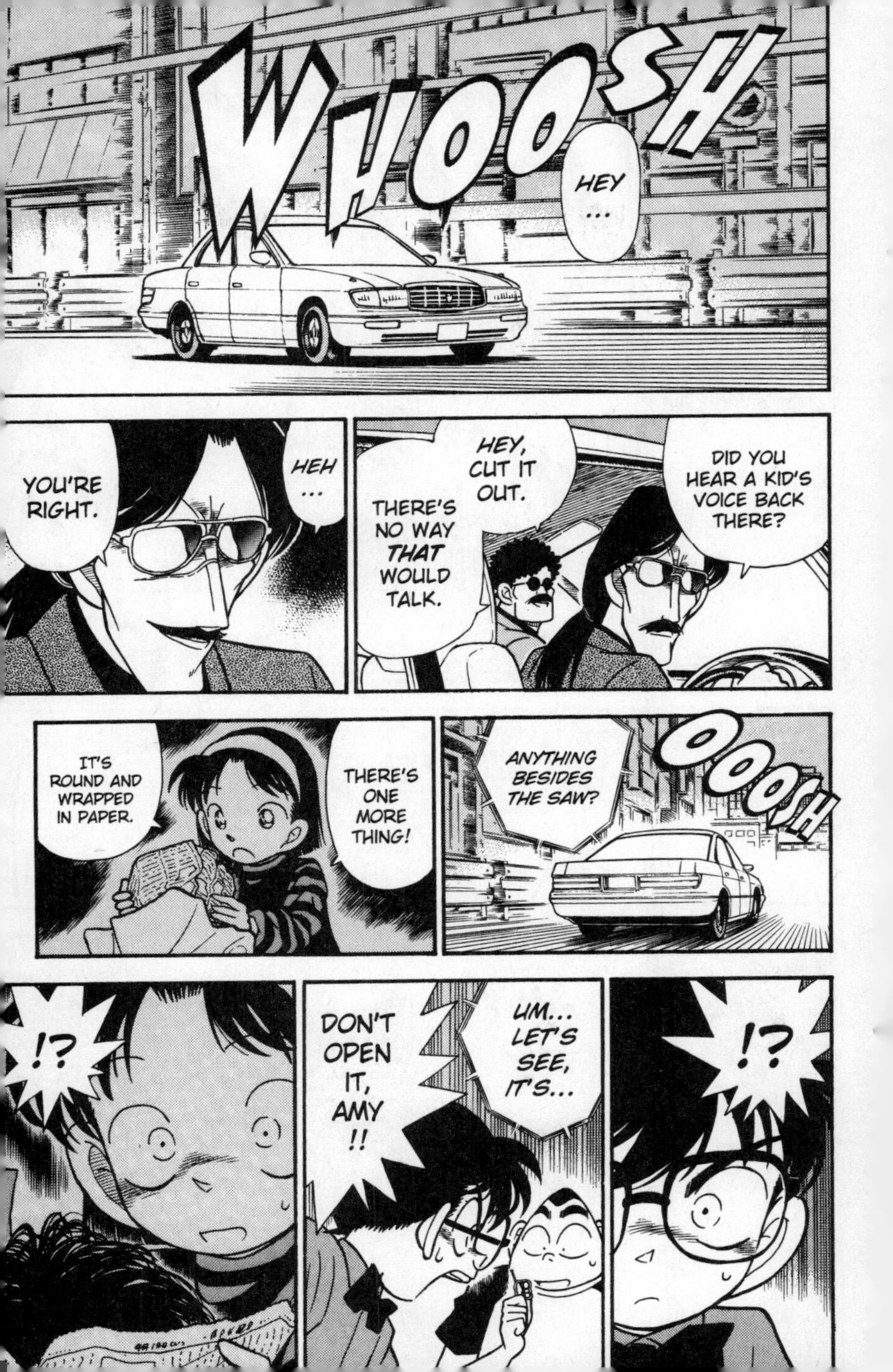
WHOOSH
HEY ...
DID YOU HEAR A KID'S VOICE BACK THERE?
HEY, CUT IT OUT.
THERE'S NO WAY THAT WOULD TALK.
HEH ...
YOU'RE RIGHT.
OOOSH
ANYTHING BESIDES THE SAW?
THERE'S ONE MORE THING!
IT'S ROUND AND WRAPPED IN PAPER.
!?
UM... LET'S SEE, IT'S...
DON'T OPEN IT, AMY !!
!?

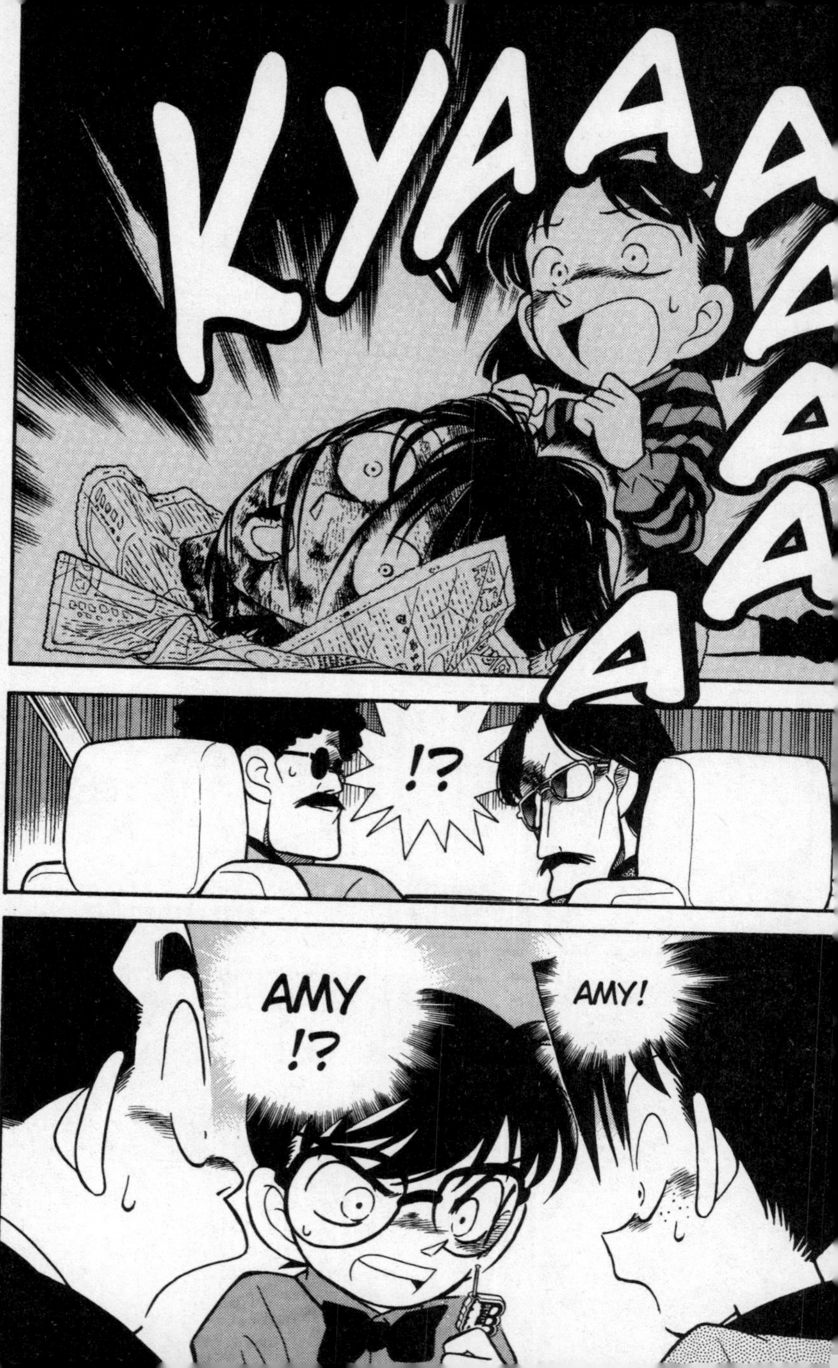
KYAAAAAAA
!?
AMY!
AMY !?

FILE 2: FOLLOW THAT VOICE!!

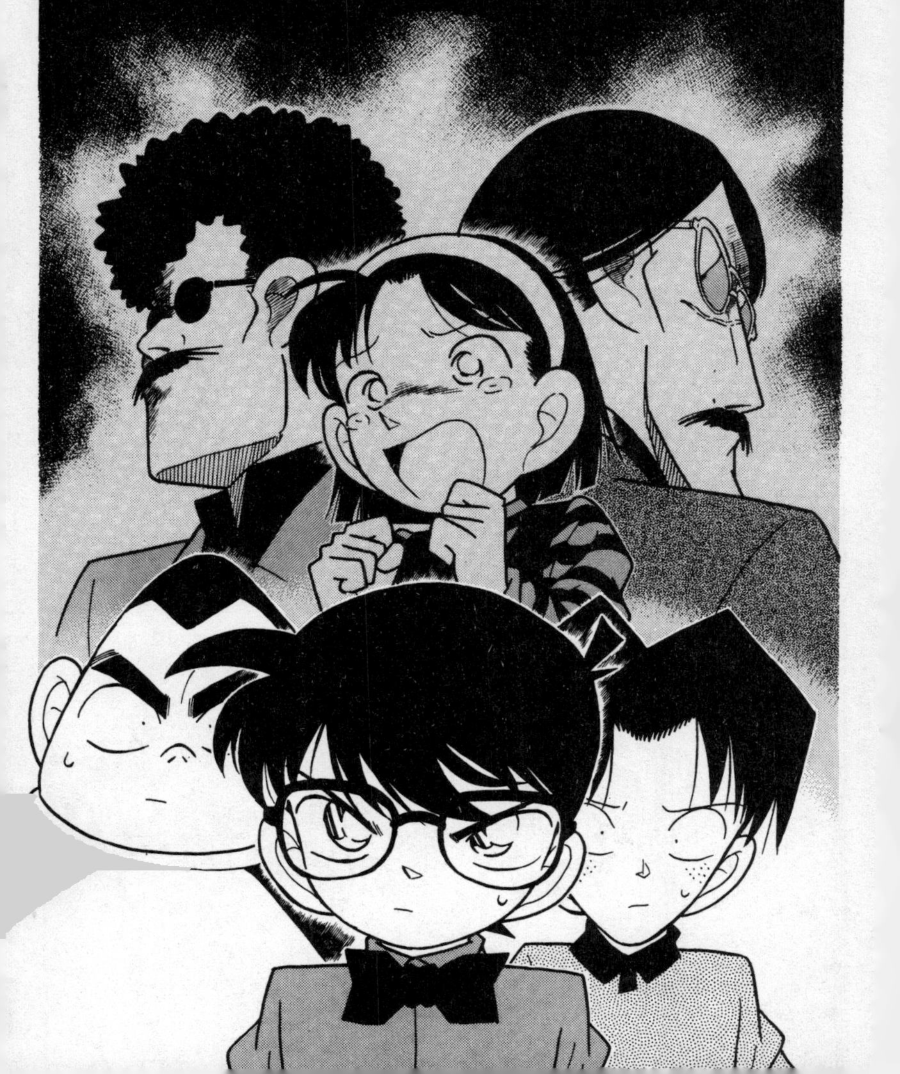

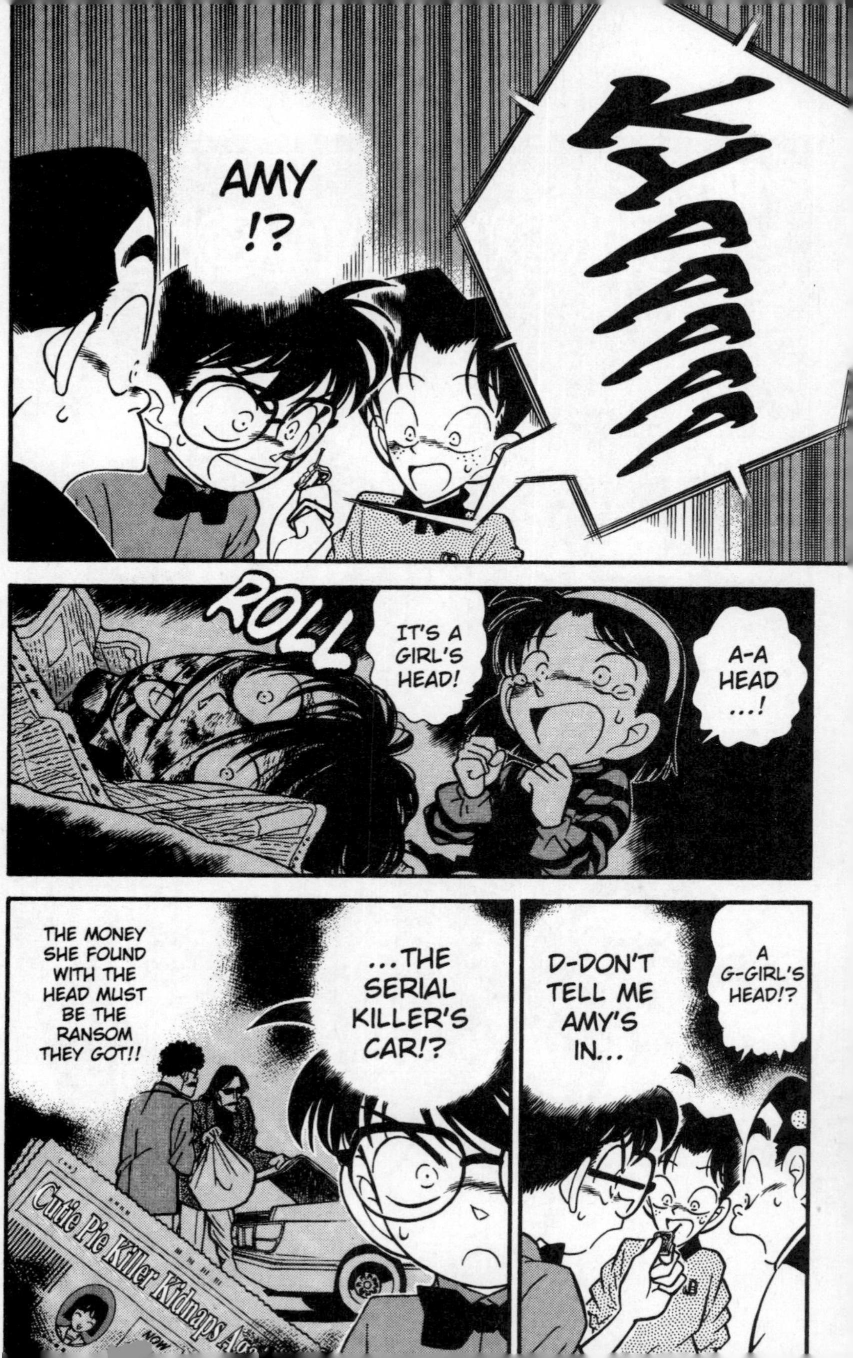
KYAAAAAA
AMY !?
A-A HEAD ...!
IT'S A GIRL'S HEAD!
ROLL
A G-GIRL'S HEAD!?
D-DON'T TELL ME AMY'S IN...
...THE SERIAL KILLER'S CAR!?
THE MONEY SHE FOUND WITH THE HEAD MUST BE THE RANSOM THEY GOT!!
Cutie Pie Killer Kidnaps
NOW

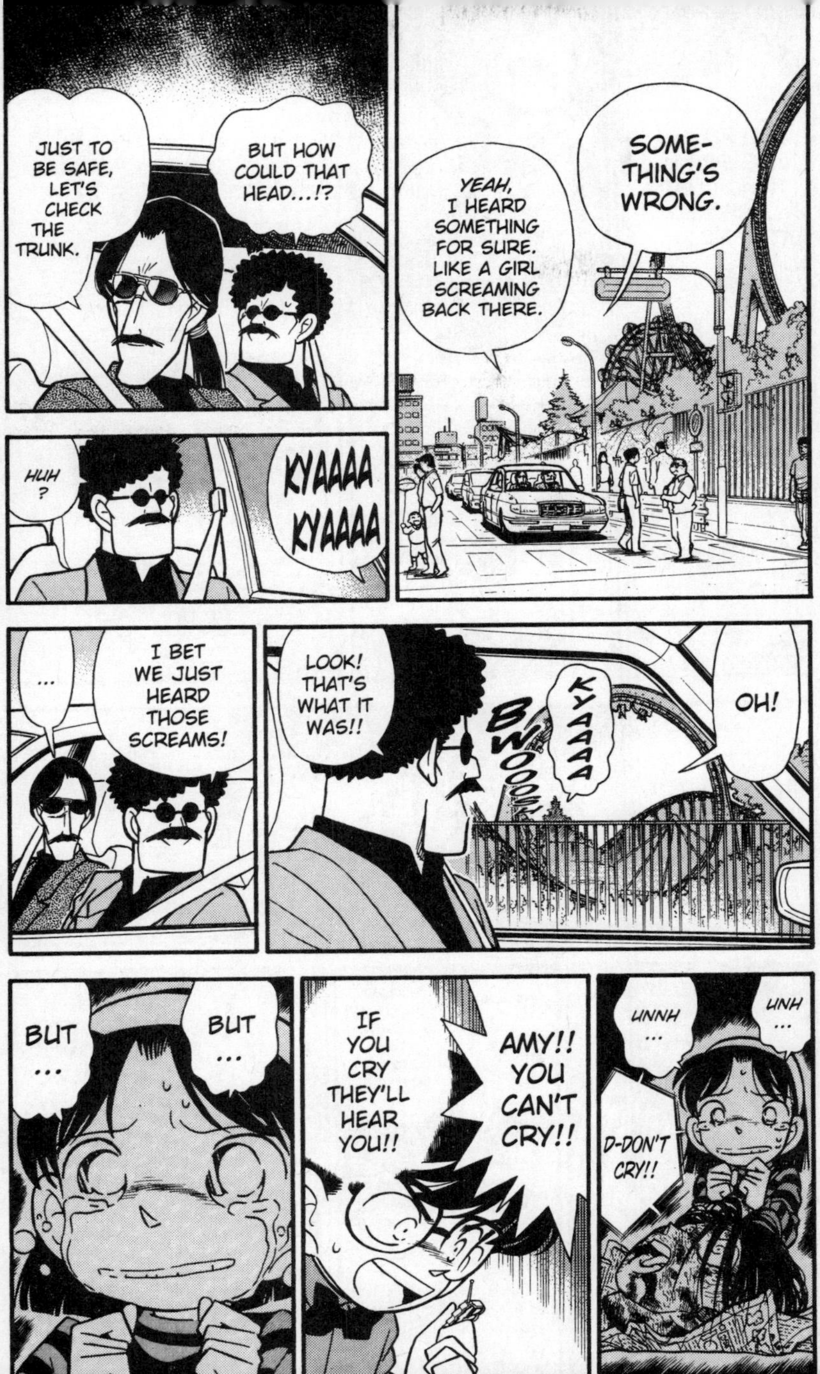
SOME-THING'S WRONG.
YEAH, I HEARD SOMETHING FOR SURE. LIKE A GIRL SCREAMING BACK THERE.
BUT HOW COULD THAT HEAD...!?
JUST TO BE SAFE, LET'S CHECK THE TRUNK.
KYAAAA KYAAAA
HUH?
OH!
KYAAAA
BWOOOSH
LOOK! THAT'S WHAT IT WAS!!
I BET WE JUST HEARD THOSE SCREAMS!
...
UNH ...
UNNH ...
D-DON'T CRY!!
AMY!! YOU CAN'T CRY!!
IF YOU CRY THEY'LL HEAR YOU!!
BUT ...
BUT ...

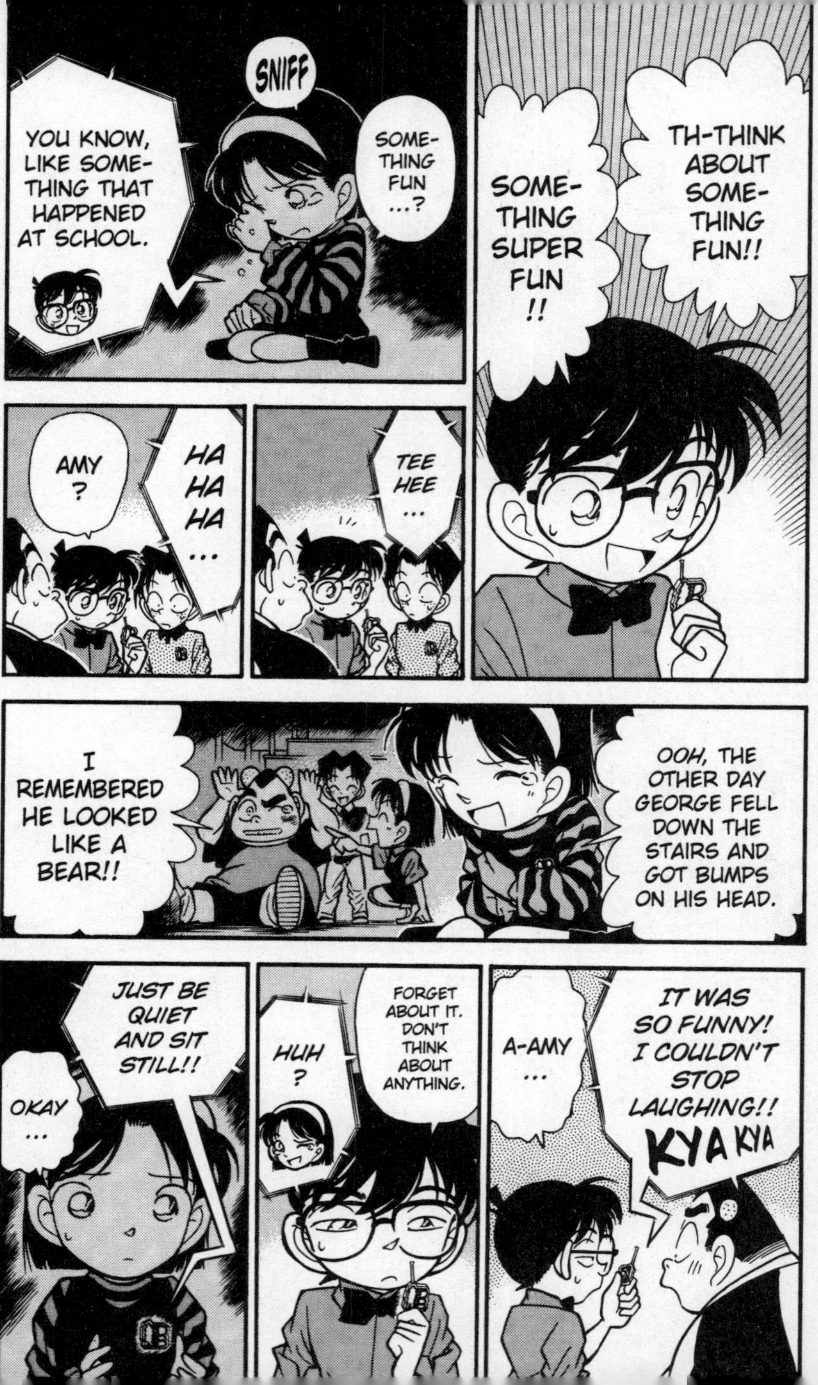
TH-THINK ABOUT SOME-THING FUN!!
SOME-THING SUPER FUN !!
SNIFF
SOME-THING FUN ...?
YOU KNOW, LIKE SOME-THING THAT HAPPENED AT SCHOOL.
TEE HEE ...
HA HA HA ...
AMY ?
OOH, THE OTHER DAY GEORGE FELL DOWN THE STAIRS AND GOT BUMPS ON HIS HEAD.
I REMEMBERED HE LOOKED LIKE A BEAR!!
IT WAS SO FUNNY! I COULDN'T STOP LAUGHING!!
KYA KYA
A-AMY ...
FORGET ABOUT IT. DON'T THINK ABOUT ANYTHING.
HUH ?
JUST BE QUIET AND SIT STILL!!
OKAY ...

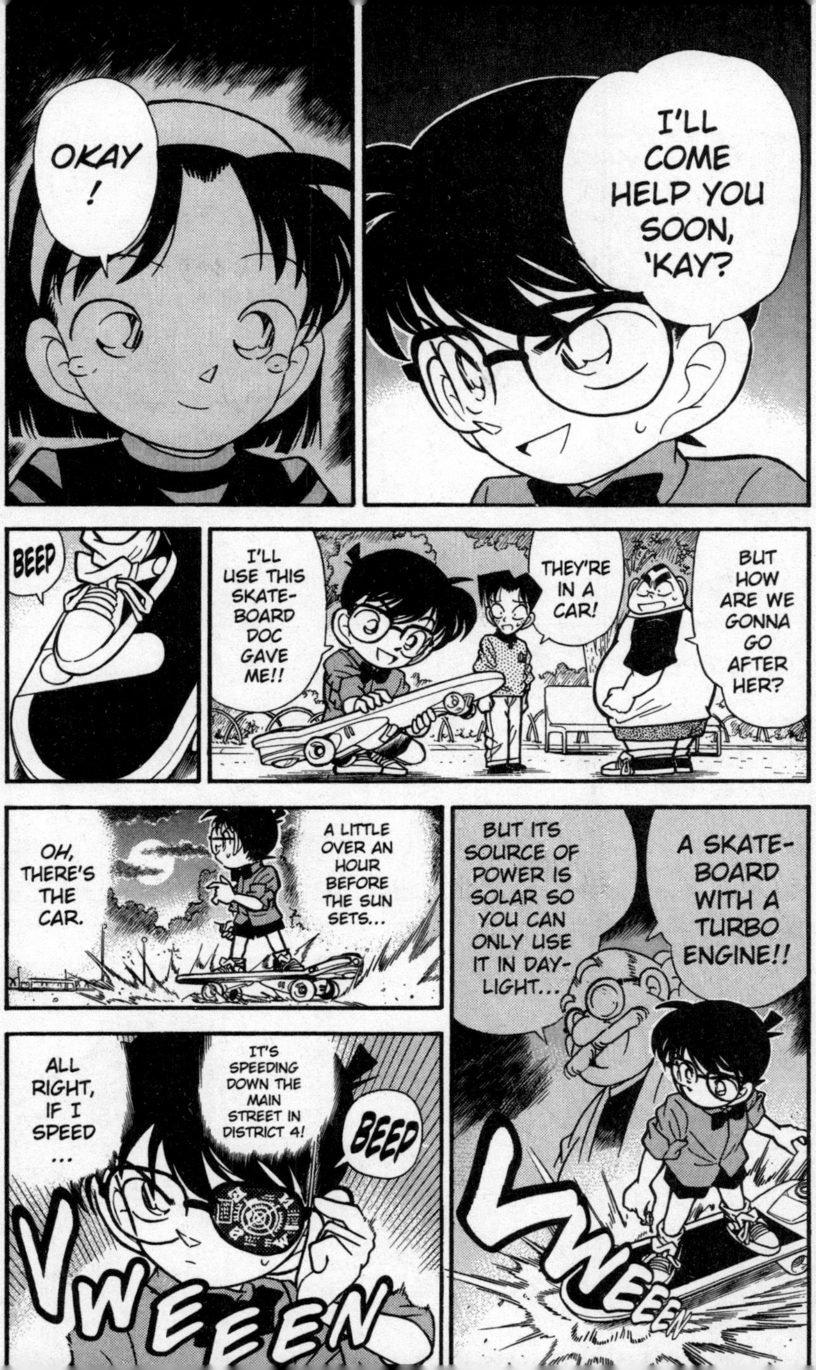
I'LL COME HELP YOU SOON, 'KAY?
OKAY!
BUT HOW ARE WE GONNA GO AFTER HER?
THEY'RE IN A CAR!
I'LL USE THIS SKATE-BOARD DOC GAVE ME!!
BEEP
A SKATE-BOARD WITH A TURBO ENGINE!!
BUT ITS SOURCE OF POWER IS SOLAR SO YOU CAN ONLY USE IT IN DAY-LIGHT...
VWEEEN
A LITTLE OVER AN HOUR BEFORE THE SUN SETS...
OH, THERE'S THE CAR.
BEEP
IT'S SPEEDING DOWN THE MAIN STREET IN DISTRICT 4!
ALL RIGHT, IF I SPEED ...
VWEEEN

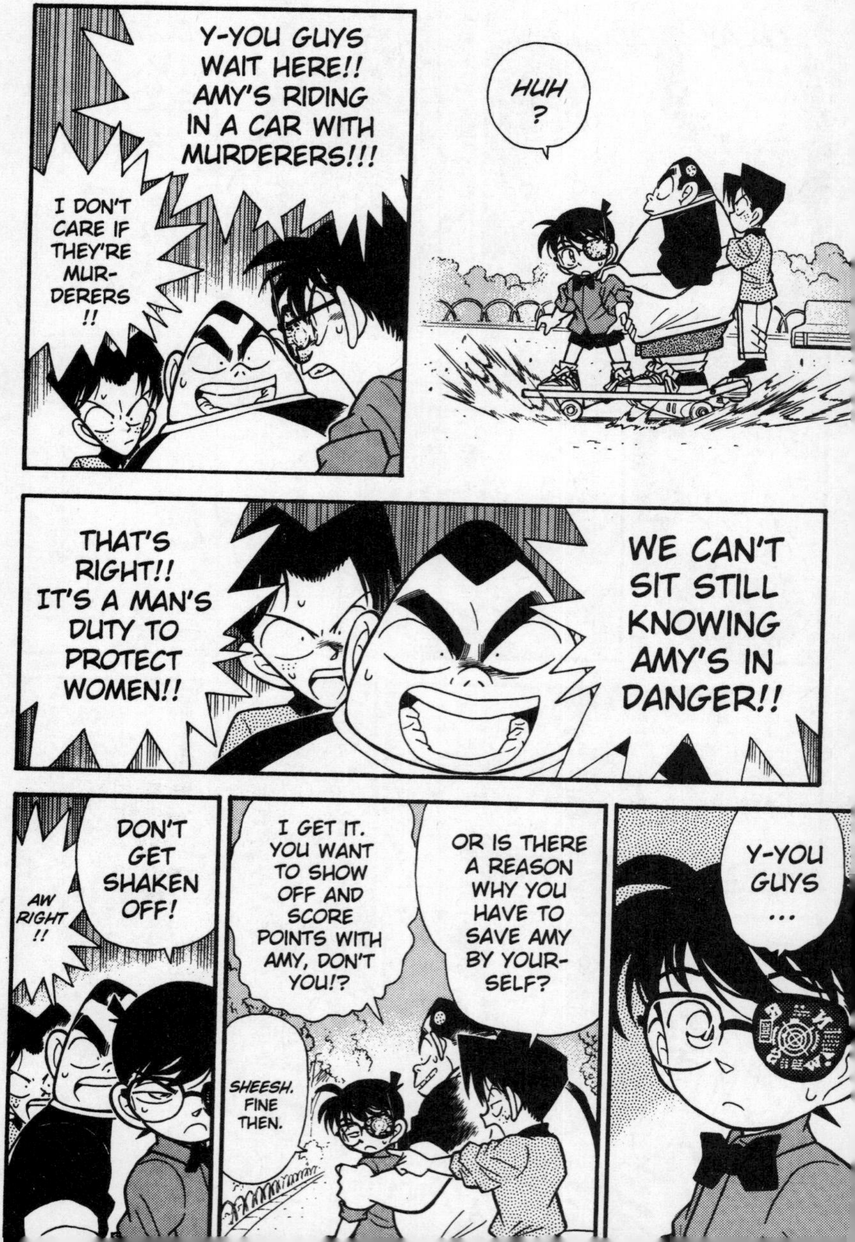
HUH ?
Y-YOU GUYS WAIT HERE!! AMY'S RIDING IN A CAR WITH MURDERERS!!!
I DON'T CARE IF THEY'RE MUR-DERERS !!
WE CAN'T SIT STILL KNOWING AMY'S IN DANGER!!
THAT'S RIGHT!! IT'S A MAN'S DUTY TO PROTECT WOMEN!!
Y-YOU GUYS ...
OR IS THERE A REASON WHY YOU HAVE TO SAVE AMY BY YOUR-SELF?
I GET IT. YOU WANT TO SHOW OFF AND SCORE POINTS WITH AMY, DON'T YOU!?
SHEESH. FINE THEN.
DON'T GET SHAKEN OFF!
AW RIGHT !!

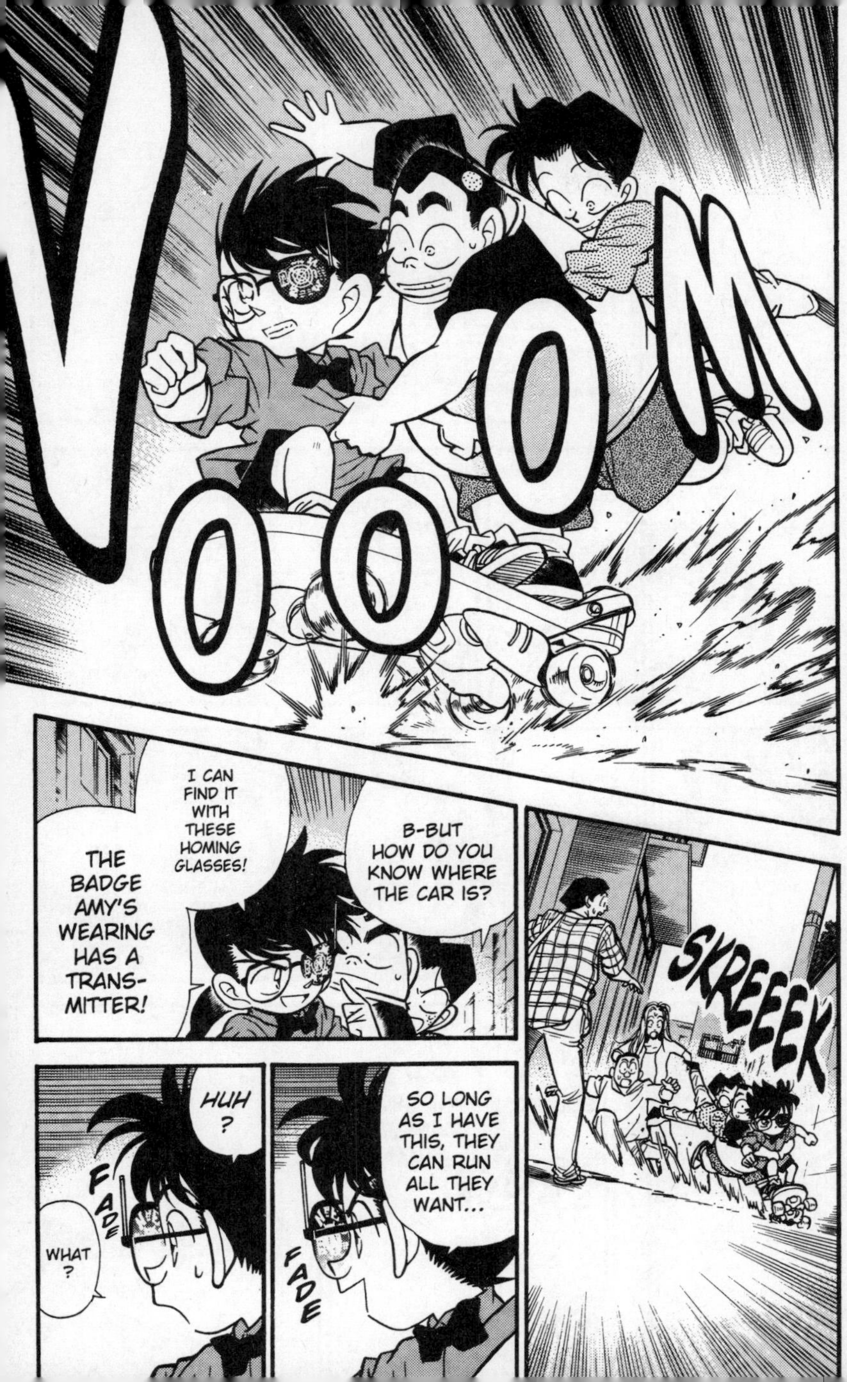
VROOOM
SKREEEK
B-BUT HOW DO YOU KNOW WHERE THE CAR IS?
I CAN FIND IT WITH THESE HOMING GLASSES!
THE BADGE AMY'S WEARING HAS A TRANSMITTER!
SO LONG AS I HAVE THIS, THEY CAN RUN ALL THEY WANT...
FADE
HUH?
FADE
WHAT?

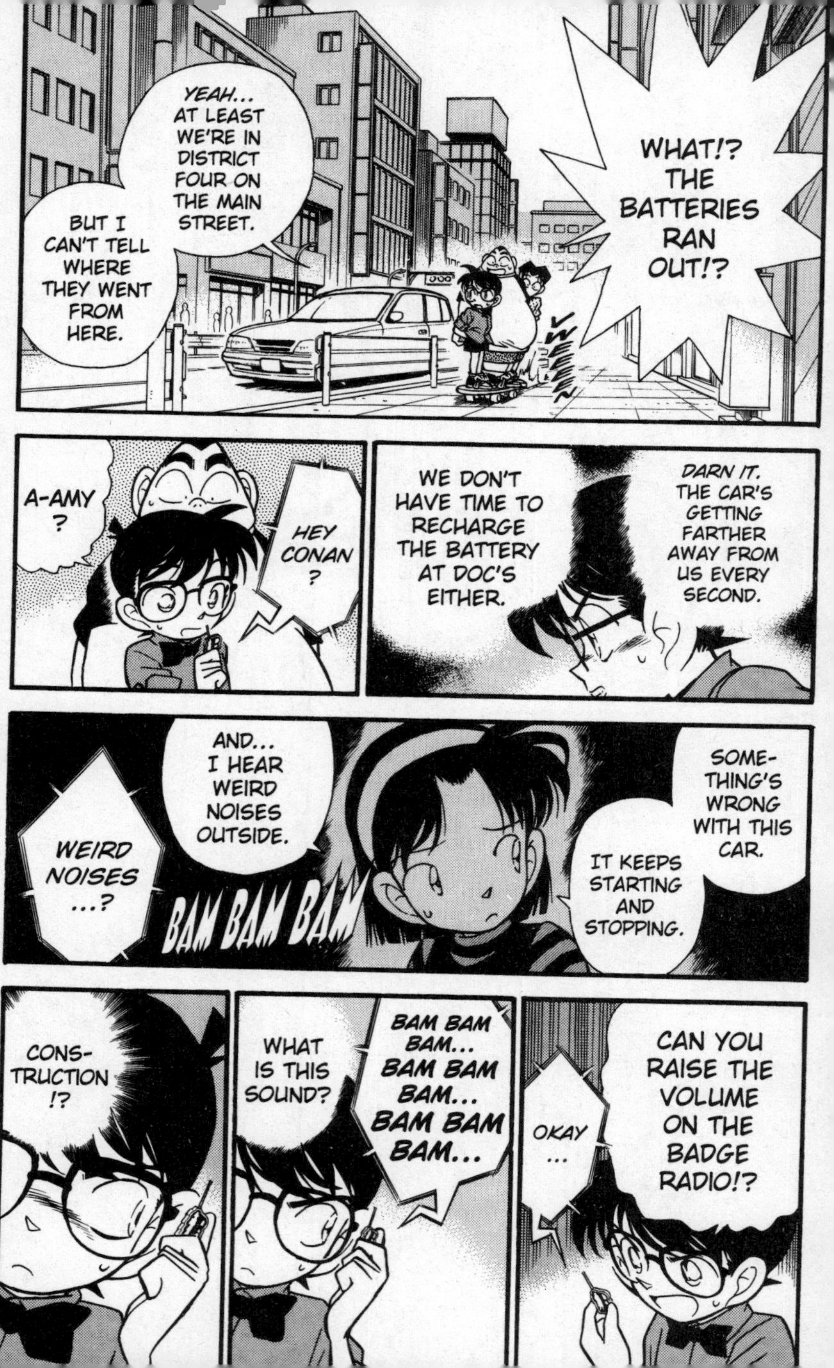
WHAT!? THE BATTERIES RAN OUT!?
VWEEEEEN
YEAH... AT LEAST WE'RE IN DISTRICT FOUR ON THE MAIN STREET.
BUT I CAN'T TELL WHERE THEY WENT FROM HERE.
DARN IT. THE CAR'S GETTING FARTHER AWAY FROM US EVERY SECOND.
WE DON'T HAVE TIME TO RECHARGE THE BATTERY AT DOC'S EITHER.
HEY CONAN?
A-AMY?
SOME-THING'S WRONG WITH THIS CAR.
IT KEEPS STARTING AND STOPPING.
AND... I HEAR WEIRD NOISES OUTSIDE.
BAM BAM BAM
WEIRD NOISES...?
CAN YOU RAISE THE VOLUME ON THE BADGE RADIO!?
OKAY...
BAM BAM BAM... BAM BAM BAM... BAM BAM BAM...
WHAT IS THIS SOUND?
CONS-TRUCTION!?

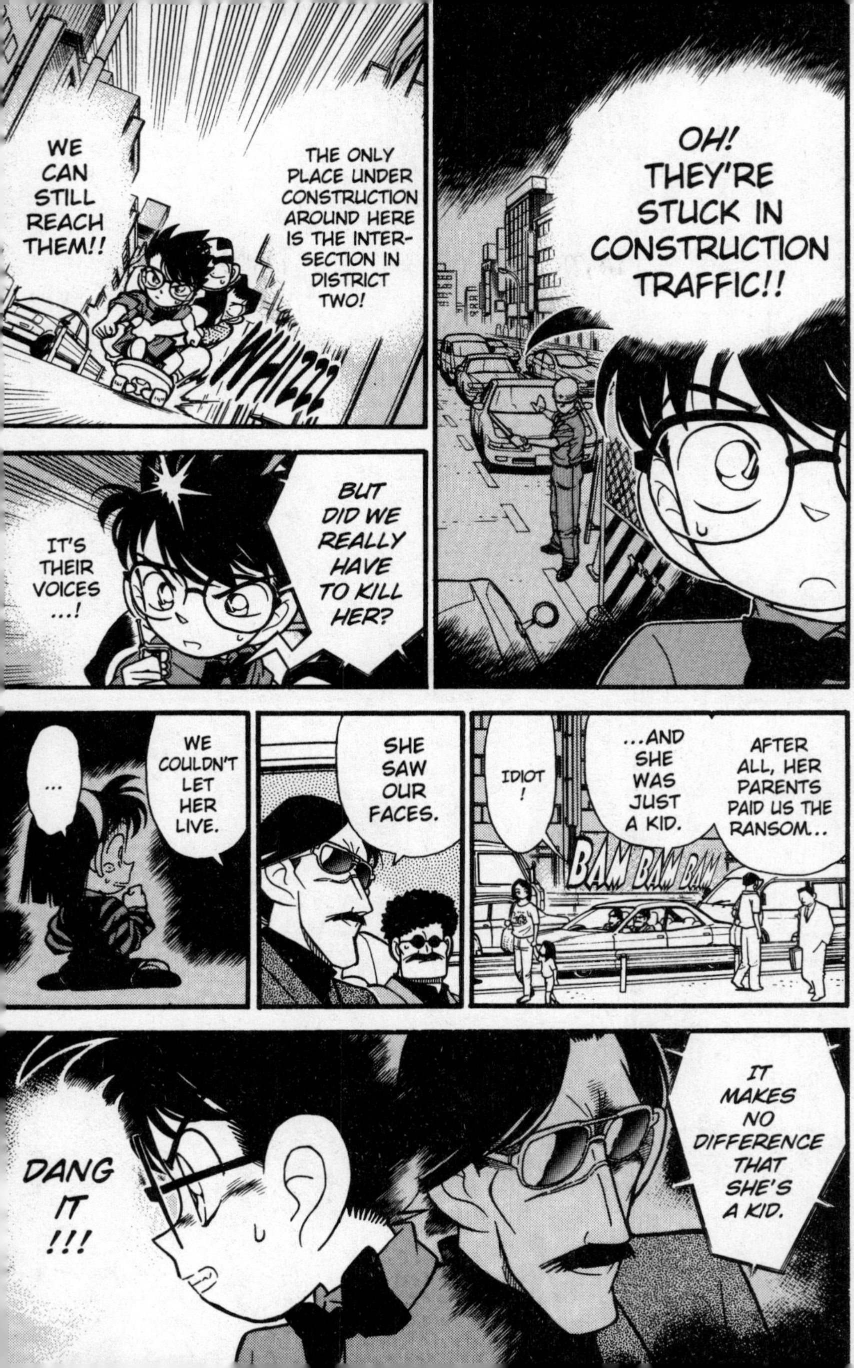
OH! THEY'RE STUCK IN CONSTRUCTION TRAFFIC!!
THE ONLY PLACE UNDER CONSTRUCTION AROUND HERE IS THE INTER-SECTION IN DISTRICT TWO!
WE CAN STILL REACH THEM!!
WHIZZZ
BUT DID WE REALLY HAVE TO KILL HER?
IT'S THEIR VOICES ...!
AFTER ALL, HER PARENTS PAID US THE RANSOM...
...AND SHE WAS JUST A KID.
IDIOT!
BAM BAM BAM
SHE SAW OUR FACES.
WE COULDN'T LET HER LIVE.
...
IT MAKES NO DIFFERENCE THAT SHE'S A KID.
DANG IT!!!

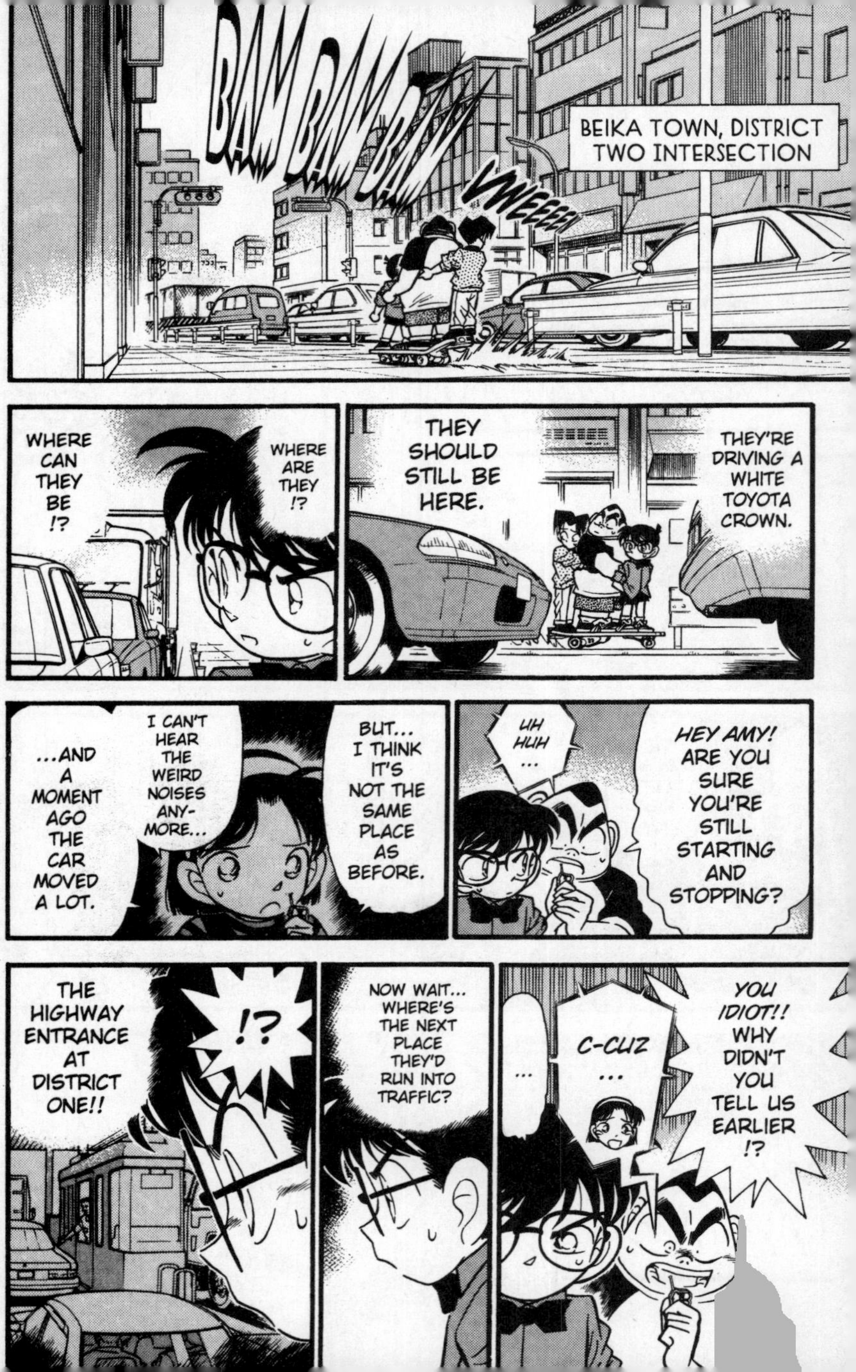
BEIKA TOWN, DISTRICT TWO INTERSECTION
BAM BAM BAM
THEY'RE DRIVING A WHITE TOYOTA CROWN.
THEY SHOULD STILL BE HERE.
WHERE ARE THEY !?
WHERE CAN THEY BE !?
HEY AMY! ARE YOU SURE YOU'RE STILL STARTING AND STOPPING?
UH HUH ...
BUT... I THINK IT'S NOT THE SAME PLACE AS BEFORE.
I CAN'T HEAR THE WEIRD NOISES ANY-MORE...
...AND A MOMENT AGO THE CAR MOVED A LOT.
YOU IDIOT!! WHY DIDN'T YOU TELL US EARLIER !?
C-CUZ ...
...
NOW WAIT... WHERE'S THE NEXT PLACE THEY'D RUN INTO TRAFFIC?
!?
THE HIGHWAY ENTRANCE AT DISTRICT ONE!!

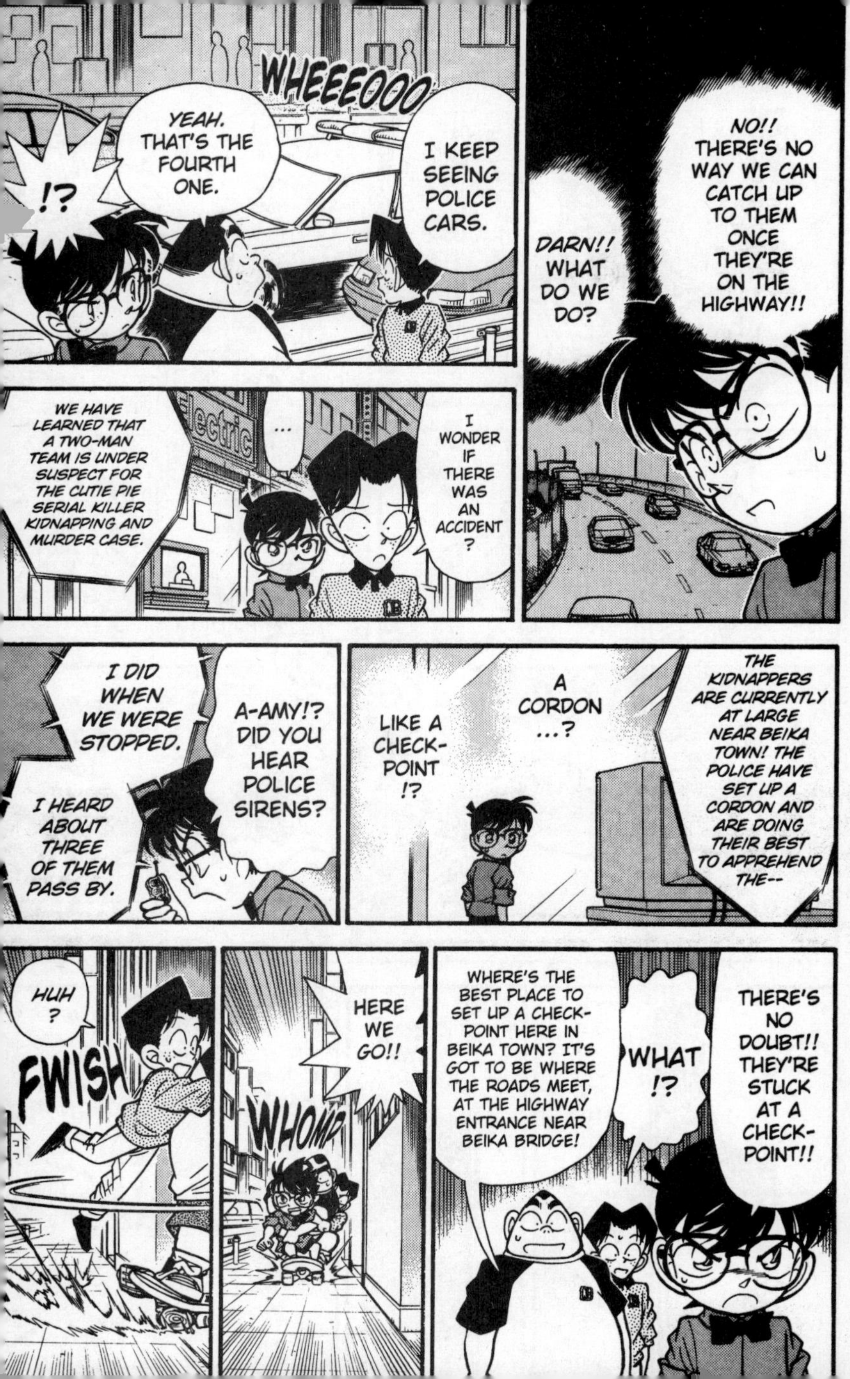

NO!! THERE'S NO WAY WE CAN CATCH UP TO THEM ONCE THEY'RE ON THE HIGHWAY!!
DARN!! WHAT DO WE DO?
WHEEEOOO
I KEEP SEEING POLICE CARS.
YEAH. THAT'S THE FOURTH ONE.
!?
I WONDER IF THERE WAS AN ACCIDENT?
...
WE HAVE LEARNED THAT A TWO-MAN TEAM IS UNDER SUSPECT FOR THE CUTIE PIE SERIAL KILLER KIDNAPPING AND MURDER CASE.
THE KIDNAPPERS ARE CURRENTLY AT LARGE NEAR BEIKA TOWN! THE POLICE HAVE SET UP A CORDON AND ARE DOING THEIR BEST TO APPREHEND THE--
A CORDON...?
LIKE A CHECK-POINT!?
A-AMY!? DID YOU HEAR POLICE SIRENS?
I DID WHEN WE WERE STOPPED.
I HEARD ABOUT THREE OF THEM PASS BY.
THERE'S NO DOUBT!! THEY'RE STUCK AT A CHECK-POINT!!
WHAT!?
WHERE'S THE BEST PLACE TO SET UP A CHECK-POINT HERE IN BEIKA TOWN? IT'S GOT TO BE WHERE THE ROADS MEET, AT THE HIGHWAY ENTRANCE NEAR BEIKA BRIDGE!
HERE WE GO!!
WHOMP
HUH?
FWISH

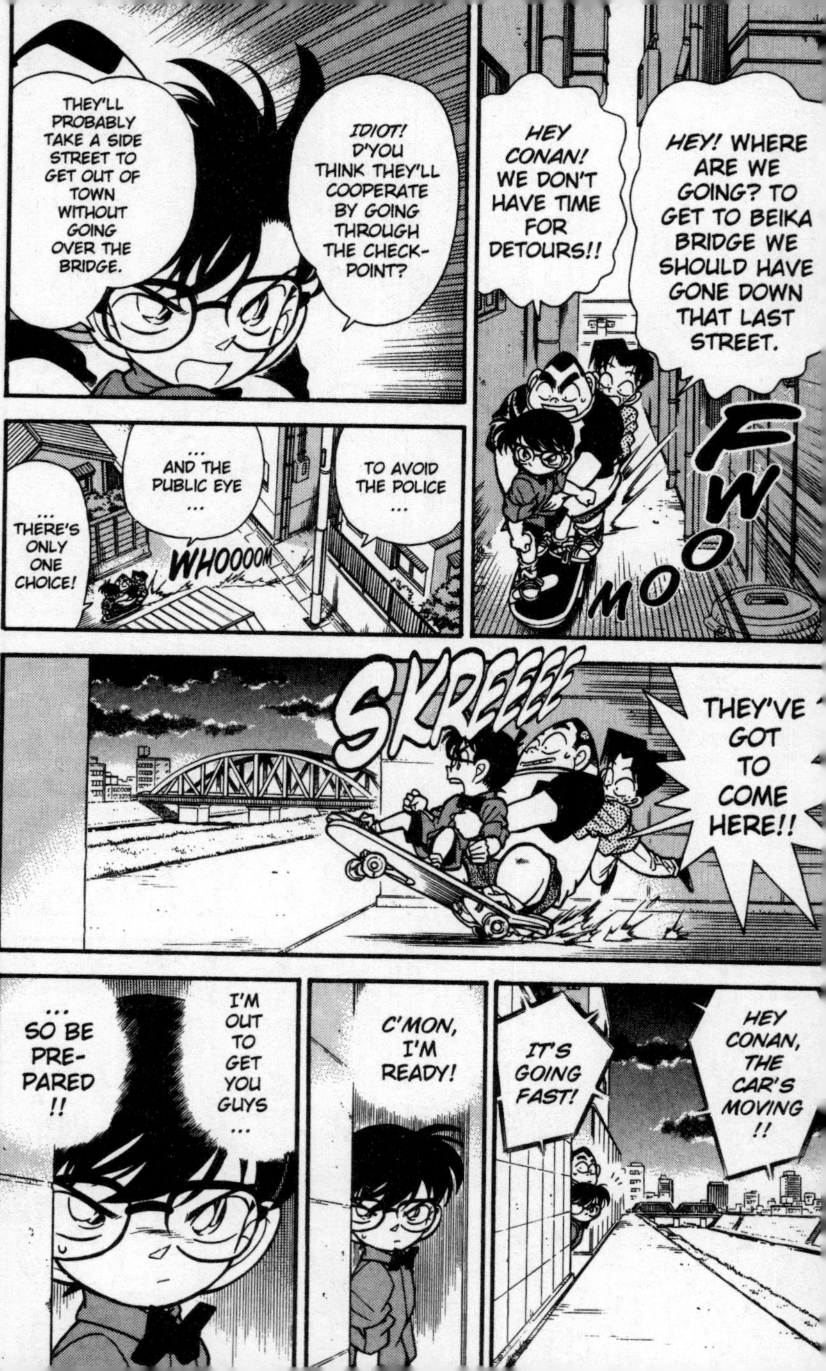
HEY! WHERE ARE WE GOING? TO GET TO BEIKA BRIDGE WE SHOULD HAVE GONE DOWN THAT LAST STREET.
HEY CONAN! WE DON'T HAVE TIME FOR DETOURS!!
FWOOM
IDIOT! D'YOU THINK THEY'LL COOPERATE BY GOING THROUGH THE CHECK-POINT?
THEY'LL PROBABLY TAKE A SIDE STREET TO GET OUT OF TOWN WITHOUT GOING OVER THE BRIDGE.
TO AVOID THE POLICE ...
... AND THE PUBLIC EYE ...
WHOOOOM
... THERE'S ONLY ONE CHOICE!
SKREEEE
THEY'VE GOT TO COME HERE!!
HEY CONAN, THE CAR'S MOVING!!
IT'S GOING FAST!
C'MON, I'M READY!
I'M OUT TO GET YOU GUYS ...
... SO BE PRE-PARED!!

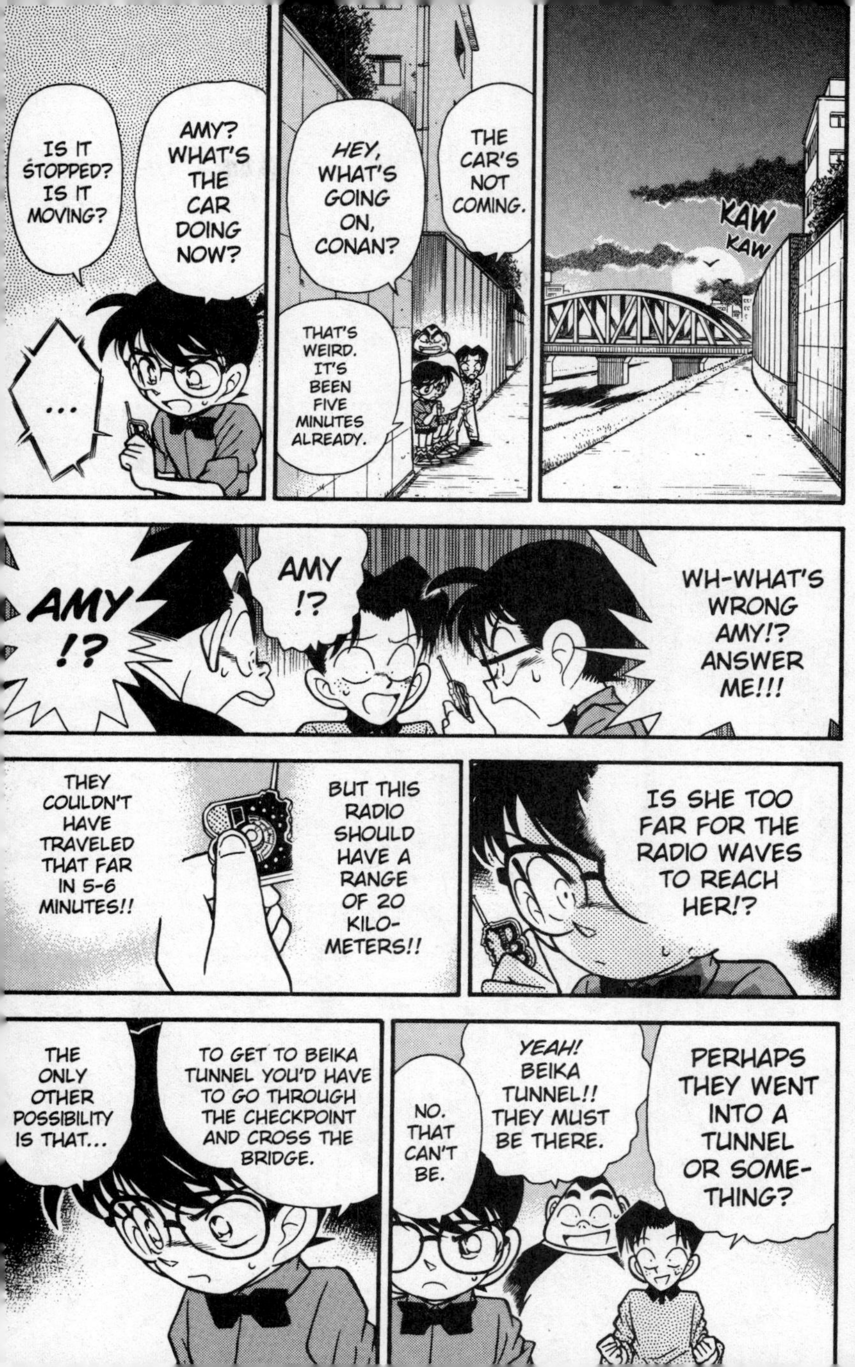
KAW KAW
THE CAR'S NOT COMING.
HEY, WHAT'S GOING ON, CONAN?
THAT'S WEIRD. IT'S BEEN FIVE MINUTES ALREADY.
AMY? WHAT'S THE CAR DOING NOW?
IS IT STOPPED? IS IT MOVING?
...
WH-WHAT'S WRONG AMY!? ANSWER ME!!!
AMY !?
AMY !?
IS SHE TOO FAR FOR THE RADIO WAVES TO REACH HER!?
BUT THIS RADIO SHOULD HAVE A RANGE OF 20 KILO-METERS!!
THEY COULDN'T HAVE TRAVELED THAT FAR IN 5-6 MINUTES!!
PERHAPS THEY WENT INTO A TUNNEL OR SOME-THING?
YEAH! BEIKA TUNNEL!! THEY MUST BE THERE.
NO. THAT CAN'T BE.
TO GET TO BEIKA TUNNEL YOU'D HAVE TO GO THROUGH THE CHECKPOINT AND CROSS THE BRIDGE.
THE ONLY OTHER POSSIBILITY IS THAT...

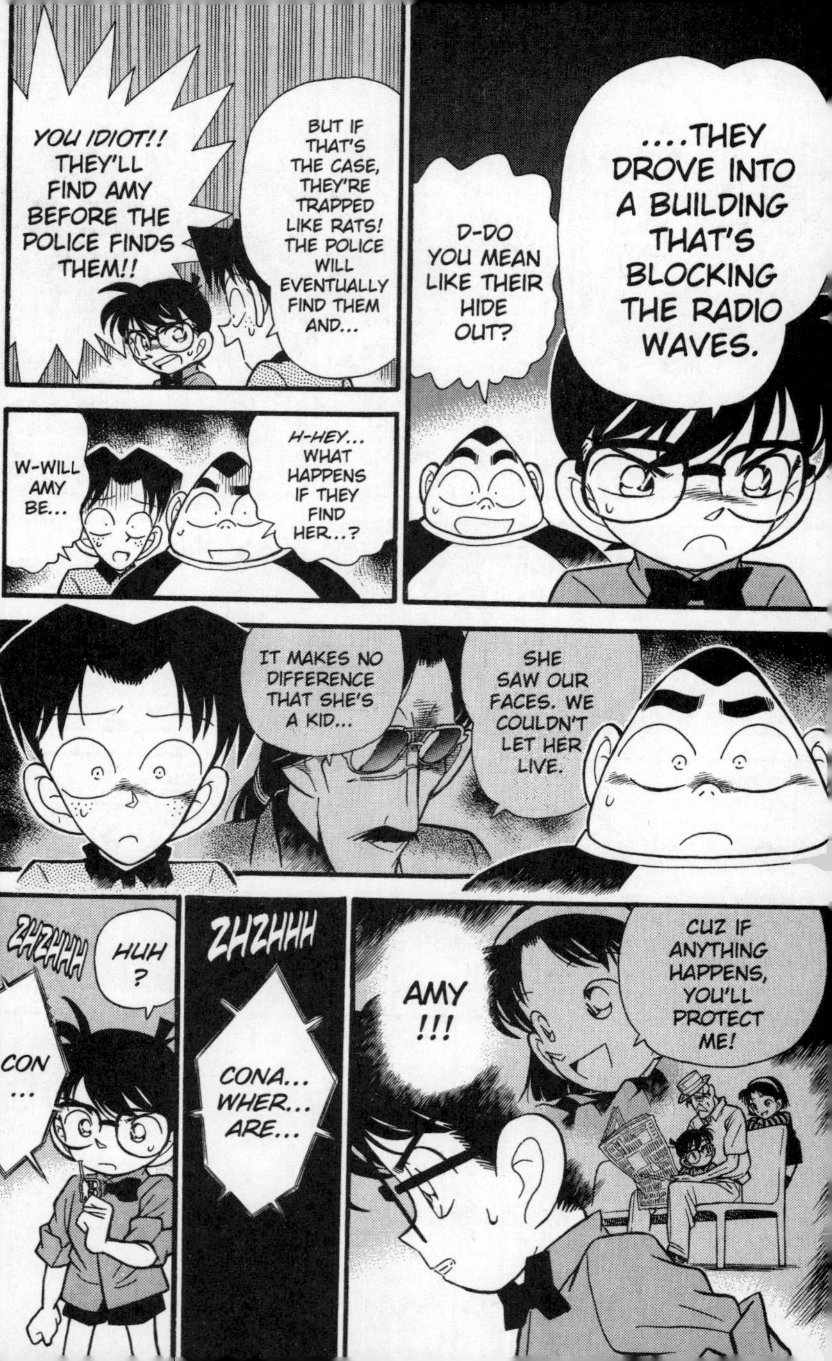
....THEY DROVE INTO A BUILDING THAT'S BLOCKING THE RADIO WAVES.
D-DO YOU MEAN LIKE THEIR HIDE OUT?
BUT IF THAT'S THE CASE, THEY'RE TRAPPED LIKE RATS! THE POLICE WILL EVENTUALLY FIND THEM AND...
YOU IDIOT!! THEY'LL FIND AMY BEFORE THE POLICE FINDS THEM!!
H-HEY... WHAT HAPPENS IF THEY FIND HER...?
W-WILL AMY BE...
SHE SAW OUR FACES. WE COULDN'T LET HER LIVE.
IT MAKES NO DIFFERENCE THAT SHE'S A KID...
CUZ IF ANYTHING HAPPENS, YOU'LL PROTECT ME!
AMY !!!
ZHZHHH
CONA... WHER... ARE...
HUH ?
ZHZHHH
CON ...

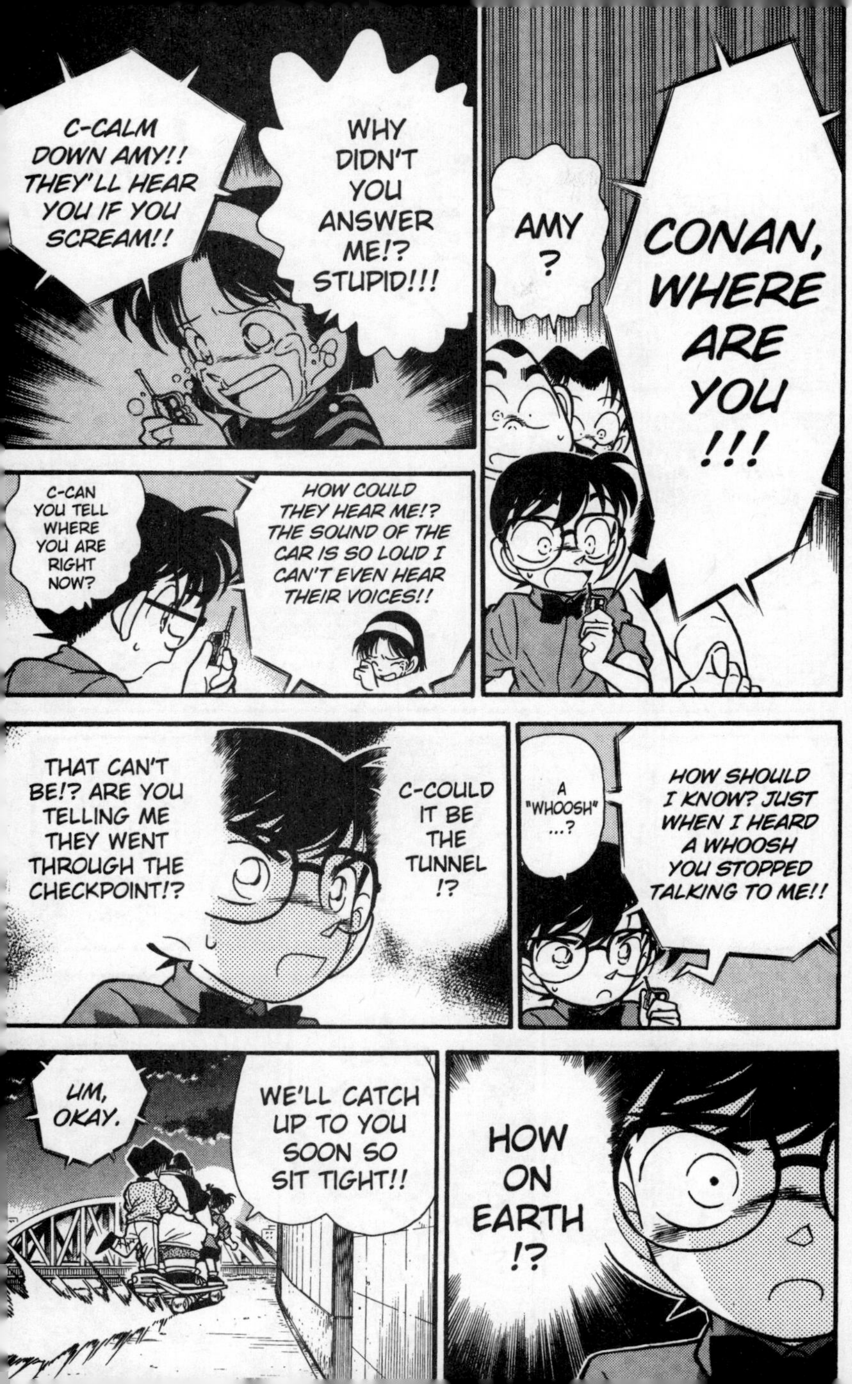
CONAN, WHERE ARE YOU!!!
AMY?
WHY DIDN'T YOU ANSWER ME!? STUPID!!!
C-CALM DOWN AMY!! THEY'LL HEAR YOU IF YOU SCREAM!!
HOW COULD THEY HEAR ME!? THE SOUND OF THE CAR IS SO LOUD I CAN'T EVEN HEAR THEIR VOICES!!
C-CAN YOU TELL WHERE YOU ARE RIGHT NOW?
HOW SHOULD I KNOW? JUST WHEN I HEARD A WHOOSH YOU STOPPED TALKING TO ME!!
A "WHOOSH" ...?
C-COULD IT BE THE TUNNEL!?
THAT CAN'T BE!? ARE YOU TELLING ME THEY WENT THROUGH THE CHECKPOINT!?
HOW ON EARTH!?
WE'LL CATCH UP TO YOU SOON SO SIT TIGHT!!
UM, OKAY.

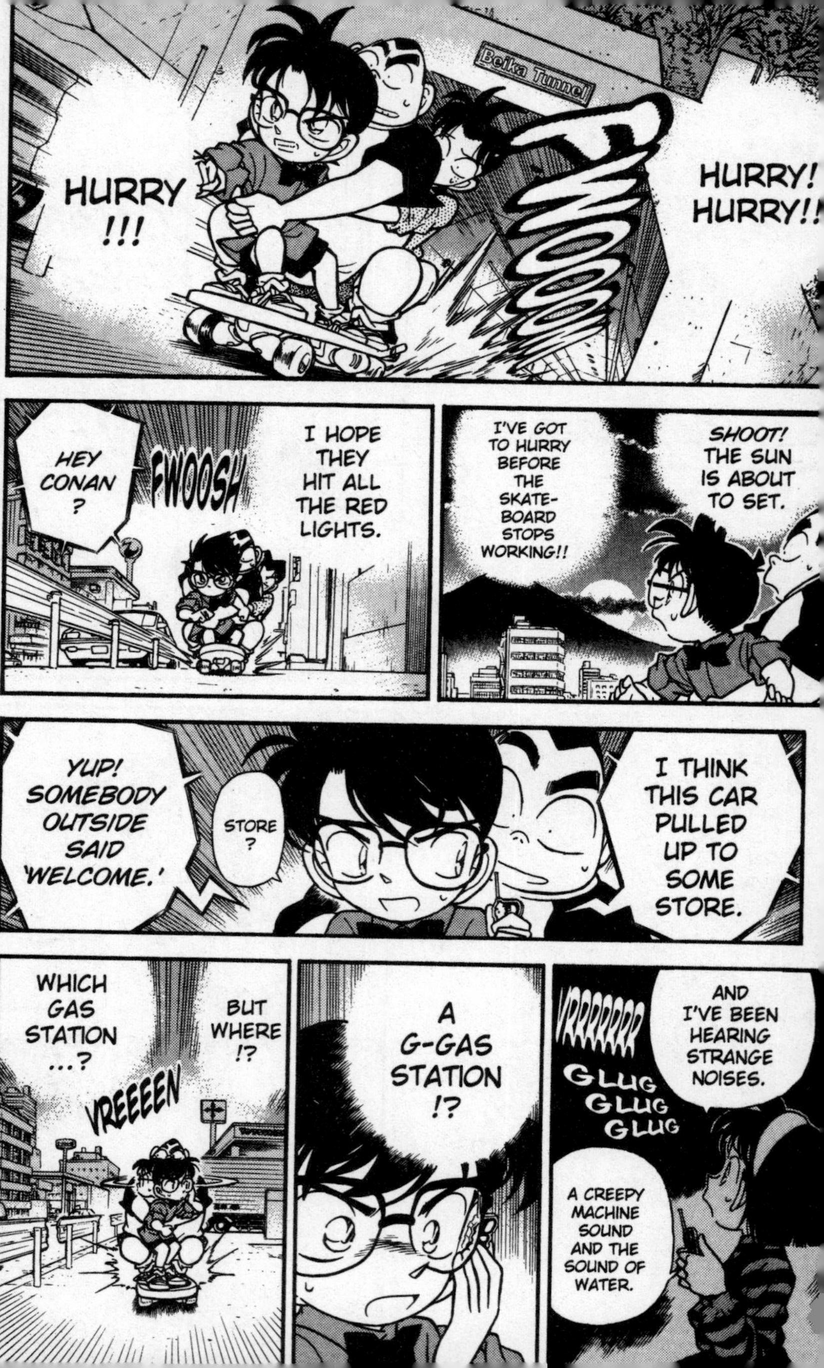
Beika Tunnel
HURRY! HURRY!!
HURRY !!!
SHOOT! THE SUN IS ABOUT TO SET.
I'VE GOT TO HURRY BEFORE THE SKATE-BOARD STOPS WORKING!!
I HOPE THEY HIT ALL THE RED LIGHTS.
FWOOSH
HEY CONAN ?
I THINK THIS CAR PULLED UP TO SOME STORE.
STORE ?
YUP! SOMEBODY OUTSIDE SAID 'WELCOME.'
AND I'VE BEEN HEARING STRANGE NOISES.
VRRRRRRR
GLUG GLUG GLUG
A CREEPY MACHINE SOUND AND THE SOUND OF WATER.
A G-GAS STATION !?
BUT WHERE !?
WHICH GAS STATION ...?
VREEEEN

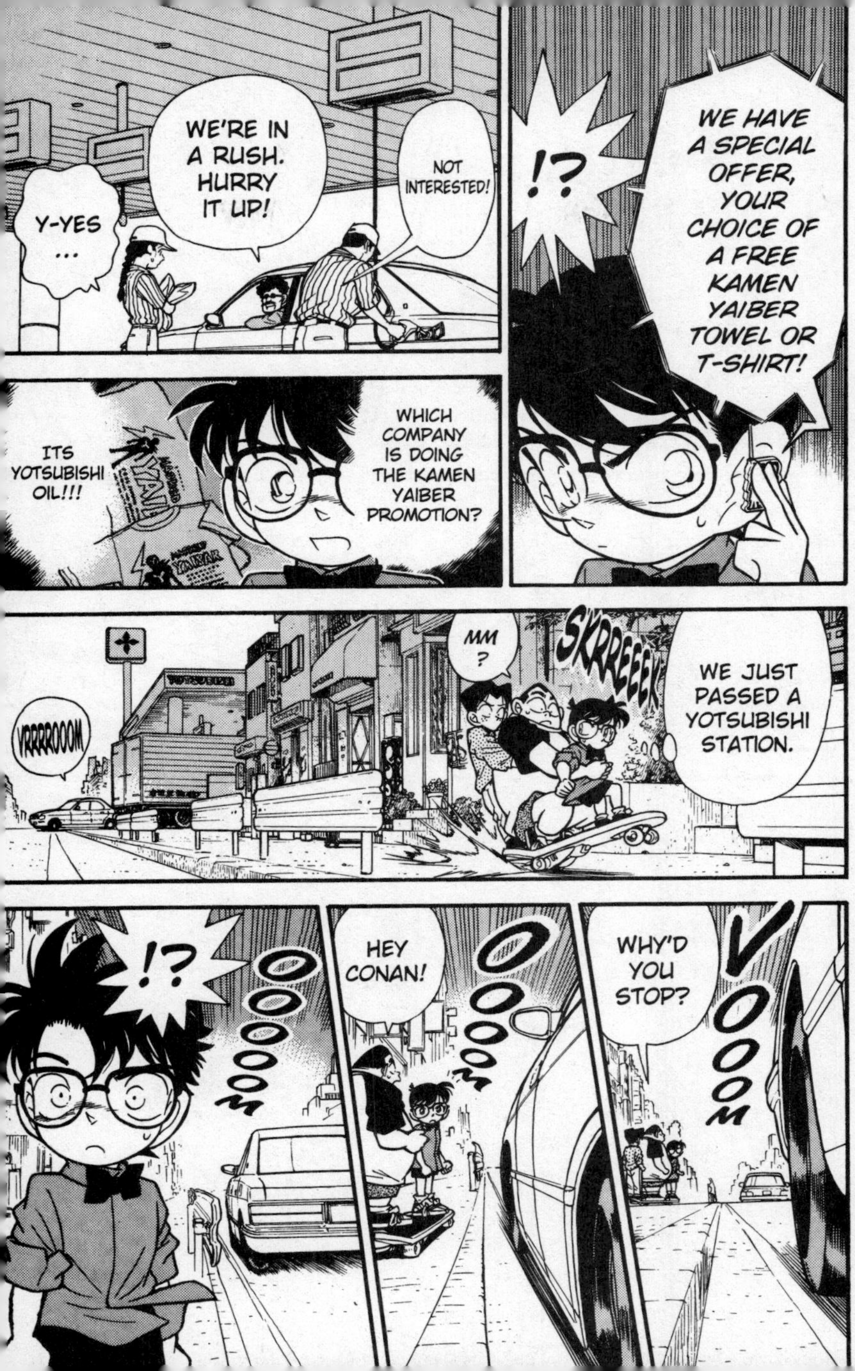
WE HAVE A SPECIAL OFFER, YOUR CHOICE OF A FREE KAMEN YAIBER TOWEL OR T-SHIRT!
!?
NOT INTERESTED!
WE'RE IN A RUSH. HURRY IT UP!
Y-YES ...
WHICH COMPANY IS DOING THE KAMEN YAIBER PROMOTION?
ITS YOTSUBISHI OIL!!!
WE JUST PASSED A YOTSUBISHI STATION.
SKRREEEK
MM ?
VRRRROOOM
VOOOOOM
WHY'D YOU STOP?
OOOOOOM
HEY CONAN!
OOOOOOM
!?

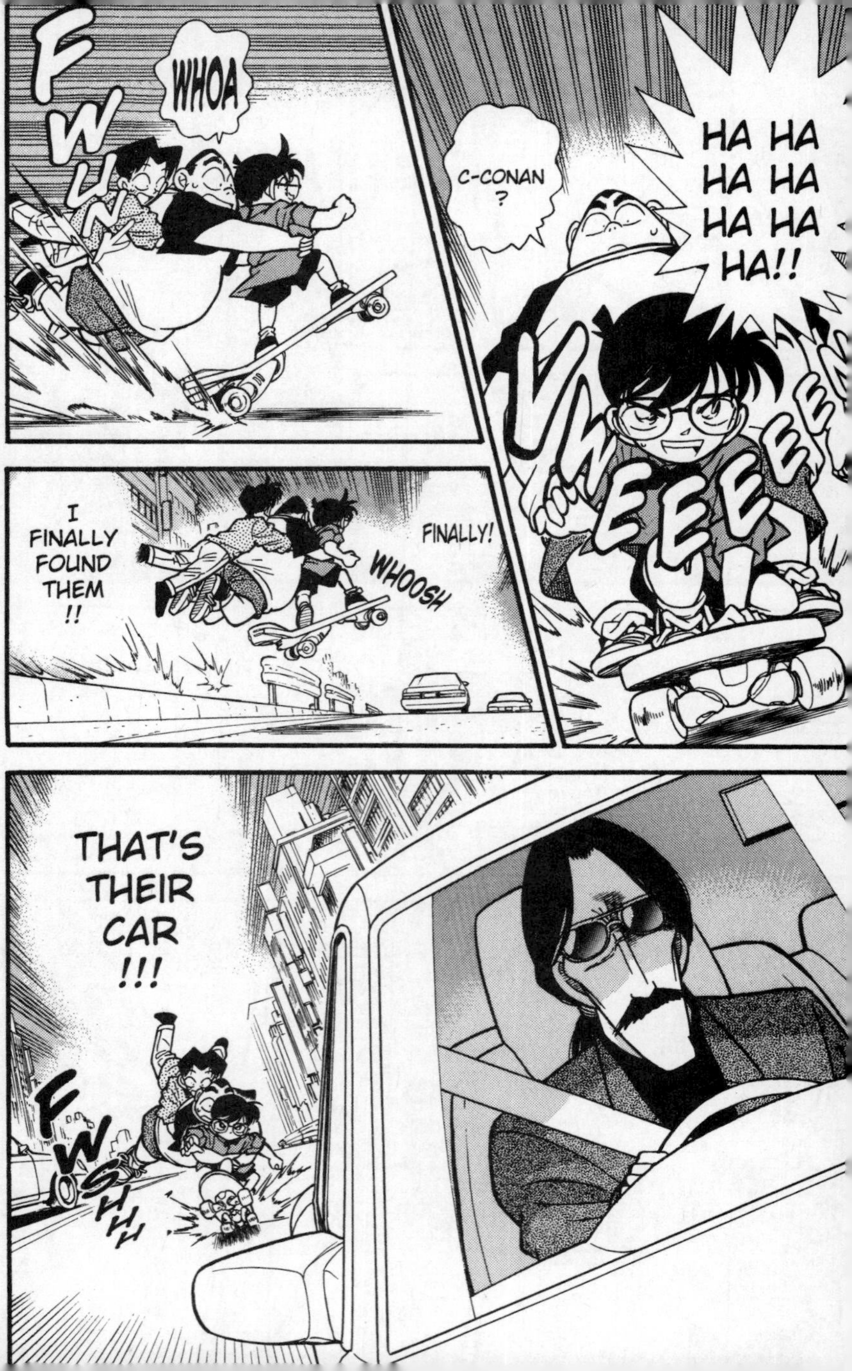
C-CONAN ?
HA HA HA HA HA HA HA!!
WEEEEEEE
FWUN
WHOA
FINALLY!
WHOOSH
I FINALLY FOUND THEM !!
THAT'S THEIR CAR !!!
FWSHHH

FILE 3:
WHAT! REALLY!?

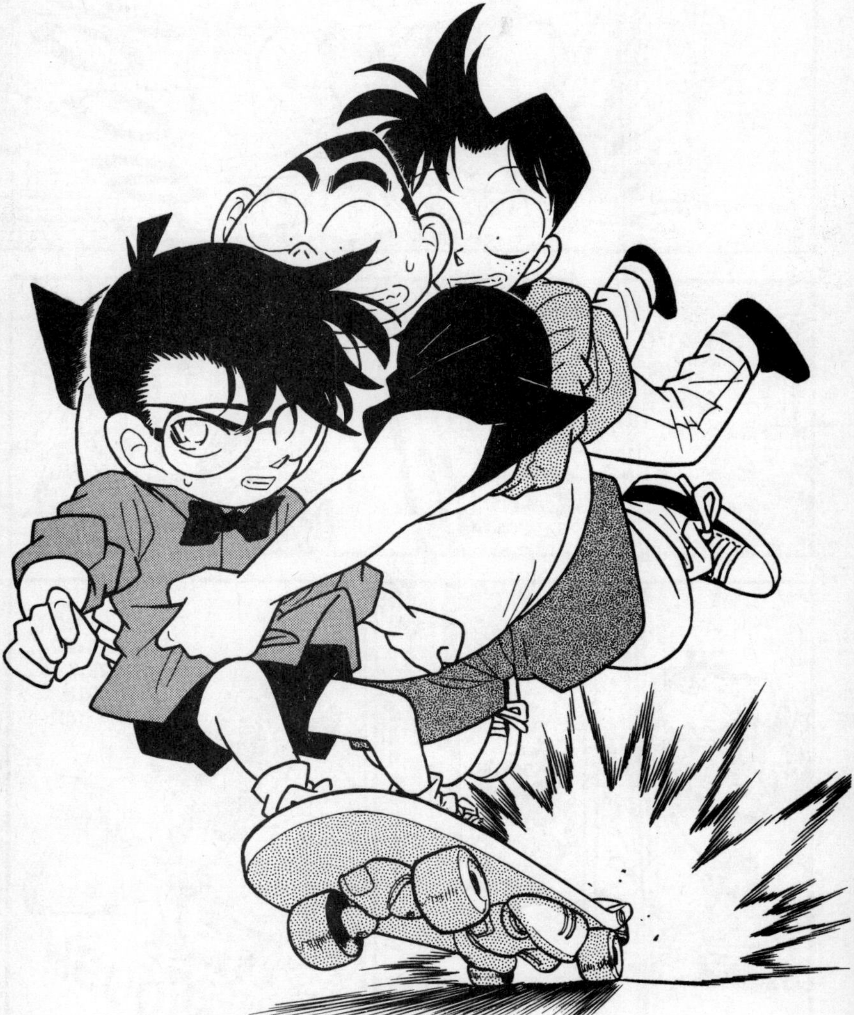

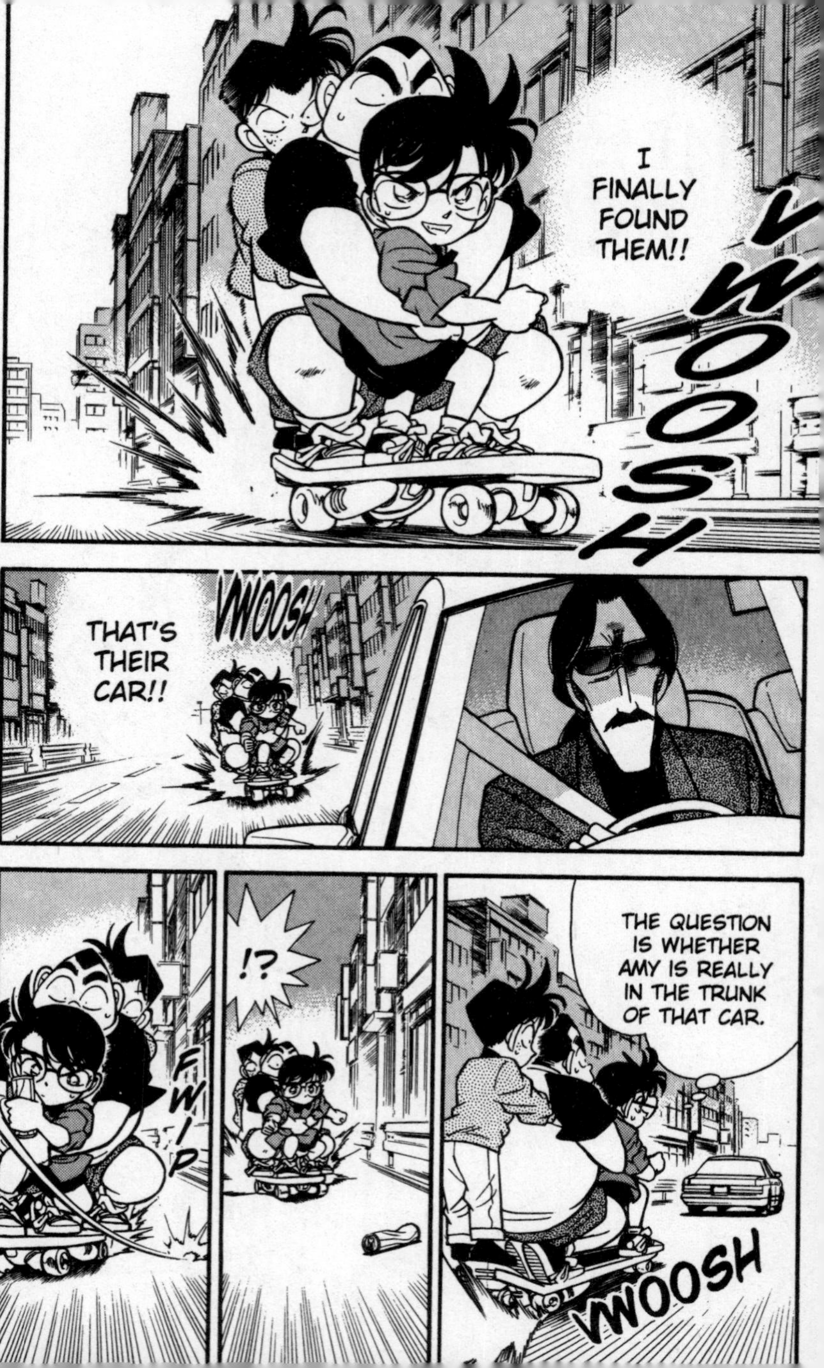
I FINALLY FOUND THEM!!
VWOOSH
VWOOSH
THAT'S THEIR CAR!!
THE QUESTION IS WHETHER AMY IS REALLY IN THE TRUNK OF THAT CAR.
VWOOSH
!?
FWIP

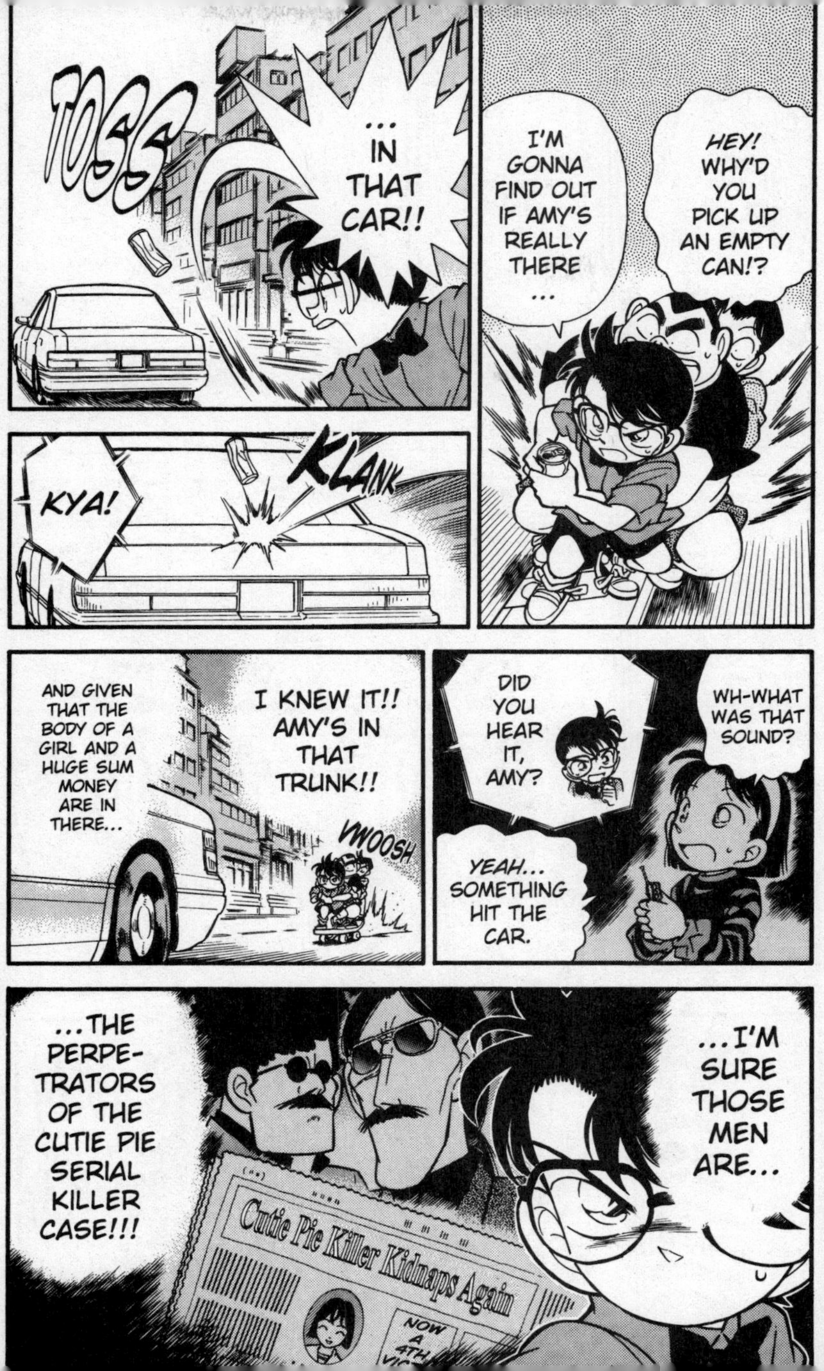
HEY! WHY'D YOU PICK UP AN EMPTY CAN!?
I'M GONNA FIND OUT IF AMY'S REALLY THERE...
TOSS
... IN THAT CAR!!
KLANK
KYA!
WH-WHAT WAS THAT SOUND?
DID YOU HEAR IT, AMY?
YEAH... SOMETHING HIT THE CAR.
I KNEW IT!! AMY'S IN THAT TRUNK!!
VWOOSH
AND GIVEN THAT THE BODY OF A GIRL AND A HUGE SUM MONEY ARE IN THERE...
...I'M SURE THOSE MEN ARE...
...THE PERPE-TRATORS OF THE CUTIE PIE SERIAL KILLER CASE!!!
Cutie Pie Killer Kidnaps Again

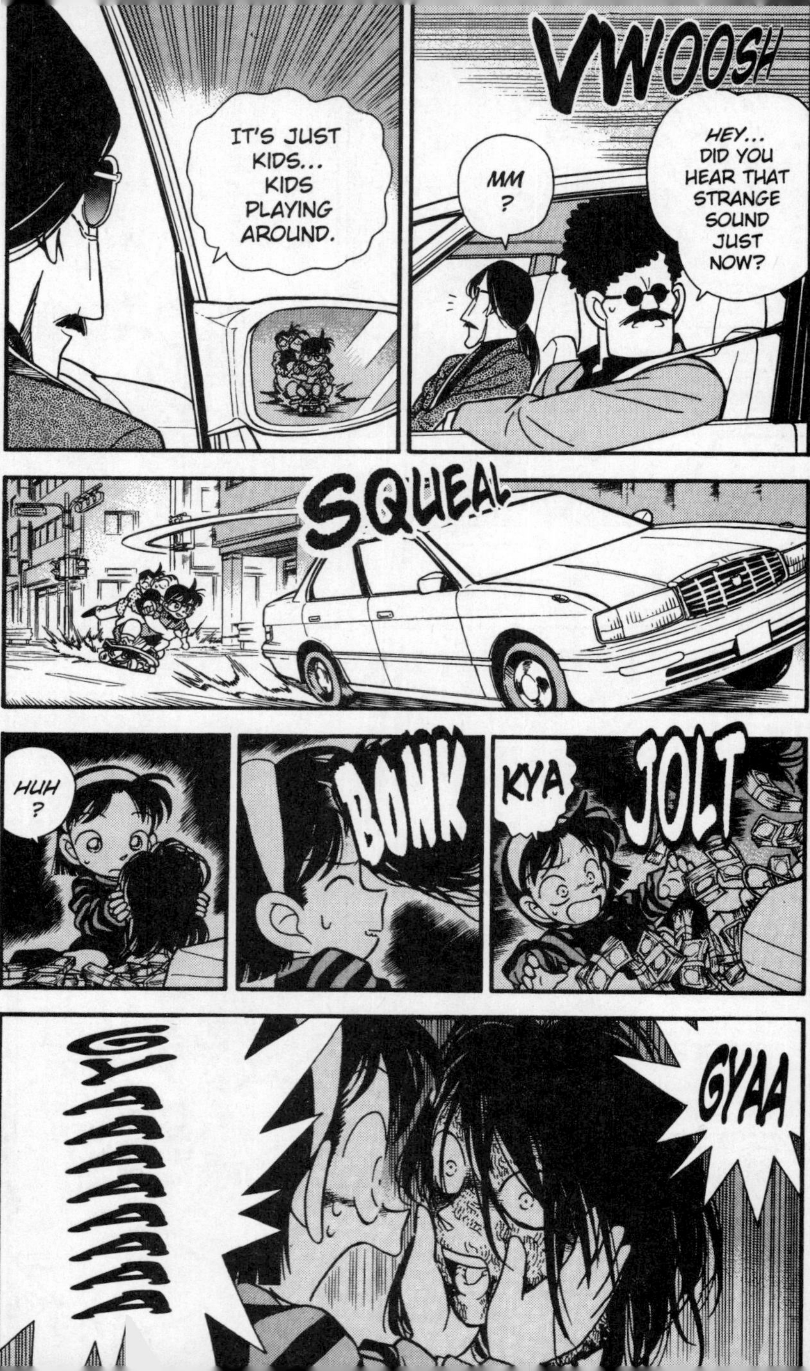
VWOOSH
HEY... DID YOU HEAR THAT STRANGE SOUND JUST NOW?
MM?
IT'S JUST KIDS... KIDS PLAYING AROUND.
SQUEAL
JOLT
KYA
BONK
HUH?
GYAA
GYAAAAAAAAA

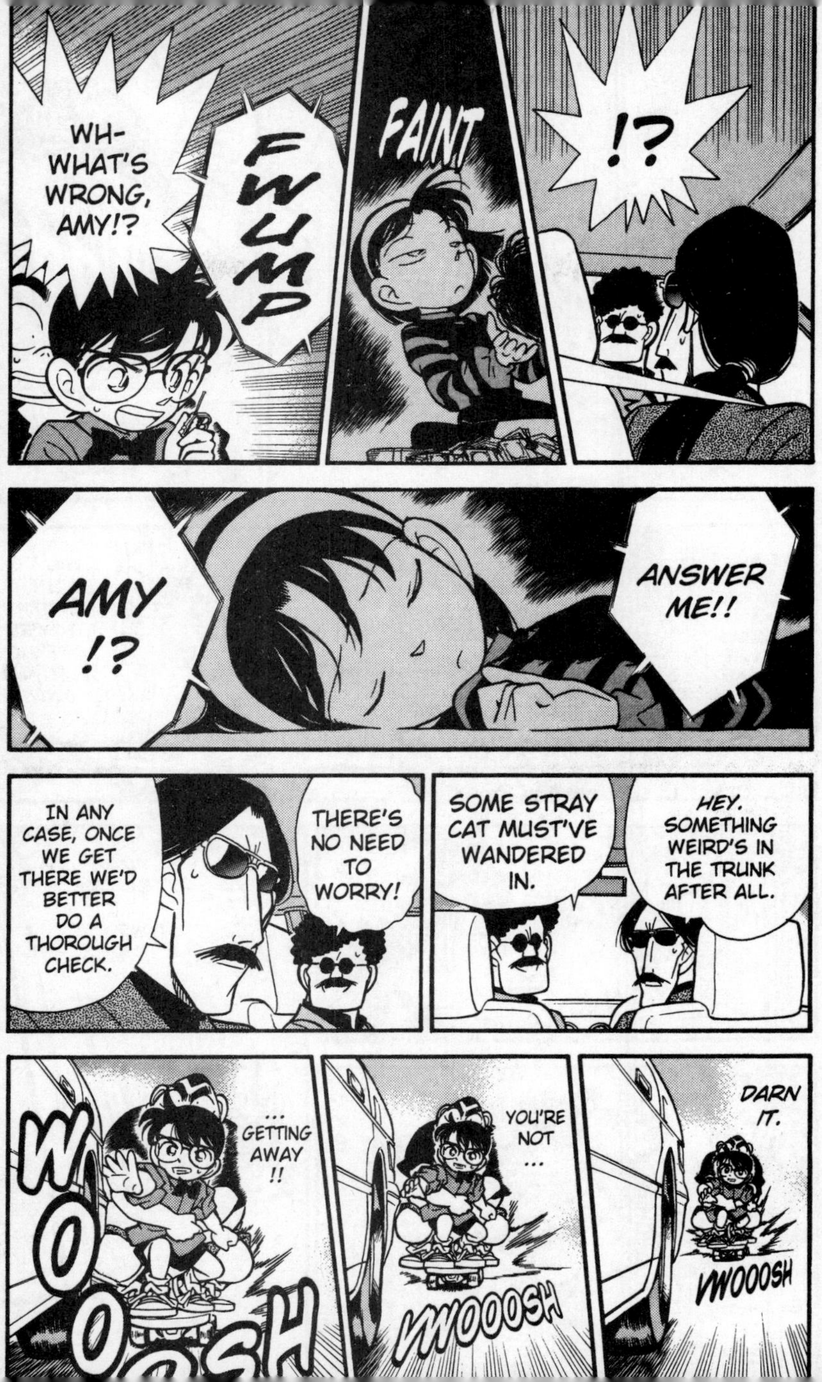
!?
FAINT
FWUMP
WH- WHAT'S WRONG, AMY!?
ANSWER ME!!
AMY !?
HEY. SOMETHING WEIRD'S IN THE TRUNK AFTER ALL.
SOME STRAY CAT MUST'VE WANDERED IN.
THERE'S NO NEED TO WORRY!
IN ANY CASE, ONCE WE GET THERE WE'D BETTER DO A THOROUGH CHECK.
DARN IT.
VWOOOSH
YOU'RE NOT ...
VWOOOSH
... GETTING AWAY !!
WOOOOSH

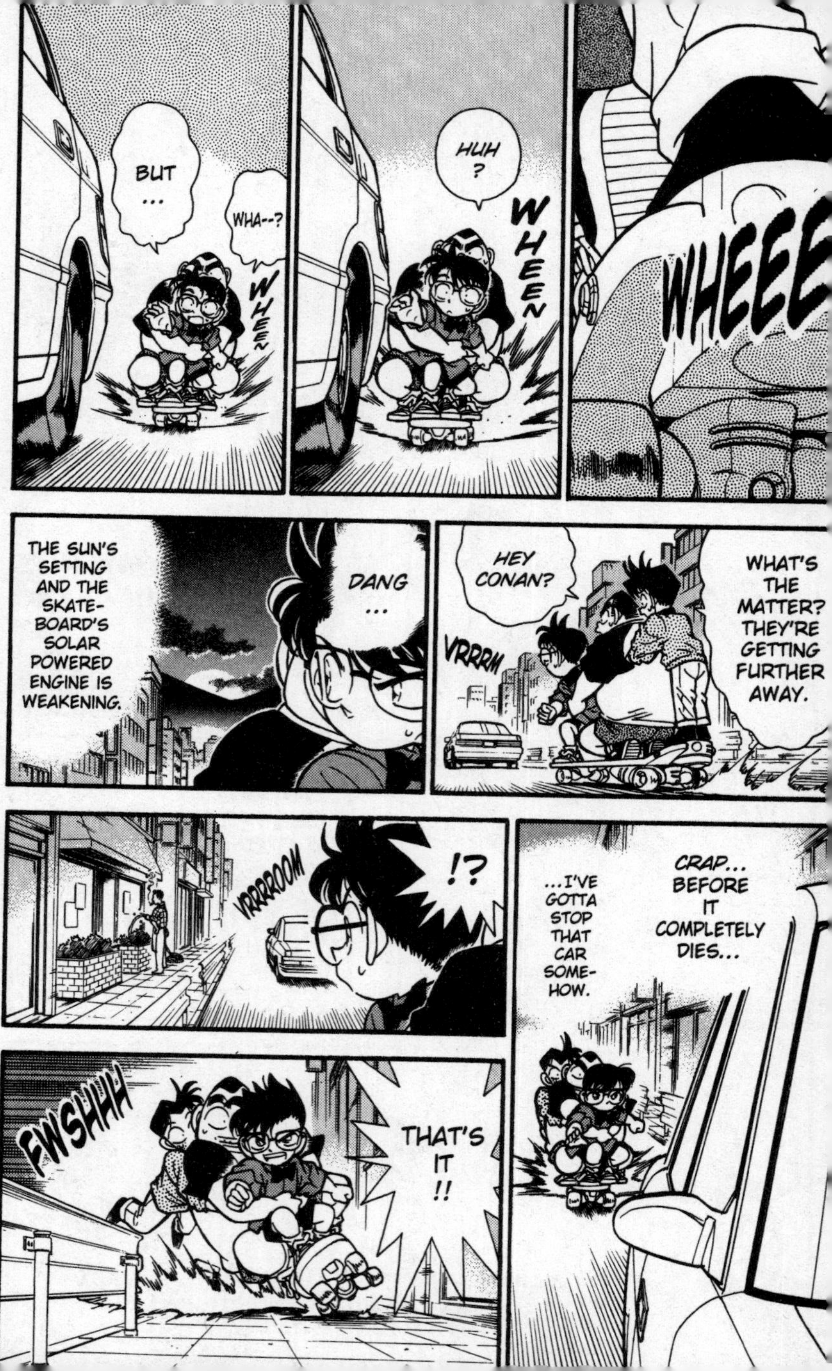
WHEEE
HUH ?
WHEEN
BUT ...
WHA--?
WHEEN
WHAT'S THE MATTER? THEY'RE GETTING FURTHER AWAY.
HEY CONAN?
VRRRM
DANG ...
THE SUN'S SETTING AND THE SKATE-BOARD'S SOLAR POWERED ENGINE IS WEAKENING.
CRAP... BEFORE IT COMPLETELY DIES...
...I'VE GOTTA STOP THAT CAR SOME-HOW.
!?
VRRRROOM
THAT'S IT !!
FWSHHH

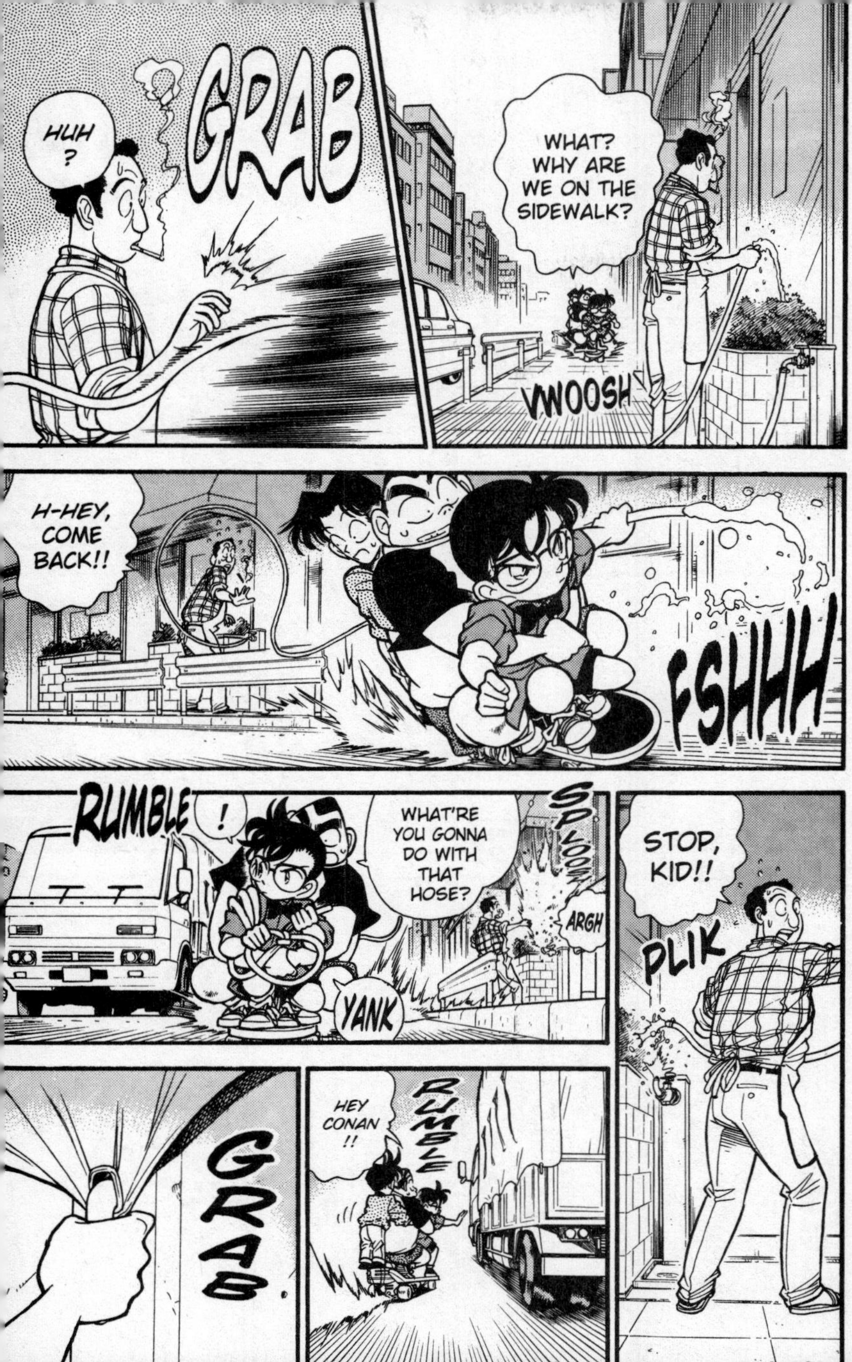
WHAT? WHY ARE WE ON THE SIDEWALK?
VWOOSH
GRAB
HUH?
H-HEY, COME BACK!!
FSHHH
STOP, KID!!
PLIK
SPLOOSH
ARGH
WHAT'RE YOU GONNA DO WITH THAT HOSE?
!
RUMBLE
YANK
RUMBLE
HEY CONAN!!
GRAB

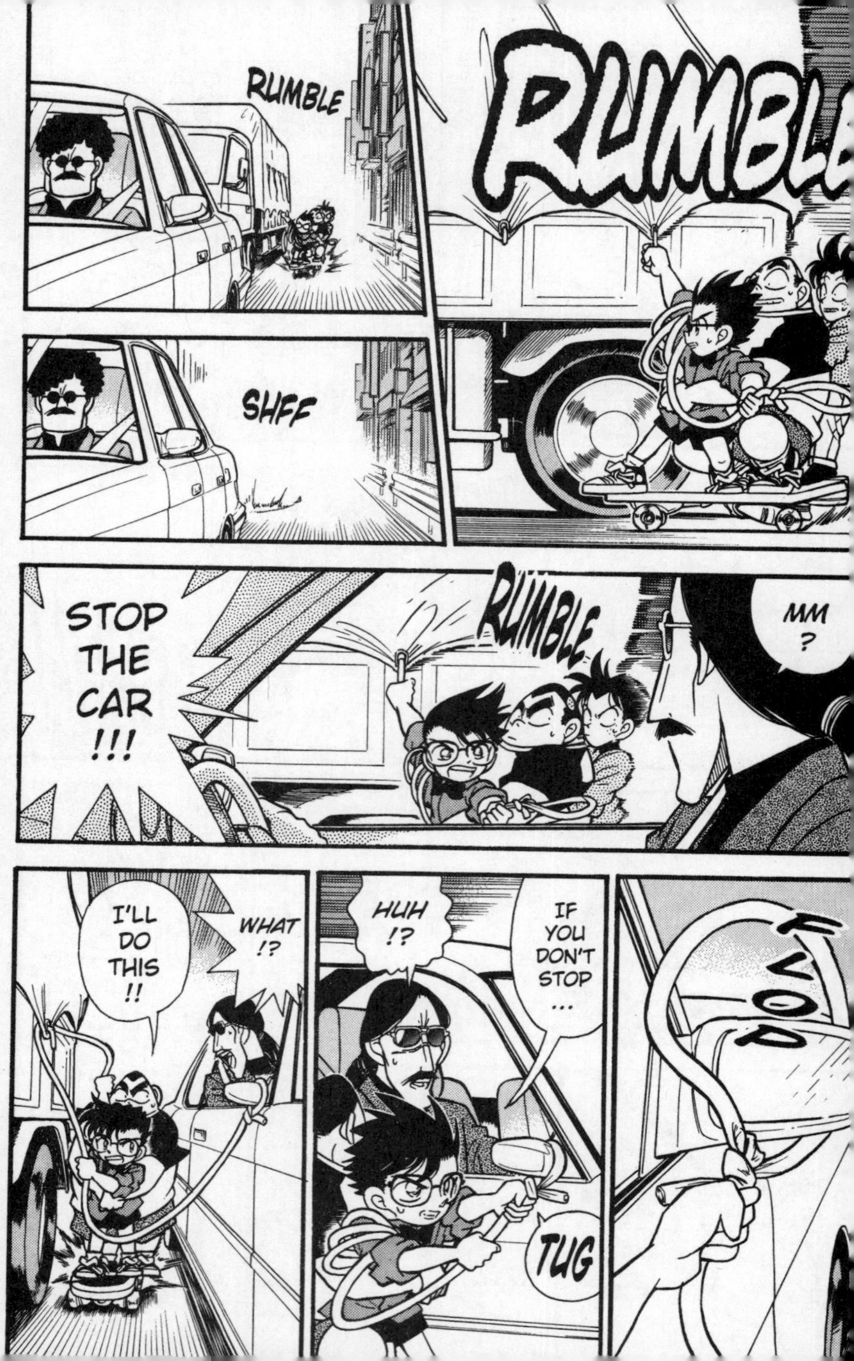
RUMBLE
RUMBLE
SHFF
MM ?
RUMBLE
STOP THE CAR !!!
FVOP
IF YOU DON'T STOP ...
HUH !?
TUG
WHAT !?
I'LL DO THIS !!

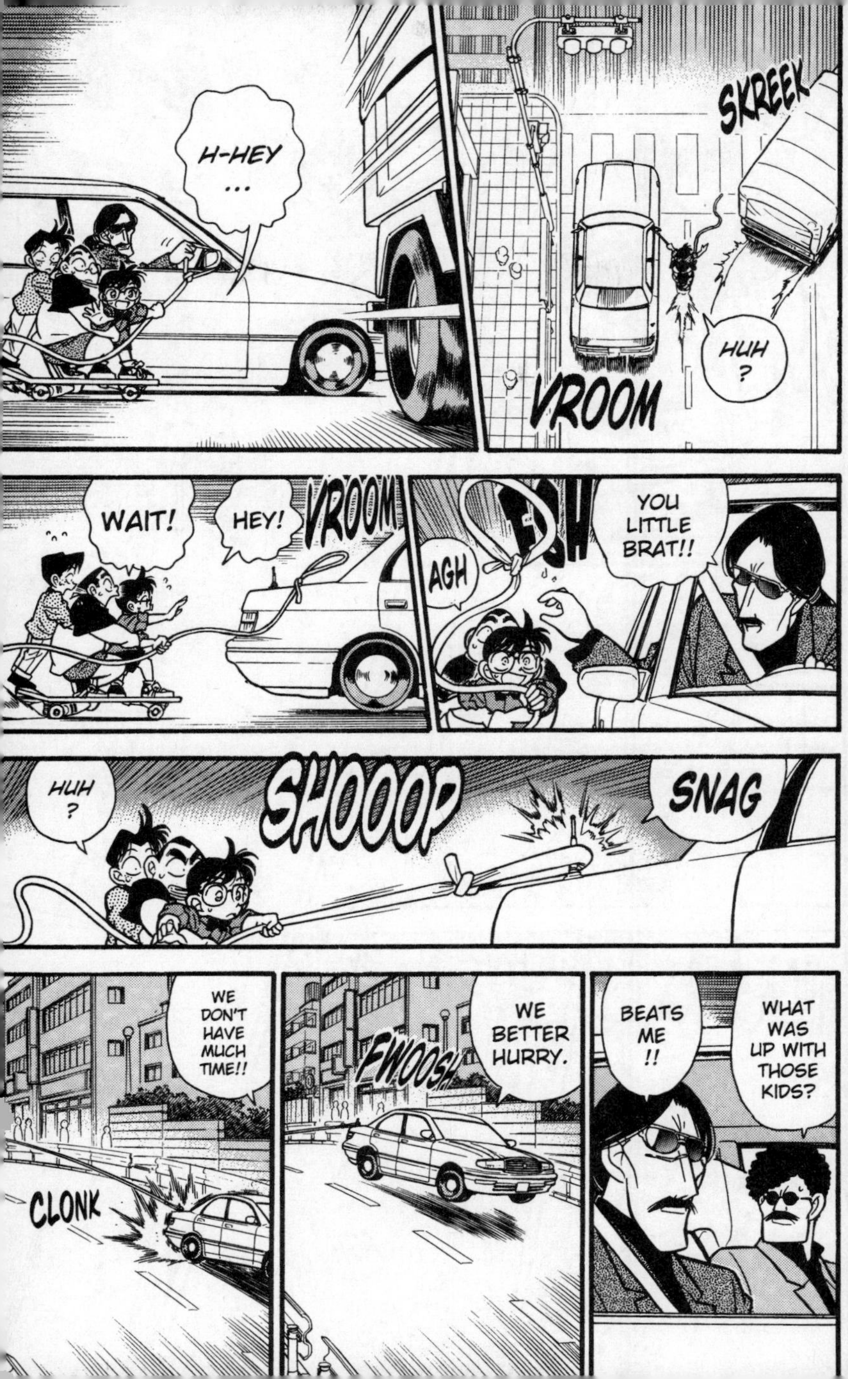
SKREEK
VROOM
HUH ?
H-HEY ...
YOU LITTLE BRAT!!
AGH
VROOM
HEY!
WAIT!
SNAG
SHOOOP
HUH ?
WHAT WAS UP WITH THOSE KIDS?
BEATS ME !!
WE BETTER HURRY.
FWOOSH
WE DON'T HAVE MUCH TIME!!
CLONK

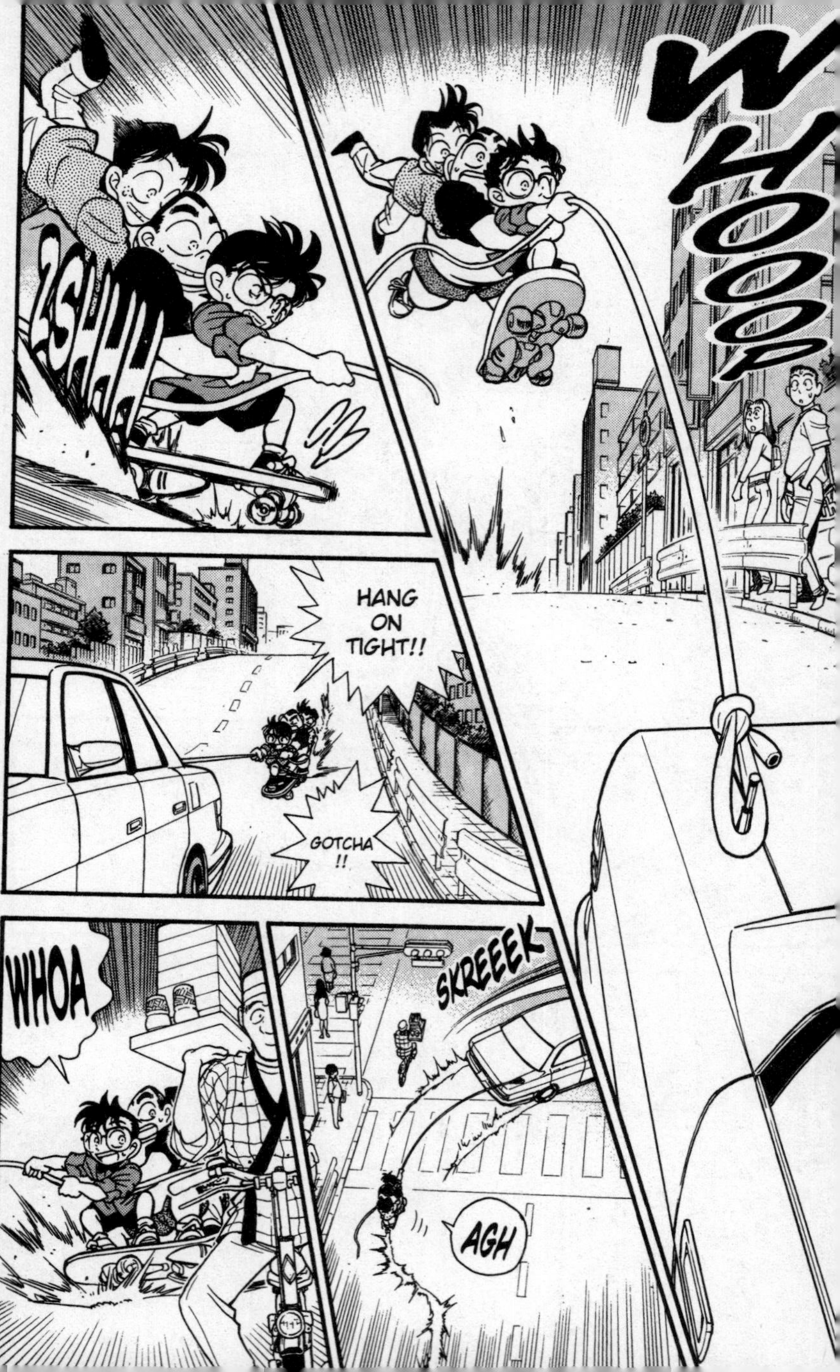
WHOOOP
HANG ON TIGHT!!
GOTCHA !!
SKREEEK
AGH
WHOA

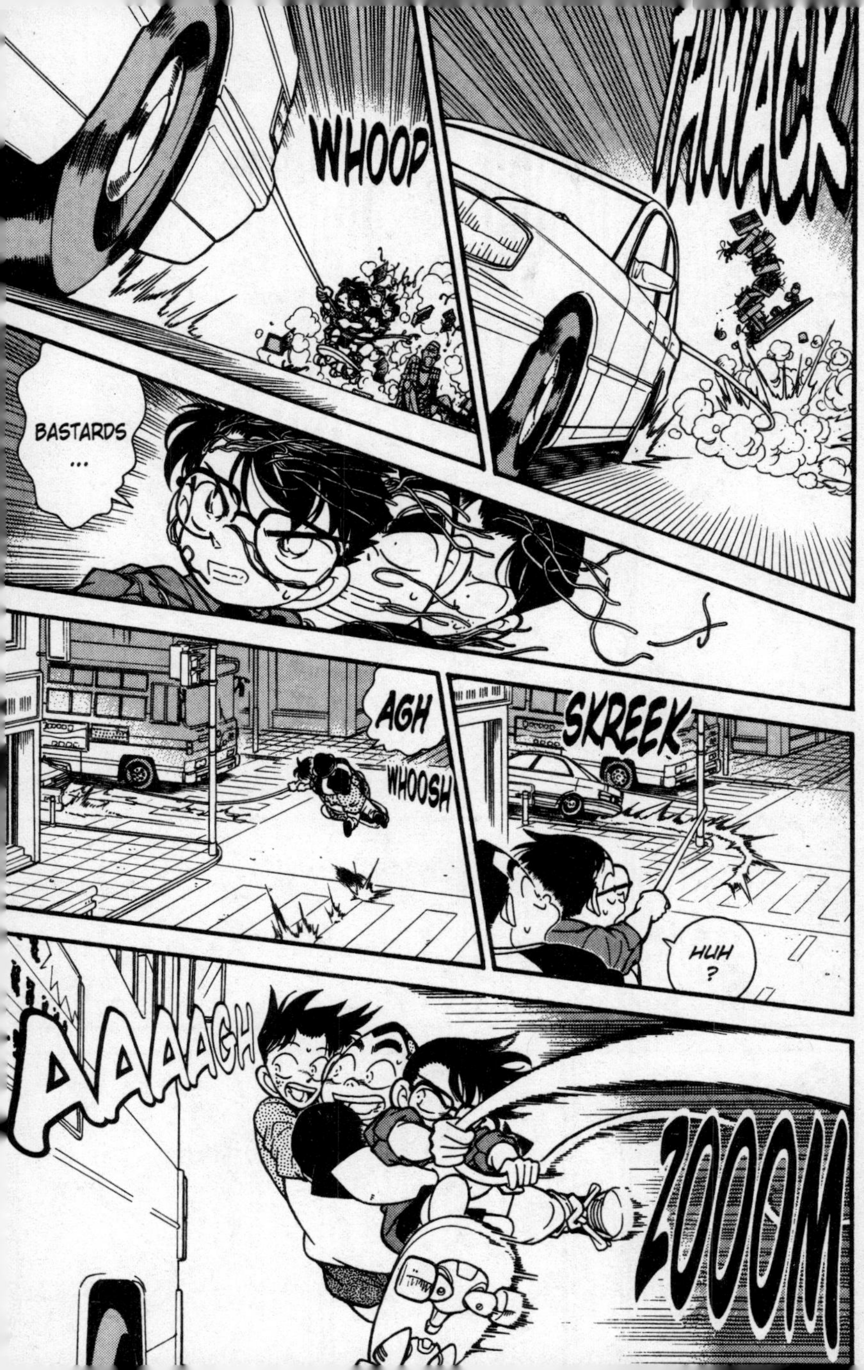
THWACK
WHOOP
BASTARDS ...
SKREEK
HUH?
AGH
WHOOSH
ZOOOM
AAAAGH

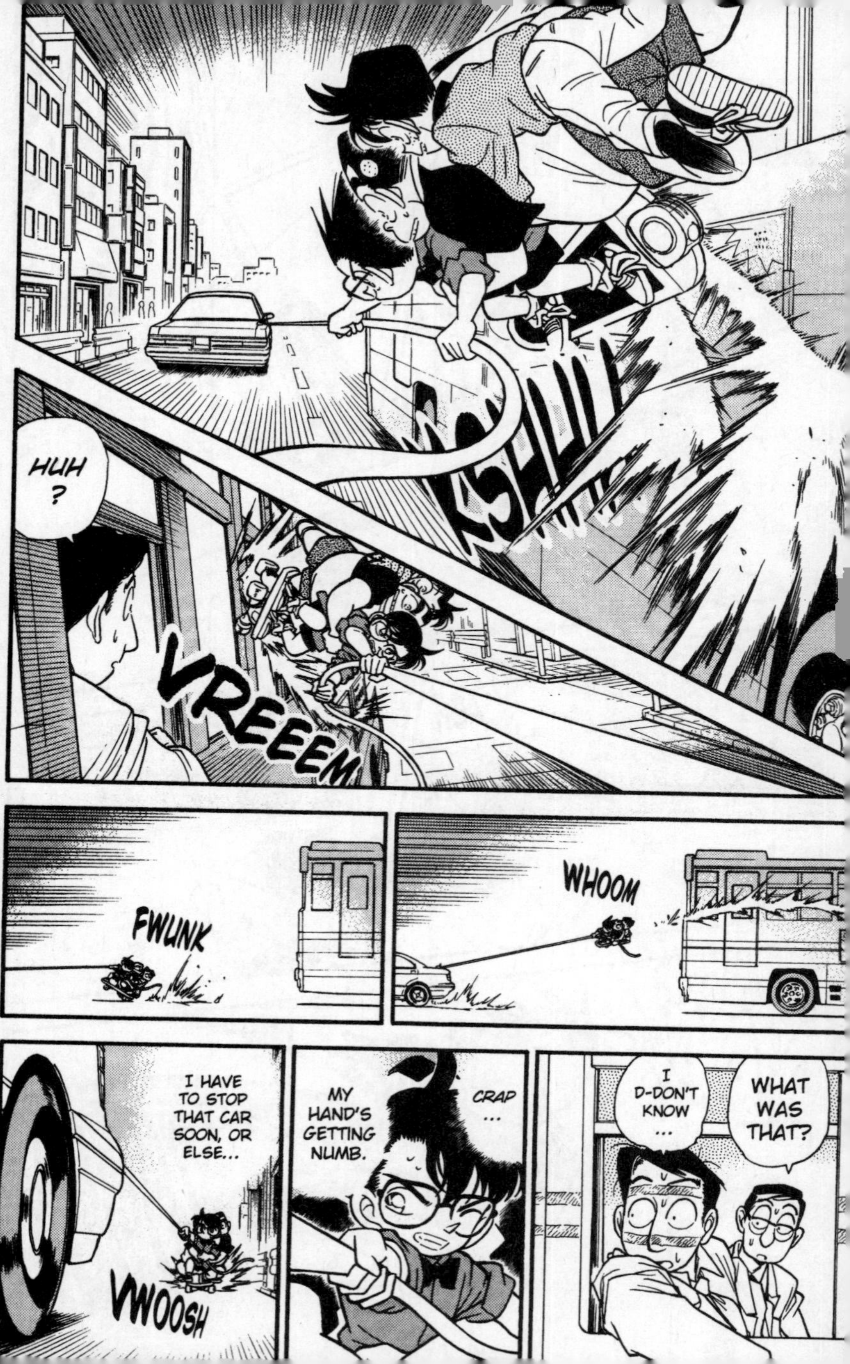
HUH ?
VREEEM
WHOOM
FWUNK
WHAT WAS THAT?
I D-DON'T KNOW ...
CRAP ...
MY HAND'S GETTING NUMB.
I HAVE TO STOP THAT CAR SOON, OR ELSE...
VWOOSH

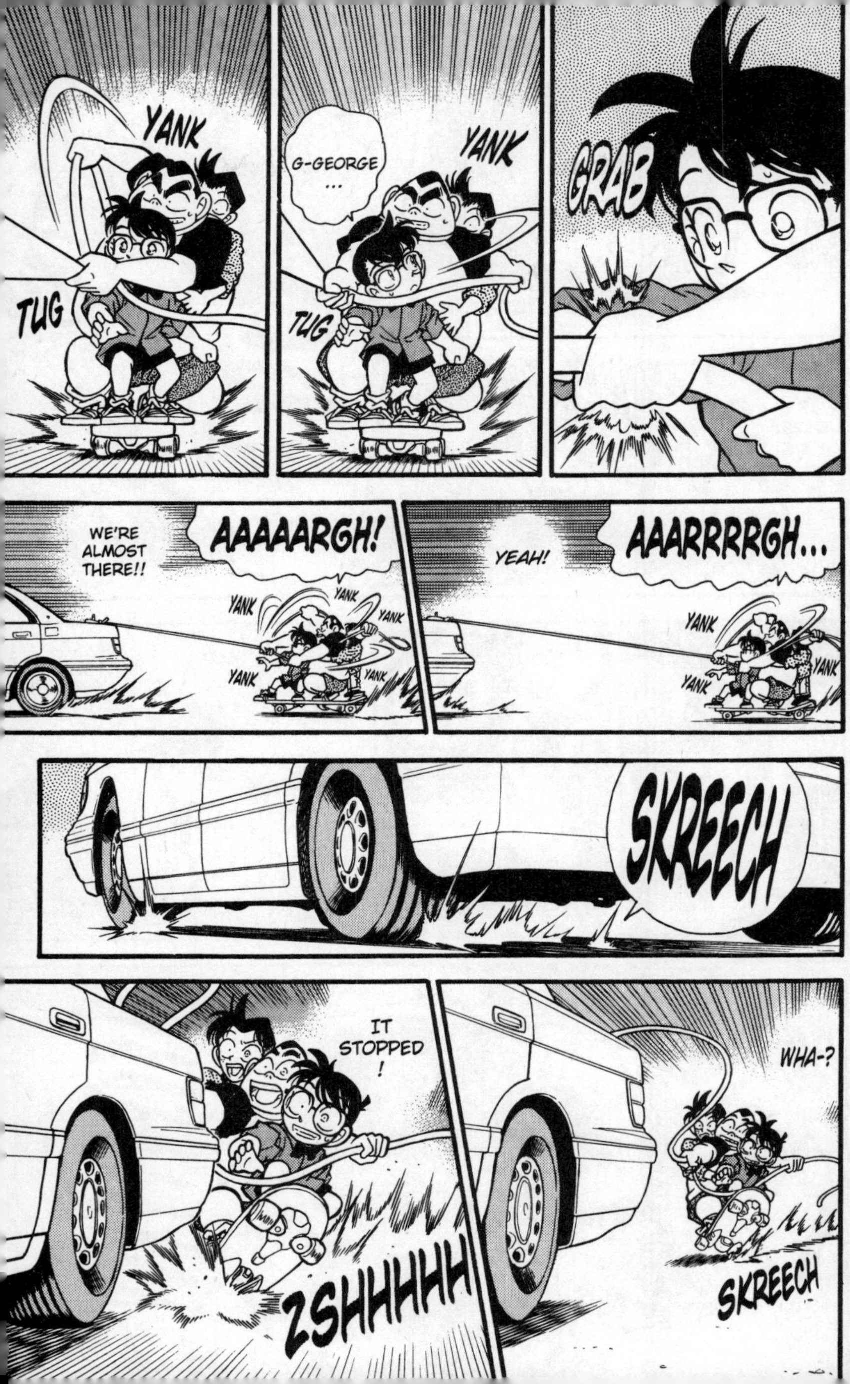
GRAB
YANK
G-GEORGE ...
TUG
YANK
TUG
AAARRRRGH...
YEAH!
YANK
YANK
YANK
AAAAARGH!
WE'RE ALMOST THERE!!
YANK
YANK
YANK
YANK
YANK
SKREECH
WHA-?
SKREECH
IT STOPPED !
ZSHHHHH

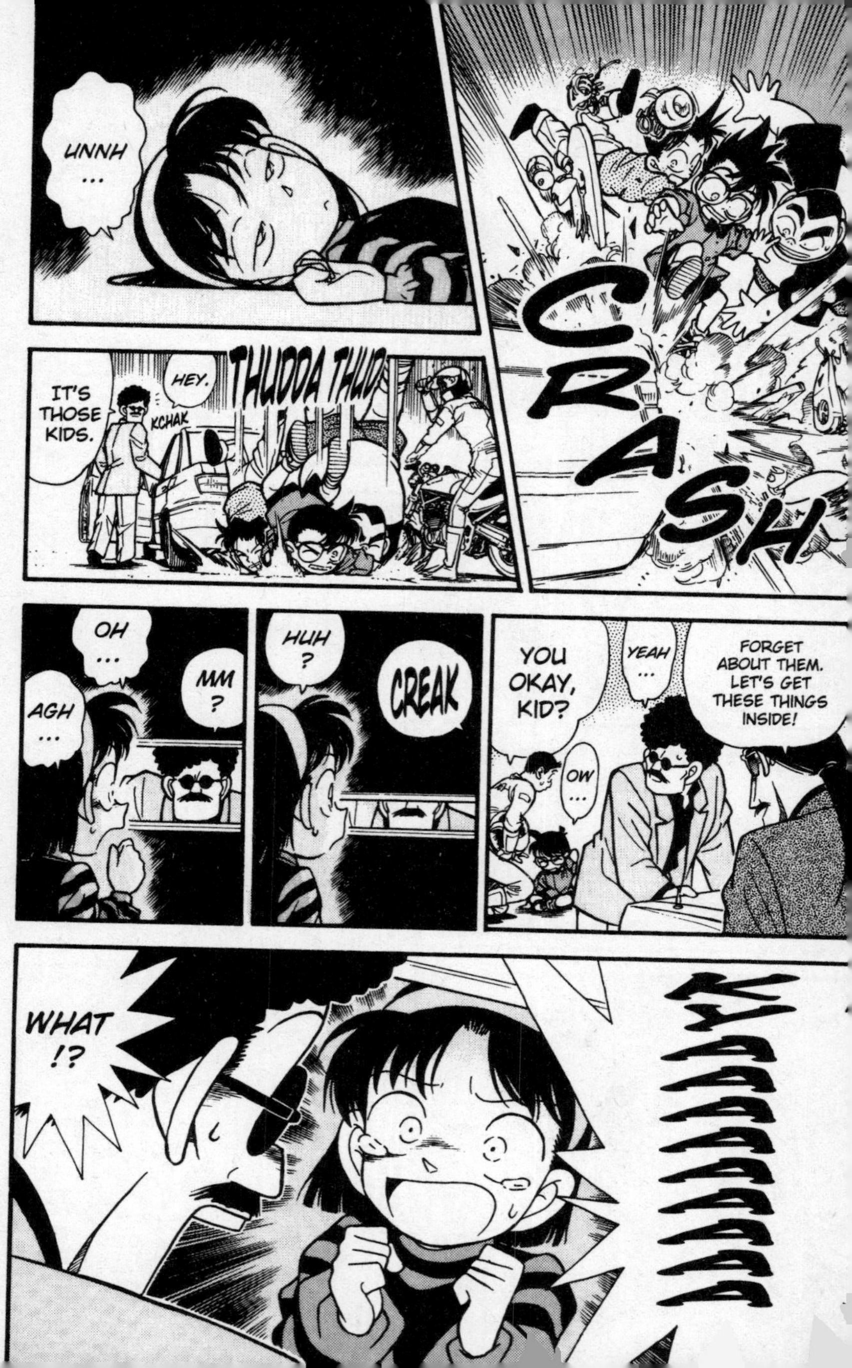

CRASH
UNNH ...
THUDDA THUD
HEY.
IT'S THOSE KIDS.
KCHAK
FORGET ABOUT THEM. LET'S GET THESE THINGS INSIDE!
YEAH ...
YOU OKAY, KID?
OW ...
CREAK
HUH ?
MM ?
OH ...
AGH ...
WHAT !?

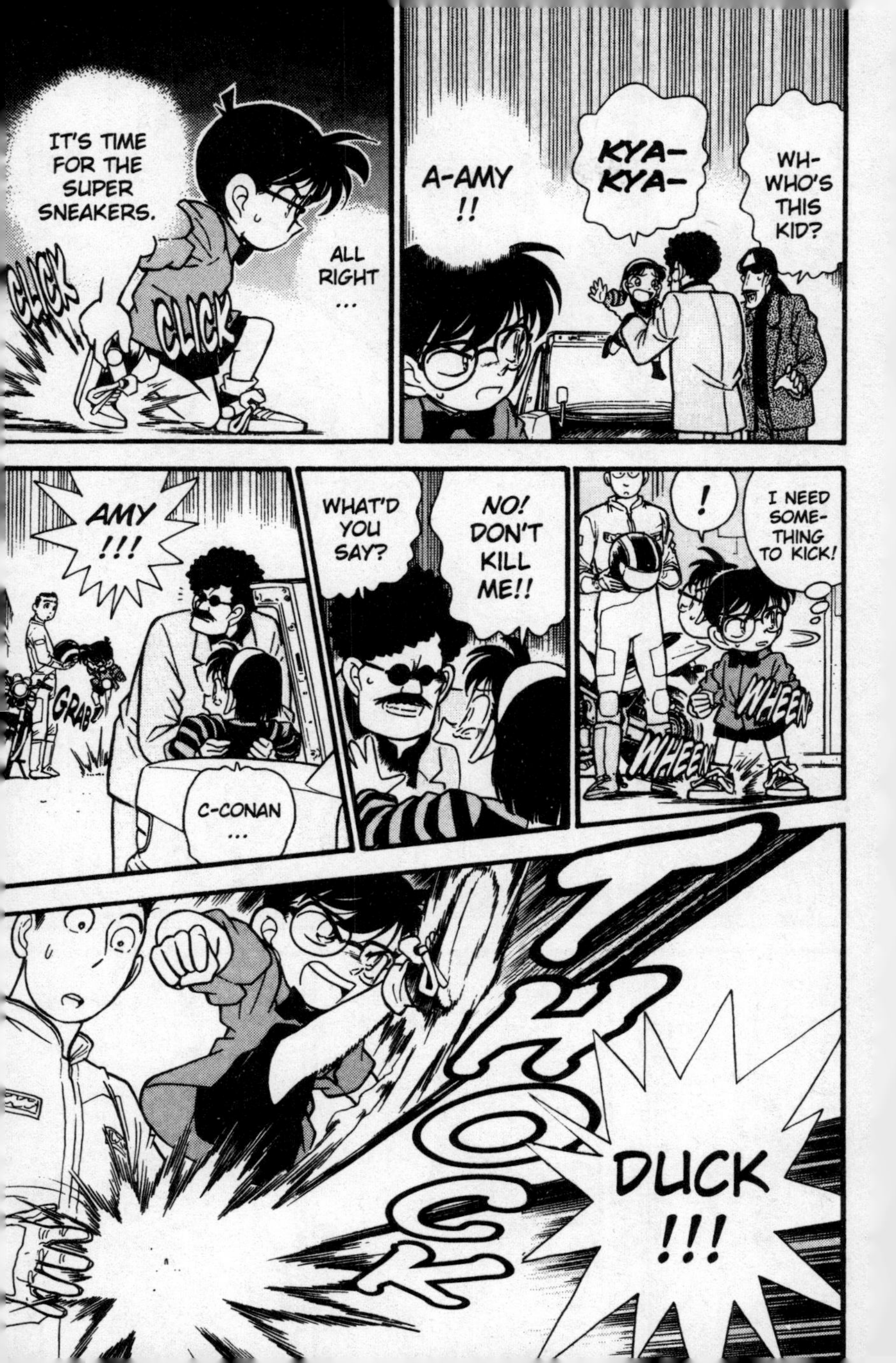

WH- WHO'S THIS KID?
KYA- KYA-
A-AMY !!
ALL RIGHT ...
IT'S TIME FOR THE SUPER SNEAKERS.
CLICK
CLICK
I NEED SOME-THING TO KICK!
!
WHEEN
WHEEN
NO! DON'T KILL ME!!
WHAT'D YOU SAY?
AMY !!!
GRAB
C-CONAN ...
DUCK !!!

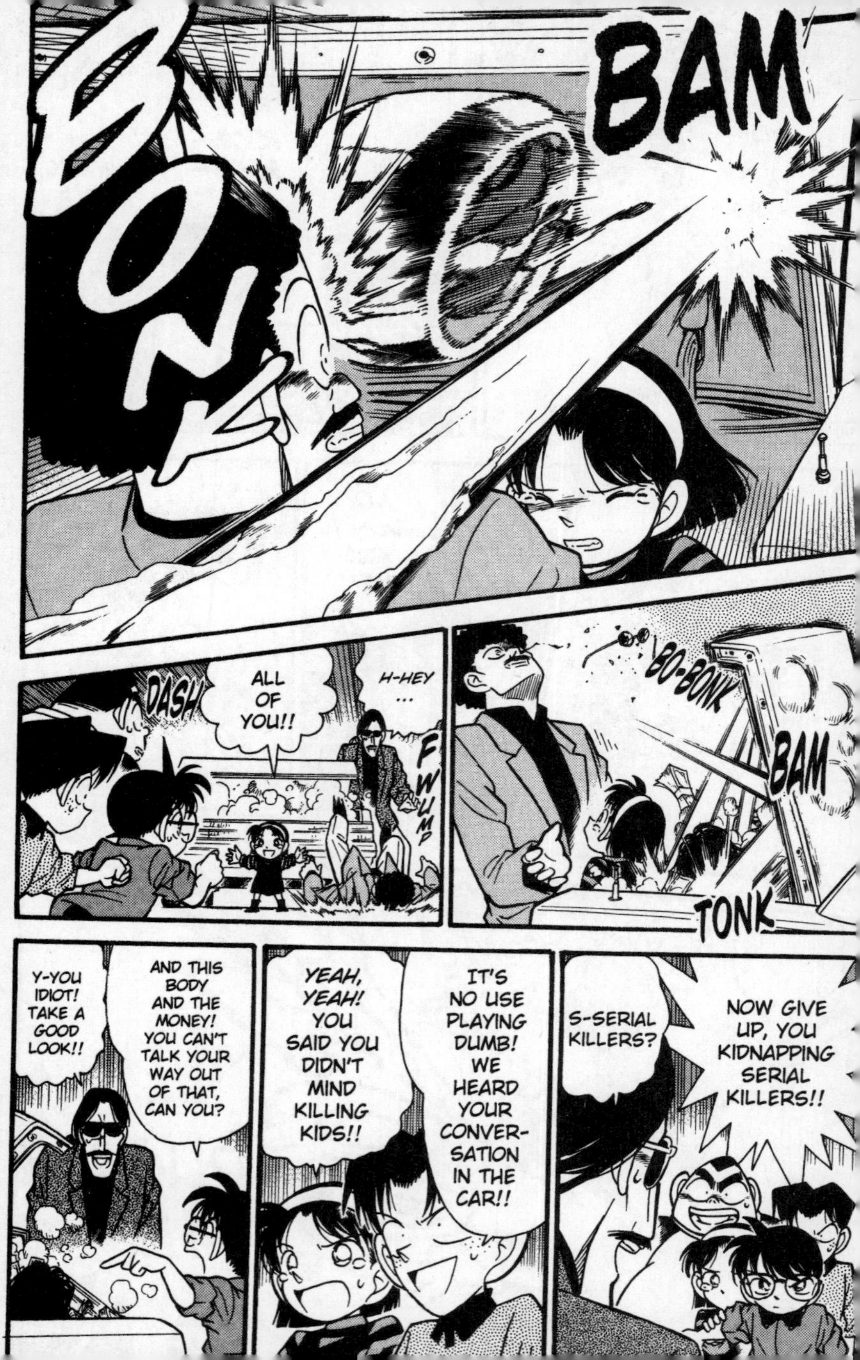
BAM
BO-BONK
BAM
TONK
H-HEY ...
FWUMP
ALL OF YOU!!
DASH
NOW GIVE UP, YOU KIDNAPPING SERIAL KILLERS!!
S-SERIAL KILLERS?
IT'S NO USE PLAYING DUMB! WE HEARD YOUR CONVERSATION IN THE CAR!!
YEAH, YEAH! YOU SAID YOU DIDN'T MIND KILLING KIDS!!
AND THIS BODY AND THE MONEY! YOU CAN'T TALK YOUR WAY OUT OF THAT, CAN YOU?
Y-YOU IDIOT! TAKE A GOOD LOOK!!

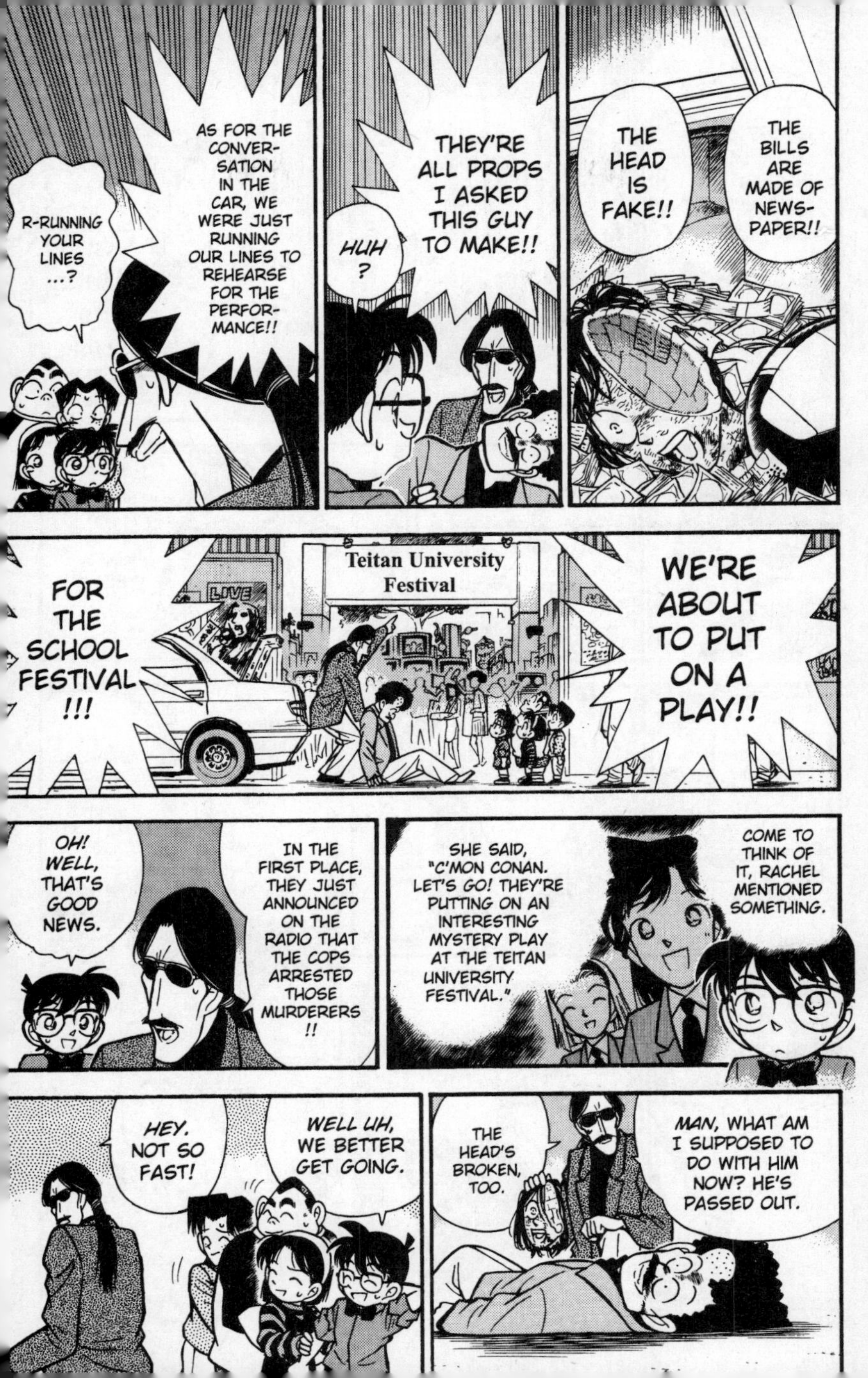
THE BILLS ARE MADE OF NEWS-PAPER!!
THE HEAD IS FAKE!!
THEY'RE ALL PROPS I ASKED THIS GUY TO MAKE!!
HUH?
AS FOR THE CONVER-SATION IN THE CAR, WE WERE JUST RUNNING OUR LINES TO REHEARSE FOR THE PERFOR-MANCE!!
R-RUNNING YOUR LINES ...?
WE'RE ABOUT TO PUT ON A PLAY!!
Teitan University Festival
LIVE
FOR THE SCHOOL FESTIVAL !!!
COME TO THINK OF IT, RACHEL MENTIONED SOMETHING.
SHE SAID, "C'MON CONAN. LET'S GO! THEY'RE PUTTING ON AN INTERESTING MYSTERY PLAY AT THE TEITAN UNIVERSITY FESTIVAL."
IN THE FIRST PLACE, THEY JUST ANNOUNCED ON THE RADIO THAT THE COPS ARRESTED THOSE MURDERERS !!
OH! WELL, THAT'S GOOD NEWS.
MAN, WHAT AM I SUPPOSED TO DO WITH HIM NOW? HE'S PASSED OUT.
THE HEAD'S BROKEN, TOO.
WELL UH, WE BETTER GET GOING.
HEY. NOT SO FAST!

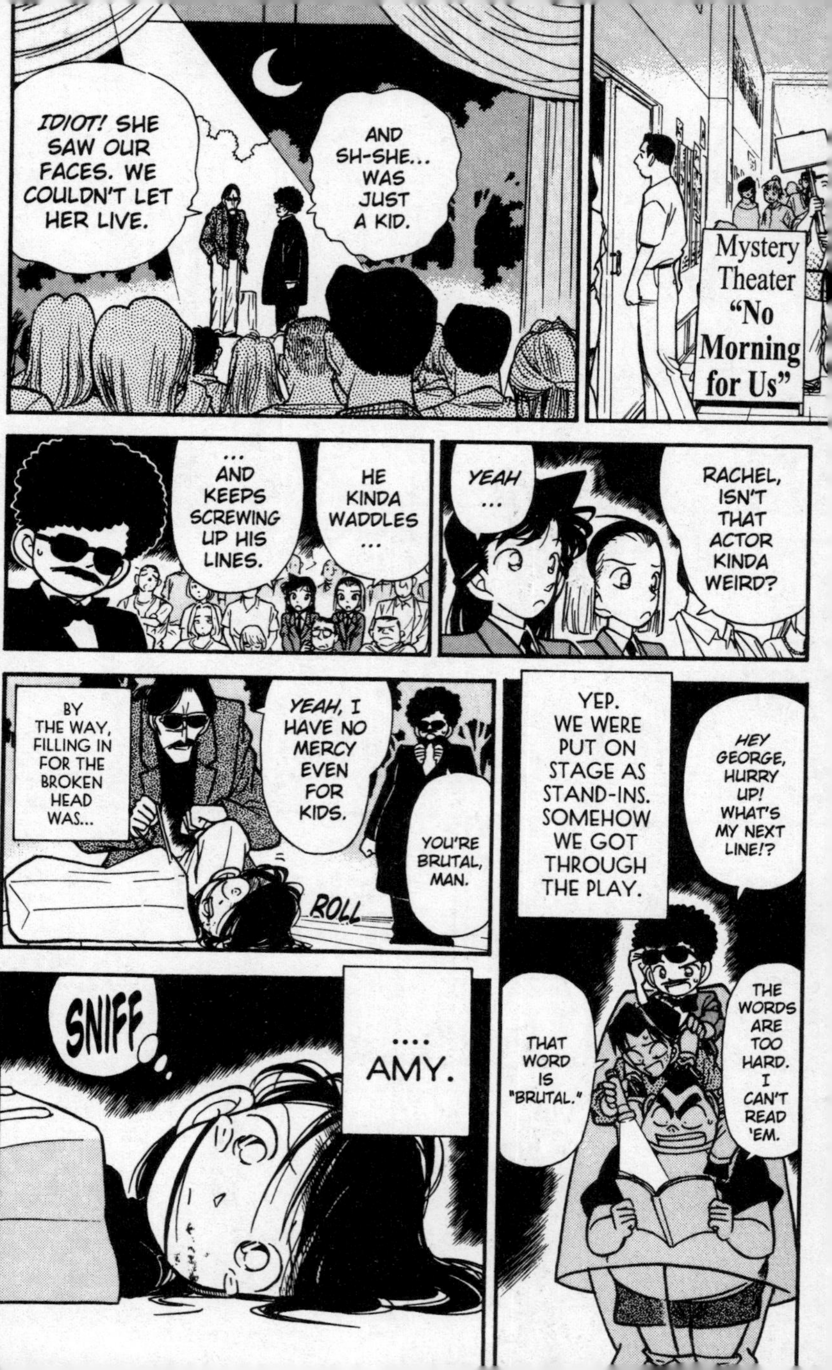
Mystery Theater "No Morning for Us"
AND SH-SHE... WAS JUST A KID.
IDIOT! SHE SAW OUR FACES. WE COULDN'T LET HER LIVE.
RACHEL, ISN'T THAT ACTOR KINDA WEIRD?
YEAH ...
HE KINDA WADDLES ...
... AND KEEPS SCREWING UP HIS LINES.
YEP. WE WERE PUT ON STAGE AS STAND-INS. SOMEHOW WE GOT THROUGH THE PLAY.
HEY GEORGE, HURRY UP! WHAT'S MY NEXT LINE!?
THE WORDS ARE TOO HARD. I CAN'T READ 'EM.
THAT WORD IS "BRUTAL."
YEAH, I HAVE NO MERCY EVEN FOR KIDS.
BY THE WAY, FILLING IN FOR THE BROKEN HEAD WAS...
YOU'RE BRUTAL, MAN.
ROLL
.... AMY.
SNIFF

FILE 4:
RICHARD'S REUNION

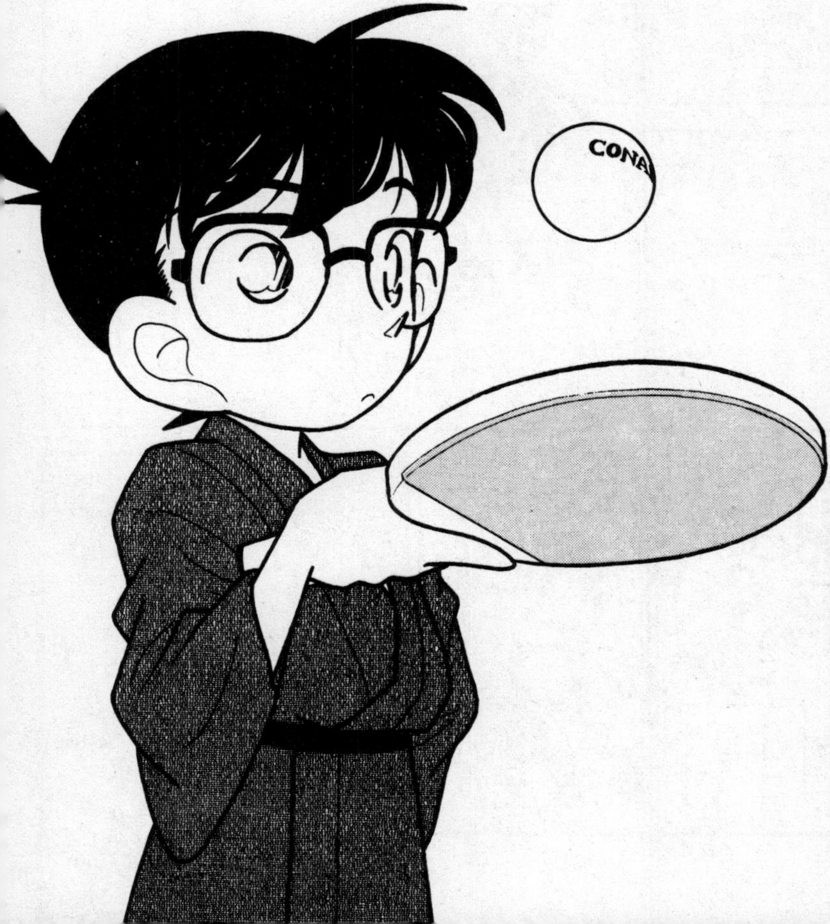
CONA

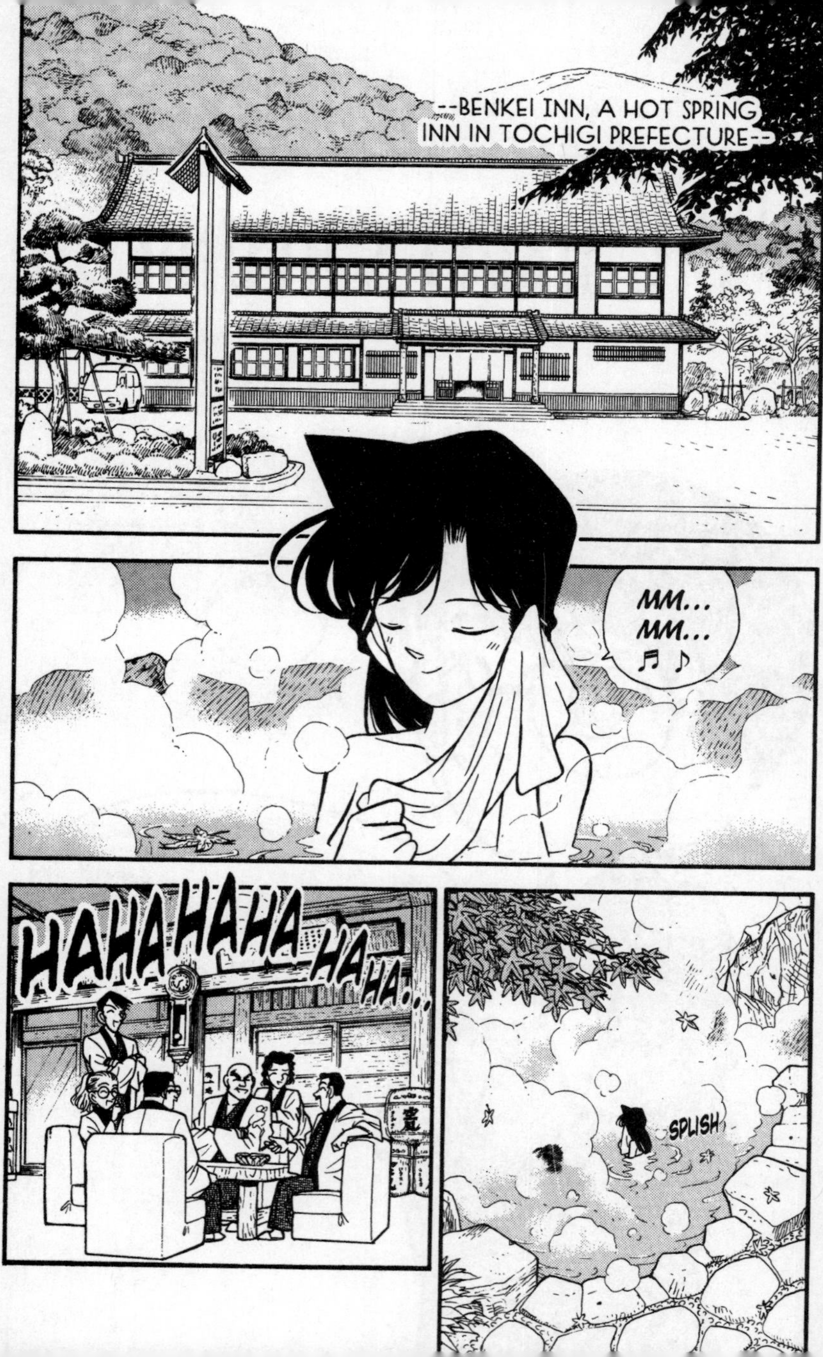
--BENKEI INN, A HOT SPRING INN IN TOCHIGI PREFECTURE--
MM... MM... ♬ ♪
SPLISH
HAHA HAHA HAHA...

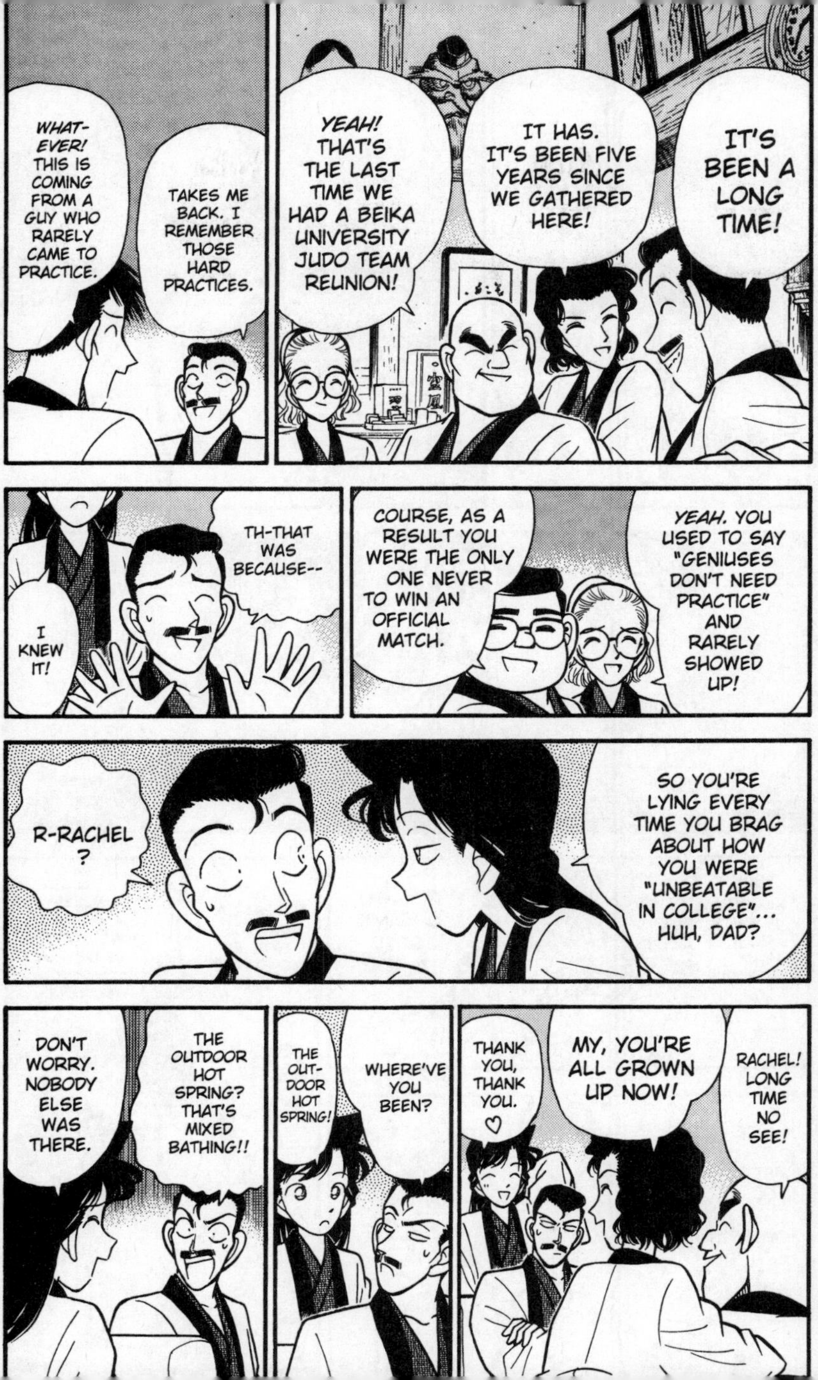
IT'S BEEN A LONG TIME!
IT HAS. IT'S BEEN FIVE YEARS SINCE WE GATHERED HERE!
YEAH! THAT'S THE LAST TIME WE HAD A BEIKA UNIVERSITY JUDO TEAM REUNION!
TAKES ME BACK. I REMEMBER THOSE HARD PRACTICES.
WHATEVER! THIS IS COMING FROM A GUY WHO RARELY CAME TO PRACTICE.
YEAH. YOU USED TO SAY "GENIUSES DON'T NEED PRACTICE" AND RARELY SHOWED UP!
COURSE, AS A RESULT YOU WERE THE ONLY ONE NEVER TO WIN AN OFFICIAL MATCH.
TH-THAT WAS BECAUSE--
I KNEW IT!
SO YOU'RE LYING EVERY TIME YOU BRAG ABOUT HOW YOU WERE "UNBEATABLE IN COLLEGE"... HUH, DAD?
R-RACHEL?
RACHEL! LONG TIME NO SEE!
MY, YOU'RE ALL GROWN UP NOW!
THANK YOU, THANK YOU. ♡
WHERE'VE YOU BEEN?
THE OUTDOOR HOT SPRING!
THE OUTDOOR HOT SPRING? THAT'S MIXED BATHING!!
DON'T WORRY. NOBODY ELSE WAS THERE.

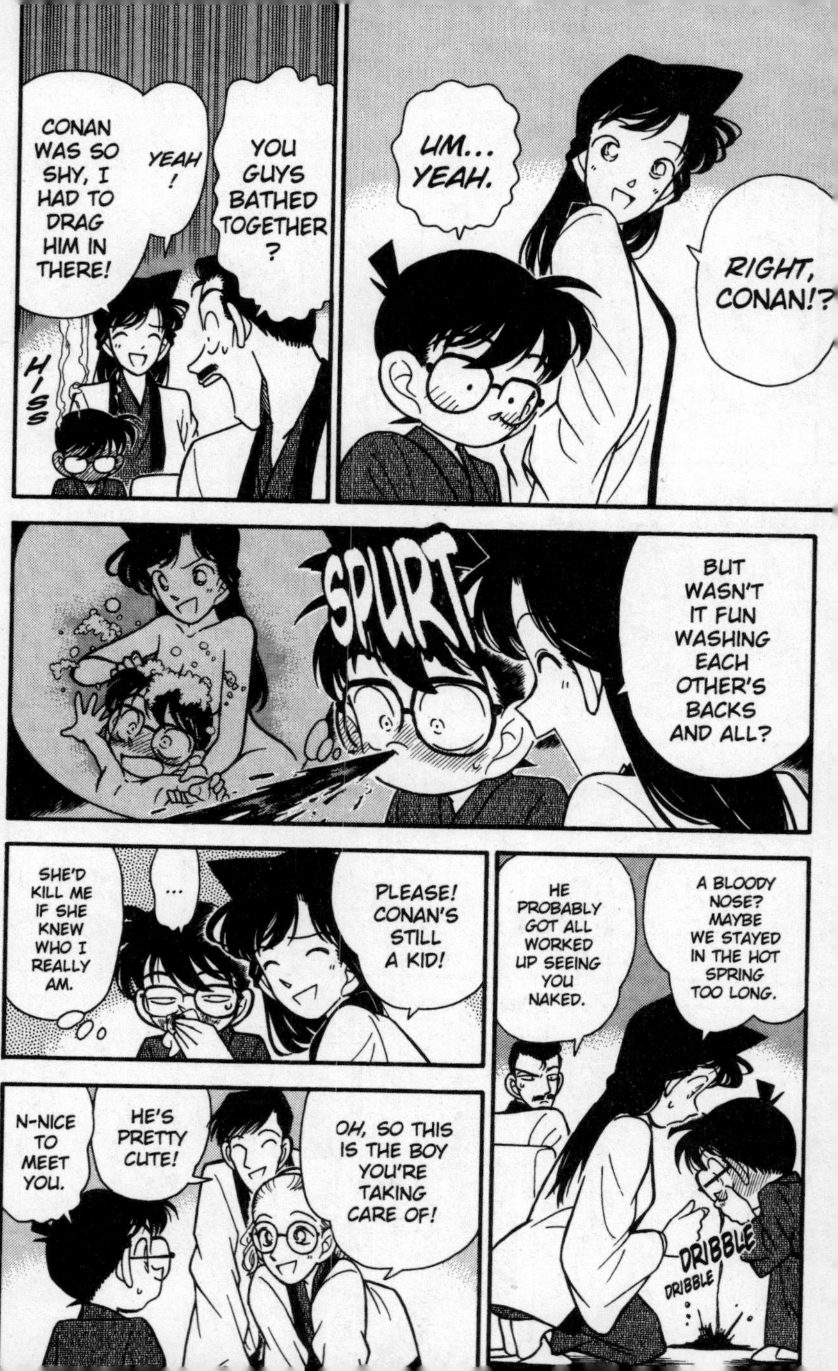
RIGHT, CONAN!?
UM... YEAH.
YOU GUYS BATHED TOGETHER?
YEAH!
CONAN WAS SO SHY, I HAD TO DRAG HIM IN THERE!
HISS
BUT WASN'T IT FUN WASHING EACH OTHER'S BACKS AND ALL?
SPURT
A BLOODY NOSE? MAYBE WE STAYED IN THE HOT SPRING TOO LONG.
HE PROBABLY GOT ALL WORKED UP SEEING YOU NAKED.
DRIBBLE
DRIBBLE
...
PLEASE! CONAN'S STILL A KID!
...
SHE'D KILL ME IF SHE KNEW WHO I REALLY AM.
OH, SO THIS IS THE BOY YOU'RE TAKING CARE OF!
HE'S PRETTY CUTE!
N-NICE TO MEET YOU.

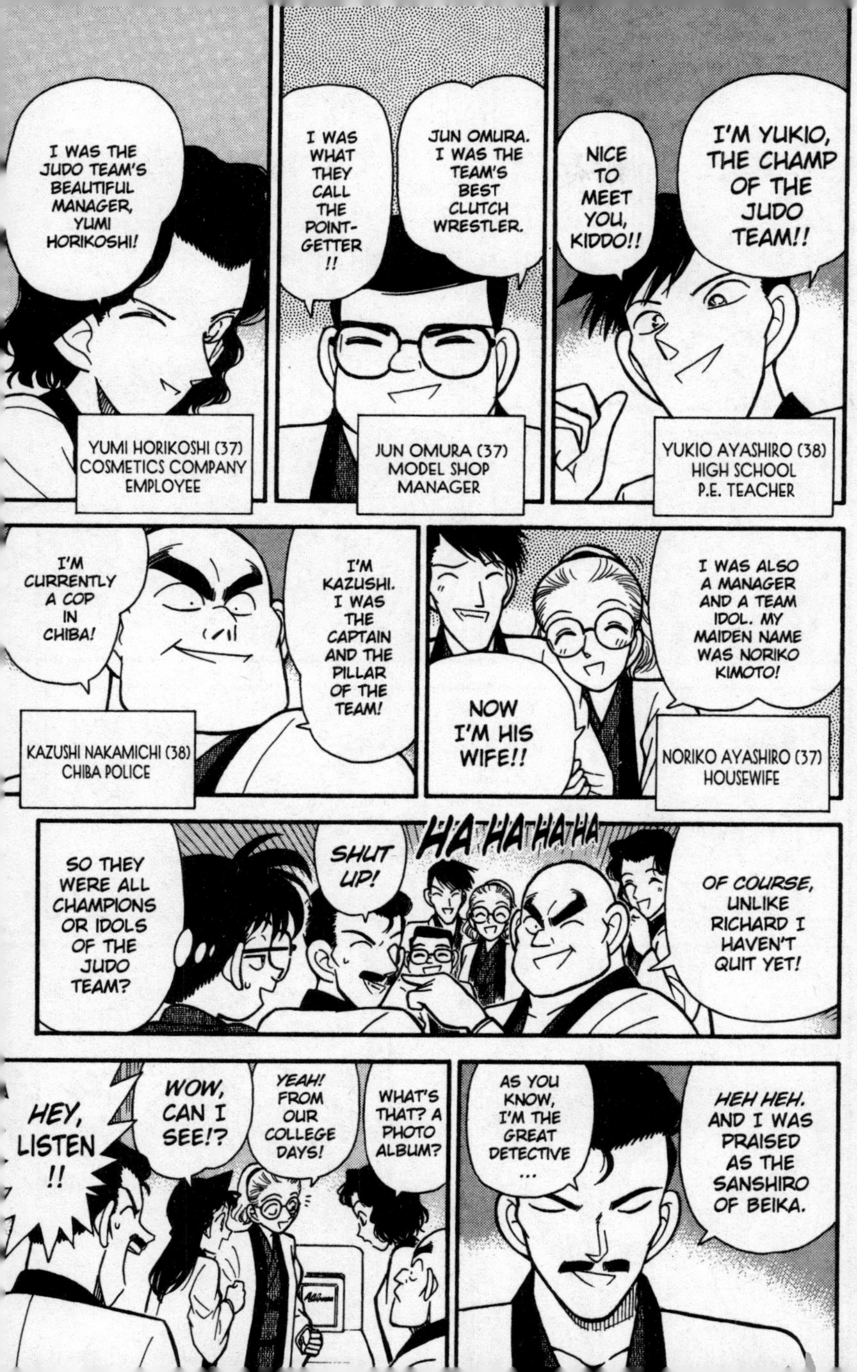
I'M YUKIO, THE CHAMP OF THE JUDO TEAM!!
NICE TO MEET YOU, KIDDO!!
YUKIO AYASHIRO (38) HIGH SCHOOL P.E. TEACHER
JUN OMURA. I WAS THE TEAM'S BEST CLUTCH WRESTLER.
I WAS WHAT THEY CALL THE POINT-GETTER!!
JUN OMURA (37) MODEL SHOP MANAGER
I WAS THE JUDO TEAM'S BEAUTIFUL MANAGER, YUMI HORIKOSHI!
YUMI HORIKOSHI (37) COSMETICS COMPANY EMPLOYEE
I WAS ALSO A MANAGER AND A TEAM IDOL. MY MAIDEN NAME WAS NORIKO KIMOTO!
NOW I'M HIS WIFE!!
NORIKO AYASHIRO (37) HOUSEWIFE
I'M KAZUSHI. I WAS THE CAPTAIN AND THE PILLAR OF THE TEAM!
I'M CURRENTLY A COP IN CHIBA!
KAZUSHI NAKAMICHI (38) CHIBA POLICE
OF COURSE, UNLIKE RICHARD I HAVEN'T QUIT YET!
HA HA HA HA
SHUT UP!
SO THEY WERE ALL CHAMPIONS OR IDOLS OF THE JUDO TEAM?
HEH HEH. AND I WAS PRAISED AS THE SANSHIRO OF BEIKA.
AS YOU KNOW, I'M THE GREAT DETECTIVE ...
WHAT'S THAT? A PHOTO ALBUM?
YEAH! FROM OUR COLLEGE DAYS!
WOW, CAN I SEE!?
HEY, LISTEN !!

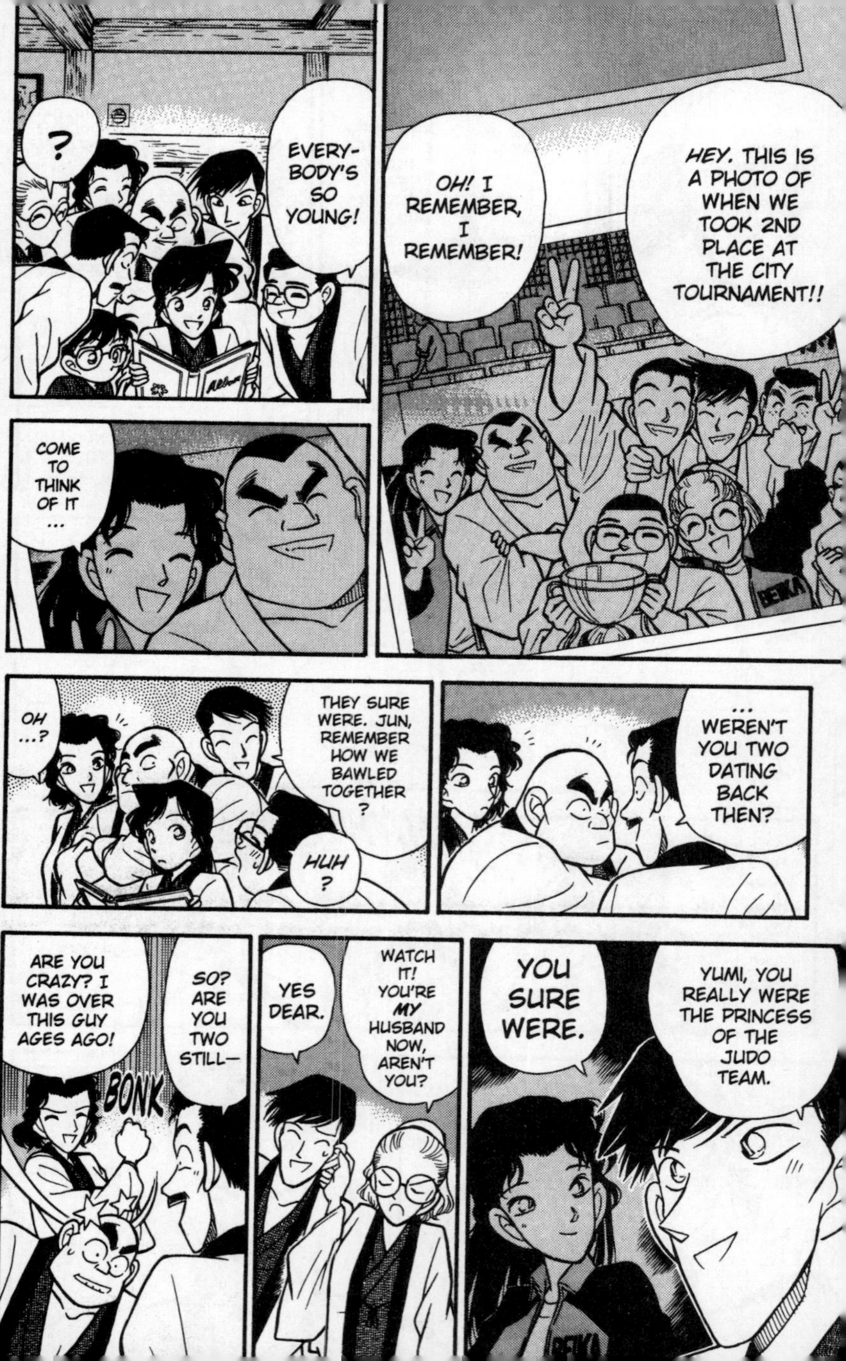
HEY. THIS IS A PHOTO OF WHEN WE TOOK 2ND PLACE AT THE CITY TOURNAMENT!!
OH! I REMEMBER, I REMEMBER!
EVERY-BODY'S SO YOUNG!
?
COME TO THINK OF IT ...
... WEREN'T YOU TWO DATING BACK THEN?
THEY SURE WERE. JUN, REMEMBER HOW WE BAWLED TOGETHER?
HUH?
OH ...?
YUMI, YOU REALLY WERE THE PRINCESS OF THE JUDO TEAM.
YOU SURE WERE.
WATCH IT! YOU'RE MY HUSBAND NOW, AREN'T YOU?
YES DEAR.
SO? ARE YOU TWO STILL—
ARE YOU CRAZY? I WAS OVER THIS GUY AGES AGO!
BONK

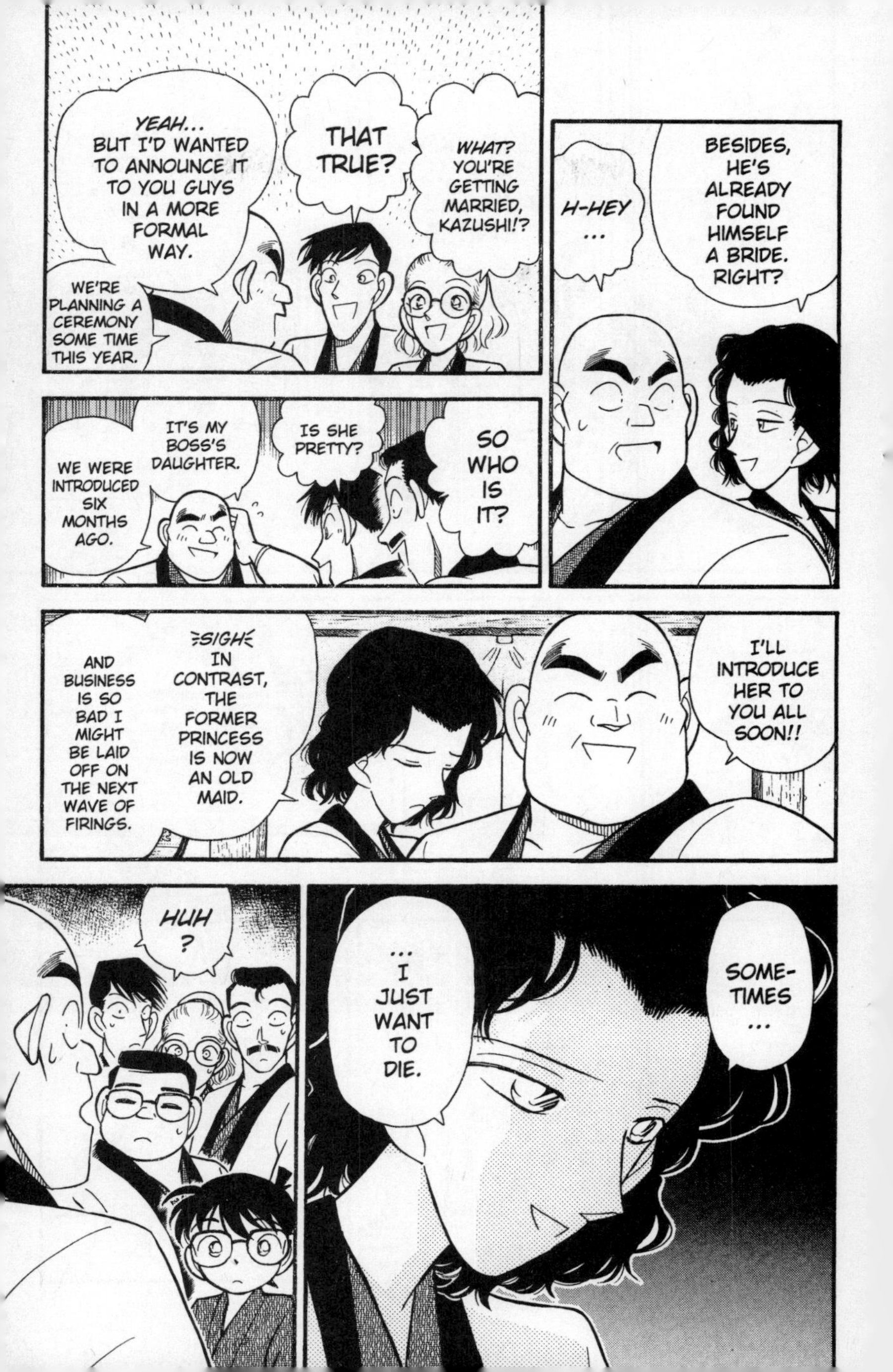
BESIDES, HE'S ALREADY FOUND HIMSELF A BRIDE. RIGHT?
H-HEY...
WHAT? YOU'RE GETTING MARRIED, KAZUSHI!?
THAT TRUE?
YEAH... BUT I'D WANTED TO ANNOUNCE IT TO YOU GUYS IN A MORE FORMAL WAY.
WE'RE PLANNING A CEREMONY SOME TIME THIS YEAR.
SO WHO IS IT?
IS SHE PRETTY?
IT'S MY BOSS'S DAUGHTER.
WE WERE INTRODUCED SIX MONTHS AGO.
I'LL INTRODUCE HER TO YOU ALL SOON!!
≡SIGH≡ IN CONTRAST, THE FORMER PRINCESS IS NOW AN OLD MAID.
AND BUSINESS IS SO BAD I MIGHT BE LAID OFF ON THE NEXT WAVE OF FIRINGS.
SOME-TIMES...
...I JUST WANT TO DIE.
HUH?

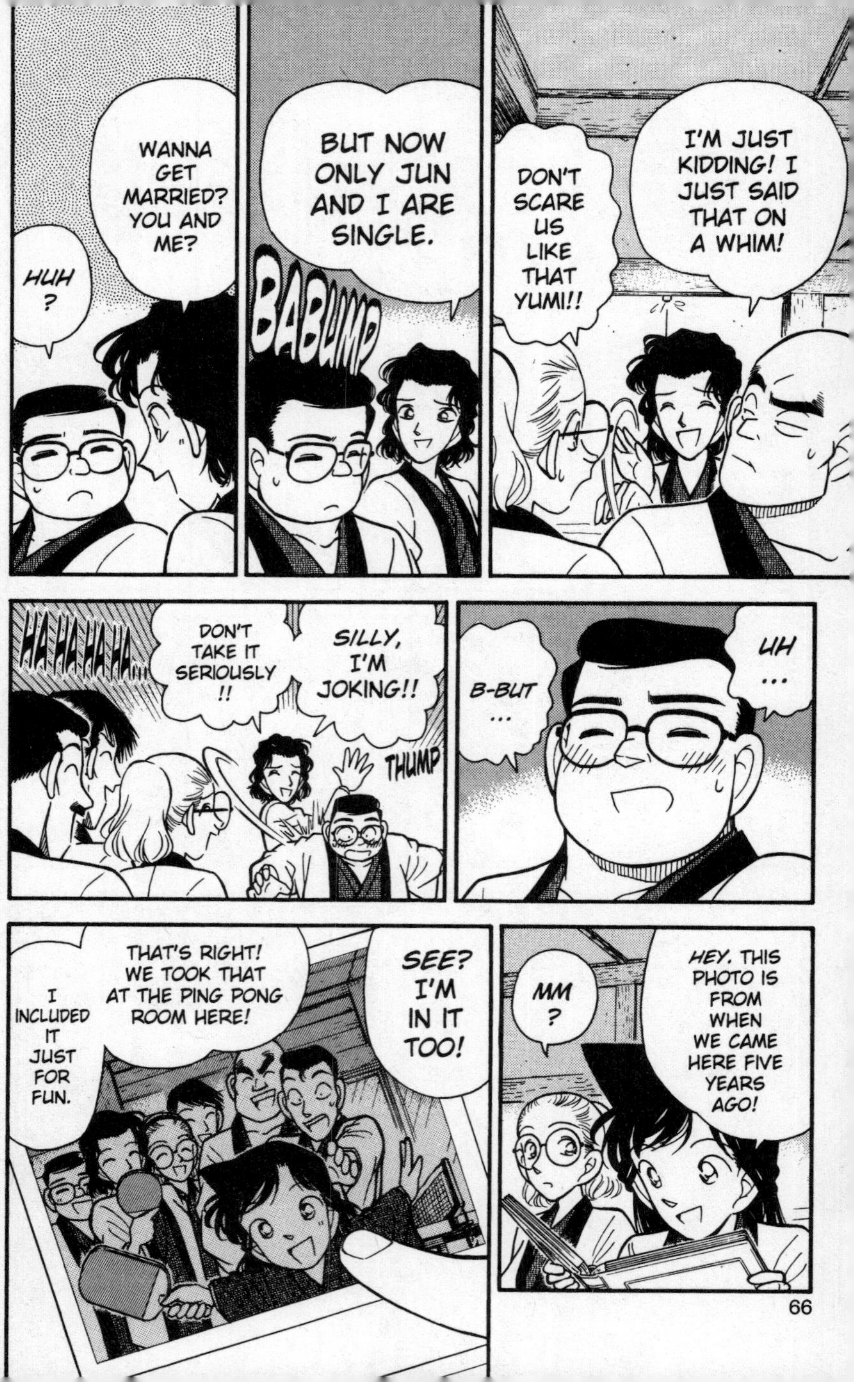
WANNA GET MARRIED? YOU AND ME?
HUH?
BUT NOW ONLY JUN AND I ARE SINGLE.
BABUMP
I'M JUST KIDDING! I JUST SAID THAT ON A WHIM!
DON'T SCARE US LIKE THAT YUMI!!
HA HA HA HA...
DON'T TAKE IT SERIOUSLY!!
SILLY, I'M JOKING!!
THUMP
UH ...
B-BUT ...
I INCLUDED IT JUST FOR FUN.
THAT'S RIGHT! WE TOOK THAT AT THE PING PONG ROOM HERE!
SEE? I'M IN IT TOO!
HEY. THIS PHOTO IS FROM WHEN WE CAME HERE FIVE YEARS AGO!
MM?

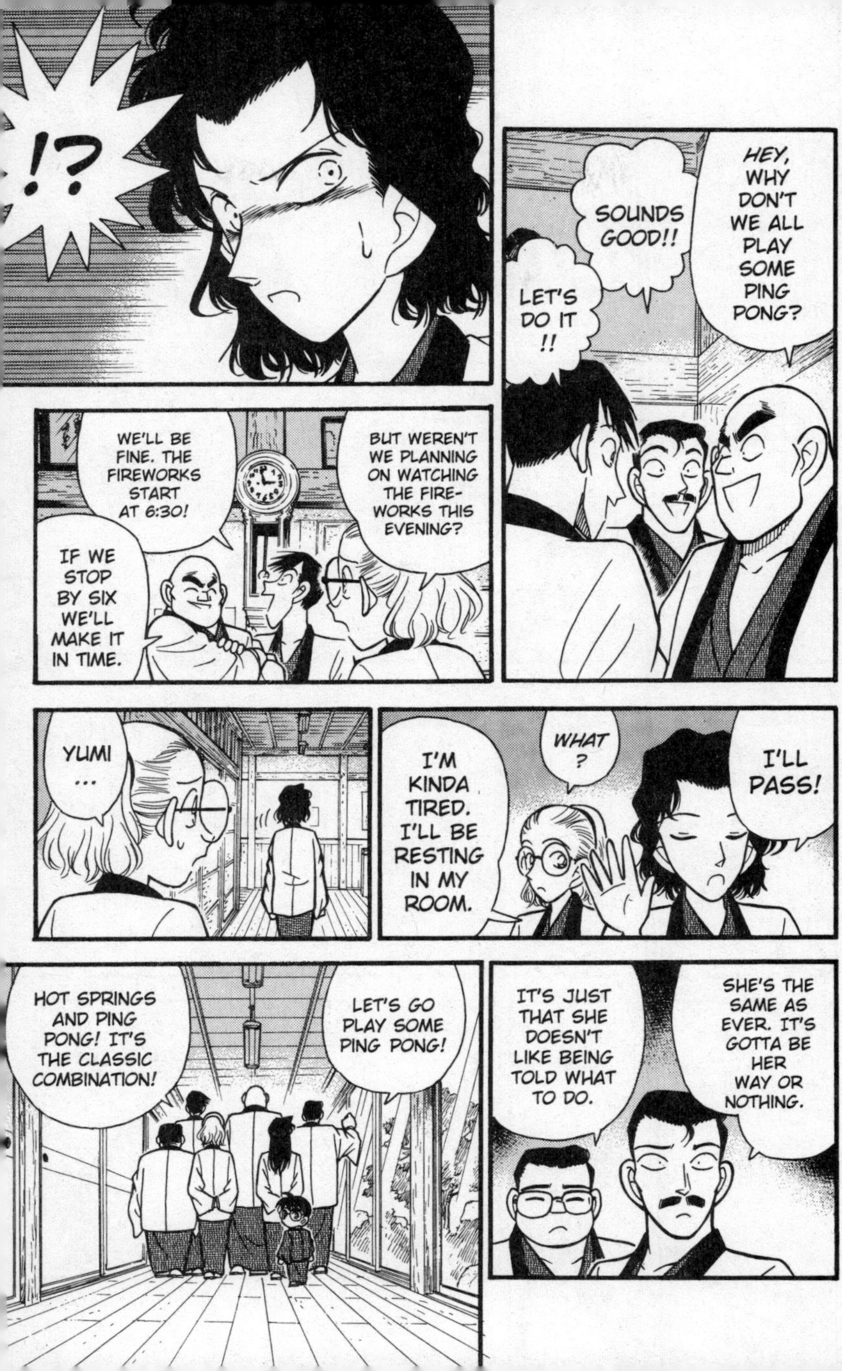
HEY, WHY DON'T WE ALL PLAY SOME PING PONG?
SOUNDS GOOD!!
LET'S DO IT !!
!?
BUT WEREN'T WE PLANNING ON WATCHING THE FIRE-WORKS THIS EVENING?
WE'LL BE FINE. THE FIREWORKS START AT 6:30!
IF WE STOP BY SIX WE'LL MAKE IT IN TIME.
I'LL PASS!
WHAT ?
I'M KINDA TIRED. I'LL BE RESTING IN MY ROOM.
YUMI ...
SHE'S THE SAME AS EVER. IT'S GOTTA BE HER WAY OR NOTHING.
IT'S JUST THAT SHE DOESN'T LIKE BEING TOLD WHAT TO DO.
LET'S GO PLAY SOME PING PONG!
HOT SPRINGS AND PING PONG! IT'S THE CLASSIC COMBINATION!

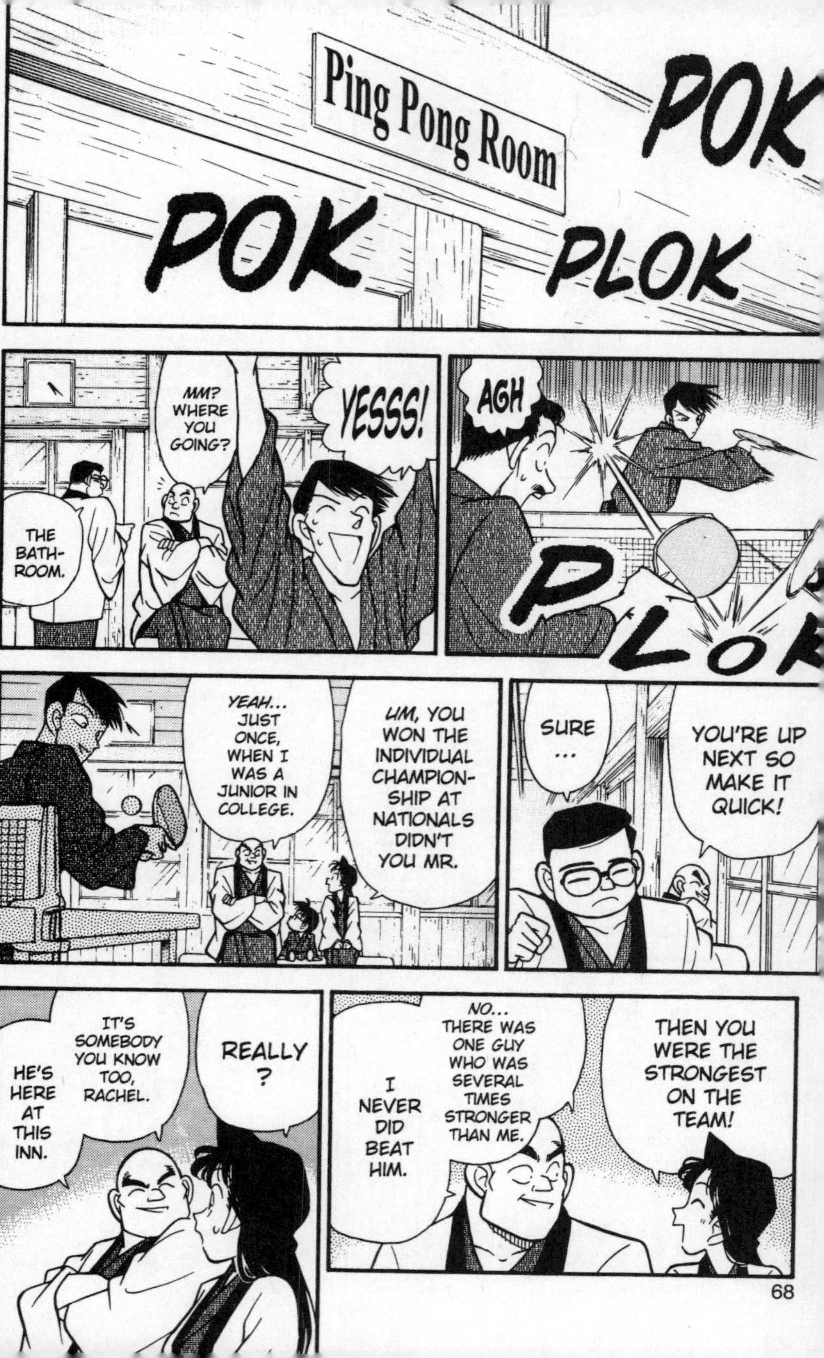
Ping Pong Room
POK
PLOK
POK
AGH
PLO
YESSS!
MM? WHERE YOU GOING?
THE BATH-ROOM.
YOU'RE UP NEXT SO MAKE IT QUICK!
SURE...
UM, YOU WON THE INDIVIDUAL CHAMPION-SHIP AT NATIONALS DIDN'T YOU MR.
YEAH... JUST ONCE, WHEN I WAS A JUNIOR IN COLLEGE.
THEN YOU WERE THE STRONGEST ON THE TEAM!
NO... THERE WAS ONE GUY WHO WAS SEVERAL TIMES STRONGER THAN ME.
I NEVER DID BEAT HIM.
REALLY?
IT'S SOMEBODY YOU KNOW TOO, RACHEL.
HE'S HERE AT THIS INN.

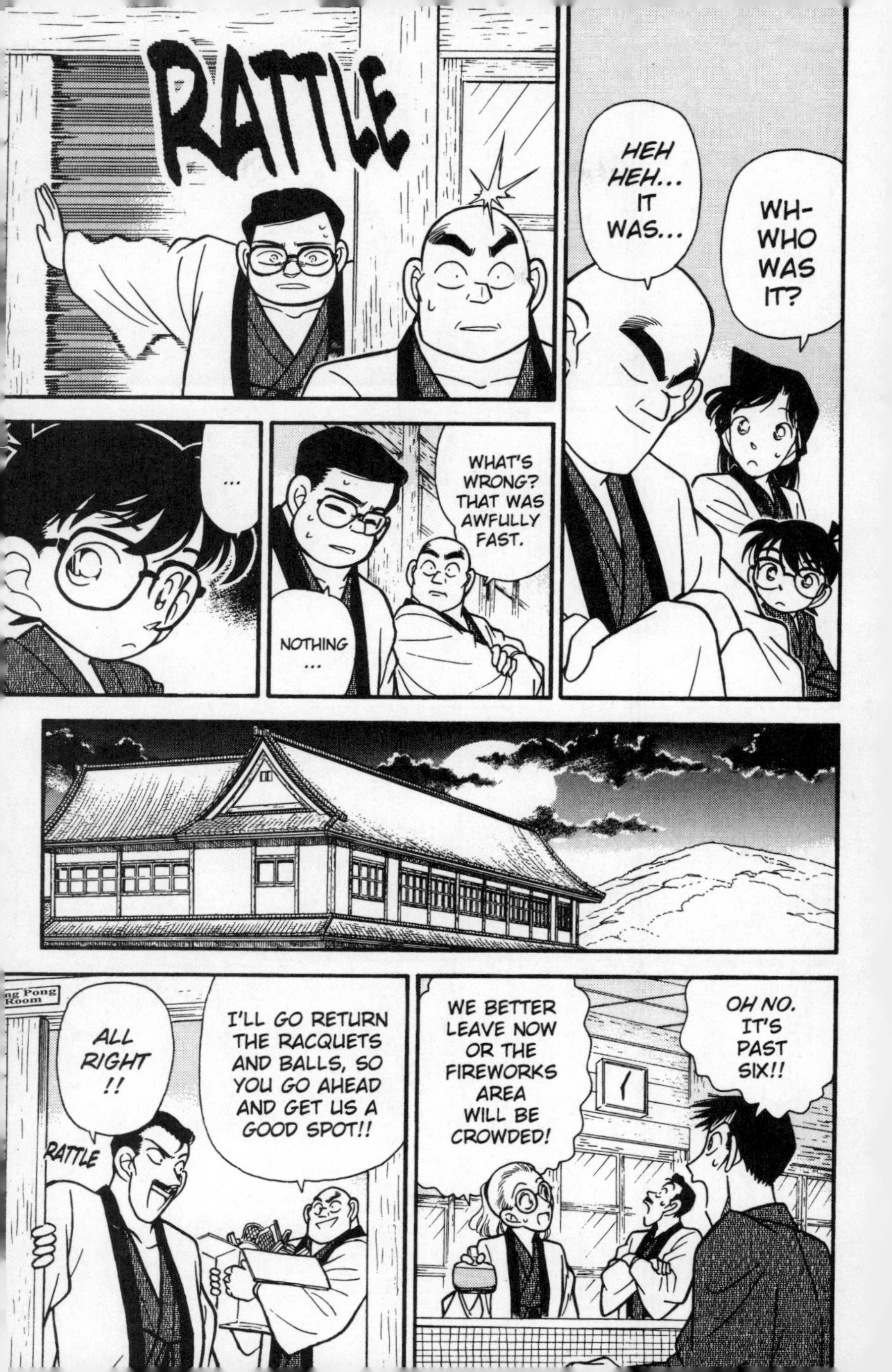
WH-WHO WAS IT?
HEH HEH... IT WAS...
RATTLE
WHAT'S WRONG? THAT WAS AWFULLY FAST.
NOTHING ...
...
OH NO. IT'S PAST SIX!!
WE BETTER LEAVE NOW OR THE FIREWORKS AREA WILL BE CROWDED!
I'LL GO RETURN THE RACQUETS AND BALLS, SO YOU GO AHEAD AND GET US A GOOD SPOT!!
ALL RIGHT !!
ng Pong Room
RATTLE

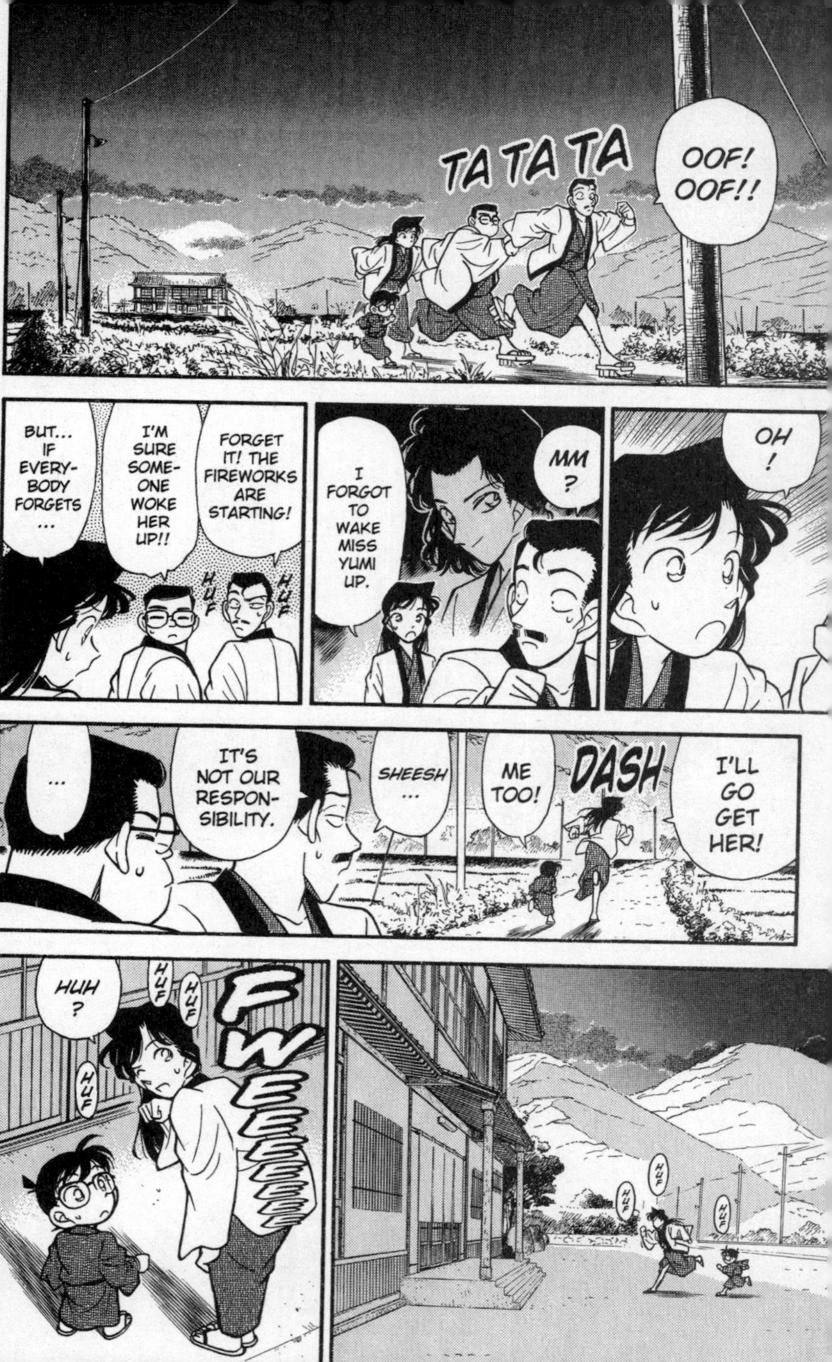
OOF! OOF!!
TA TA TA
OH!
MM?
I FORGOT TO WAKE MISS YUMI UP.
FORGET IT! THE FIREWORKS ARE STARTING!
HUF
I'M SURE SOME-ONE WOKE HER UP!!
HUF
BUT... IF EVERY-BODY FORGETS...
I'LL GO GET HER!
DASH
ME TOO!
SHEESH...
IT'S NOT OUR RESPON-SIBILITY.
...
HUF
HUF
HUF
FWEEEEEE
HUF
HUF
HUH?
HUF

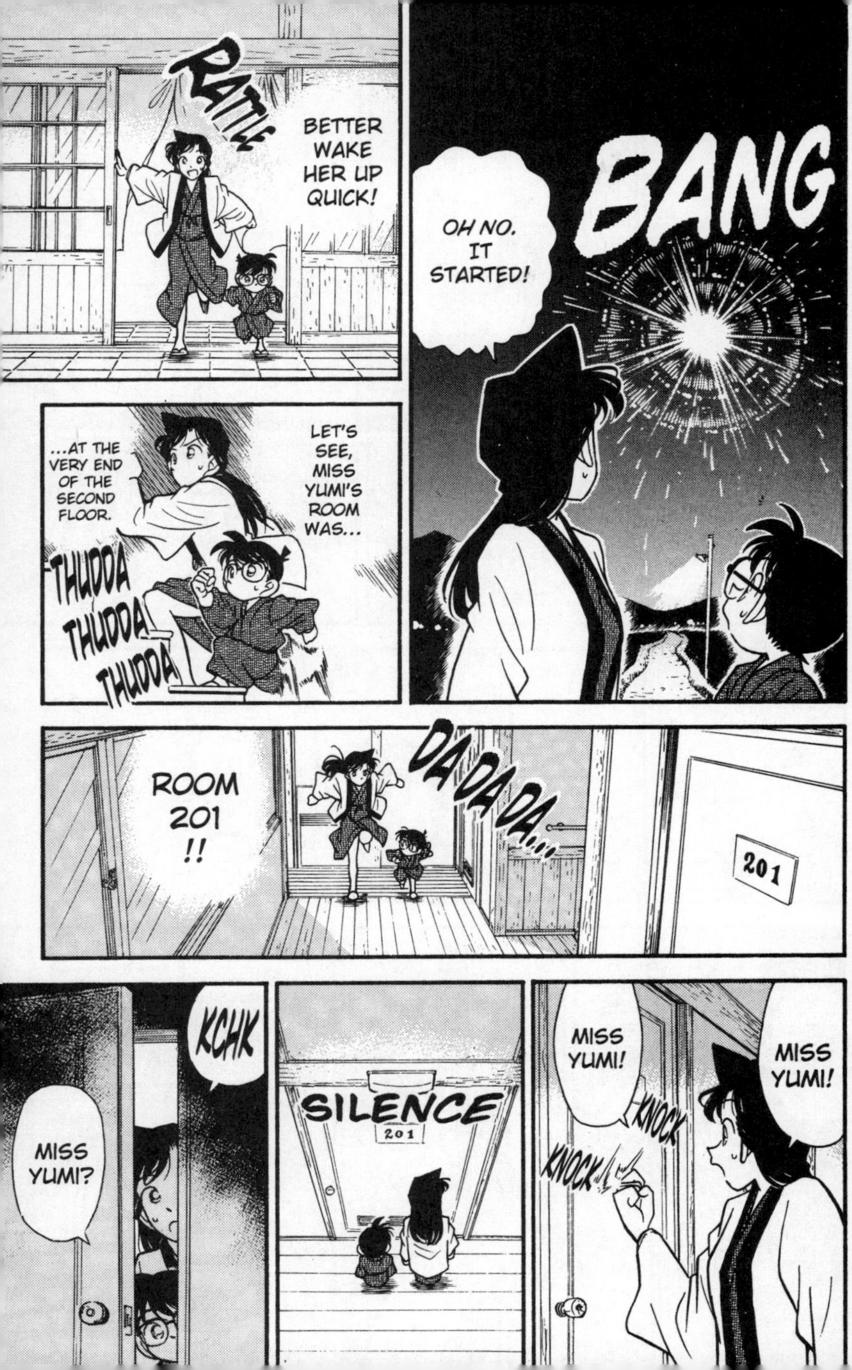
BANG
OH NO. IT STARTED!
RATTLE
BETTER WAKE HER UP QUICK!
LET'S SEE, MISS YUMI'S ROOM WAS...
...AT THE VERY END OF THE SECOND FLOOR.
THUDDA THUDDA THUDDA
201
DA DA DA...
ROOM 201 !!
MISS YUMI!
KNOCK
KNOCK
MISS YUMI!
SILENCE
201
KCHK
MISS YUMI?

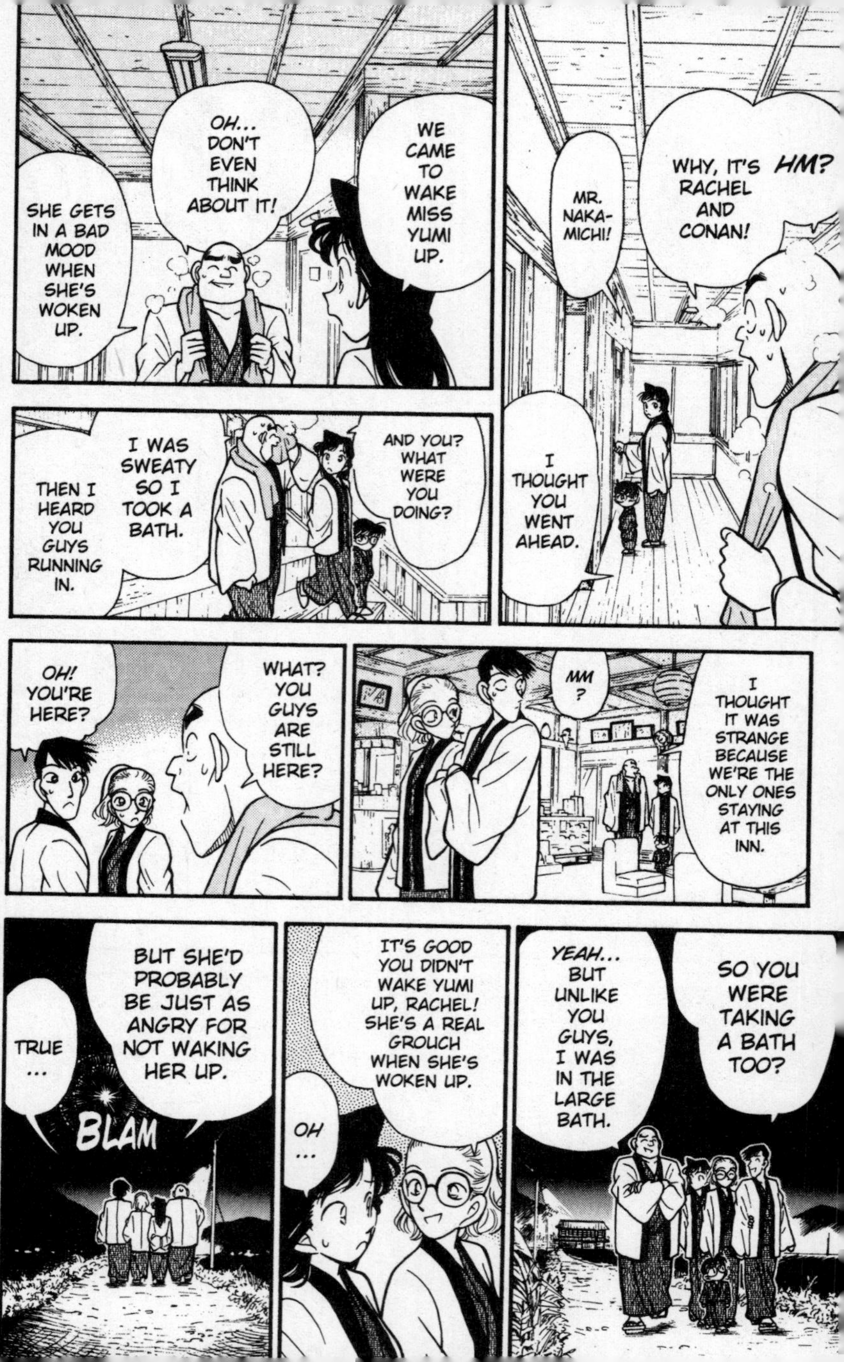
HM?
WHY, IT'S RACHEL AND CONAN!
MR. NAKAMICHI!
I THOUGHT YOU WENT AHEAD.
WE CAME TO WAKE MISS YUMI UP.
OH... DON'T EVEN THINK ABOUT IT!
SHE GETS IN A BAD MOOD WHEN SHE'S WOKEN UP.
AND YOU? WHAT WERE YOU DOING?
I WAS SWEATY SO I TOOK A BATH.
THEN I HEARD YOU GUYS RUNNING IN.
I THOUGHT IT WAS STRANGE BECAUSE WE'RE THE ONLY ONES STAYING AT THIS INN.
MM?
WHAT? YOU GUYS ARE STILL HERE?
OH! YOU'RE HERE?
SO YOU WERE TAKING A BATH TOO?
YEAH... BUT UNLIKE YOU GUYS, I WAS IN THE LARGE BATH.
IT'S GOOD YOU DIDN'T WAKE YUMI UP, RACHEL! SHE'S A REAL GROUCH WHEN SHE'S WOKEN UP.
OH...
BUT SHE'D PROBABLY BE JUST AS ANGRY FOR NOT WAKING HER UP.
TRUE...
BLAM

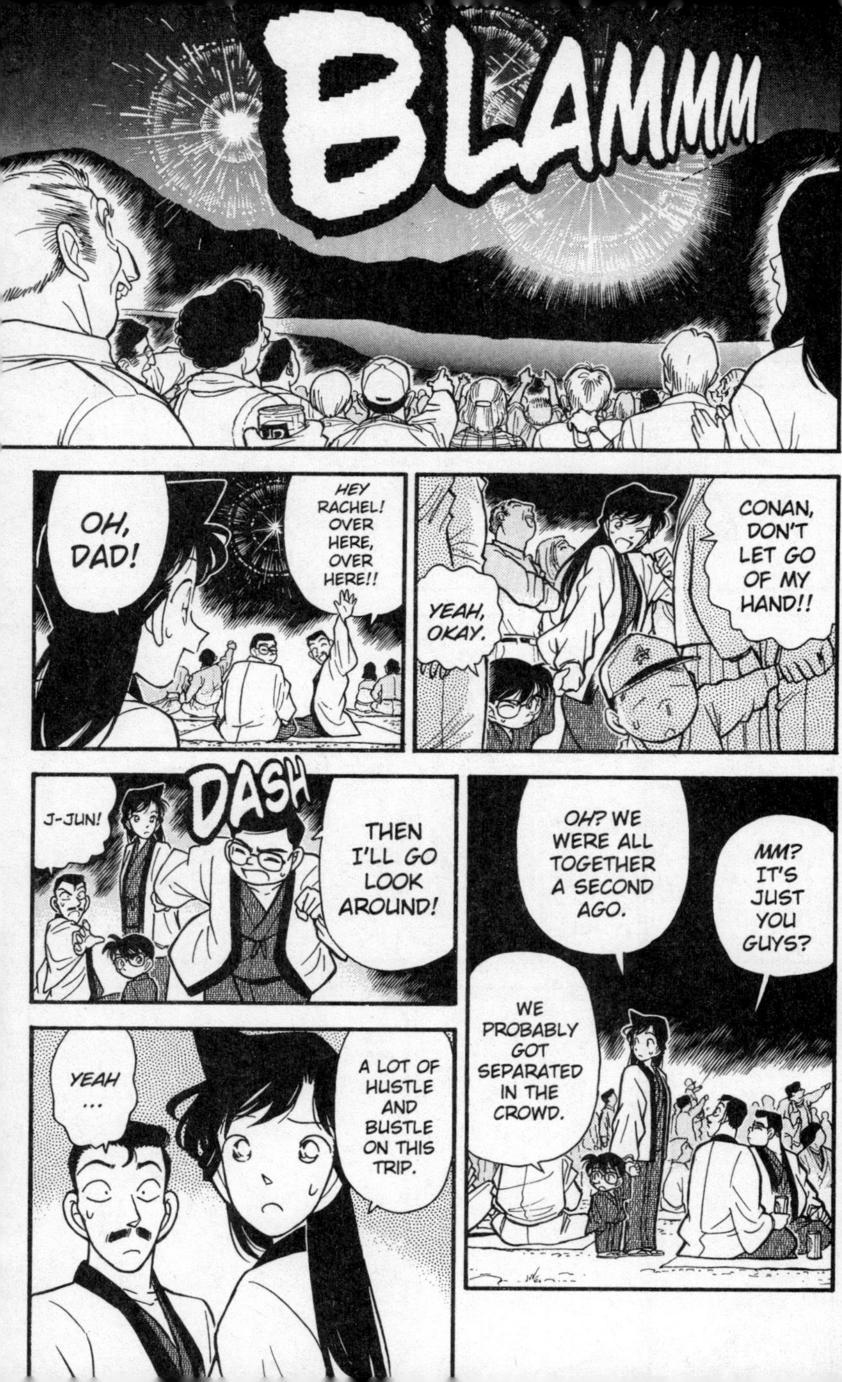
BLAMMM
CONAN, DON'T LET GO OF MY HAND!!
YEAH, OKAY.
HEY RACHEL! OVER HERE, OVER HERE!!
OH, DAD!
MM? IT'S JUST YOU GUYS?
OH? WE WERE ALL TOGETHER A SECOND AGO.
WE PROBABLY GOT SEPARATED IN THE CROWD.
THEN I'LL GO LOOK AROUND!
DASH
J-JUN!
A LOT OF HUSTLE AND BUSTLE ON THIS TRIP.
YEAH ...

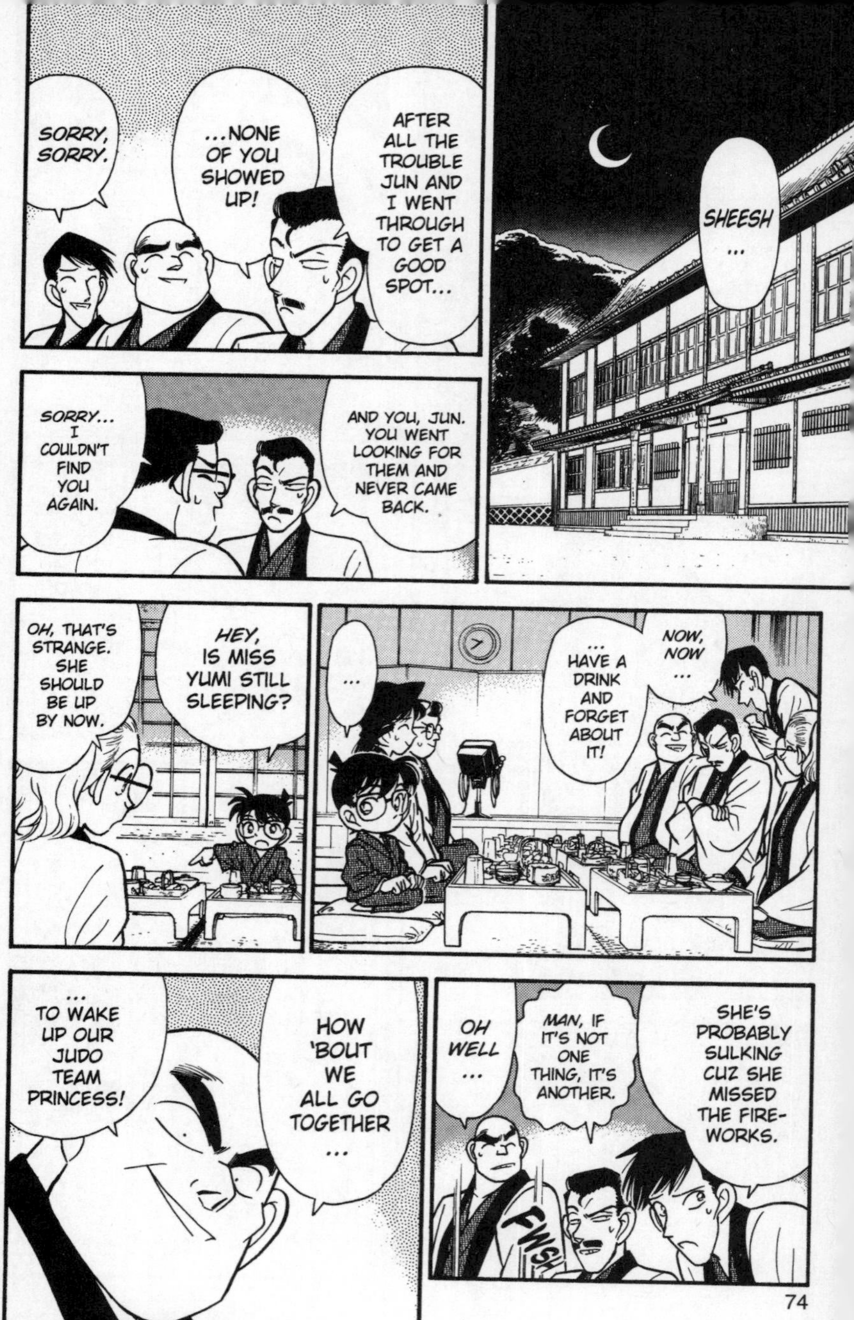
SHEESH ...
AFTER ALL THE TROUBLE JUN AND I WENT THROUGH TO GET A GOOD SPOT...
...NONE OF YOU SHOWED UP!
SORRY, SORRY.
AND YOU, JUN. YOU WENT LOOKING FOR THEM AND NEVER CAME BACK.
SORRY... I COULDN'T FIND YOU AGAIN.
NOW, NOW ...
... HAVE A DRINK AND FORGET ABOUT IT!
...
HEY, IS MISS YUMI STILL SLEEPING?
OH, THAT'S STRANGE. SHE SHOULD BE UP BY NOW.
SHE'S PROBABLY SULKING CUZ SHE MISSED THE FIRE-WORKS.
MAN, IF IT'S NOT ONE THING, IT'S ANOTHER.
OH WELL ...
FWSH
HOW 'BOUT WE ALL GO TOGETHER ...
... TO WAKE UP OUR JUDO TEAM PRINCESS!

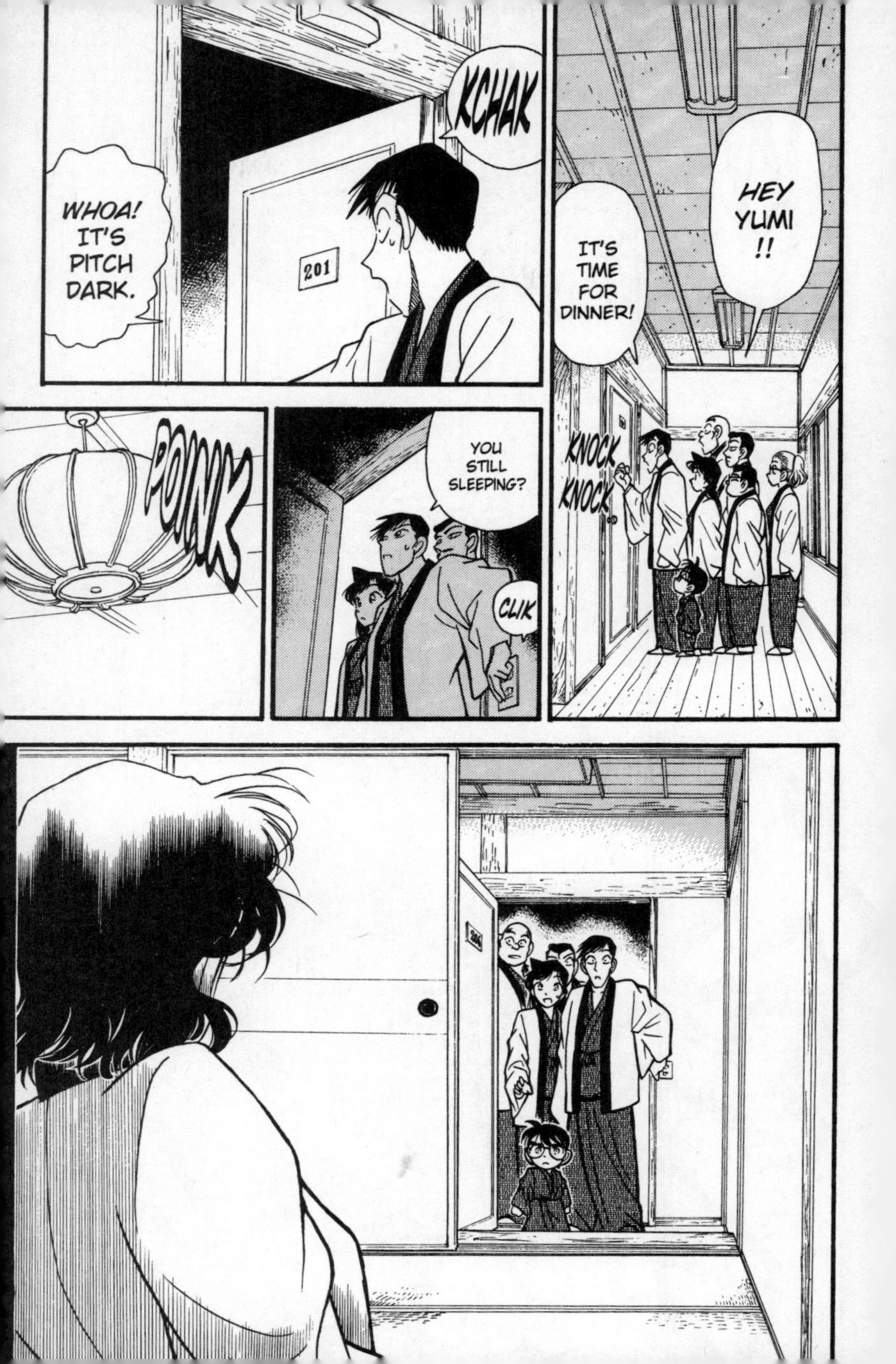
HEY YUMI !!
IT'S TIME FOR DINNER!
KNOCK KNOCK
KCHAK
WHOA! IT'S PITCH DARK.
201
YOU STILL SLEEPING?
CLIK
POINK

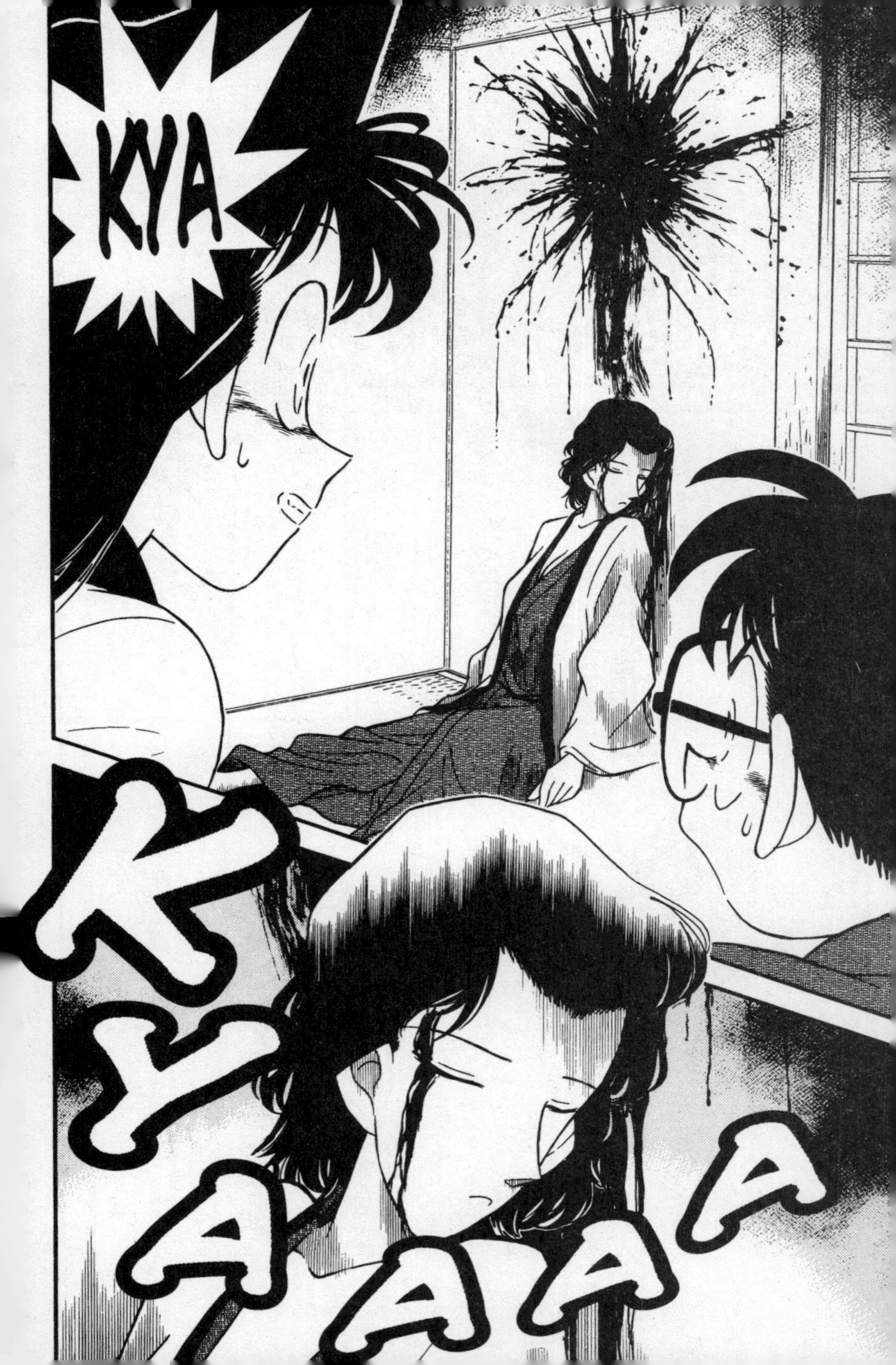
KYA
KYAAAAA

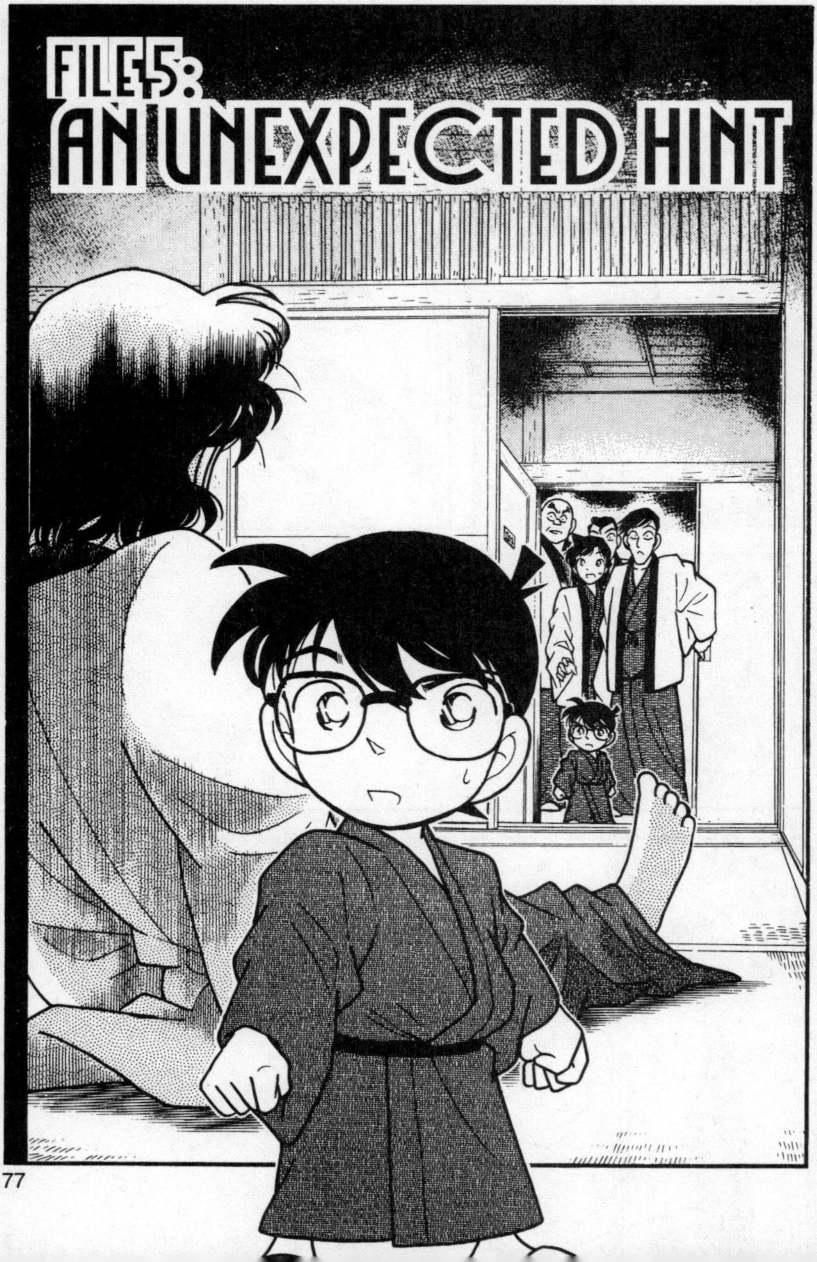
FILE 5:
AN UNEXPECTED HINT

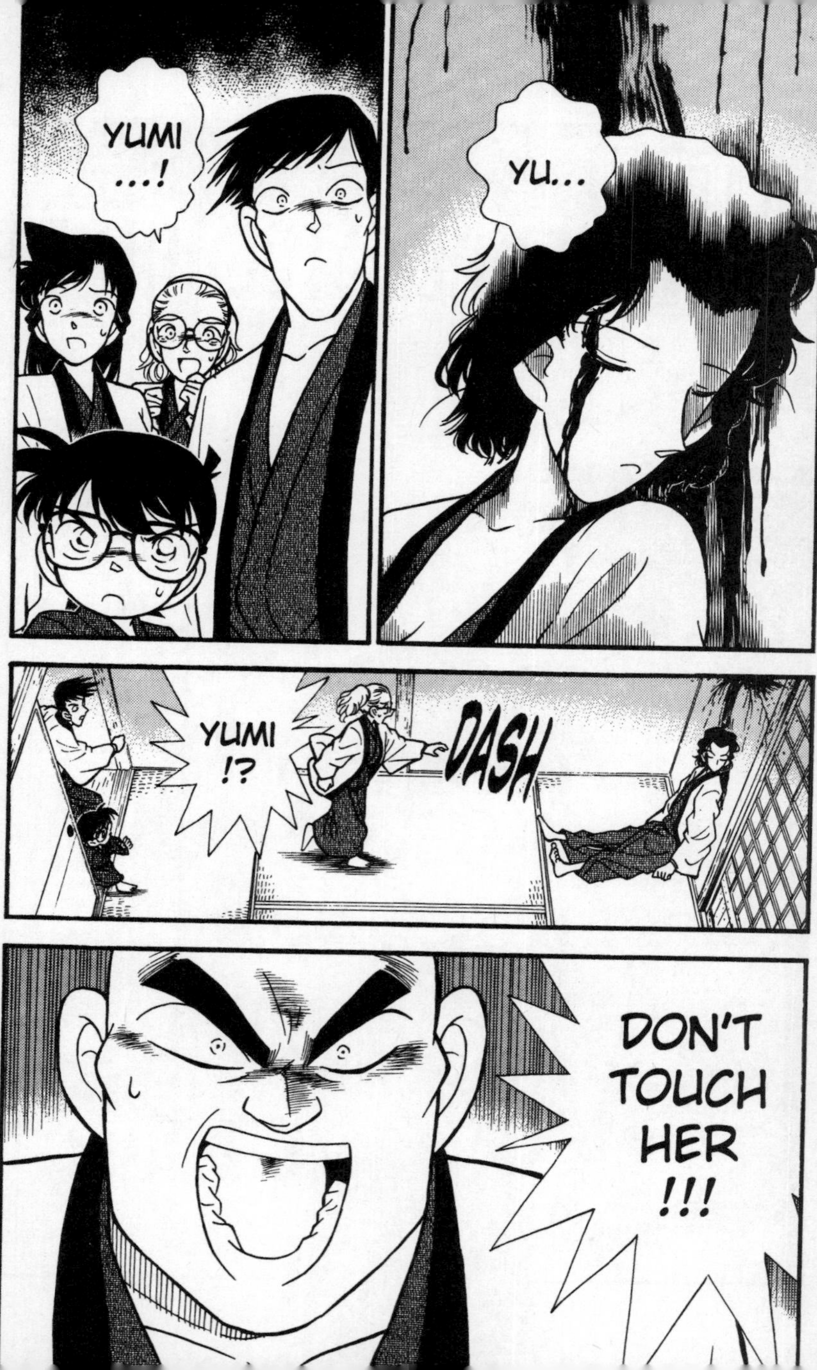
YU...
YUMI ...!
DASH
YUMI !?
DON'T TOUCH HER !!!

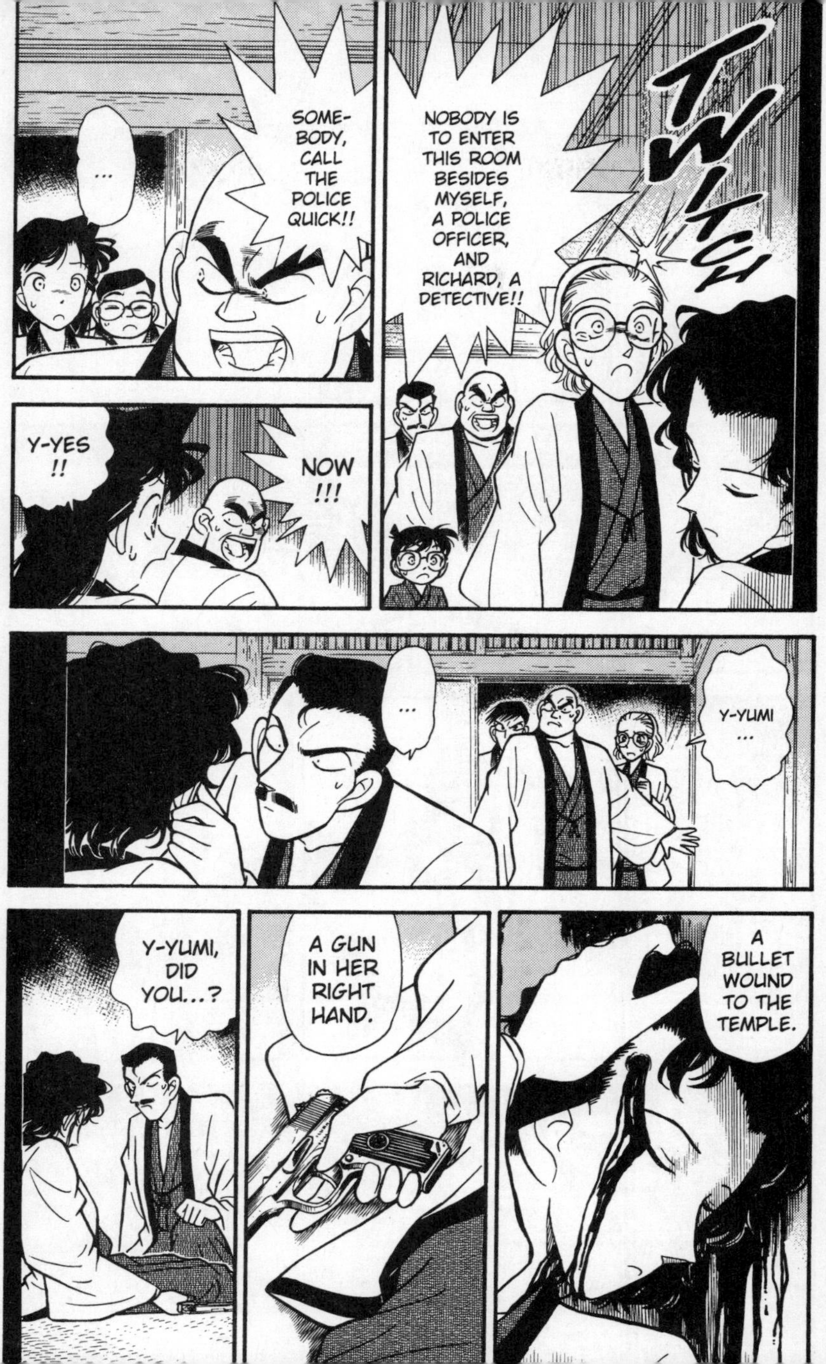
TWITCH
NOBODY IS TO ENTER THIS ROOM BESIDES MYSELF, A POLICE OFFICER, AND RICHARD, A DETECTIVE!!
SOME-BODY, CALL THE POLICE QUICK!!
...
NOW !!!
Y-YES !!
Y-YUMI ...
...
A BULLET WOUND TO THE TEMPLE.
A GUN IN HER RIGHT HAND.
Y-YUMI, DID YOU...?

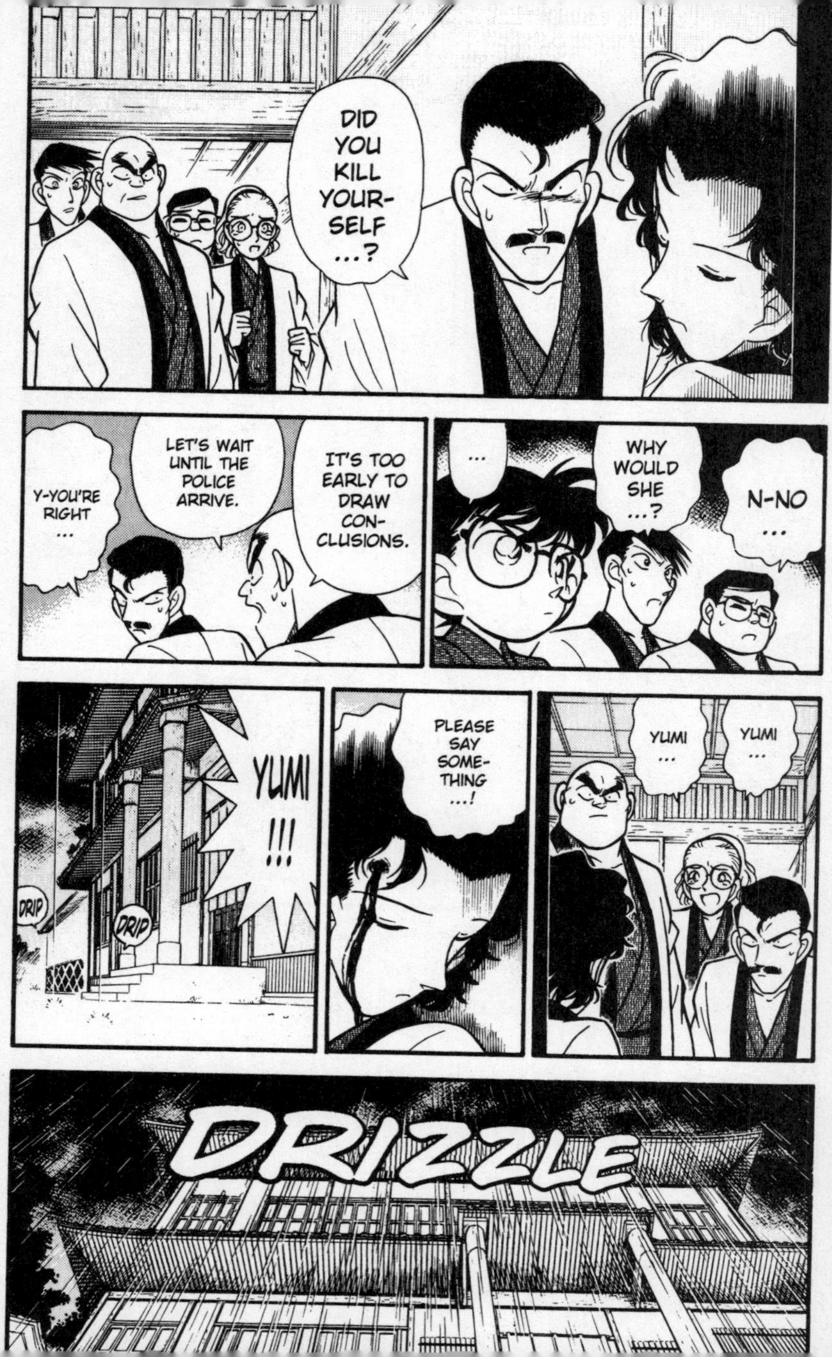
DID YOU KILL YOUR-SELF ...?
N-NO ...
WHY WOULD SHE ...?
...
IT'S TOO EARLY TO DRAW CON-CLUSIONS.
LET'S WAIT UNTIL THE POLICE ARRIVE.
Y-YOU'RE RIGHT ...
YUMI ...
YUMI ...
PLEASE SAY SOME-THING ...!
YUMI !!!
DRIP
DRIP
DRIZZLE

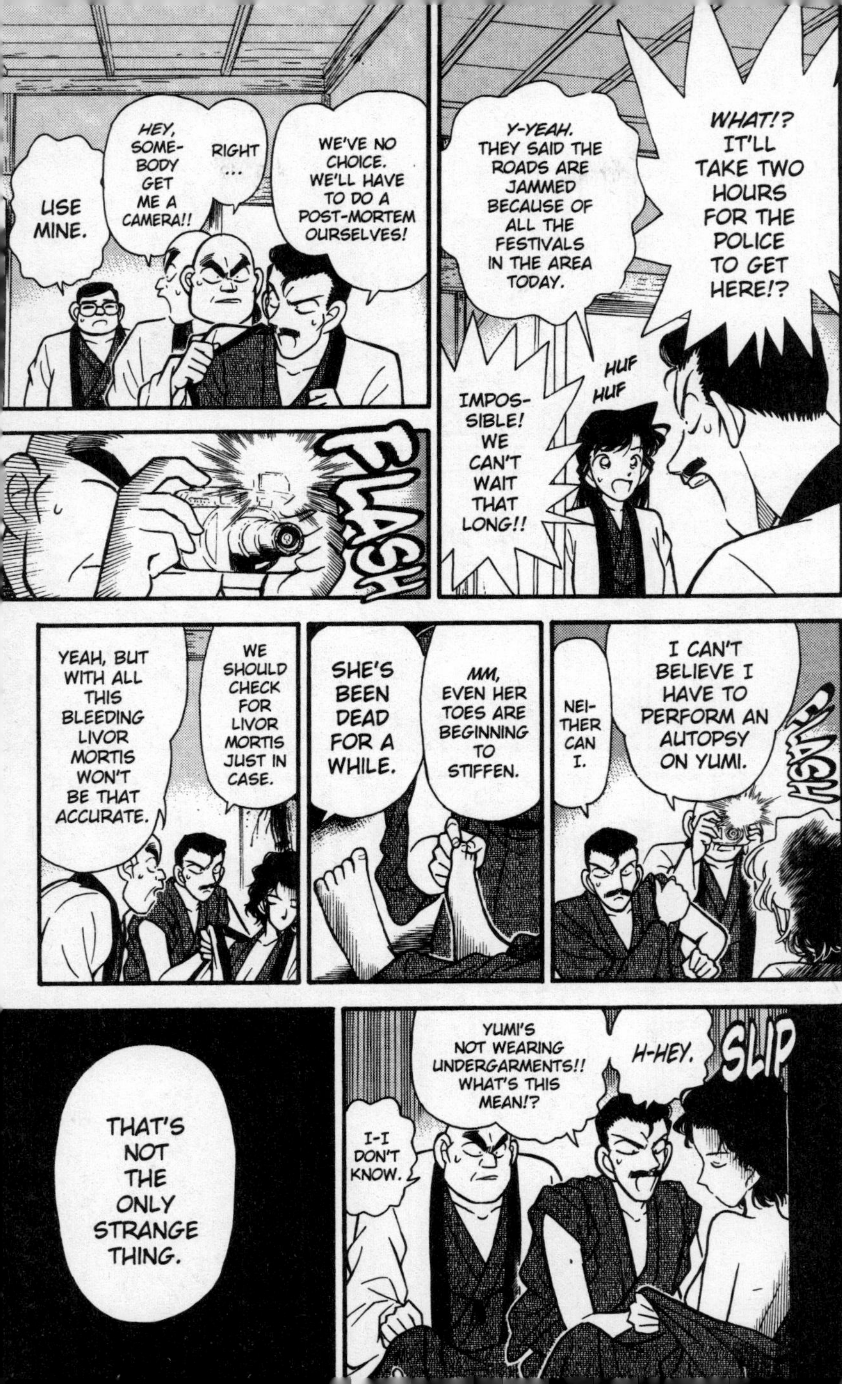
WHAT!? IT'LL TAKE TWO HOURS FOR THE POLICE TO GET HERE!?
Y-YEAH. THEY SAID THE ROADS ARE JAMMED BECAUSE OF ALL THE FESTIVALS IN THE AREA TODAY.
HUF HUF
IMPOSSIBLE! WE CAN'T WAIT THAT LONG!!
WE'VE NO CHOICE. WE'LL HAVE TO DO A POST-MORTEM OURSELVES!
RIGHT...
HEY, SOMEBODY GET ME A CAMERA!!
USE MINE.
FLASH
I CAN'T BELIEVE I HAVE TO PERFORM AN AUTOPSY ON YUMI.
FLASH
NEITHER CAN I.
MM, EVEN HER TOES ARE BEGINNING TO STIFFEN.
SHE'S BEEN DEAD FOR A WHILE.
WE SHOULD CHECK FOR LIVOR MORTIS JUST IN CASE.
YEAH, BUT WITH ALL THIS BLEEDING LIVOR MORTIS WON'T BE THAT ACCURATE.
SLIP
H-HEY.
YUMI'S NOT WEARING UNDERGARMENTS!! WHAT'S THIS MEAN!?
I-I DON'T KNOW.
THAT'S NOT THE ONLY STRANGE THING.

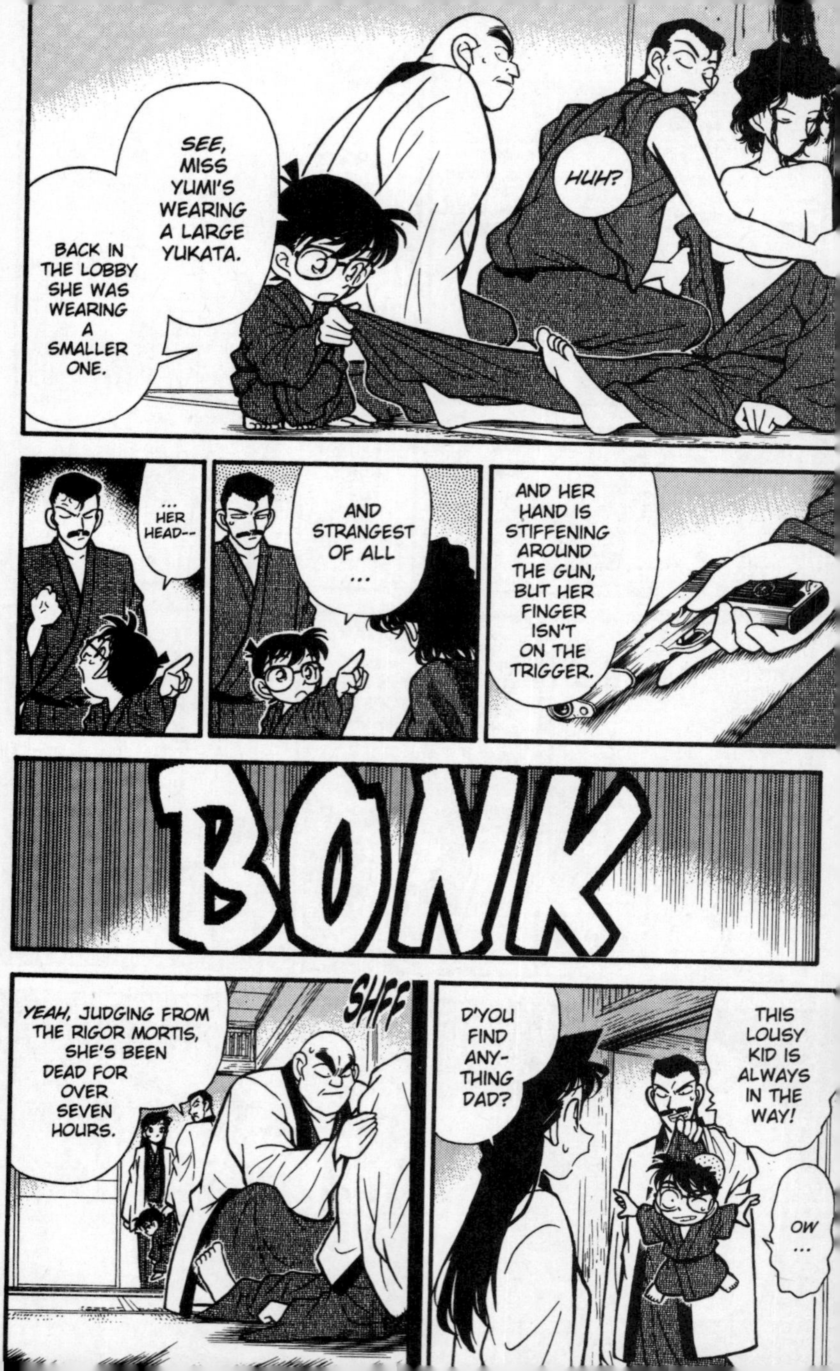
HUH?
SEE, MISS YUMI'S WEARING A LARGE YUKATA.
BACK IN THE LOBBY SHE WAS WEARING A SMALLER ONE.
AND HER HAND IS STIFFENING AROUND THE GUN, BUT HER FINGER ISN'T ON THE TRIGGER.
AND STRANGEST OF ALL ...
... HER HEAD--
BONK
THIS LOUSY KID IS ALWAYS IN THE WAY!
OW ...
D'YOU FIND ANY-THING DAD?
SHFF
YEAH, JUDGING FROM THE RIGOR MORTIS, SHE'S BEEN DEAD FOR OVER SEVEN HOURS.

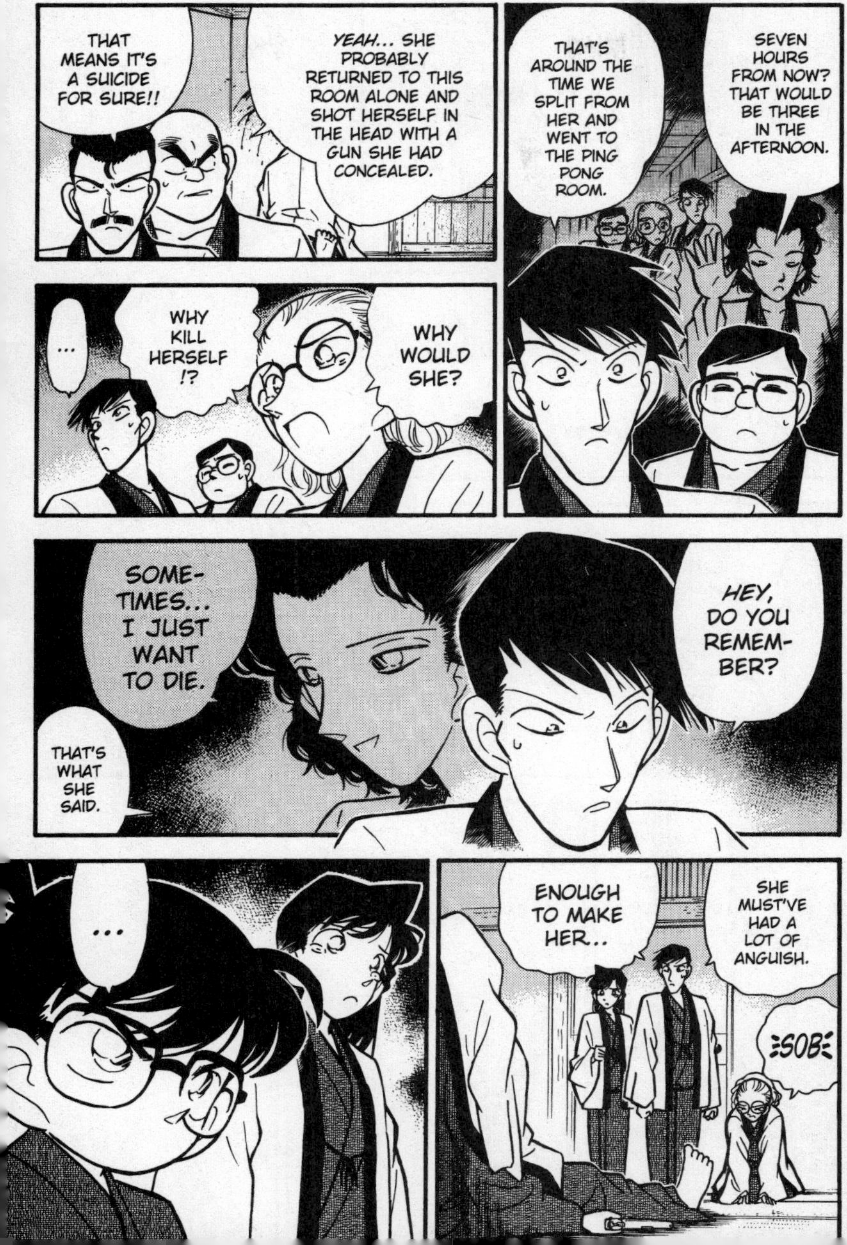
SEVEN HOURS FROM NOW? THAT WOULD BE THREE IN THE AFTERNOON.
THAT'S AROUND THE TIME WE SPLIT FROM HER AND WENT TO THE PING PONG ROOM.
YEAH... SHE PROBABLY RETURNED TO THIS ROOM ALONE AND SHOT HERSELF IN THE HEAD WITH A GUN SHE HAD CONCEALED.
THAT MEANS IT'S A SUICIDE FOR SURE!!
WHY WOULD SHE?
WHY KILL HERSELF !?
...
HEY, DO YOU REMEMBER?
SOME-TIMES... I JUST WANT TO DIE.
THAT'S WHAT SHE SAID.
SHE MUST'VE HAD A LOT OF ANGUISH.
ENOUGH TO MAKE HER...
SOB
...

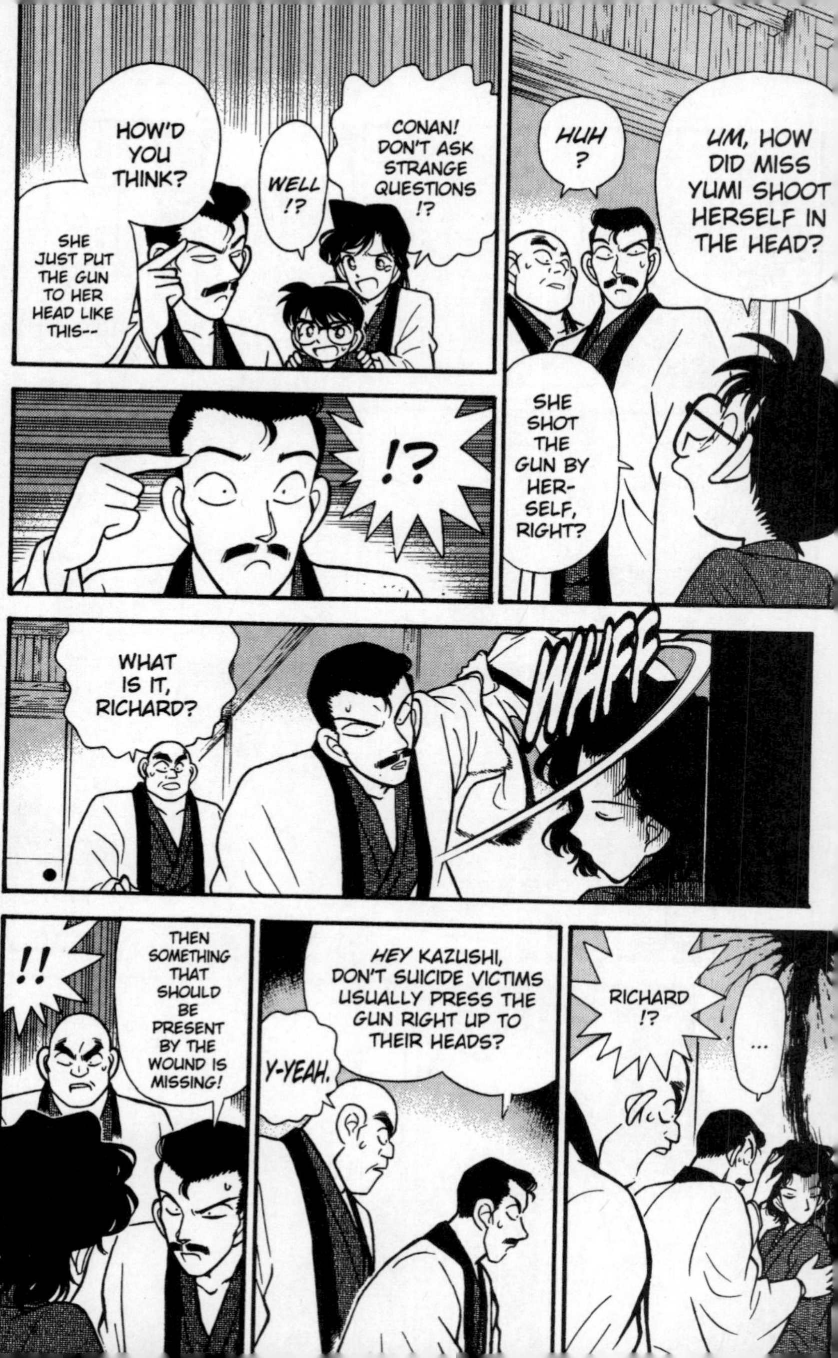
UM, HOW DID MISS YUMI SHOOT HERSELF IN THE HEAD?
HUH ?
SHE SHOT THE GUN BY HER-SELF, RIGHT?
CONAN! DON'T ASK STRANGE QUESTIONS !?
WELL !?
HOW'D YOU THINK?
SHE JUST PUT THE GUN TO HER HEAD LIKE THIS--
!?
WHIFF
WHAT IS IT, RICHARD?
...
RICHARD !?
HEY KAZUSHI, DON'T SUICIDE VICTIMS USUALLY PRESS THE GUN RIGHT UP TO THEIR HEADS?
Y-YEAH.
THEN SOMETHING THAT SHOULD BE PRESENT BY THE WOUND IS MISSING!
!!

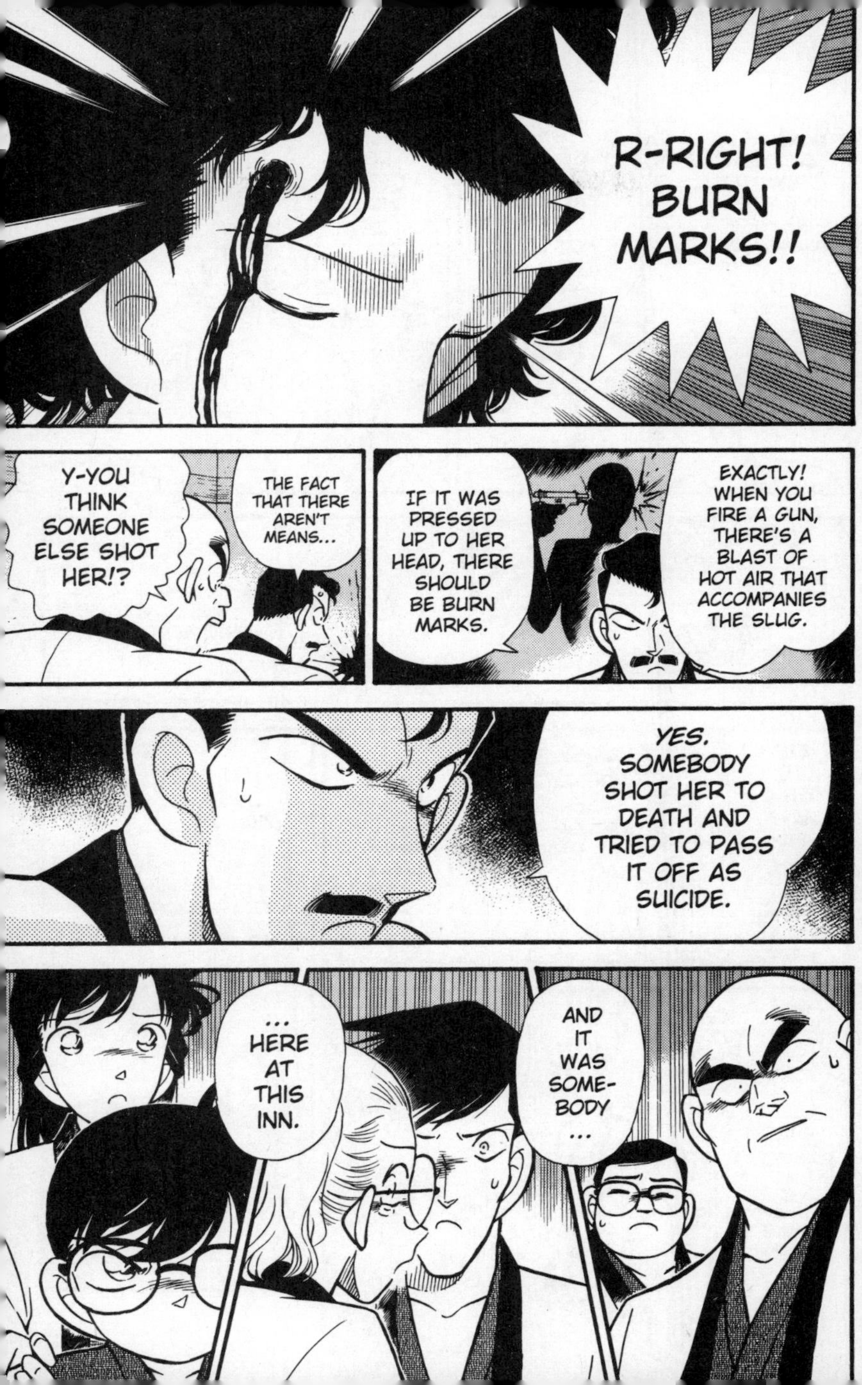
R-RIGHT! BURN MARKS!!
EXACTLY! WHEN YOU FIRE A GUN, THERE'S A BLAST OF HOT AIR THAT ACCOMPANIES THE SLUG.
IF IT WAS PRESSED UP TO HER HEAD, THERE SHOULD BE BURN MARKS.
THE FACT THAT THERE AREN'T MEANS...
Y-YOU THINK SOMEONE ELSE SHOT HER!?
YES. SOMEBODY SHOT HER TO DEATH AND TRIED TO PASS IT OFF AS SUICIDE.
AND IT WAS SOME-BODY ...
... HERE AT THIS INN.

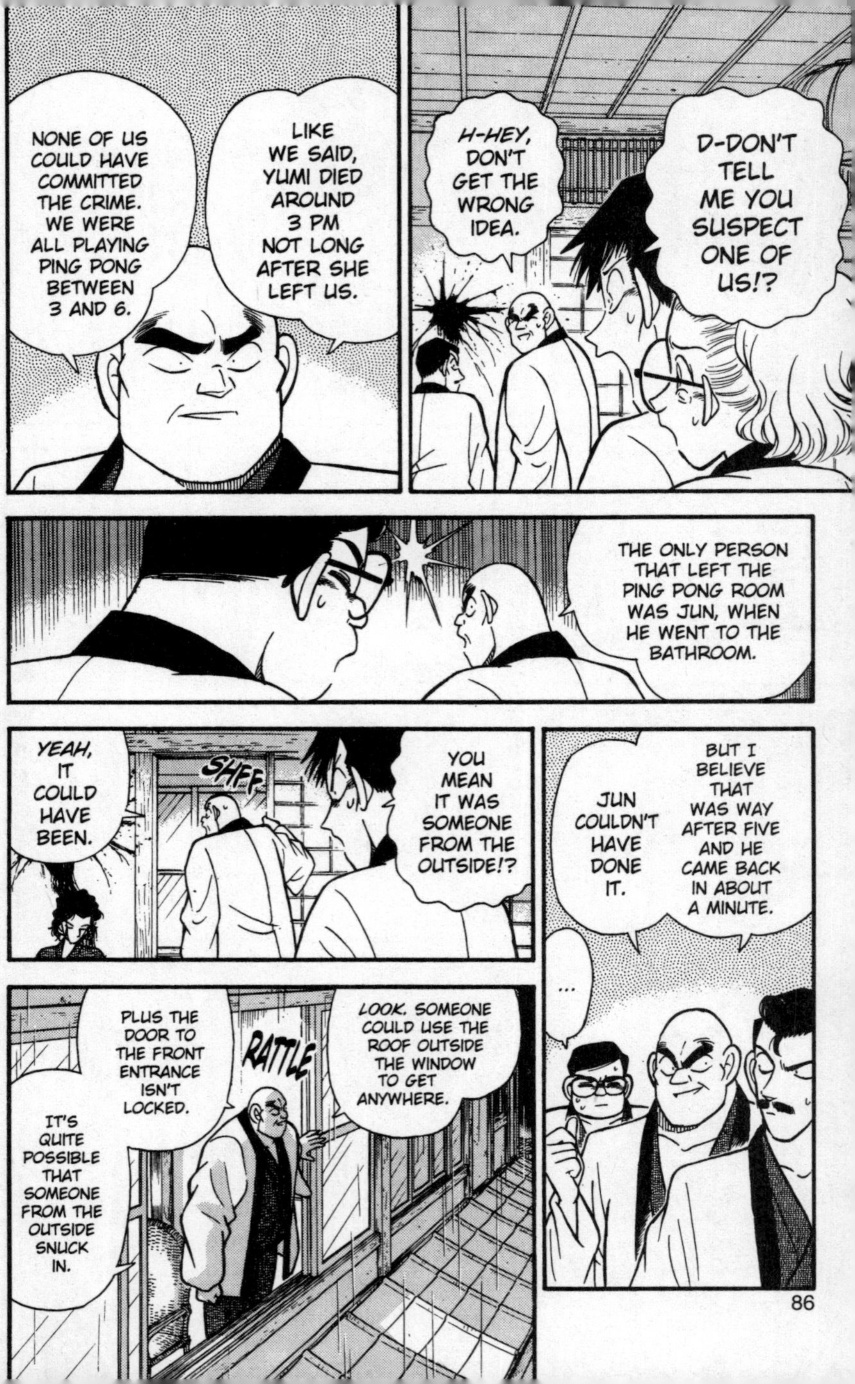
D-DON'T TELL ME YOU SUSPECT ONE OF US!?
H-HEY, DON'T GET THE WRONG IDEA.
LIKE WE SAID, YUMI DIED AROUND 3 PM NOT LONG AFTER SHE LEFT US.
NONE OF US COULD HAVE COMMITTED THE CRIME. WE WERE ALL PLAYING PING PONG BETWEEN 3 AND 6.
THE ONLY PERSON THAT LEFT THE PING PONG ROOM WAS JUN, WHEN HE WENT TO THE BATHROOM.
BUT I BELIEVE THAT WAS WAY AFTER FIVE AND HE CAME BACK IN ABOUT A MINUTE.
JUN COULDN'T HAVE DONE IT.
...
YOU MEAN IT WAS SOMEONE FROM THE OUTSIDE!?
SHFF
YEAH, IT COULD HAVE BEEN.
LOOK. SOMEONE COULD USE THE ROOF OUTSIDE THE WINDOW TO GET ANYWHERE.
RATTLE
PLUS THE DOOR TO THE FRONT ENTRANCE ISN'T LOCKED.
IT'S QUITE POSSIBLE THAT SOMEONE FROM THE OUTSIDE SNUCK IN.

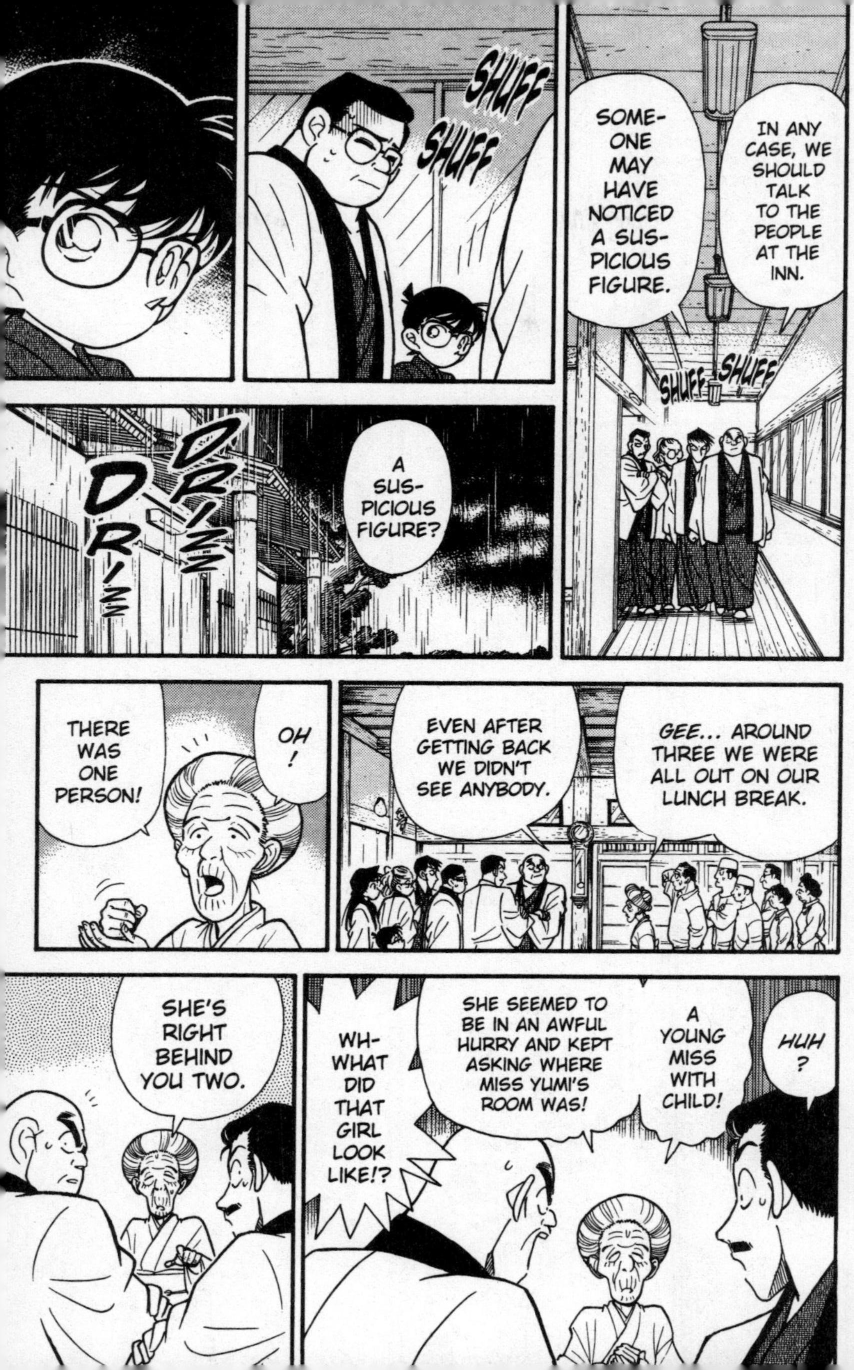
IN ANY CASE, WE SHOULD TALK TO THE PEOPLE AT THE INN.
SOME-ONE MAY HAVE NOTICED A SUS-PICIOUS FIGURE.
SHUFF SHUFF
SHUFF SHUFF
DRIZZ DRIZZ
A SUS-PICIOUS FIGURE?
GEE... AROUND THREE WE WERE ALL OUT ON OUR LUNCH BREAK.
EVEN AFTER GETTING BACK WE DIDN'T SEE ANYBODY.
OH!
THERE WAS ONE PERSON!
HUH?
A YOUNG MISS WITH CHILD!
SHE SEEMED TO BE IN AN AWFUL HURRY AND KEPT ASKING WHERE MISS YUMI'S ROOM WAS!
WH-WHAT DID THAT GIRL LOOK LIKE!?
SHE'S RIGHT BEHIND YOU TWO.

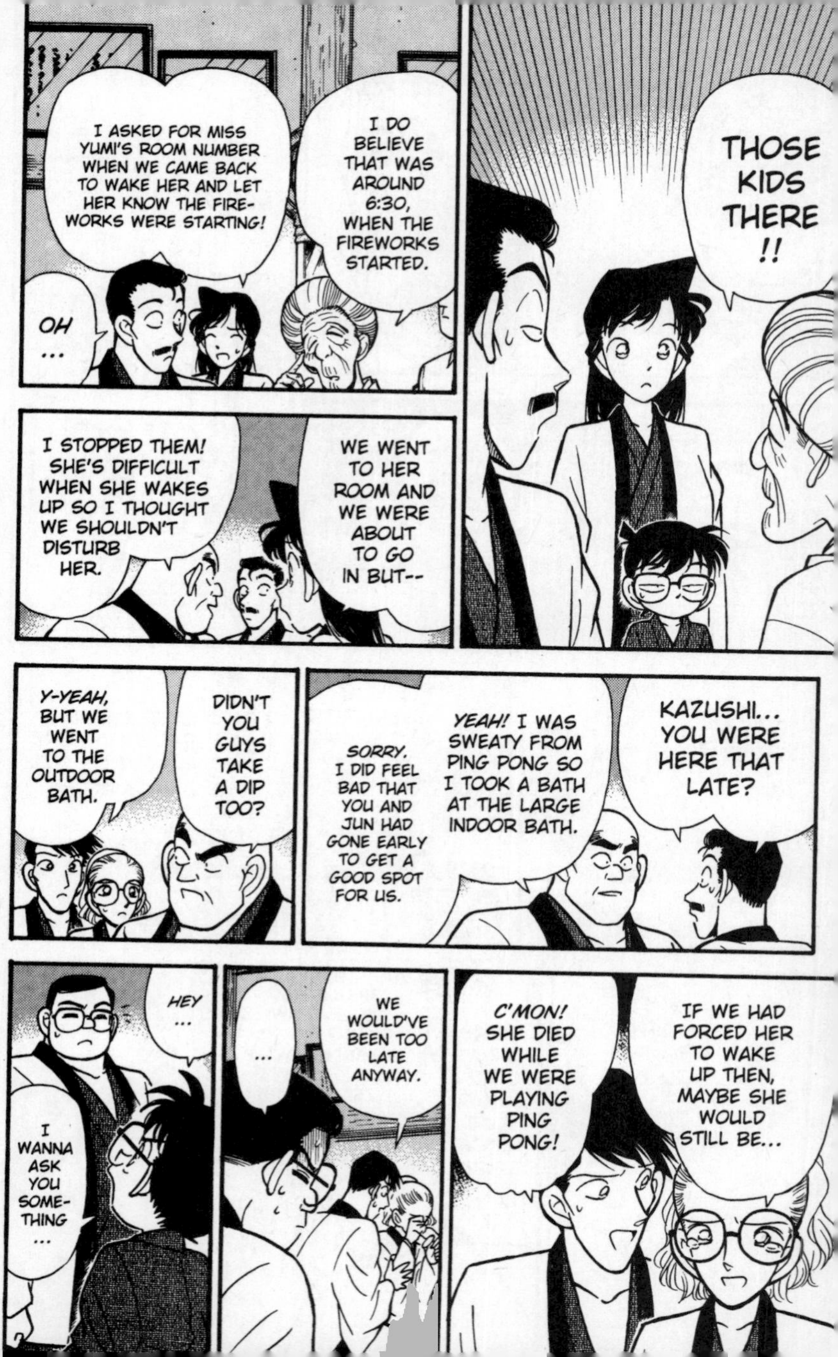
THOSE KIDS THERE!!
I DO BELIEVE THAT WAS AROUND 6:30, WHEN THE FIREWORKS STARTED.
I ASKED FOR MISS YUMI'S ROOM NUMBER WHEN WE CAME BACK TO WAKE HER AND LET HER KNOW THE FIRE-WORKS WERE STARTING!
OH...
WE WENT TO HER ROOM AND WE WERE ABOUT TO GO IN BUT--
I STOPPED THEM! SHE'S DIFFICULT WHEN SHE WAKES UP SO I THOUGHT WE SHOULDN'T DISTURB HER.
KAZUSHI... YOU WERE HERE THAT LATE?
YEAH! I WAS SWEATY FROM PING PONG SO I TOOK A BATH AT THE LARGE INDOOR BATH.
SORRY. I DID FEEL BAD THAT YOU AND JUN HAD GONE EARLY TO GET A GOOD SPOT FOR US.
DIDN'T YOU GUYS TAKE A DIP TOO?
Y-YEAH, BUT WE WENT TO THE OUTDOOR BATH.
IF WE HAD FORCED HER TO WAKE UP THEN, MAYBE SHE WOULD STILL BE...
C'MON! SHE DIED WHILE WE WERE PLAYING PING PONG!
WE WOULD'VE BEEN TOO LATE ANYWAY.
...
HEY...
I WANNA ASK YOU SOMETHING...

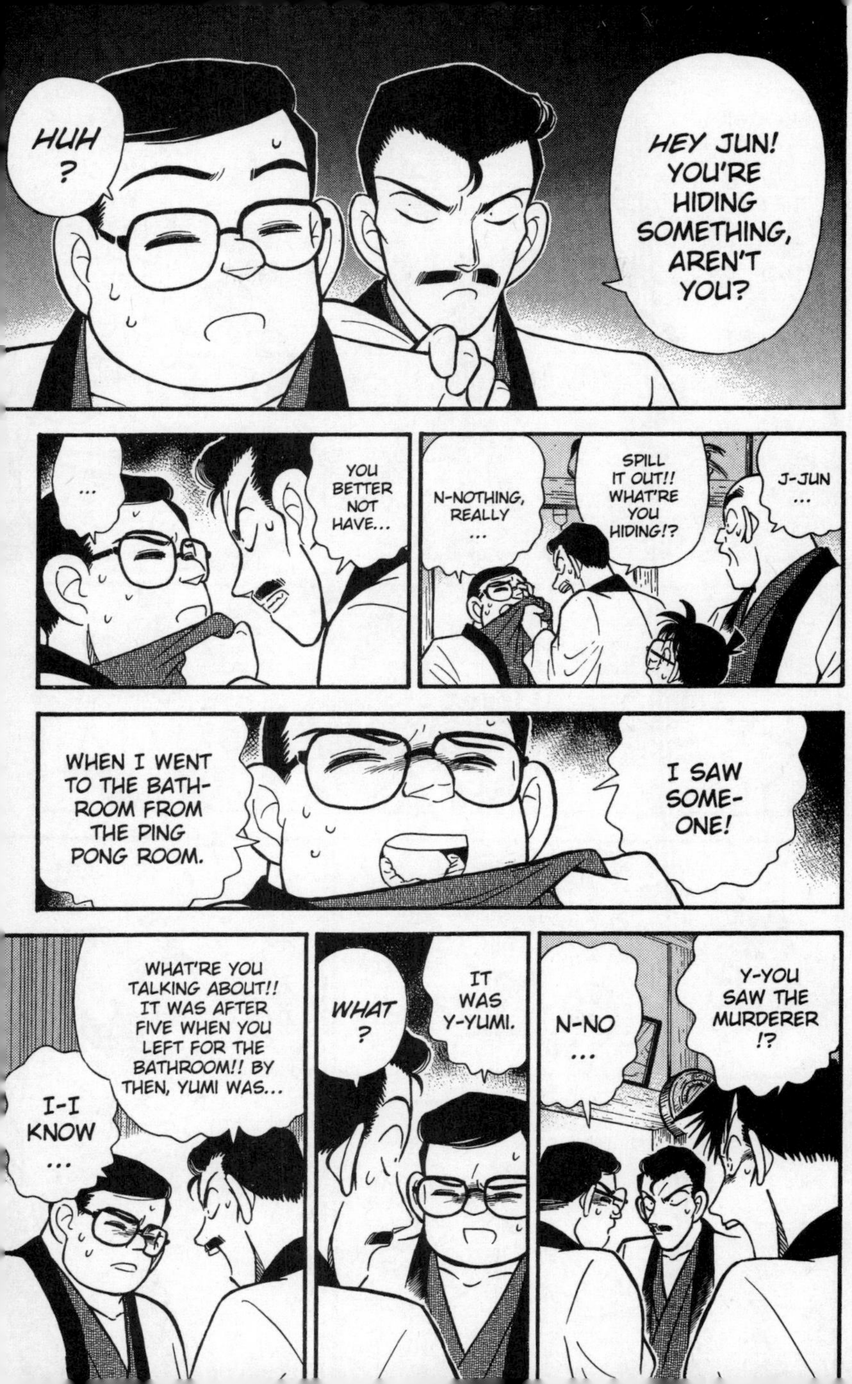
HEY JUN! YOU'RE HIDING SOMETHING, AREN'T YOU?
HUH ?
J-JUN ...
SPILL IT OUT!! WHAT'RE YOU HIDING!?
N-NOTHING, REALLY ...
YOU BETTER NOT HAVE...
...
I SAW SOME-ONE!
WHEN I WENT TO THE BATH-ROOM FROM THE PING PONG ROOM.
Y-YOU SAW THE MURDERER !?
N-NO ...
IT WAS Y-YUMI.
WHAT ?
WHAT'RE YOU TALKING ABOUT!! IT WAS AFTER FIVE WHEN YOU LEFT FOR THE BATHROOM!! BY THEN, YUMI WAS...
I-I KNOW ...

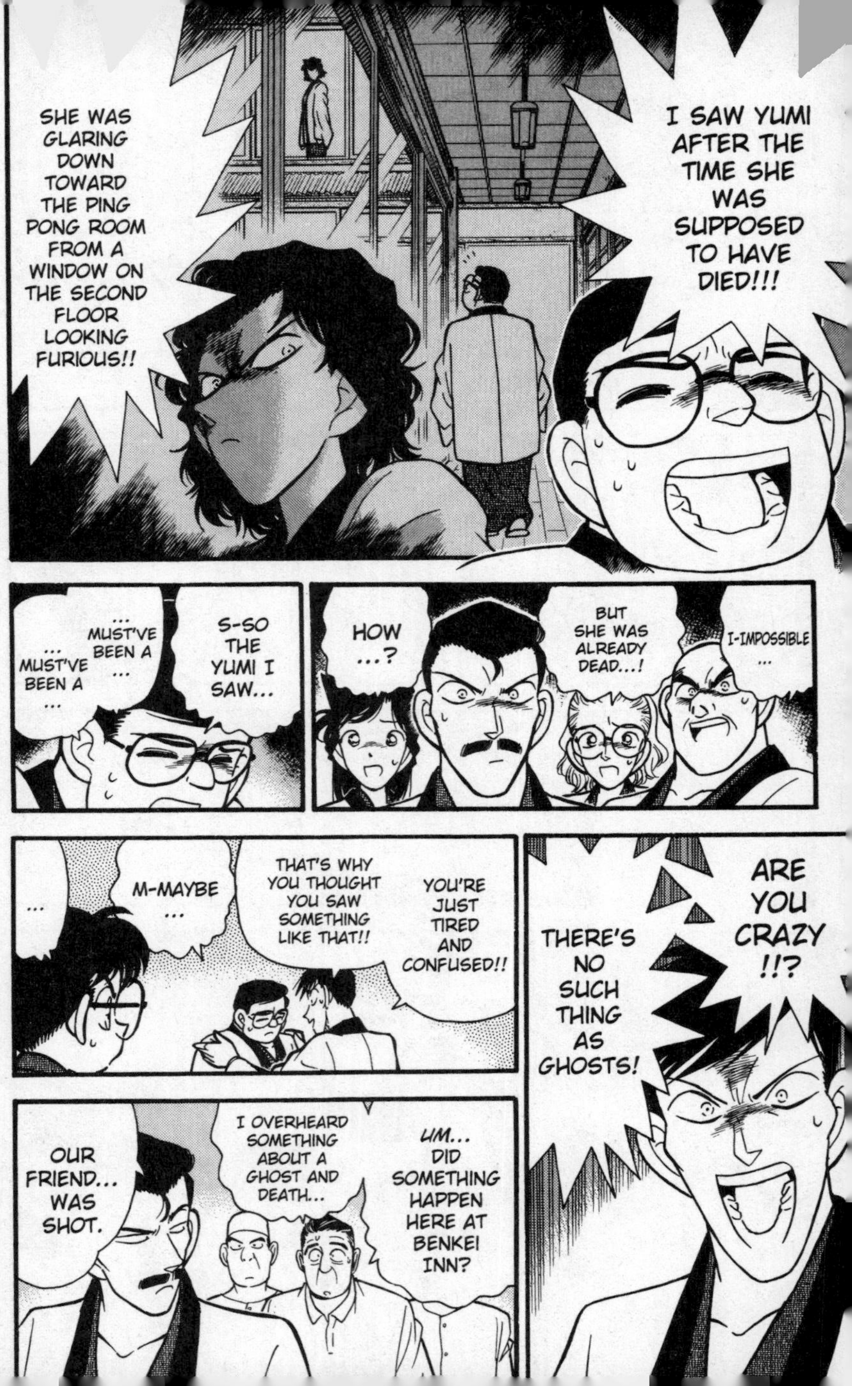
I SAW YUMI AFTER THE TIME SHE WAS SUPPOSED TO HAVE DIED!!!
SHE WAS GLARING DOWN TOWARD THE PING PONG ROOM FROM A WINDOW ON THE SECOND FLOOR LOOKING FURIOUS!!
I-IMPOSSIBLE ...
BUT SHE WAS ALREADY DEAD...!
HOW ...?
S-SO THE YUMI I SAW...
... MUST'VE BEEN A ...
... MUST'VE BEEN A ...
ARE YOU CRAZY !!?
THERE'S NO SUCH THING AS GHOSTS!
YOU'RE JUST TIRED AND CONFUSED!!
THAT'S WHY YOU THOUGHT YOU SAW SOMETHING LIKE THAT!!
M-MAYBE ...
...
UM... DID SOMETHING HAPPEN HERE AT BENKEI INN?
I OVERHEARD SOMETHING ABOUT A GHOST AND DEATH...
OUR FRIEND... WAS SHOT.

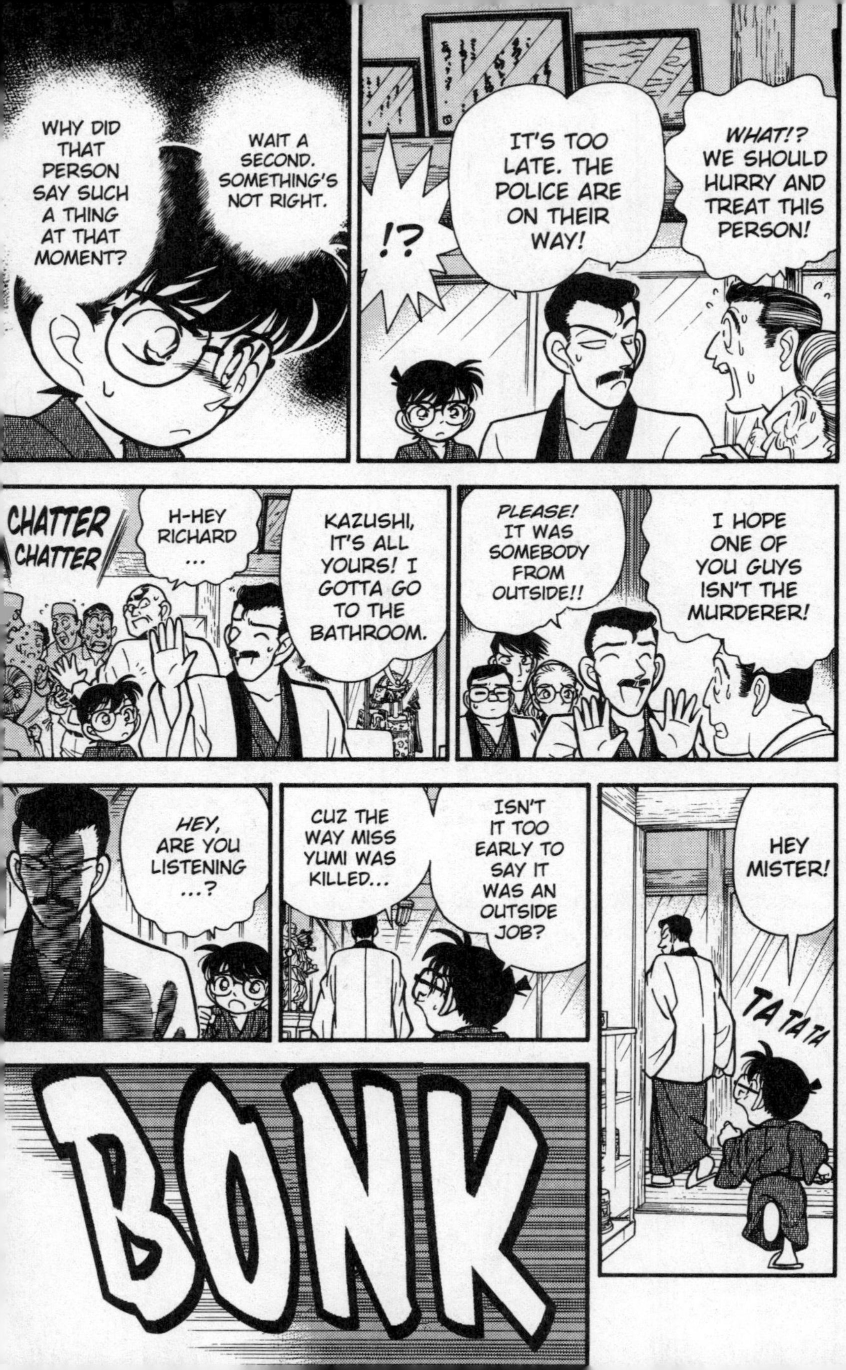
WHAT!? WE SHOULD HURRY AND TREAT THIS PERSON!
IT'S TOO LATE. THE POLICE ARE ON THEIR WAY!
!?
WAIT A SECOND. SOMETHING'S NOT RIGHT.
WHY DID THAT PERSON SAY SUCH A THING AT THAT MOMENT?
I HOPE ONE OF YOU GUYS ISN'T THE MURDERER!
PLEASE! IT WAS SOMEBODY FROM OUTSIDE!!
KAZUSHI, IT'S ALL YOURS! I GOTTA GO TO THE BATHROOM.
H-HEY RICHARD ...
CHATTER CHATTER
HEY MISTER!
TA TA TA
ISN'T IT TOO EARLY TO SAY IT WAS AN OUTSIDE JOB?
CUZ THE WAY MISS YUMI WAS KILLED...
HEY, ARE YOU LISTENING ...?
BONK

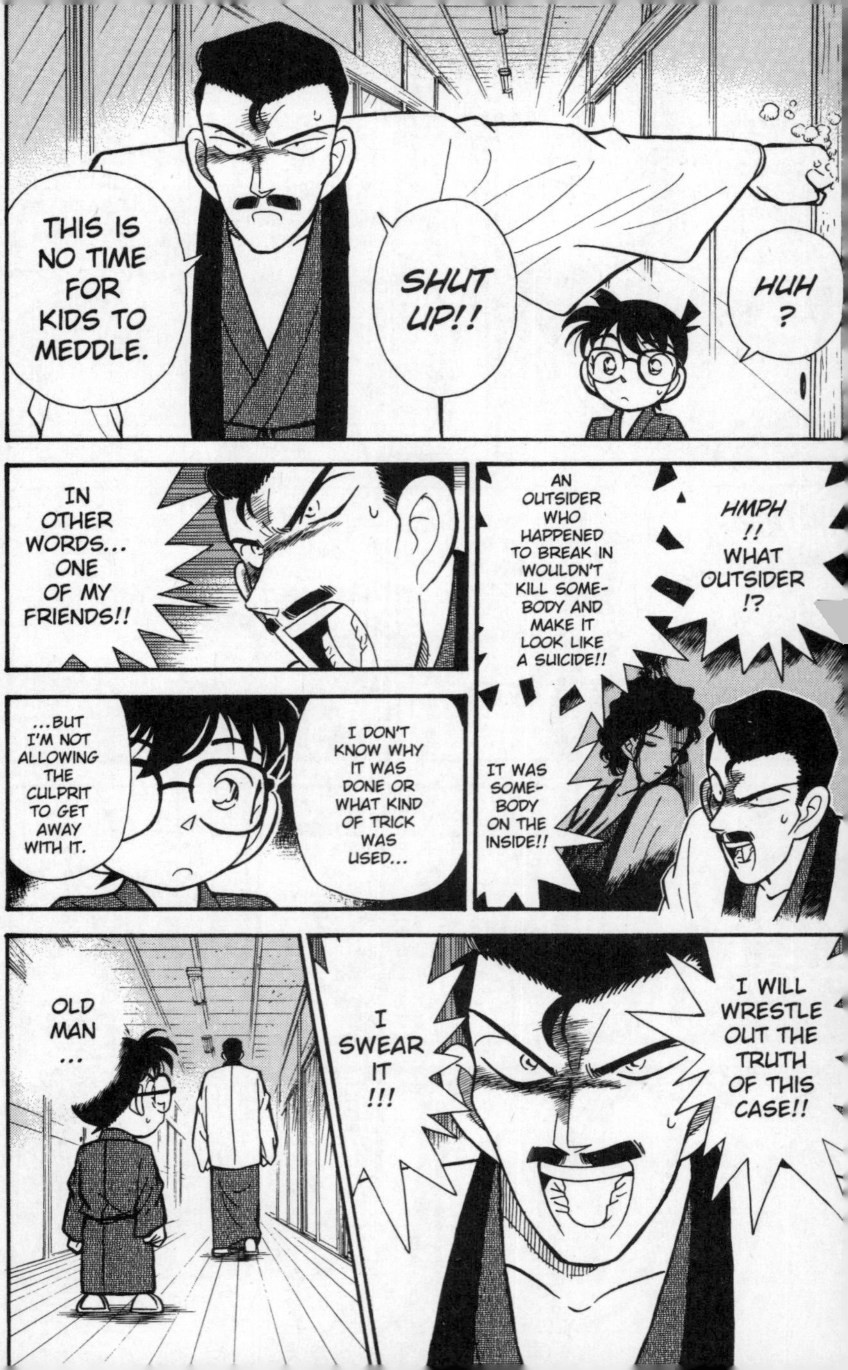

HUH ?
SHUT UP!!
THIS IS NO TIME FOR KIDS TO MEDDLE.
HMPH!! WHAT OUTSIDER !?
AN OUTSIDER WHO HAPPENED TO BREAK IN WOULDN'T KILL SOME-BODY AND MAKE IT LOOK LIKE A SUICIDE!!
IT WAS SOME-BODY ON THE INSIDE!!
IN OTHER WORDS... ONE OF MY FRIENDS!!
I DON'T KNOW WHY IT WAS DONE OR WHAT KIND OF TRICK WAS USED...
...BUT I'M NOT ALLOWING THE CULPRIT TO GET AWAY WITH IT.
I WILL WRESTLE OUT THE TRUTH OF THIS CASE!!
I SWEAR IT !!!
OLD MAN ...

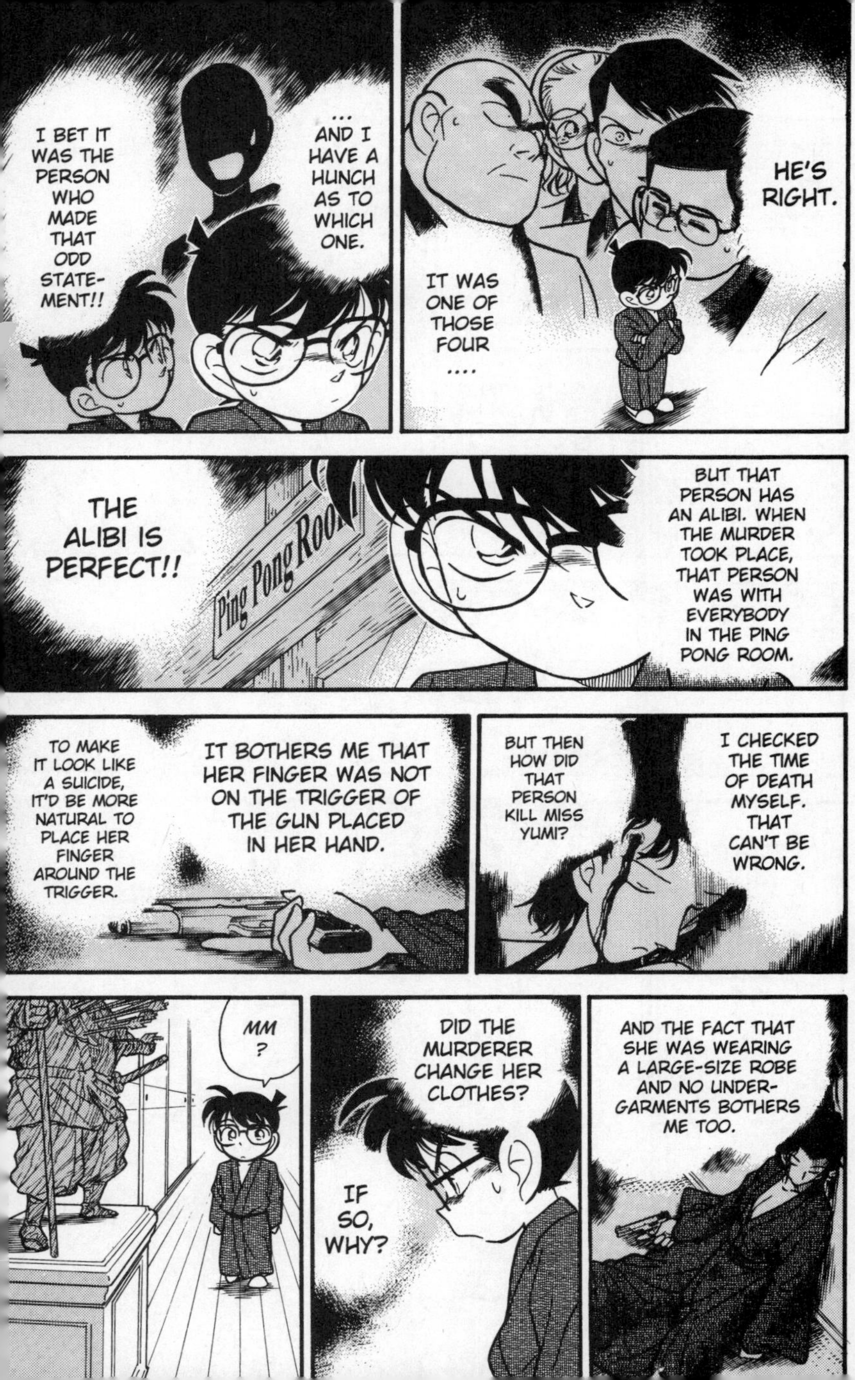
HE'S RIGHT.
IT WAS ONE OF THOSE FOUR ....
... AND I HAVE A HUNCH AS TO WHICH ONE.
I BET IT WAS THE PERSON WHO MADE THAT ODD STATEMENT!!
BUT THAT PERSON HAS AN ALIBI. WHEN THE MURDER TOOK PLACE, THAT PERSON WAS WITH EVERYBODY IN THE PING PONG ROOM.
Ping Pong Room
THE ALIBI IS PERFECT!!
I CHECKED THE TIME OF DEATH MYSELF. THAT CAN'T BE WRONG.
BUT THEN HOW DID THAT PERSON KILL MISS YUMI?
IT BOTHERS ME THAT HER FINGER WAS NOT ON THE TRIGGER OF THE GUN PLACED IN HER HAND.
TO MAKE IT LOOK LIKE A SUICIDE, IT'D BE MORE NATURAL TO PLACE HER FINGER AROUND THE TRIGGER.
AND THE FACT THAT SHE WAS WEARING A LARGE-SIZE ROBE AND NO UNDER-GARMENTS BOTHERS ME TOO.
DID THE MURDERER CHANGE HER CLOTHES?
IF SO, WHY?
MM ?

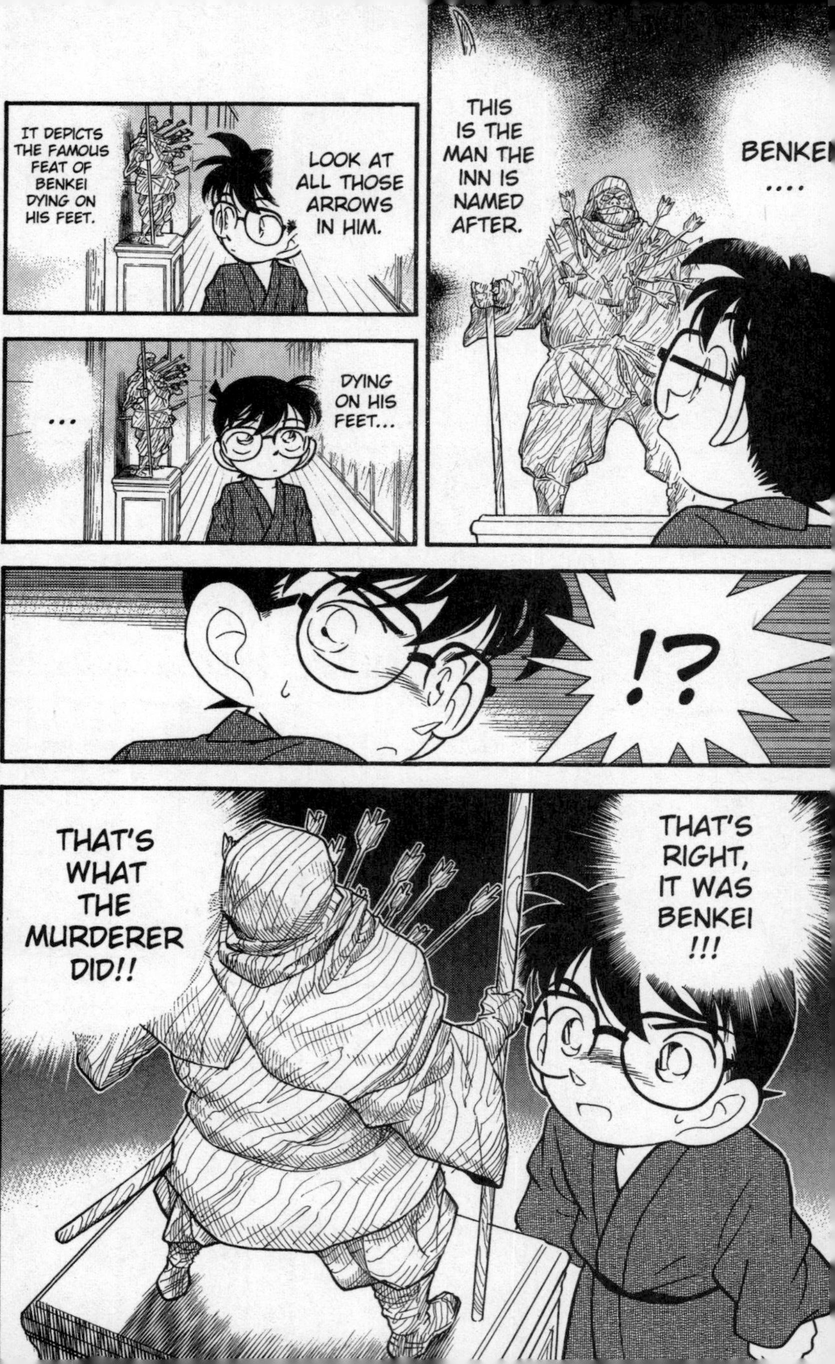
BENKE
....
THIS IS THE MAN THE INN IS NAMED AFTER.
LOOK AT ALL THOSE ARROWS IN HIM.
IT DEPICTS THE FAMOUS FEAT OF BENKEI DYING ON HIS FEET.
DYING ON HIS FEET...
...
!?
THAT'S RIGHT, IT WAS BENKEI !!!
THAT'S WHAT THE MURDERER DID!!

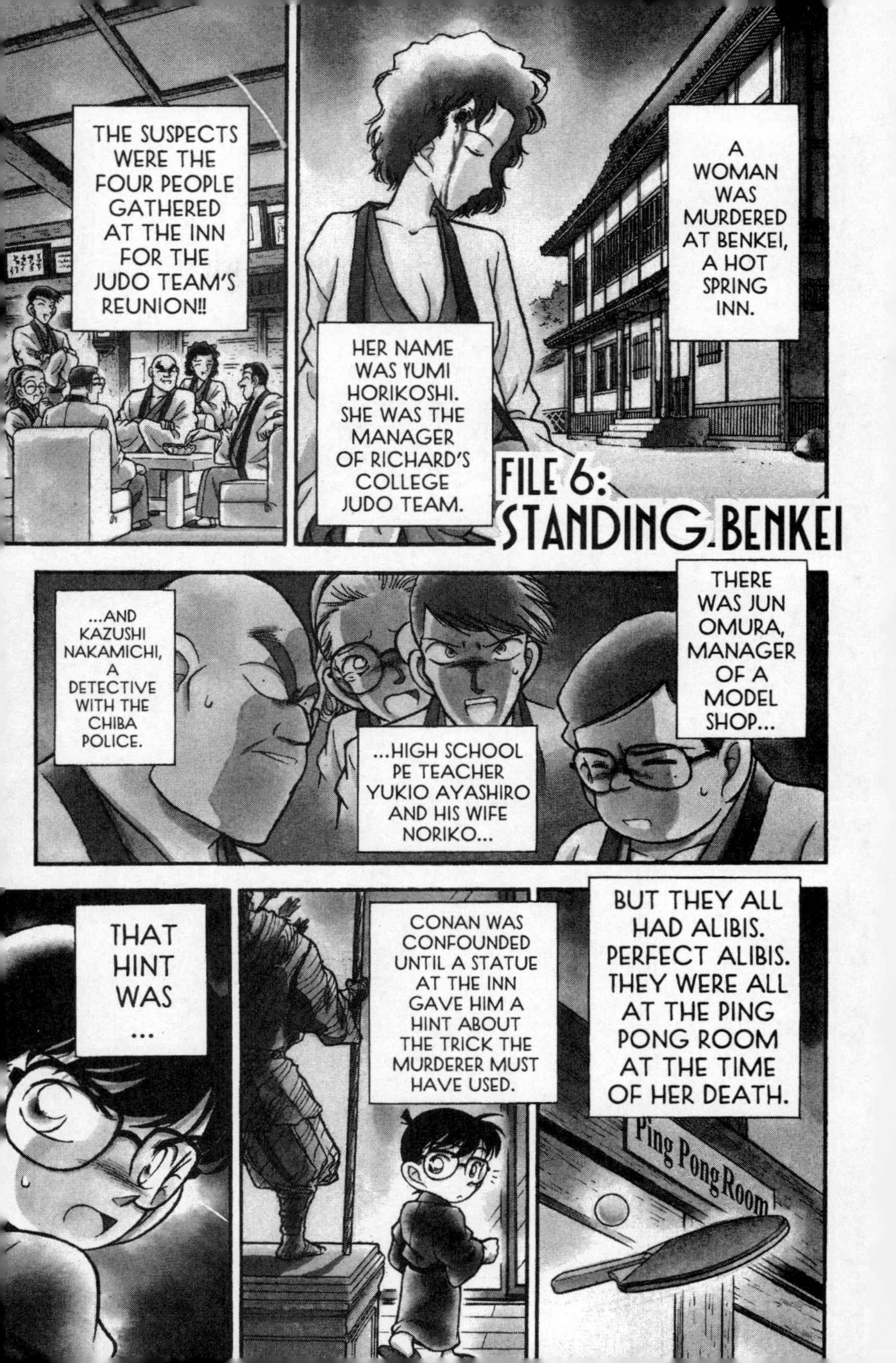
A WOMAN WAS MURDERED AT BENKEI, A HOT SPRING INN.
FILE 6: STANDING BENKEI
HER NAME WAS YUMI HORIKOSHI. SHE WAS THE MANAGER OF RICHARD'S COLLEGE JUDO TEAM.
THE SUSPECTS WERE THE FOUR PEOPLE GATHERED AT THE INN FOR THE JUDO TEAM'S REUNION!!
THERE WAS JUN OMURA, MANAGER OF A MODEL SHOP...
...HIGH SCHOOL PE TEACHER YUKIO AYASHIRO AND HIS WIFE NORIKO...
...AND KAZUSHI NAKAMICHI, A DETECTIVE WITH THE CHIBA POLICE.
BUT THEY ALL HAD ALIBIS. PERFECT ALIBIS. THEY WERE ALL AT THE PING PONG ROOM AT THE TIME OF HER DEATH.
Ping Pong Room
CONAN WAS CONFOUNDED UNTIL A STATUE AT THE INN GAVE HIM A HINT ABOUT THE TRICK THE MURDERER MUST HAVE USED.
THAT HINT WAS ...

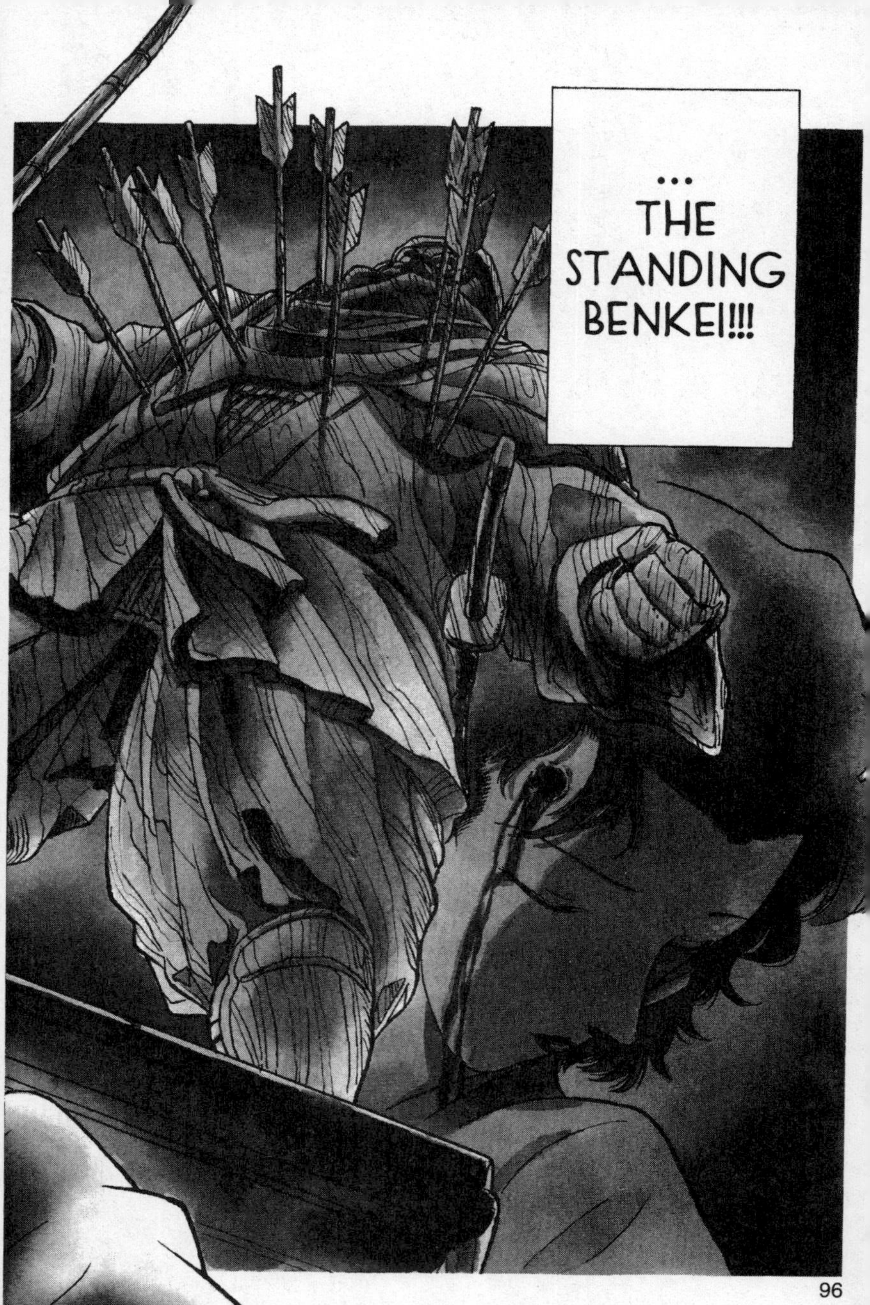
...
THE
STANDING
BENKEI!!!

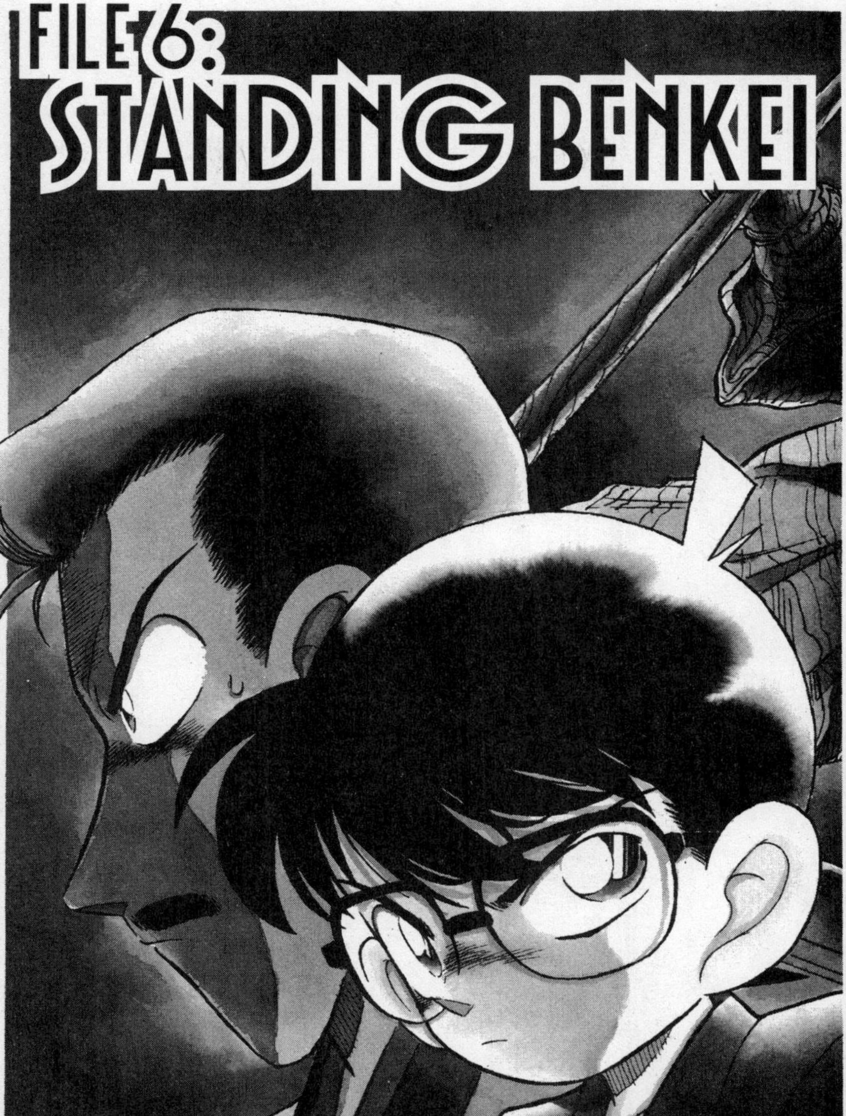
FILE 6:
STANDING BENKEI

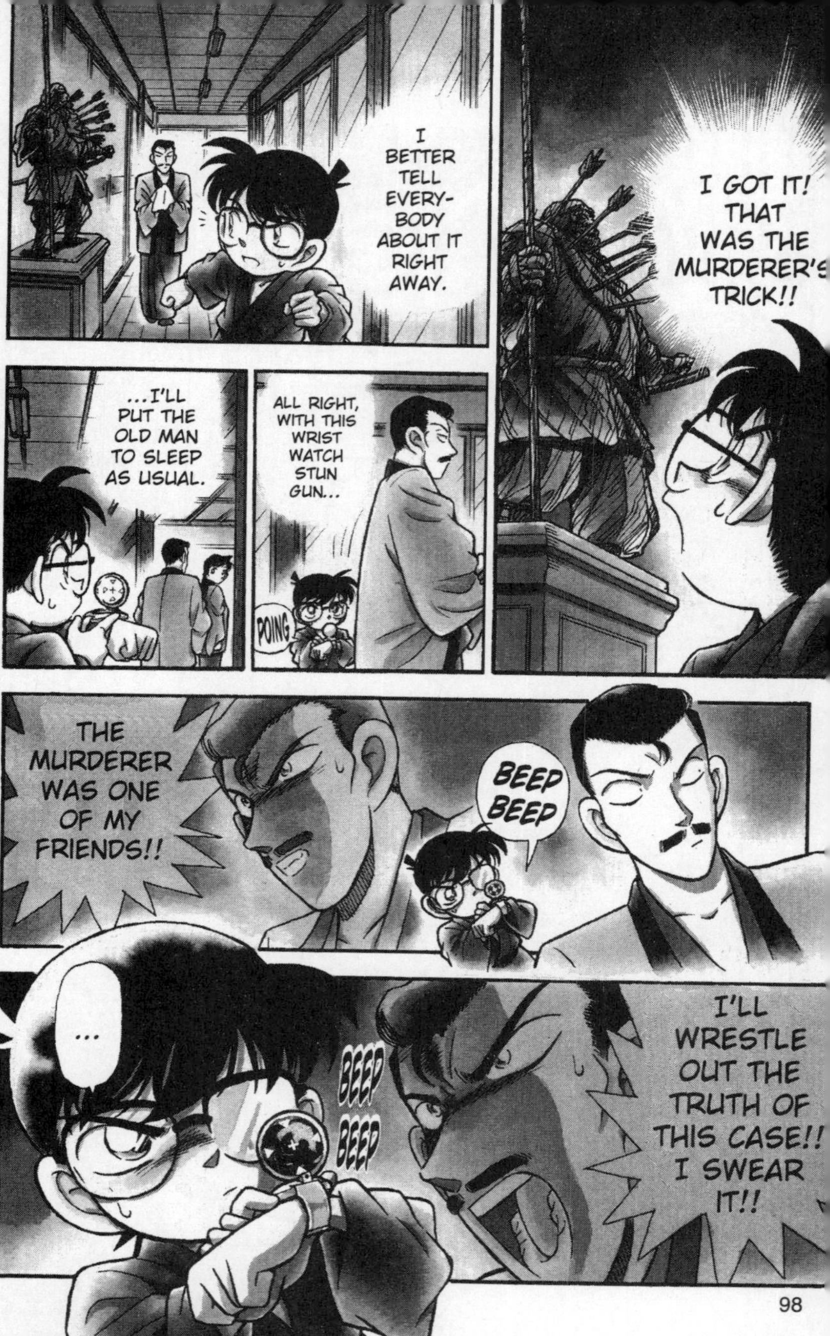
I GOT IT! THAT WAS THE MURDERER'S TRICK!!
I BETTER TELL EVERY-BODY ABOUT IT RIGHT AWAY.
ALL RIGHT, WITH THIS WRIST WATCH STUN GUN...
POING
...I'LL PUT THE OLD MAN TO SLEEP AS USUAL.
BEEP BEEP
THE MURDERER WAS ONE OF MY FRIENDS!!
I'LL WRESTLE OUT THE TRUTH OF THIS CASE!! I SWEAR IT!!
BEEP BEEP
...

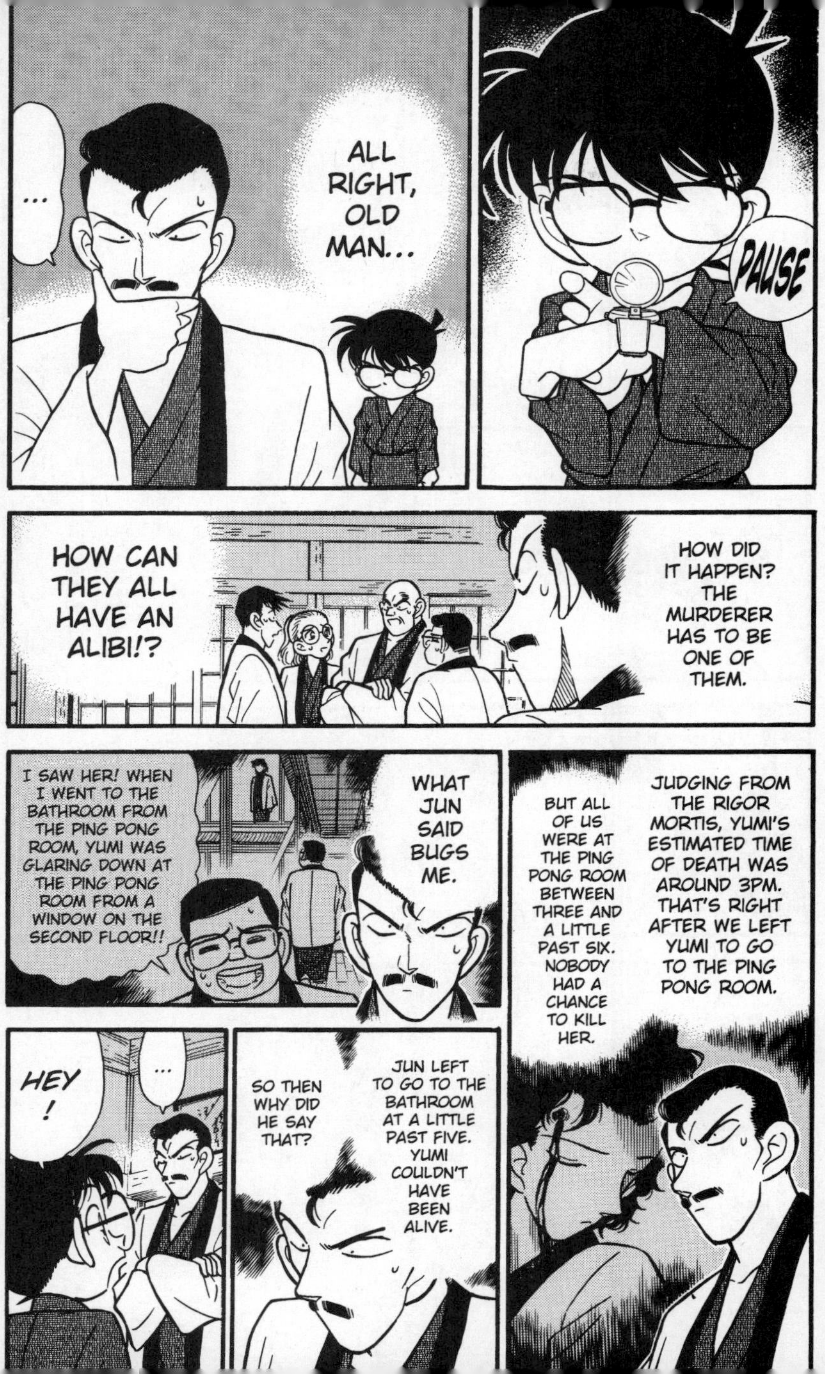
PAUSE
ALL RIGHT, OLD MAN...
...
HOW DID IT HAPPEN? THE MURDERER HAS TO BE ONE OF THEM.
HOW CAN THEY ALL HAVE AN ALIBI!?
JUDGING FROM THE RIGOR MORTIS, YUMI'S ESTIMATED TIME OF DEATH WAS AROUND 3PM. THAT'S RIGHT AFTER WE LEFT YUMI TO GO TO THE PING PONG ROOM.
BUT ALL OF US WERE AT THE PING PONG ROOM BETWEEN THREE AND A LITTLE PAST SIX. NOBODY HAD A CHANCE TO KILL HER.
WHAT JUN SAID BUGS ME.
I SAW HER! WHEN I WENT TO THE BATHROOM FROM THE PING PONG ROOM, YUMI WAS GLARING DOWN AT THE PING PONG ROOM FROM A WINDOW ON THE SECOND FLOOR!!
JUN LEFT TO GO TO THE BATHROOM AT A LITTLE PAST FIVE. YUMI COULDN'T HAVE BEEN ALIVE.
SO THEN WHY DID HE SAY THAT?
...
HEY!

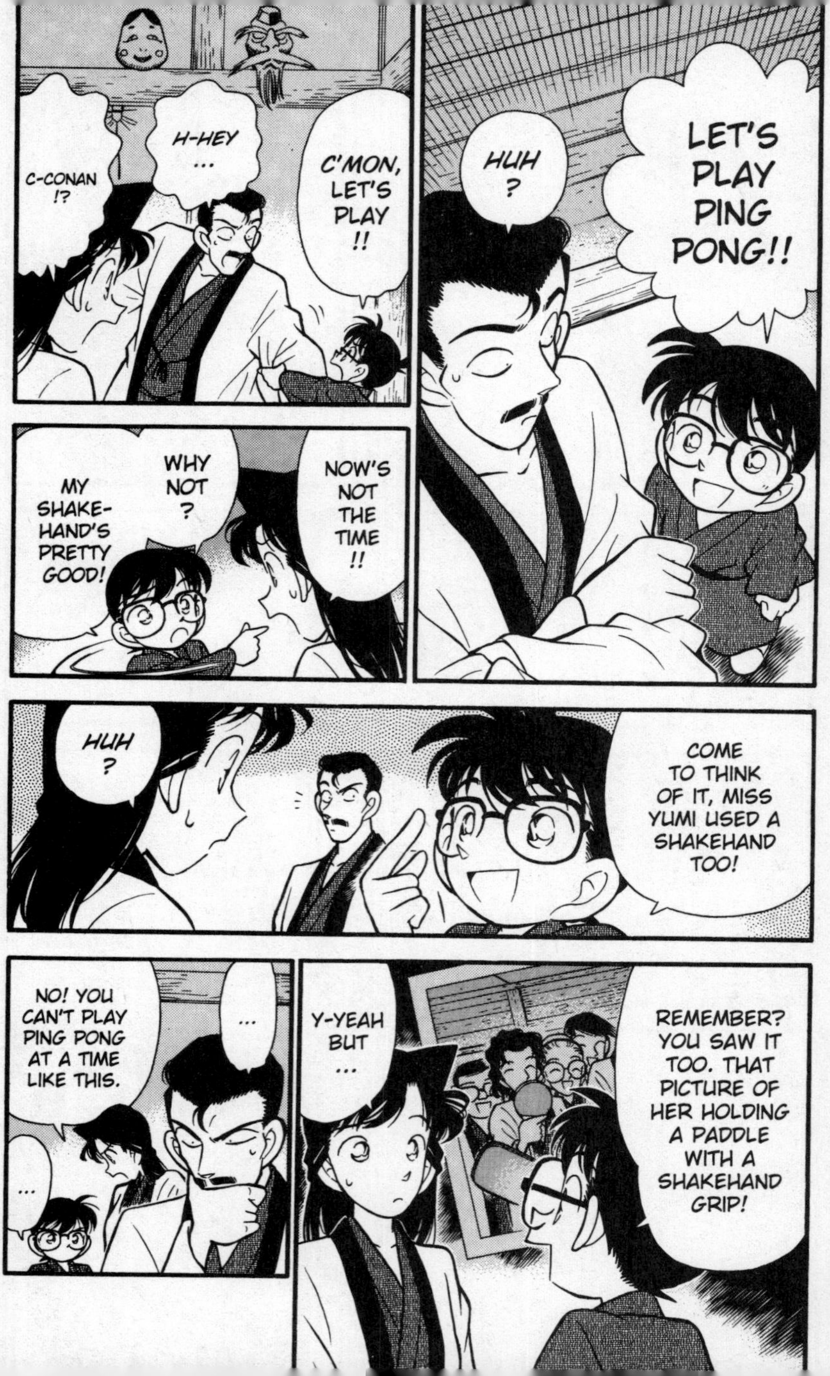
LET'S PLAY PING PONG!!
HUH ?
C'MON, LET'S PLAY !!
H-HEY ...
C-CONAN !?
NOW'S NOT THE TIME !!
WHY NOT ?
MY SHAKE-HAND'S PRETTY GOOD!
COME TO THINK OF IT, MISS YUMI USED A SHAKEHAND TOO!
HUH ?
REMEMBER? YOU SAW IT TOO. THAT PICTURE OF HER HOLDING A PADDLE WITH A SHAKEHAND GRIP!
Y-YEAH BUT ...
...
NO! YOU CAN'T PLAY PING PONG AT A TIME LIKE THIS.
...

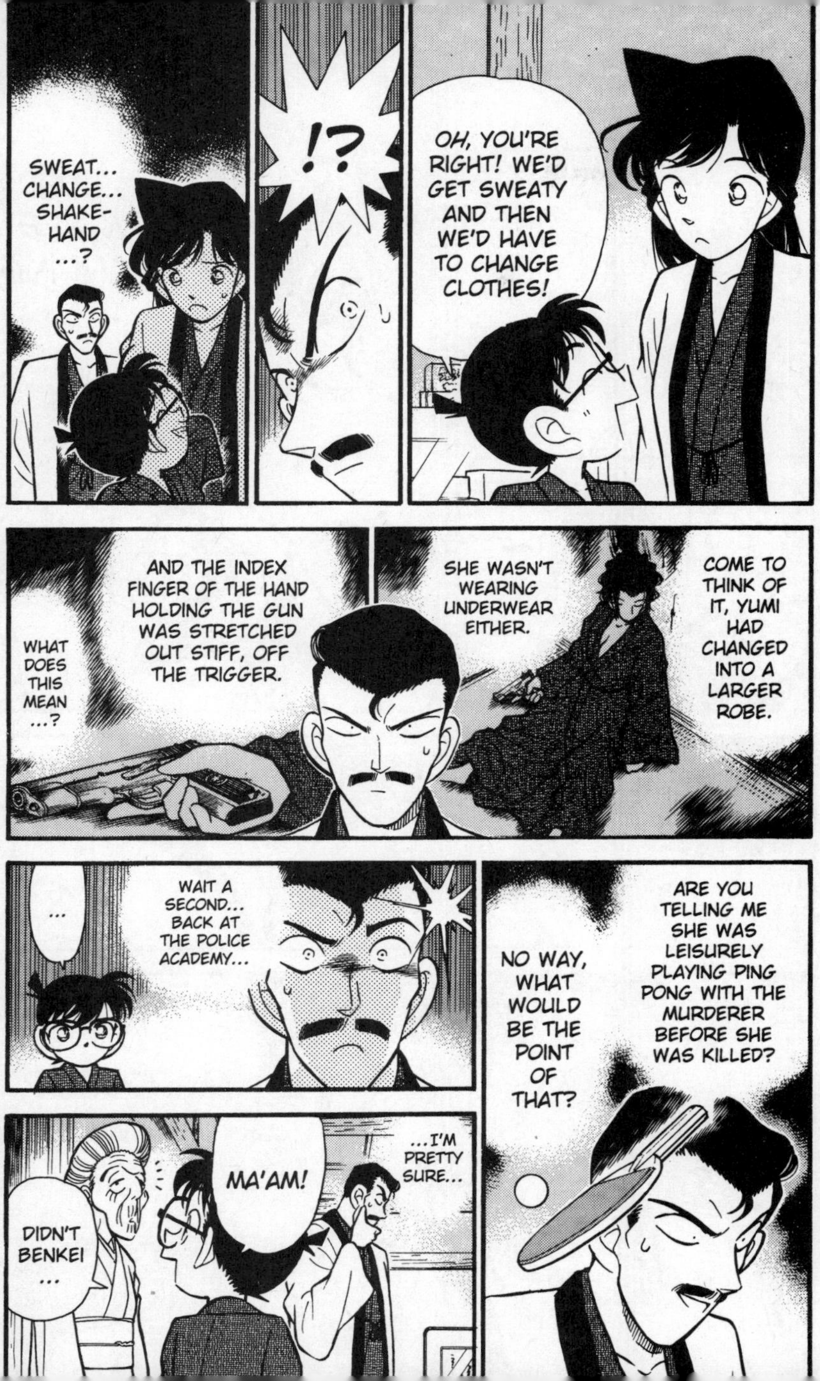
OH, YOU'RE RIGHT! WE'D GET SWEATY AND THEN WE'D HAVE TO CHANGE CLOTHES!
!?
SWEAT... CHANGE... SHAKE-HAND ...?
COME TO THINK OF IT, YUMI HAD CHANGED INTO A LARGER ROBE.
SHE WASN'T WEARING UNDERWEAR EITHER.
AND THE INDEX FINGER OF THE HAND HOLDING THE GUN WAS STRETCHED OUT STIFF, OFF THE TRIGGER.
WHAT DOES THIS MEAN ...?
ARE YOU TELLING ME SHE WAS LEISURELY PLAYING PING PONG WITH THE MURDERER BEFORE SHE WAS KILLED?
NO WAY, WHAT WOULD BE THE POINT OF THAT?
WAIT A SECOND... BACK AT THE POLICE ACADEMY...
...
...I'M PRETTY SURE...
MA'AM!
DIDN'T BENKEI ...

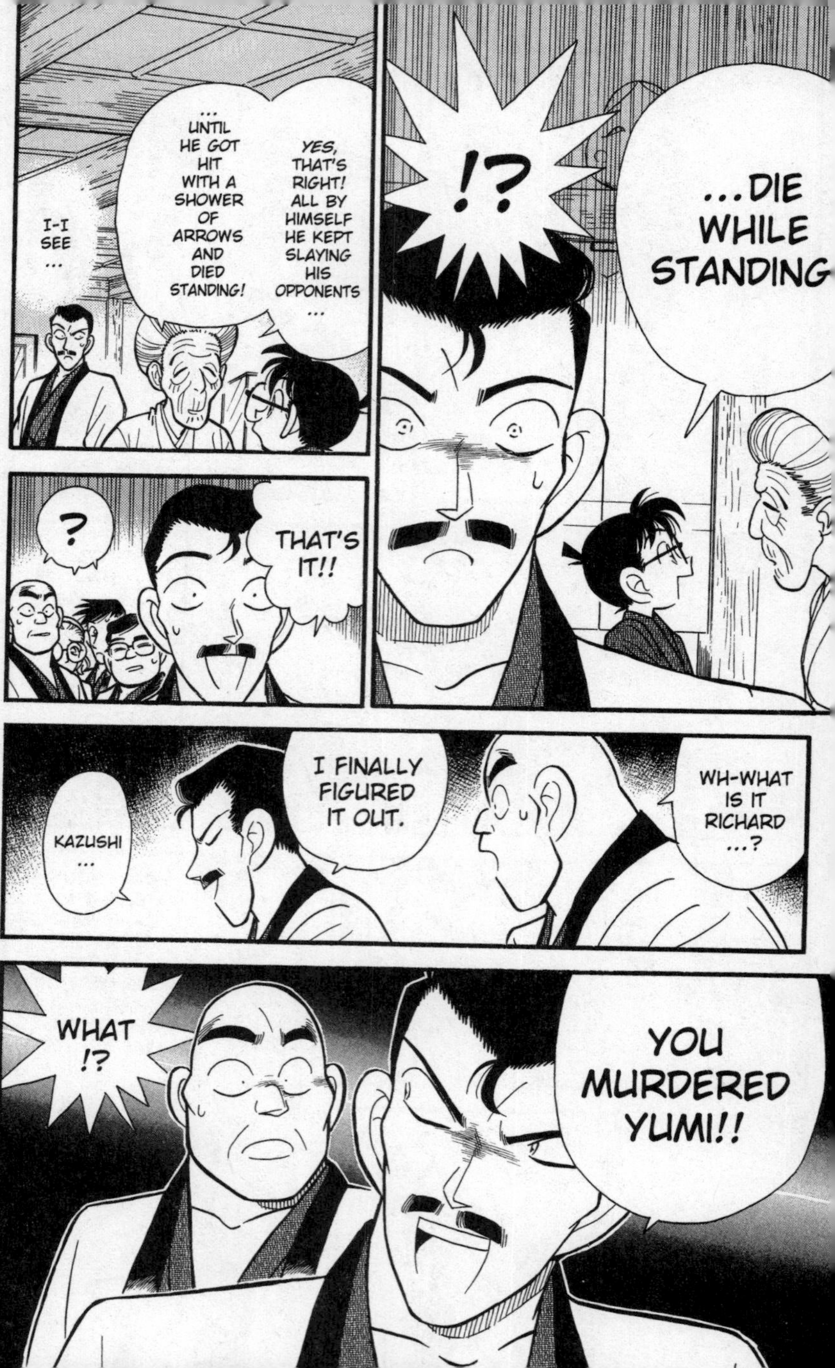
...DIE WHILE STANDING
!?
YES, THAT'S RIGHT! ALL BY HIMSELF HE KEPT SLAYING HIS OPPONENTS ...
... UNTIL HE GOT HIT WITH A SHOWER OF ARROWS AND DIED STANDING!
I-I SEE ...
THAT'S IT!!
?
WH-WHAT IS IT RICHARD ...?
I FINALLY FIGURED IT OUT.
KAZUSHI ...
YOU MURDERED YUMI!!
WHAT !?

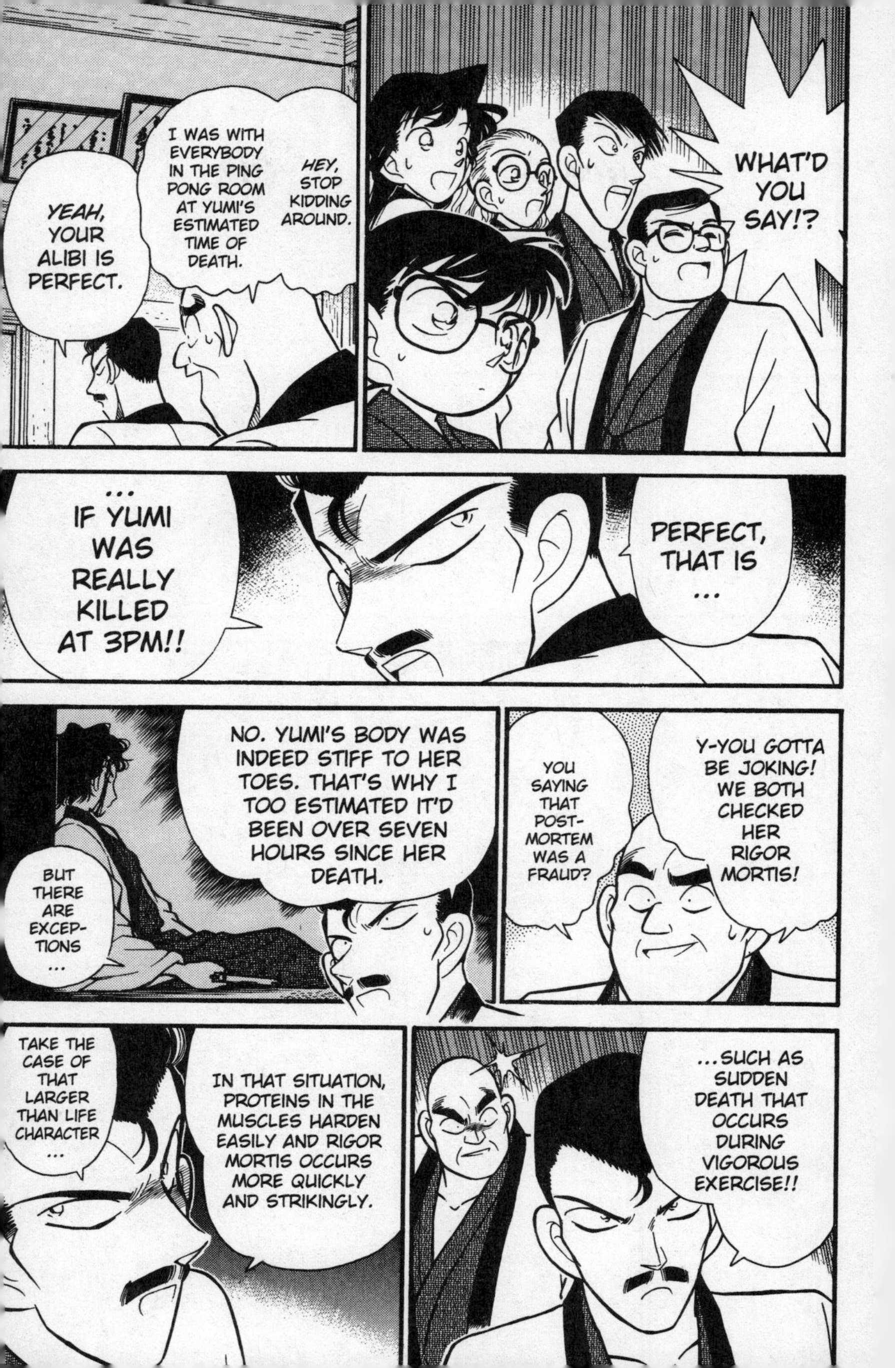
WHAT'D YOU SAY!?
HEY, STOP KIDDING AROUND.
I WAS WITH EVERYBODY IN THE PING PONG ROOM AT YUMI'S ESTIMATED TIME OF DEATH.
YEAH, YOUR ALIBI IS PERFECT.
PERFECT, THAT IS ...
... IF YUMI WAS REALLY KILLED AT 3PM!!
Y-YOU GOTTA BE JOKING! WE BOTH CHECKED HER RIGOR MORTIS!
YOU SAYING THAT POST-MORTEM WAS A FRAUD?
NO. YUMI'S BODY WAS INDEED STIFF TO HER TOES. THAT'S WHY I TOO ESTIMATED IT'D BEEN OVER SEVEN HOURS SINCE HER DEATH.
BUT THERE ARE EXCEPTIONS ...
...SUCH AS SUDDEN DEATH THAT OCCURS DURING VIGOROUS EXERCISE!!
IN THAT SITUATION, PROTEINS IN THE MUSCLES HARDEN EASILY AND RIGOR MORTIS OCCURS MORE QUICKLY AND STRIKINGLY.
TAKE THE CASE OF THAT LARGER THAN LIFE CHARACTER ...

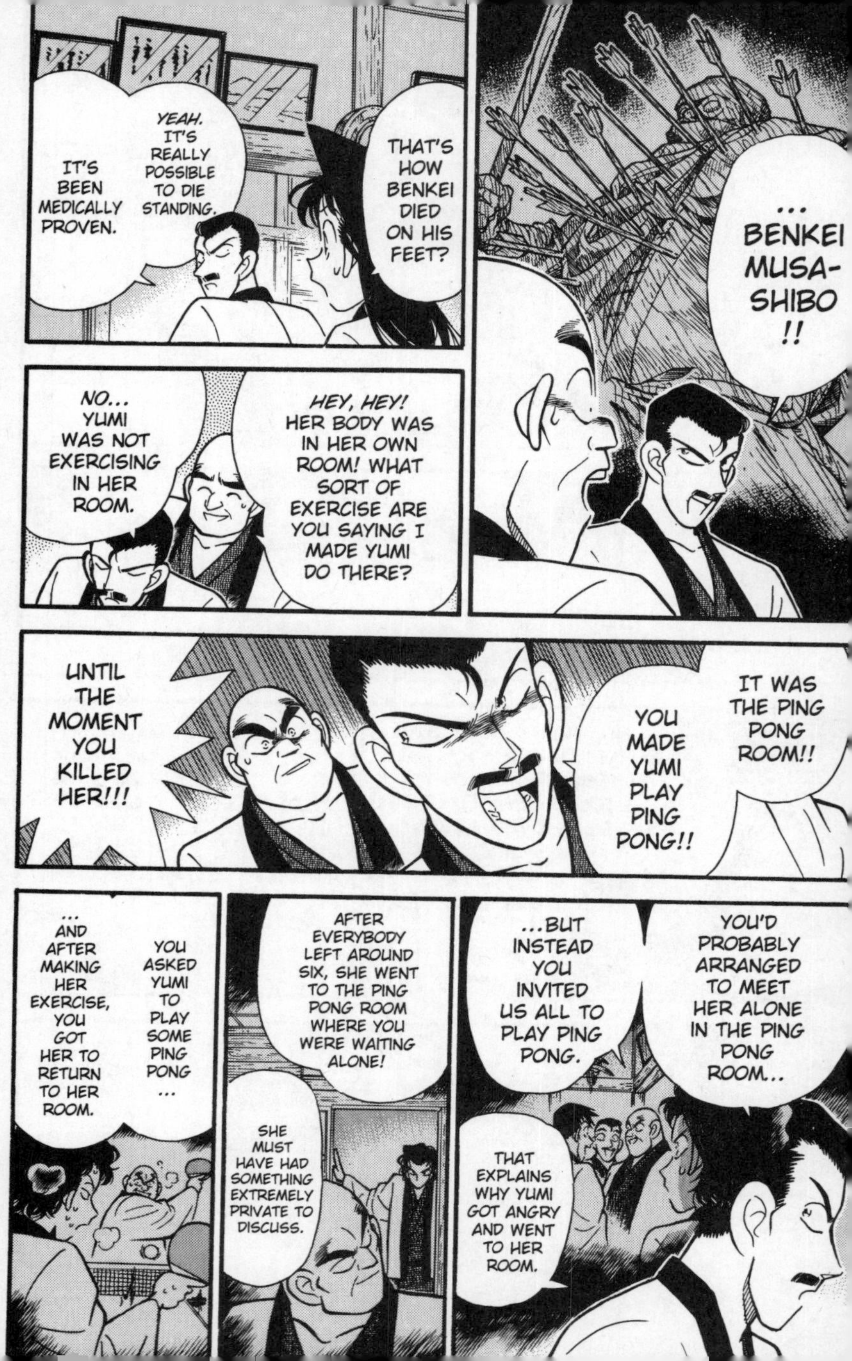
...BENKEI MUSASHIBO!!
THAT'S HOW BENKEI DIED ON HIS FEET?
YEAH. IT'S REALLY POSSIBLE TO DIE STANDING.
IT'S BEEN MEDICALLY PROVEN.
HEY, HEY! HER BODY WAS IN HER OWN ROOM! WHAT SORT OF EXERCISE ARE YOU SAYING I MADE YUMI DO THERE?
NO... YUMI WAS NOT EXERCISING IN HER ROOM.
IT WAS THE PING PONG ROOM!!
YOU MADE YUMI PLAY PING PONG!!
UNTIL THE MOMENT YOU KILLED HER!!!
YOU'D PROBABLY ARRANGED TO MEET HER ALONE IN THE PING PONG ROOM...
...BUT INSTEAD YOU INVITED US ALL TO PLAY PING PONG.
THAT EXPLAINS WHY YUMI GOT ANGRY AND WENT TO HER ROOM.
AFTER EVERYBODY LEFT AROUND SIX, SHE WENT TO THE PING PONG ROOM WHERE YOU WERE WAITING ALONE!
SHE MUST HAVE HAD SOMETHING EXTREMELY PRIVATE TO DISCUSS.
YOU ASKED YUMI TO PLAY SOME PING PONG ...
... AND AFTER MAKING HER EXERCISE, YOU GOT HER TO RETURN TO HER ROOM.

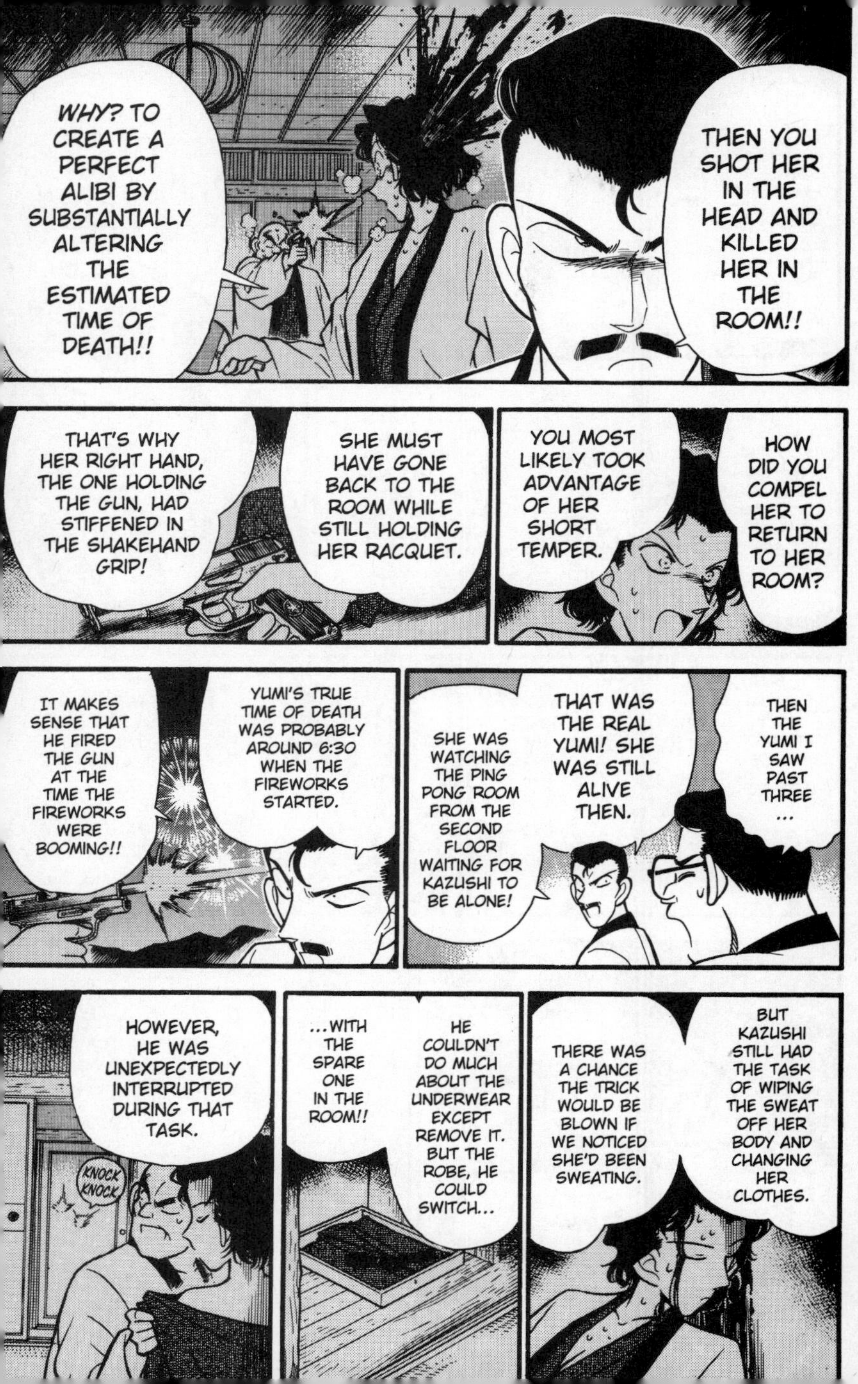
THEN YOU SHOT HER IN THE HEAD AND KILLED HER IN THE ROOM!!
WHY? TO CREATE A PERFECT ALIBI BY SUBSTANTIALLY ALTERING THE ESTIMATED TIME OF DEATH!!
HOW DID YOU COMPEL HER TO RETURN TO HER ROOM?
YOU MOST LIKELY TOOK ADVANTAGE OF HER SHORT TEMPER.
SHE MUST HAVE GONE BACK TO THE ROOM WHILE STILL HOLDING HER RACQUET.
THAT'S WHY HER RIGHT HAND, THE ONE HOLDING THE GUN, HAD STIFFENED IN THE SHAKEHAND GRIP!
THEN THE YUMI I SAW PAST THREE ...
THAT WAS THE REAL YUMI! SHE WAS STILL ALIVE THEN.
SHE WAS WATCHING THE PING PONG ROOM FROM THE SECOND FLOOR WAITING FOR KAZUSHI TO BE ALONE!
YUMI'S TRUE TIME OF DEATH WAS PROBABLY AROUND 6:30 WHEN THE FIREWORKS STARTED.
IT MAKES SENSE THAT HE FIRED THE GUN AT THE TIME THE FIREWORKS WERE BOOMING!!
BUT KAZUSHI STILL HAD THE TASK OF WIPING THE SWEAT OFF HER BODY AND CHANGING HER CLOTHES.
THERE WAS A CHANCE THE TRICK WOULD BE BLOWN IF WE NOTICED SHE'D BEEN SWEATING.
HE COULDN'T DO MUCH ABOUT THE UNDERWEAR EXCEPT REMOVE IT. BUT THE ROBE, HE COULD SWITCH...
...WITH THE SPARE ONE IN THE ROOM!!
HOWEVER, HE WAS UNEXPECTEDLY INTERRUPTED DURING THAT TASK.
KNOCK KNOCK

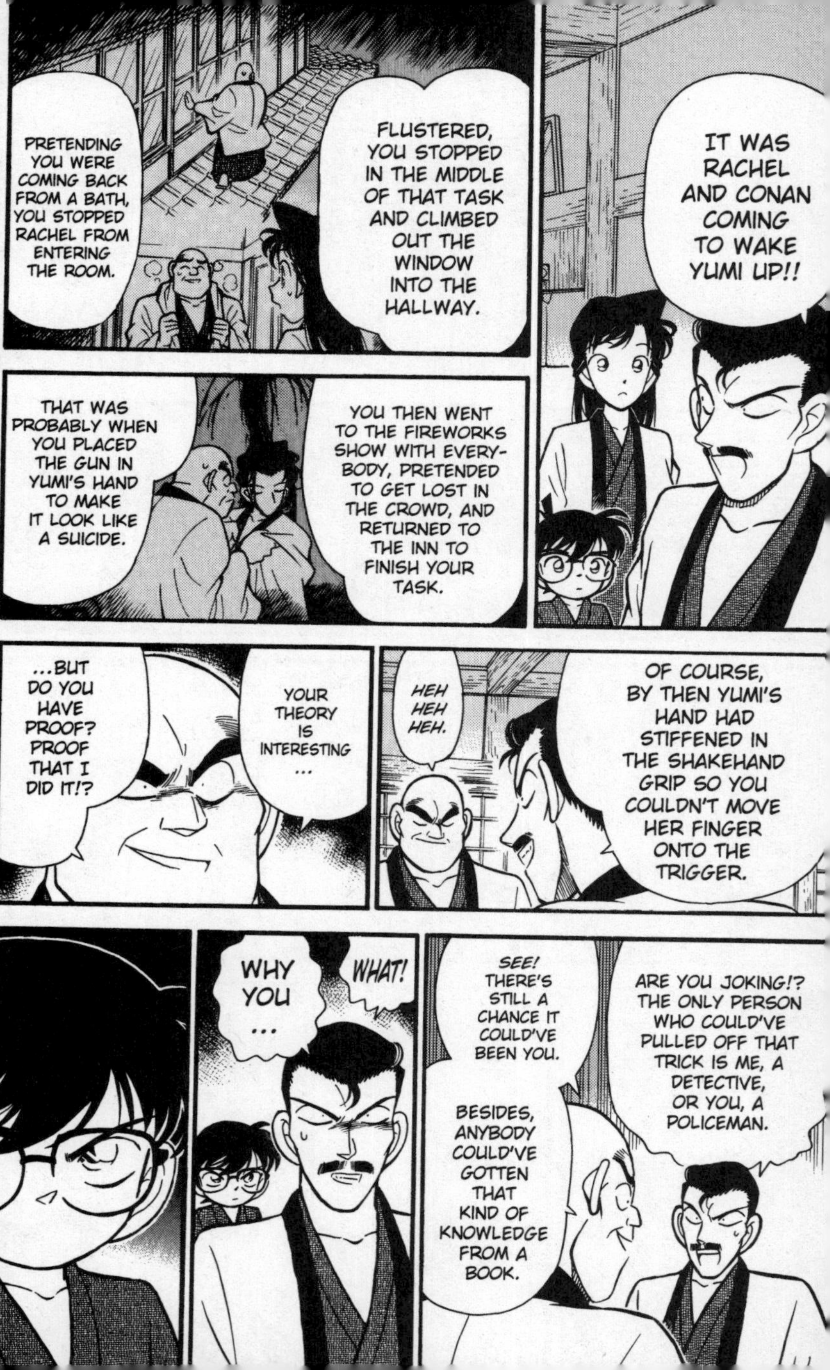
IT WAS RACHEL AND CONAN COMING TO WAKE YUMI UP!!
FLUSTERED, YOU STOPPED IN THE MIDDLE OF THAT TASK AND CLIMBED OUT THE WINDOW INTO THE HALLWAY.
PRETENDING YOU WERE COMING BACK FROM A BATH, YOU STOPPED RACHEL FROM ENTERING THE ROOM.
YOU THEN WENT TO THE FIREWORKS SHOW WITH EVERY-BODY, PRETENDED TO GET LOST IN THE CROWD, AND RETURNED TO THE INN TO FINISH YOUR TASK.
THAT WAS PROBABLY WHEN YOU PLACED THE GUN IN YUMI'S HAND TO MAKE IT LOOK LIKE A SUICIDE.
OF COURSE, BY THEN YUMI'S HAND HAD STIFFENED IN THE SHAKEHAND GRIP SO YOU COULDN'T MOVE HER FINGER ONTO THE TRIGGER.
HEH HEH HEH.
YOUR THEORY IS INTERESTING ...
...BUT DO YOU HAVE PROOF? PROOF THAT I DID IT!?
ARE YOU JOKING!? THE ONLY PERSON WHO COULD'VE PULLED OFF THAT TRICK IS ME, A DETECTIVE, OR YOU, A POLICEMAN.
SEE! THERE'S STILL A CHANCE IT COULD'VE BEEN YOU.
BESIDES, ANYBODY COULD'VE GOTTEN THAT KIND OF KNOWLEDGE FROM A BOOK.
WHAT!
WHY YOU ...

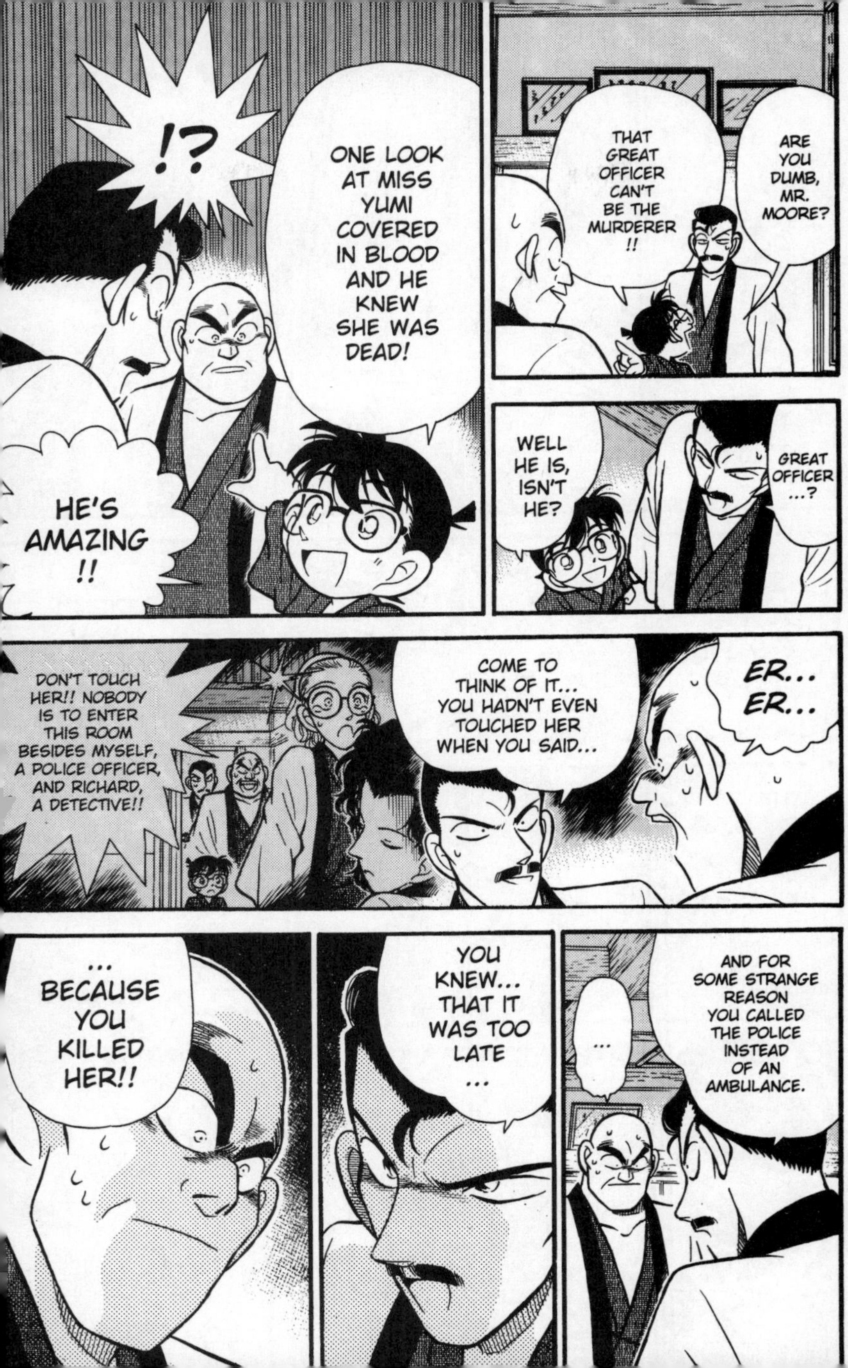
ARE YOU DUMB, MR. MOORE?
THAT GREAT OFFICER CAN'T BE THE MURDERER!!
GREAT OFFICER...?
WELL HE IS, ISN'T HE?
!?
ONE LOOK AT MISS YUMI COVERED IN BLOOD AND HE KNEW SHE WAS DEAD!
HE'S AMAZING!!
ER... ER...
COME TO THINK OF IT... YOU HADN'T EVEN TOUCHED HER WHEN YOU SAID...
DON'T TOUCH HER!! NOBODY IS TO ENTER THIS ROOM BESIDES MYSELF, A POLICE OFFICER, AND RICHARD, A DETECTIVE!!
AND FOR SOME STRANGE REASON YOU CALLED THE POLICE INSTEAD OF AN AMBULANCE.
...
YOU KNEW... THAT IT WAS TOO LATE...
... BECAUSE YOU KILLED HER!!

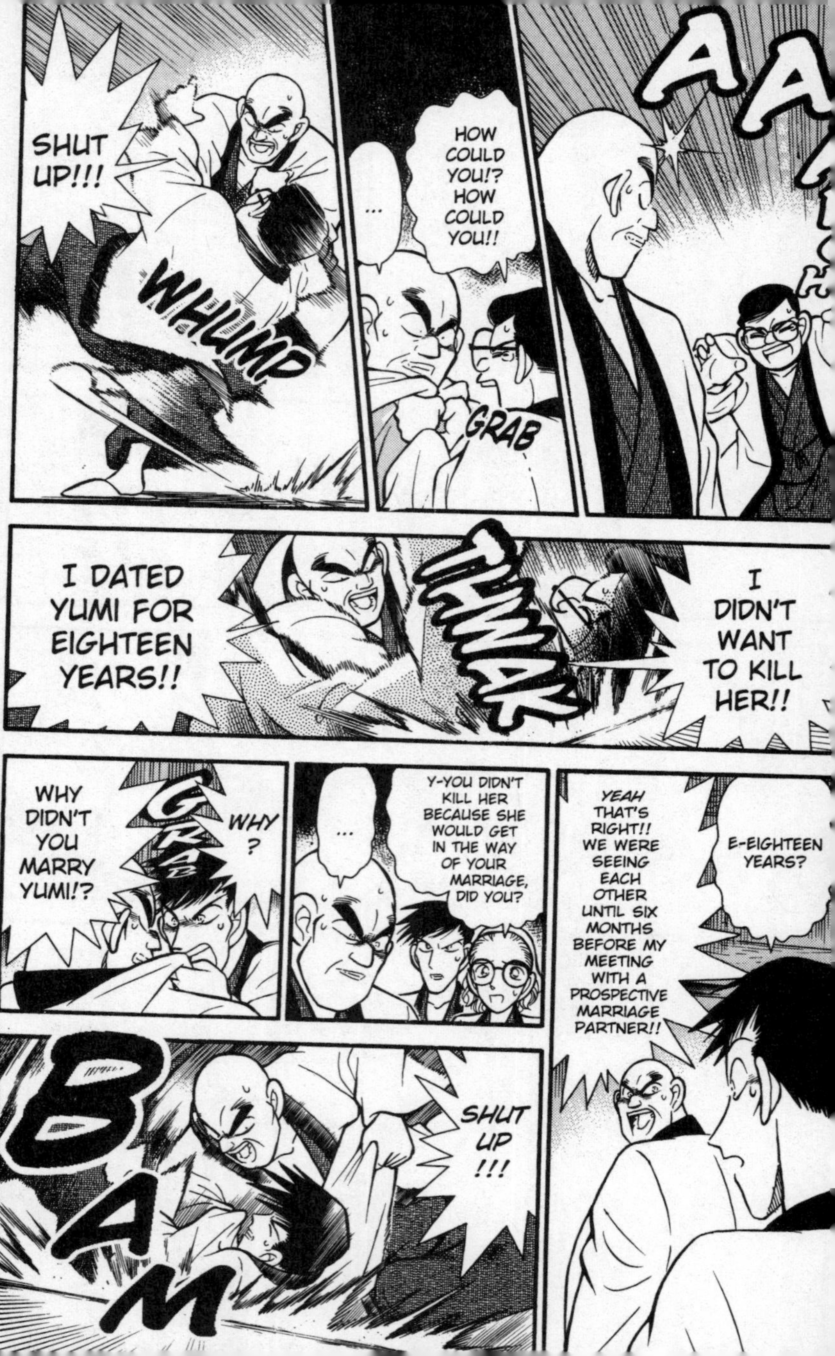

AA
HOW COULD YOU!? HOW COULD YOU!!
...
GRAB
SHUT UP!!!
WHUMP
I DIDN'T WANT TO KILL HER!!
THWAK
I DATED YUMI FOR EIGHTEEN YEARS!!
E-EIGHTEEN YEARS?
YEAH THAT'S RIGHT!! WE WERE SEEING EACH OTHER UNTIL SIX MONTHS BEFORE MY MEETING WITH A PROSPECTIVE MARRIAGE PARTNER!!
Y-YOU DIDN'T KILL HER BECAUSE SHE WOULD GET IN THE WAY OF YOUR MARRIAGE, DID YOU?
...
WHY?
GRAB
WHY DIDN'T YOU MARRY YUMI!?
SHUT UP!!!
BAM

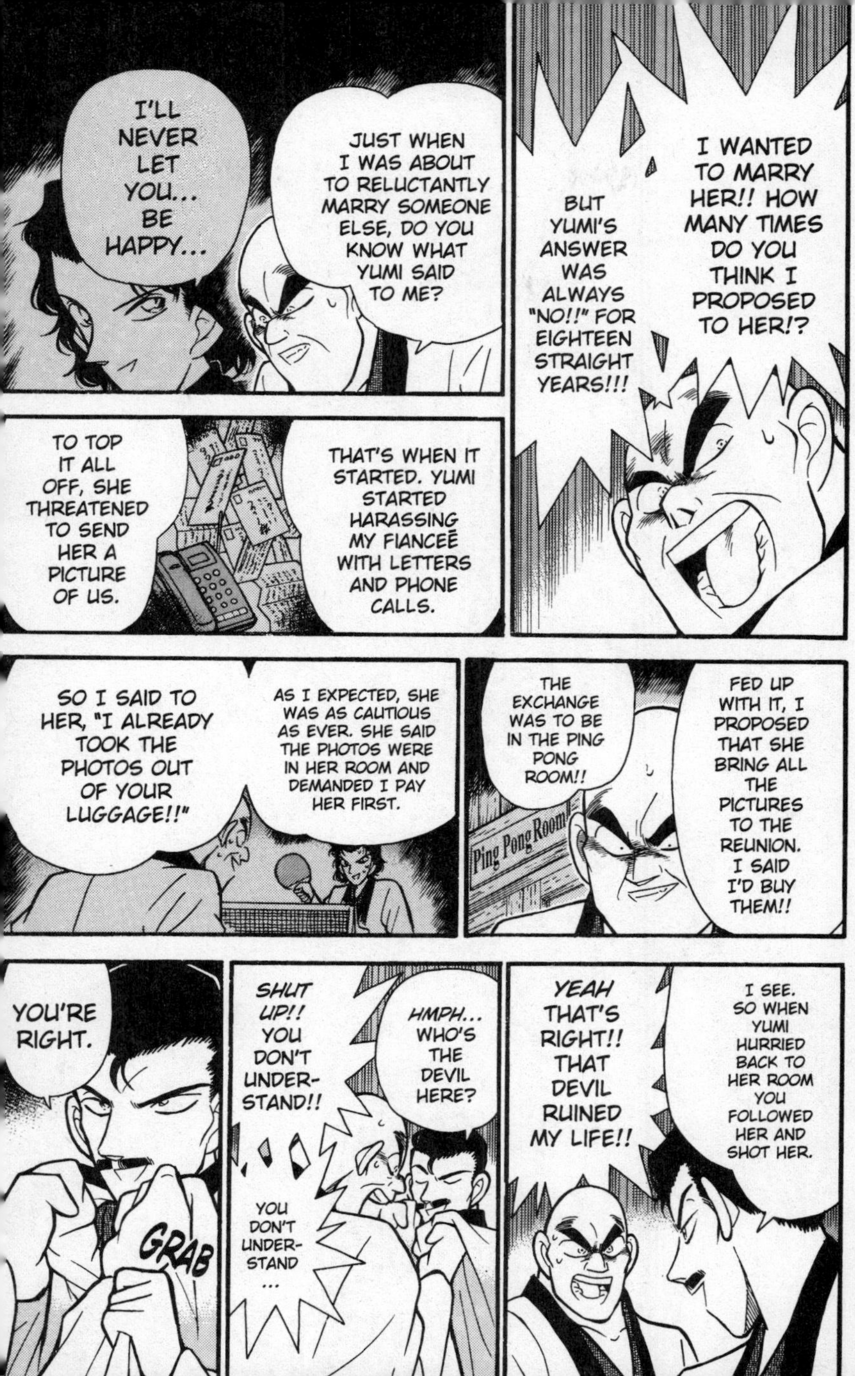
I WANTED TO MARRY HER!! HOW MANY TIMES DO YOU THINK I PROPOSED TO HER!?
BUT YUMI'S ANSWER WAS ALWAYS "NO!!" FOR EIGHTEEN STRAIGHT YEARS!!!
JUST WHEN I WAS ABOUT TO RELUCTANTLY MARRY SOMEONE ELSE, DO YOU KNOW WHAT YUMI SAID TO ME?
I'LL NEVER LET YOU... BE HAPPY...
THAT'S WHEN IT STARTED. YUMI STARTED HARASSING MY FIANCEE WITH LETTERS AND PHONE CALLS.
TO TOP IT ALL OFF, SHE THREATENED TO SEND HER A PICTURE OF US.
FED UP WITH IT, I PROPOSED THAT SHE BRING ALL THE PICTURES TO THE REUNION. I SAID I'D BUY THEM!!
THE EXCHANGE WAS TO BE IN THE PING PONG ROOM!!
Ping Pong Room
AS I EXPECTED, SHE WAS AS CAUTIOUS AS EVER. SHE SAID THE PHOTOS WERE IN HER ROOM AND DEMANDED I PAY HER FIRST.
SO I SAID TO HER, "I ALREADY TOOK THE PHOTOS OUT OF YOUR LUGGAGE!!"
I SEE. SO WHEN YUMI HURRIED BACK TO HER ROOM YOU FOLLOWED HER AND SHOT HER.
YEAH THAT'S RIGHT!! THAT DEVIL RUINED MY LIFE!!
HMPH... WHO'S THE DEVIL HERE?
SHUT UP!! YOU DON'T UNDERSTAND!!
YOU DON'T UNDER-STAND ...
YOU'RE RIGHT.
GRAB

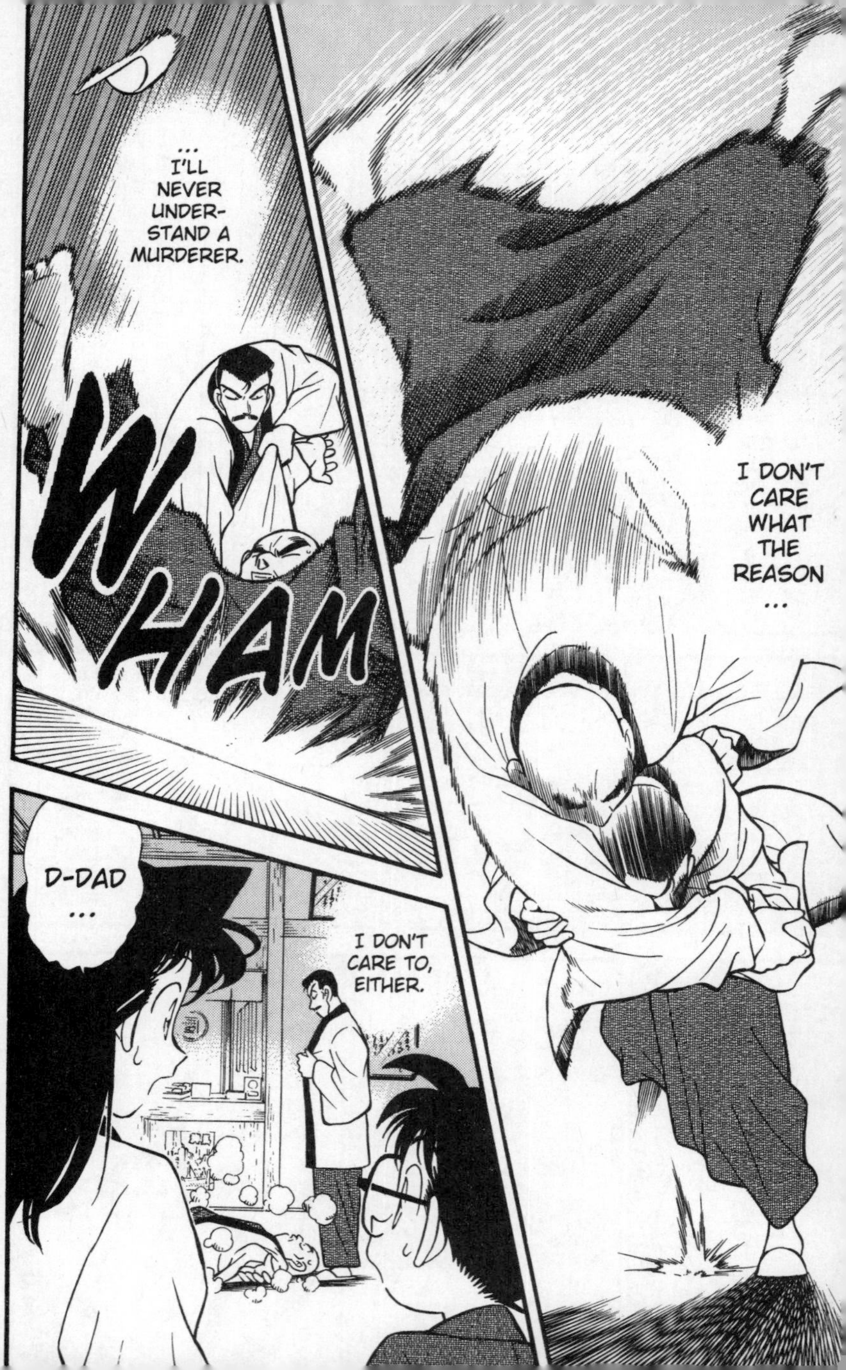
I DON'T CARE WHAT THE REASON ...
... I'LL NEVER UNDER-STAND A MURDERER.
WHAM
I DON'T CARE TO, EITHER.
D-DAD ...

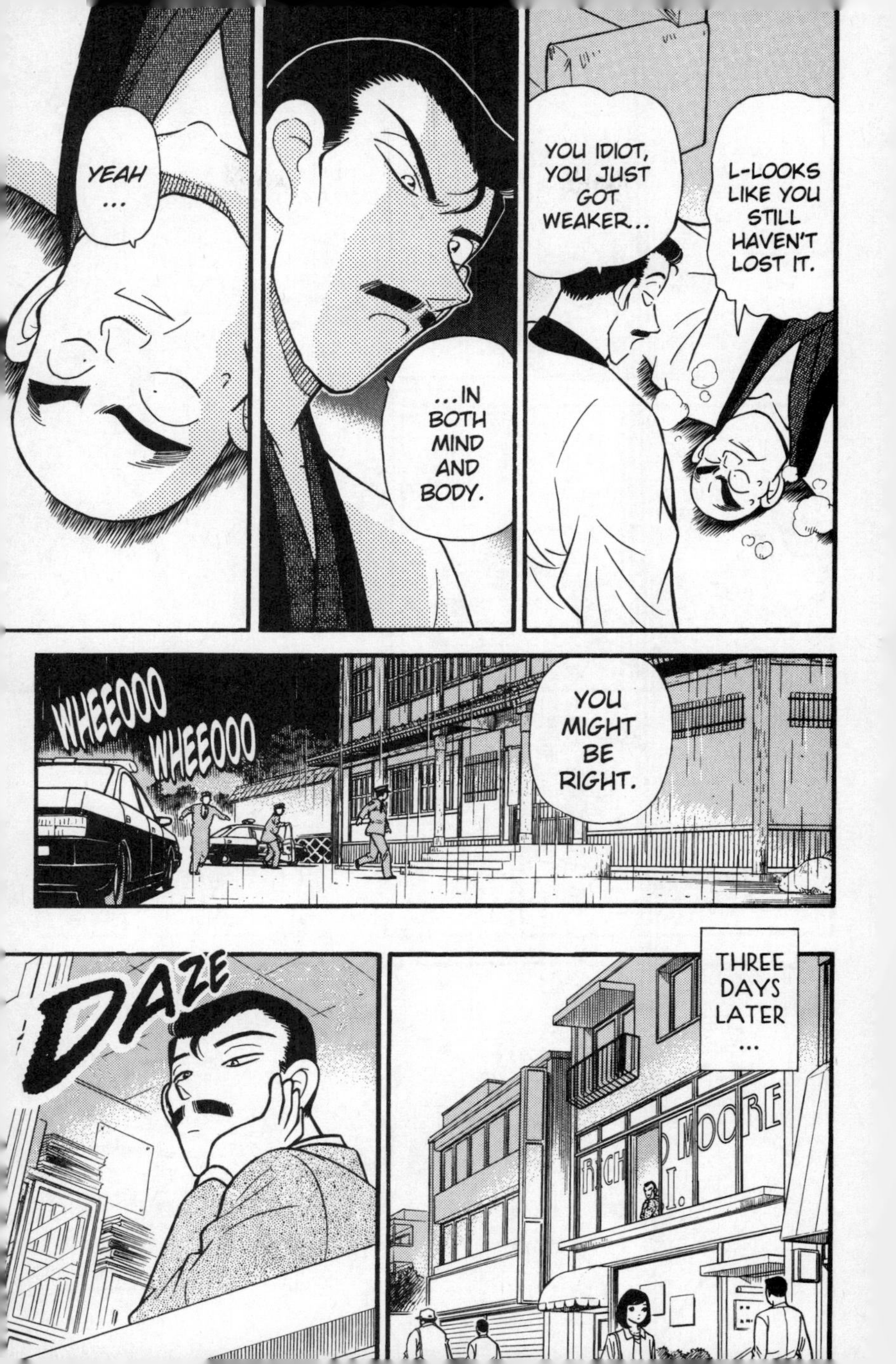
L-LOOKS LIKE YOU STILL HAVEN'T LOST IT.
YOU IDIOT, YOU JUST GOT WEAKER...
...IN BOTH MIND AND BODY.
YEAH ...
YOU MIGHT BE RIGHT.
WHEEOOO WHEEOOO
THREE DAYS LATER ...
DAZE

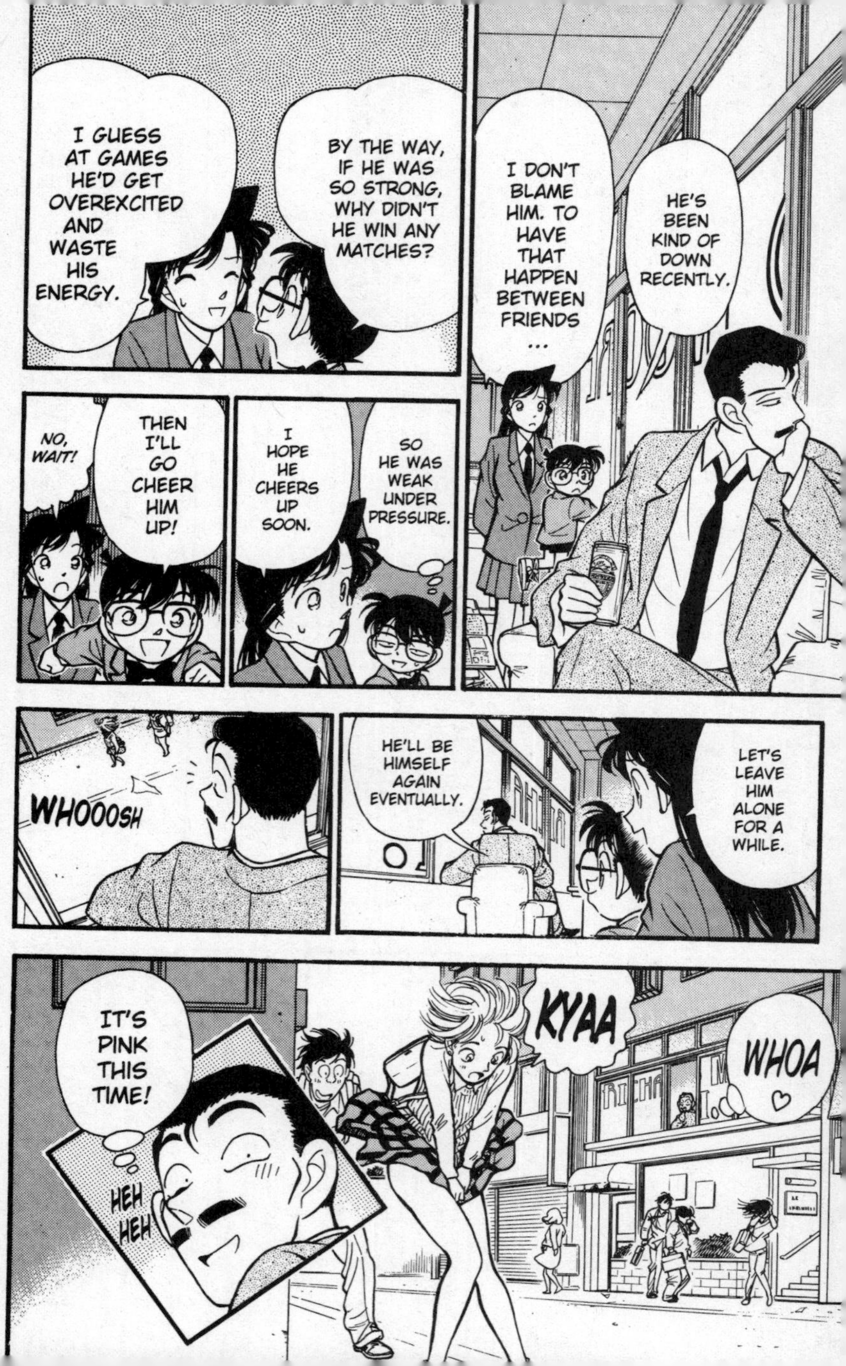
HE'S BEEN KIND OF DOWN RECENTLY.
I DON'T BLAME HIM. TO HAVE THAT HAPPEN BETWEEN FRIENDS ...
BY THE WAY, IF HE WAS SO STRONG, WHY DIDN'T HE WIN ANY MATCHES?
I GUESS AT GAMES HE'D GET OVEREXCITED AND WASTE HIS ENERGY.
SO HE WAS WEAK UNDER PRESSURE.
I HOPE HE CHEERS UP SOON.
THEN I'LL GO CHEER HIM UP!
NO, WAIT!
LET'S LEAVE HIM ALONE FOR A WHILE.
HE'LL BE HIMSELF AGAIN EVENTUALLY.
WHOOOSH
WHOA ♡
KYAA
IT'S PINK THIS TIME!
HEH HEH

FILE 7:
GROOM SELECTION

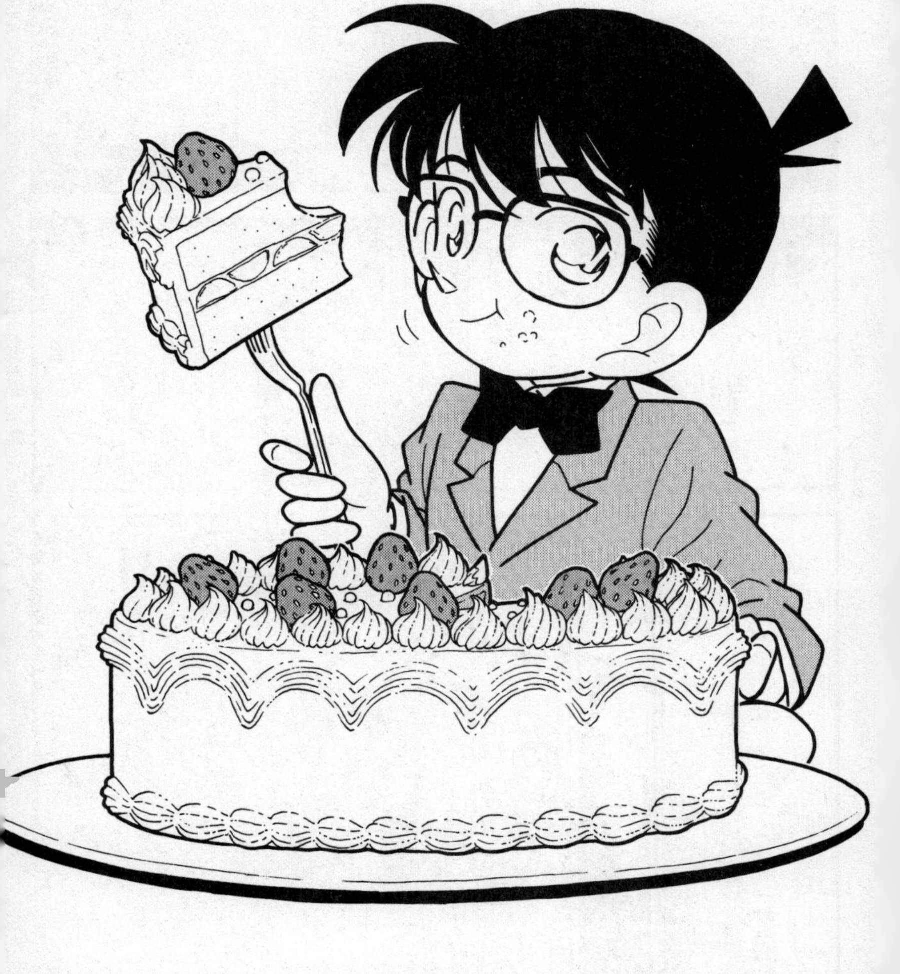

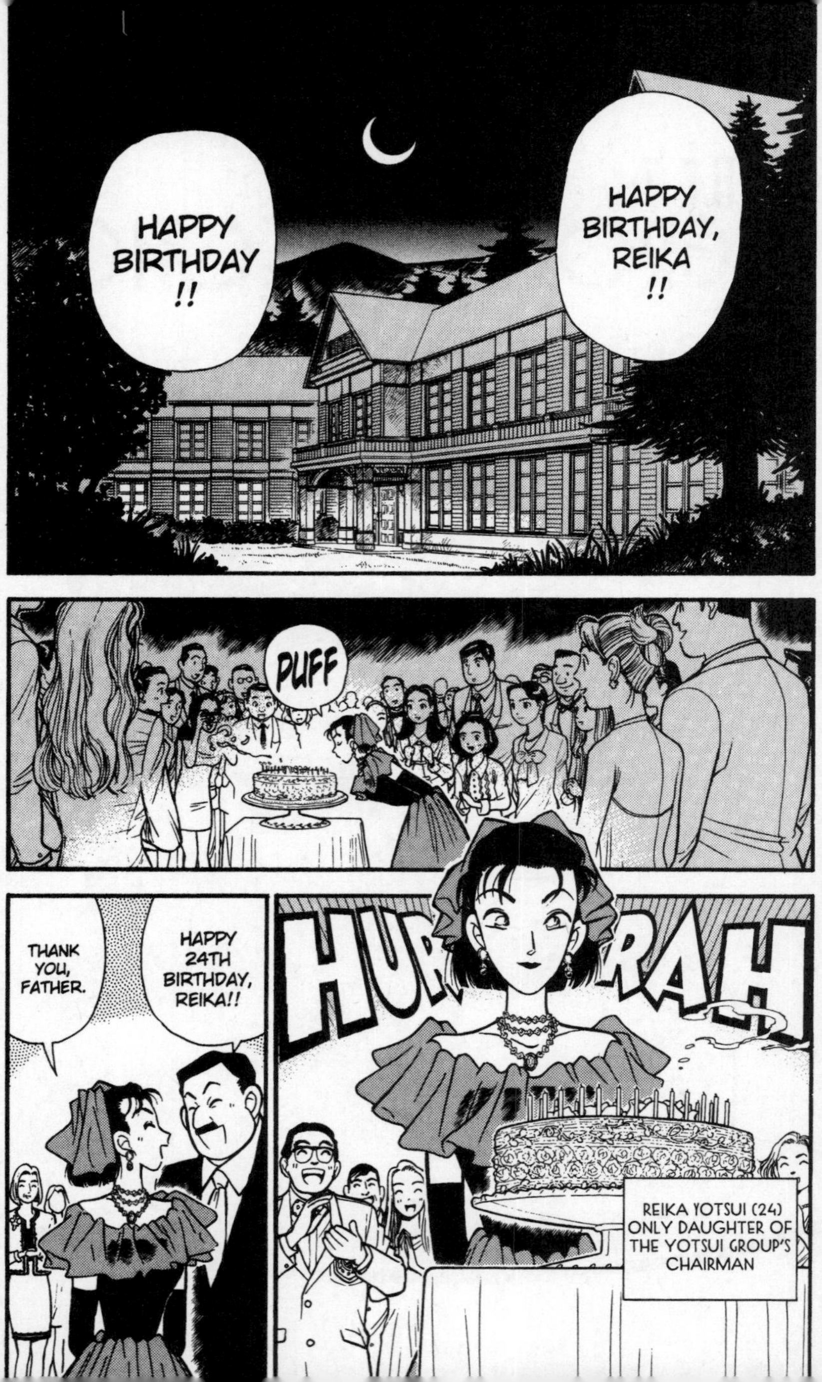
HAPPY BIRTHDAY, REIKA !!
HAPPY BIRTHDAY !!
PUFF
HURRAH
REIKA YOTSUI (24) ONLY DAUGHTER OF THE YOTSUI GROUP'S CHAIRMAN
HAPPY 24TH BIRTHDAY, REIKA!!
THANK YOU, FATHER.

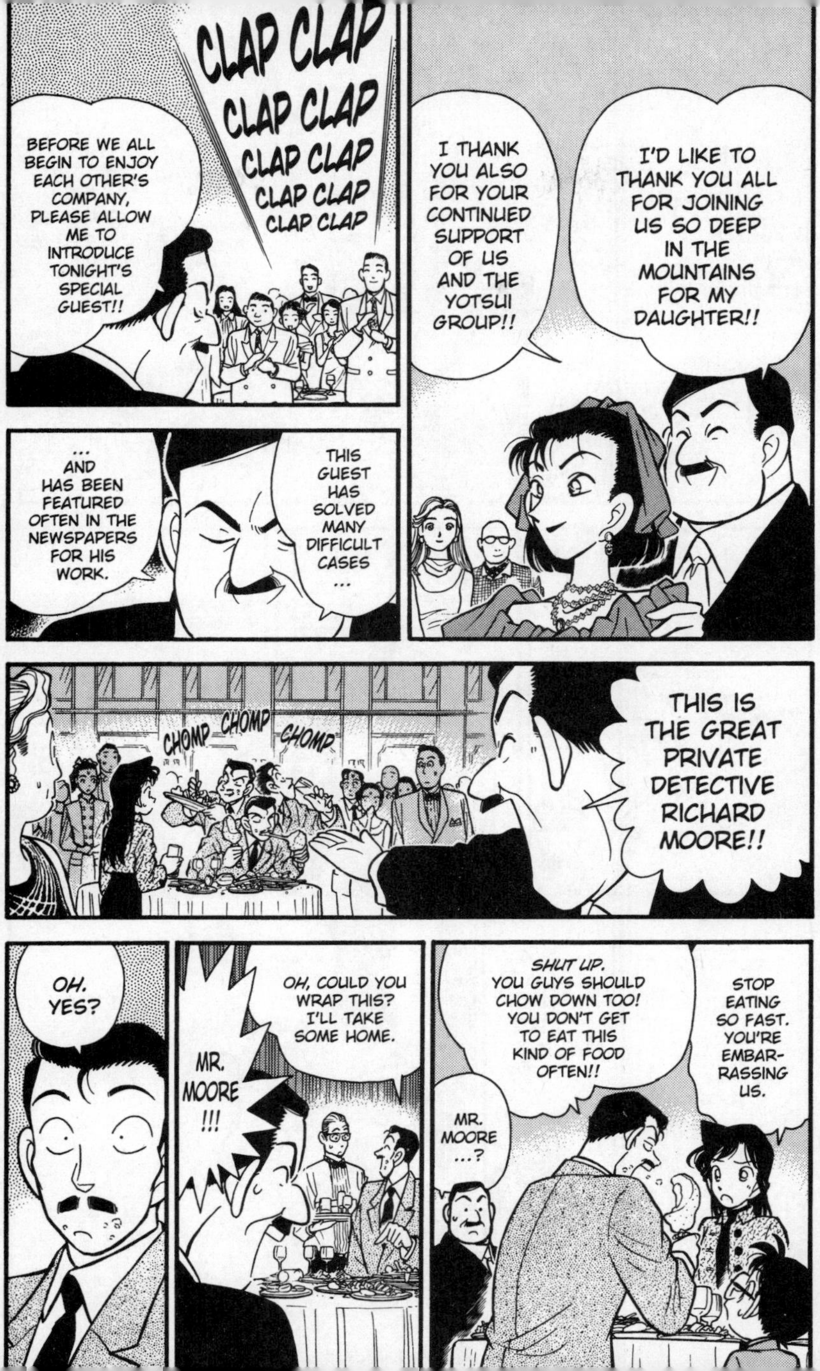
I'D LIKE TO THANK YOU ALL FOR JOINING US SO DEEP IN THE MOUNTAINS FOR MY DAUGHTER!!
I THANK YOU ALSO FOR YOUR CONTINUED SUPPORT OF US AND THE YOTSUI GROUP!!
CLAP CLAP CLAP CLAP CLAP CLAP CLAP CLAP CLAP CLAP
BEFORE WE ALL BEGIN TO ENJOY EACH OTHER'S COMPANY, PLEASE ALLOW ME TO INTRODUCE TONIGHT'S SPECIAL GUEST!!
THIS GUEST HAS SOLVED MANY DIFFICULT CASES ...
... AND HAS BEEN FEATURED OFTEN IN THE NEWSPAPERS FOR HIS WORK.
THIS IS THE GREAT PRIVATE DETECTIVE RICHARD MOORE!!
CHOMP CHOMP CHOMP
STOP EATING SO FAST. YOU'RE EMBAR-RASSING US.
SHUT UP. YOU GUYS SHOULD CHOW DOWN TOO! YOU DON'T GET TO EAT THIS KIND OF FOOD OFTEN!!
MR. MOORE ...?
OH, COULD YOU WRAP THIS? I'LL TAKE SOME HOME.
MR. MOORE !!!
OH. YES?

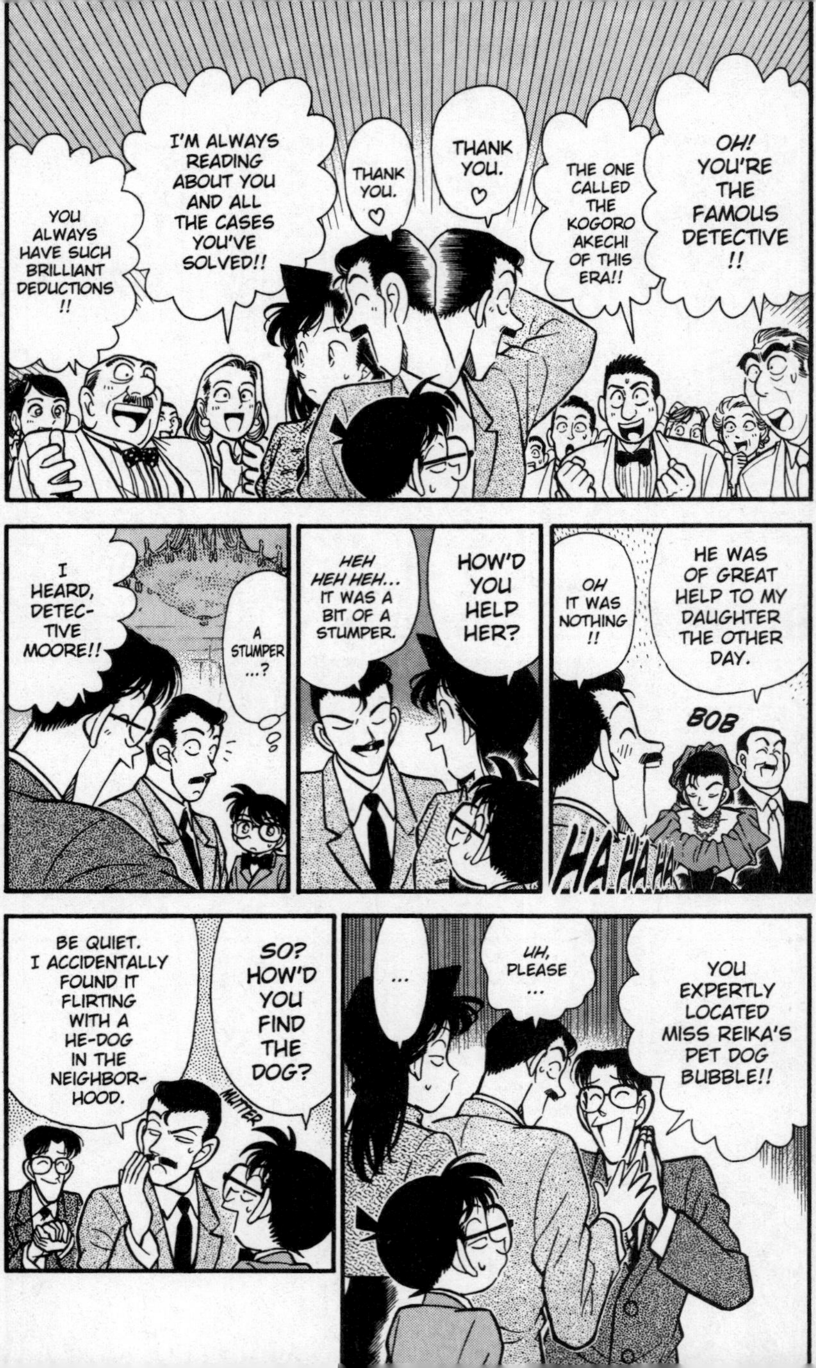
OH! YOU'RE THE FAMOUS DETECTIVE!!
THE ONE CALLED THE KOGORO AKECHI OF THIS ERA!!
THANK YOU. ♡
THANK YOU. ♡
I'M ALWAYS READING ABOUT YOU AND ALL THE CASES YOU'VE SOLVED!!
YOU ALWAYS HAVE SUCH BRILLIANT DEDUCTIONS!!
HE WAS OF GREAT HELP TO MY DAUGHTER THE OTHER DAY.
OH IT WAS NOTHING!!
BOB
HA HA HA
HOW'D YOU HELP HER?
HEH HEH HEH... IT WAS A BIT OF A STUMPER.
A STUMPER...?
I HEARD, DETECTIVE MOORE!!
YOU EXPERTLY LOCATED MISS REIKA'S PET DOG BUBBLE!!
UH, PLEASE...
...
SO? HOW'D YOU FIND THE DOG?
MUTTER
BE QUIET. I ACCIDENTALLY FOUND IT FLIRTING WITH A HE-DOG IN THE NEIGHBORHOOD.

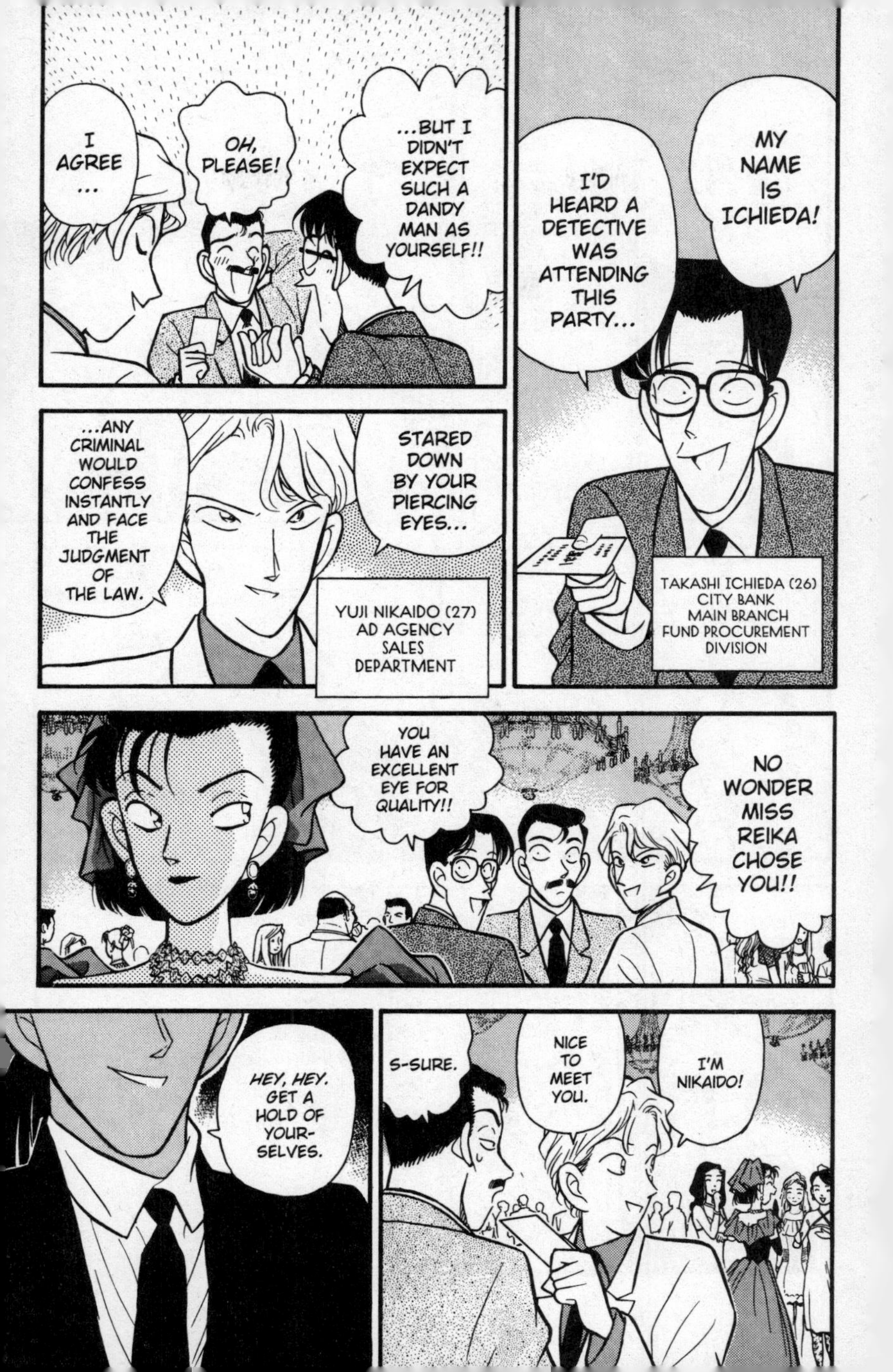
MY NAME IS ICHIEDA!
I'D HEARD A DETECTIVE WAS ATTENDING THIS PARTY...
TAKASHI ICHIEDA (26) CITY BANK MAIN BRANCH FUND PROCUREMENT DIVISION
...BUT I DIDN'T EXPECT SUCH A DANDY MAN AS YOURSELF!!
OH, PLEASE!
I AGREE...
STARED DOWN BY YOUR PIERCING EYES...
...ANY CRIMINAL WOULD CONFESS INSTANTLY AND FACE THE JUDGMENT OF THE LAW.
YUJI NIKAIDO (27) AD AGENCY SALES DEPARTMENT
NO WONDER MISS REIKA CHOSE YOU!!
YOU HAVE AN EXCELLENT EYE FOR QUALITY!!
I'M NIKAIDO!
NICE TO MEET YOU.
S-SURE.
HEY, HEY. GET A HOLD OF YOUR-SELVES.

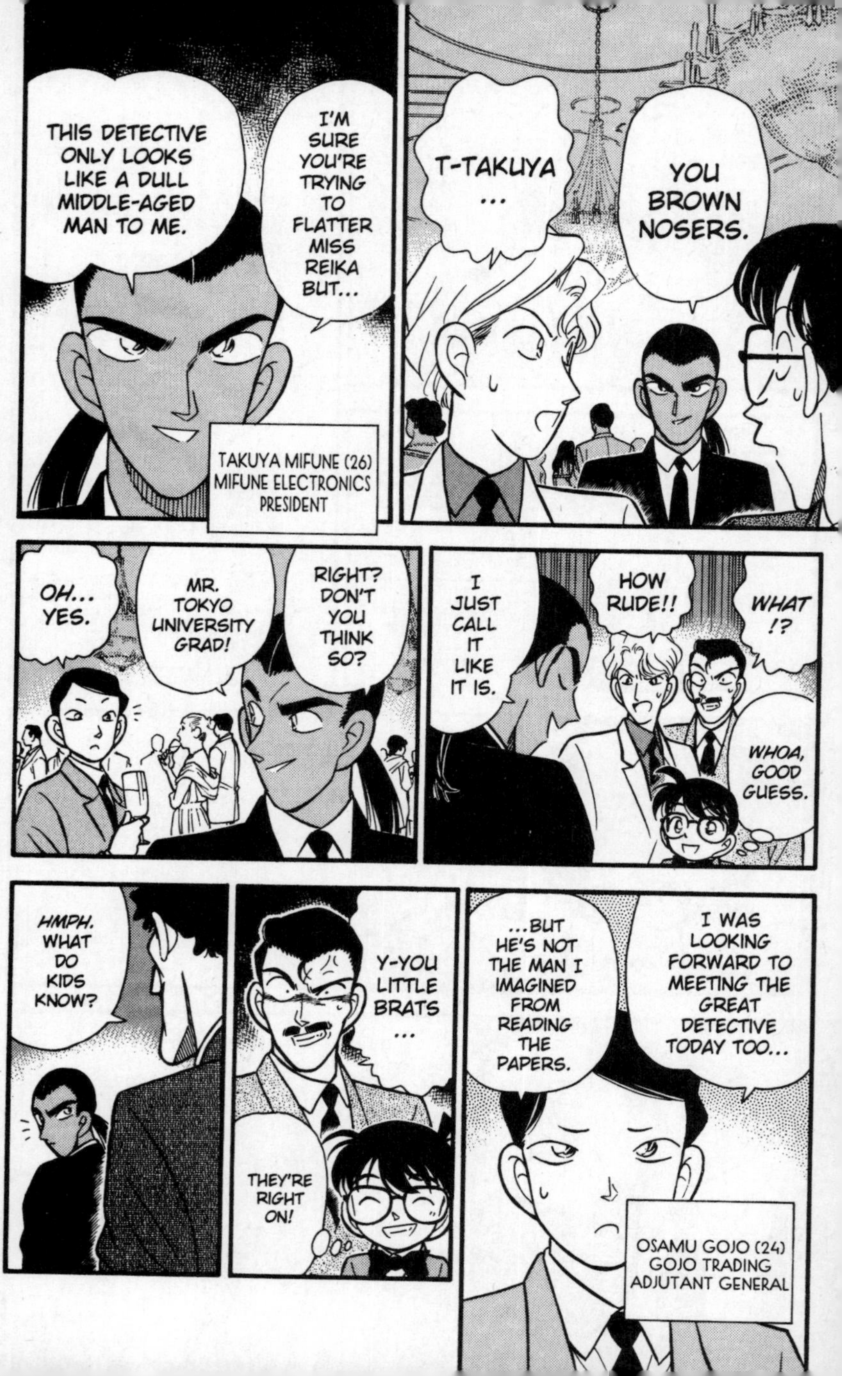
YOU BROWN NOSERS.
T-TAKUYA ...
I'M SURE YOU'RE TRYING TO FLATTER MISS REIKA BUT...
THIS DETECTIVE ONLY LOOKS LIKE A DULL MIDDLE-AGED MAN TO ME.
TAKUYA MIFUNE (26) MIFUNE ELECTRONICS PRESIDENT
WHAT!?
HOW RUDE!!
I JUST CALL IT LIKE IT IS.
WHOA, GOOD GUESS.
RIGHT? DON'T YOU THINK SO?
MR. TOKYO UNIVERSITY GRAD!
OH... YES.
I WAS LOOKING FORWARD TO MEETING THE GREAT DETECTIVE TODAY TOO...
...BUT HE'S NOT THE MAN I IMAGINED FROM READING THE PAPERS.
OSAMU GOJO (24) GOJO TRADING ADJUTANT GENERAL
Y-YOU LITTLE BRATS ...
THEY'RE RIGHT ON!
HMPH. WHAT DO KIDS KNOW?

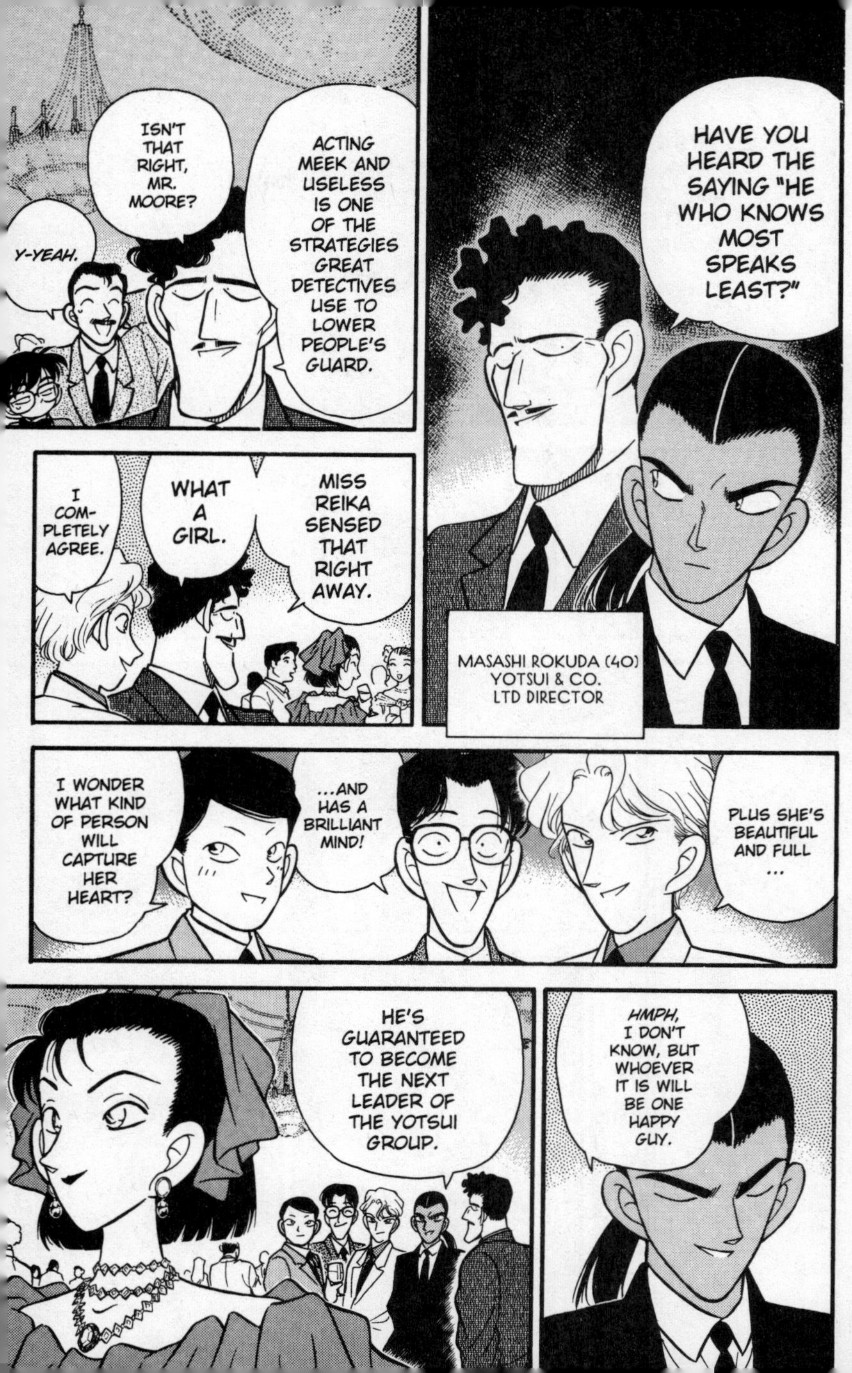
HAVE YOU HEARD THE SAYING "HE WHO KNOWS MOST SPEAKS LEAST?"
MASASHI ROKUDA (40) YOTSUI & CO. LTD DIRECTOR
ACTING MEEK AND USELESS IS ONE OF THE STRATEGIES GREAT DETECTIVES USE TO LOWER PEOPLE'S GUARD.
ISN'T THAT RIGHT, MR. MOORE?
Y-YEAH.
MISS REIKA SENSED THAT RIGHT AWAY.
WHAT A GIRL.
I COMPLETELY AGREE.
PLUS SHE'S BEAUTIFUL AND FULL ...
...AND HAS A BRILLIANT MIND!
I WONDER WHAT KIND OF PERSON WILL CAPTURE HER HEART?
HMPH, I DON'T KNOW, BUT WHOEVER IT IS WILL BE ONE HAPPY GUY.
HE'S GUARANTEED TO BECOME THE NEXT LEADER OF THE YOTSUI GROUP.

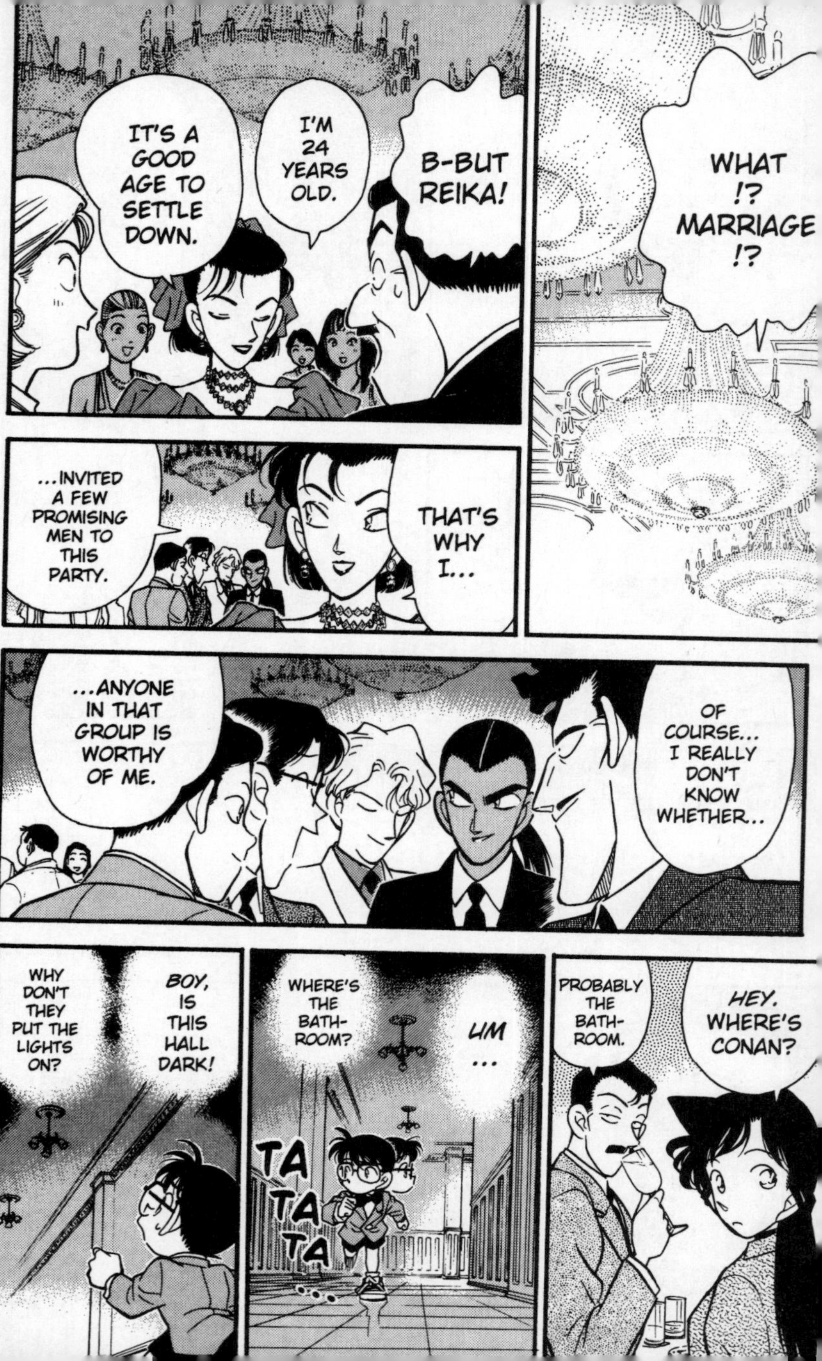
WHAT!? MARRIAGE!?
B-BUT REIKA!
I'M 24 YEARS OLD.
IT'S A GOOD AGE TO SETTLE DOWN.
THAT'S WHY I...
...INVITED A FEW PROMISING MEN TO THIS PARTY.
OF COURSE... I REALLY DON'T KNOW WHETHER...
...ANYONE IN THAT GROUP IS WORTHY OF ME.
HEY. WHERE'S CONAN?
PROBABLY THE BATH-ROOM.
UM...
WHERE'S THE BATH-ROOM?
TA TA TA
BOY, IS THIS HALL DARK!
WHY DON'T THEY PUT THE LIGHTS ON?

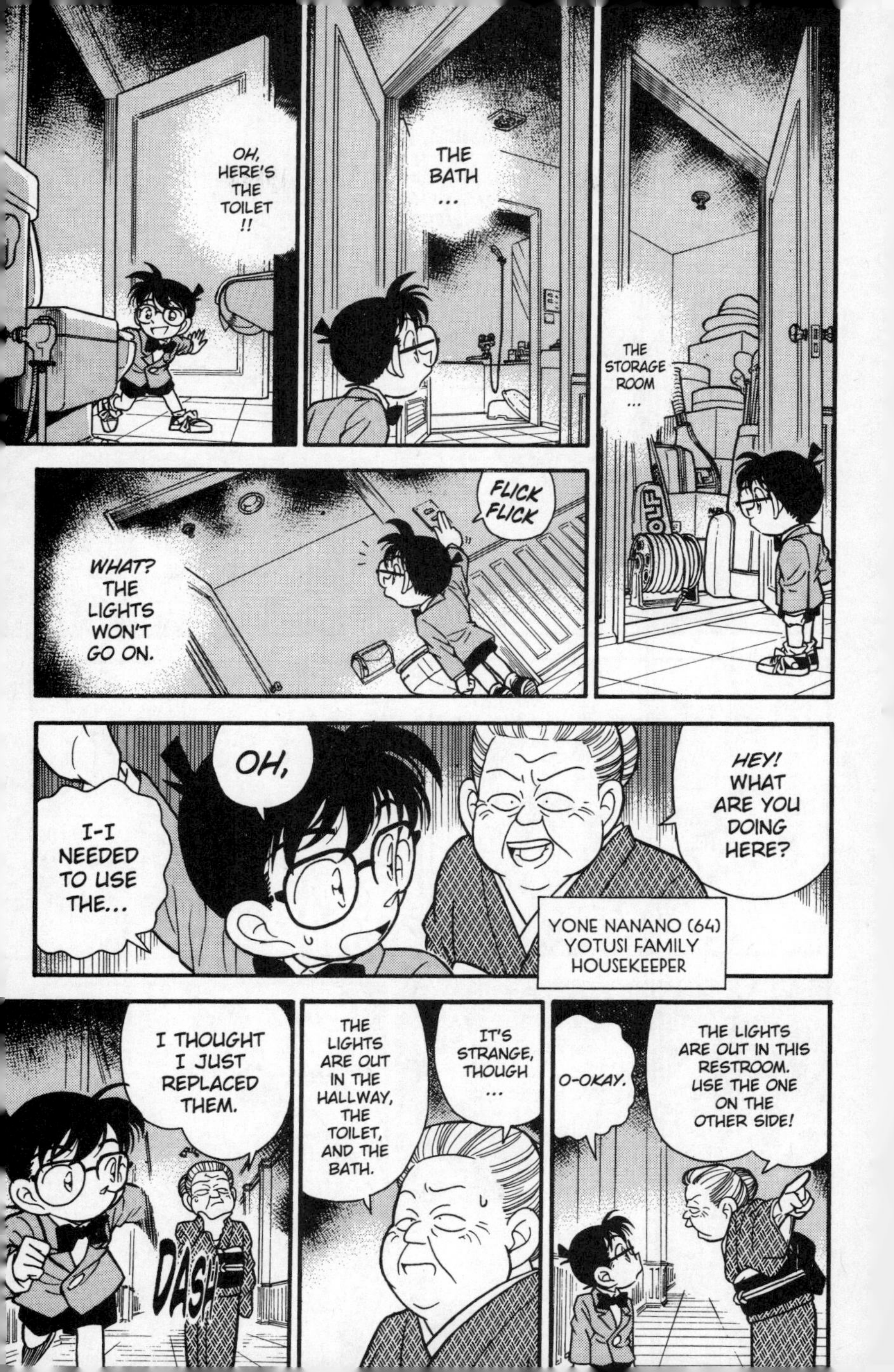
THE STORAGE ROOM ...
THE BATH ...
OH, HERE'S THE TOILET !!
FLICK FLICK
WHAT? THE LIGHTS WON'T GO ON.
HEY! WHAT ARE YOU DOING HERE?
YONE NANANO (64) YOTUSI FAMILY HOUSEKEEPER
OH,
I-I NEEDED TO USE THE...
THE LIGHTS ARE OUT IN THIS RESTROOM. USE THE ONE ON THE OTHER SIDE!
O-OKAY.
IT'S STRANGE, THOUGH ...
THE LIGHTS ARE OUT IN THE HALLWAY, THE TOILET, AND THE BATH.
I THOUGHT I JUST REPLACED THEM.
DASH

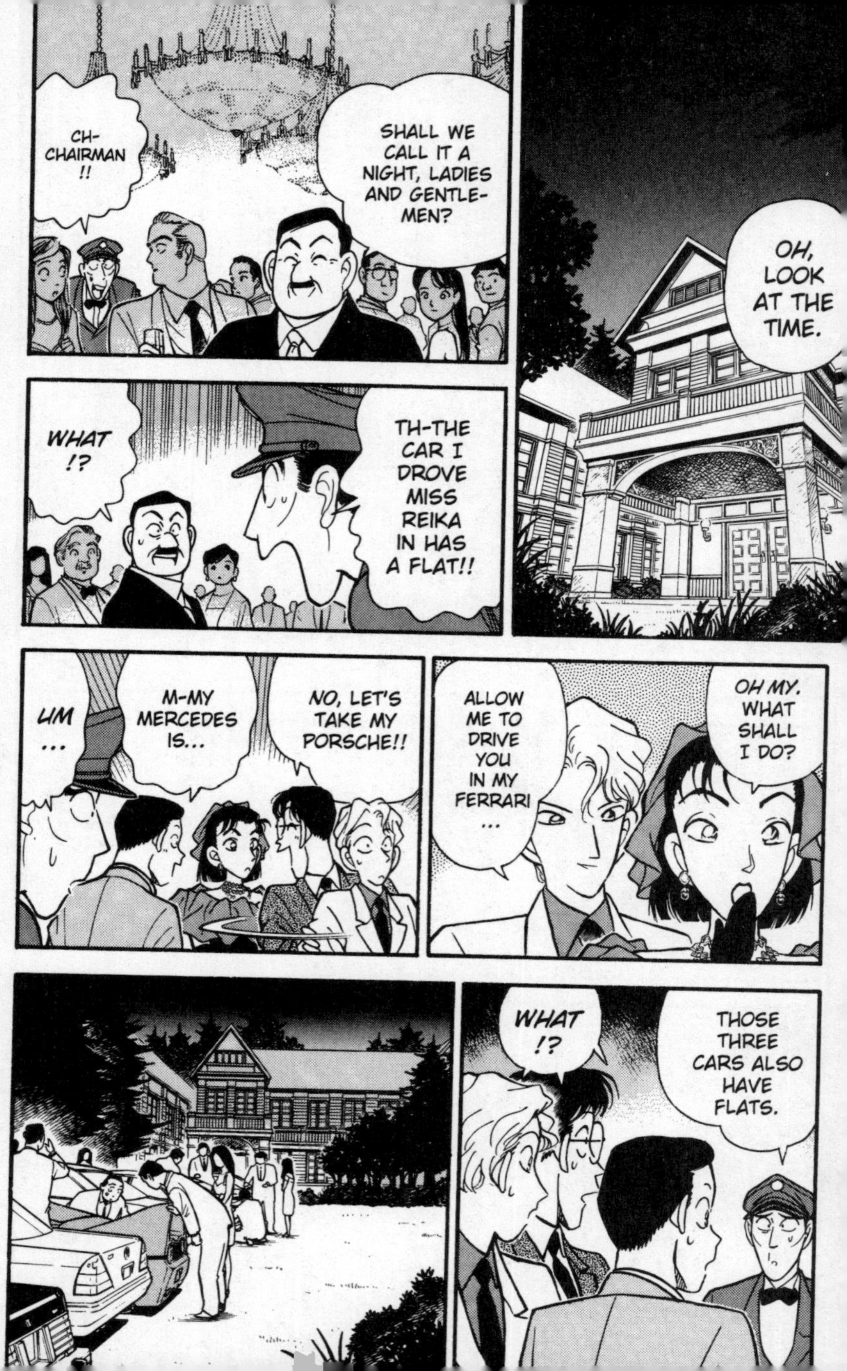
OH, LOOK AT THE TIME.
SHALL WE CALL IT A NIGHT, LADIES AND GENTLE-MEN?
CH-CHAIRMAN!!
TH-THE CAR I DROVE MISS REIKA IN HAS A FLAT!!
WHAT!?
OH MY. WHAT SHALL I DO?
ALLOW ME TO DRIVE YOU IN MY FERRARI...
NO, LET'S TAKE MY PORSCHE!!
M-MY MERCEDES IS...
UM...
THOSE THREE CARS ALSO HAVE FLATS.
WHAT!?

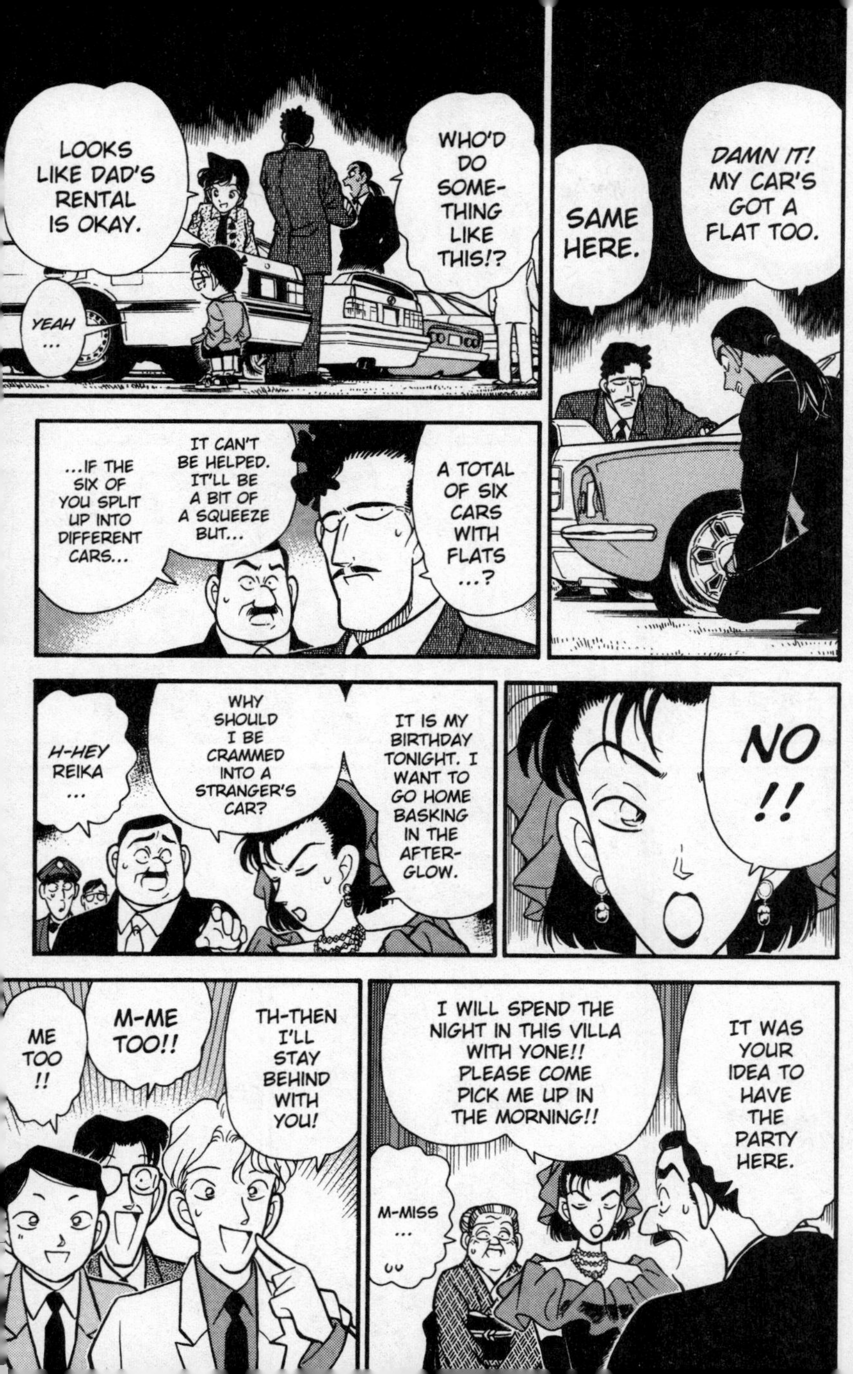
DAMN IT! MY CAR'S GOT A FLAT TOO.
SAME HERE.
WHO'D DO SOME-THING LIKE THIS!?
LOOKS LIKE DAD'S RENTAL IS OKAY.
YEAH ...
A TOTAL OF SIX CARS WITH FLATS ...?
IT CAN'T BE HELPED. IT'LL BE A BIT OF A SQUEEZE BUT...
...IF THE SIX OF YOU SPLIT UP INTO DIFFERENT CARS...
NO !!
IT IS MY BIRTHDAY TONIGHT. I WANT TO GO HOME BASKING IN THE AFTER-GLOW.
WHY SHOULD I BE CRAMMED INTO A STRANGER'S CAR?
H-HEY REIKA ...
IT WAS YOUR IDEA TO HAVE THE PARTY HERE.
I WILL SPEND THE NIGHT IN THIS VILLA WITH YONE!! PLEASE COME PICK ME UP IN THE MORNING!!
M-MISS ...
TH-THEN I'LL STAY BEHIND WITH YOU!
M-ME TOO!!
ME TOO !!

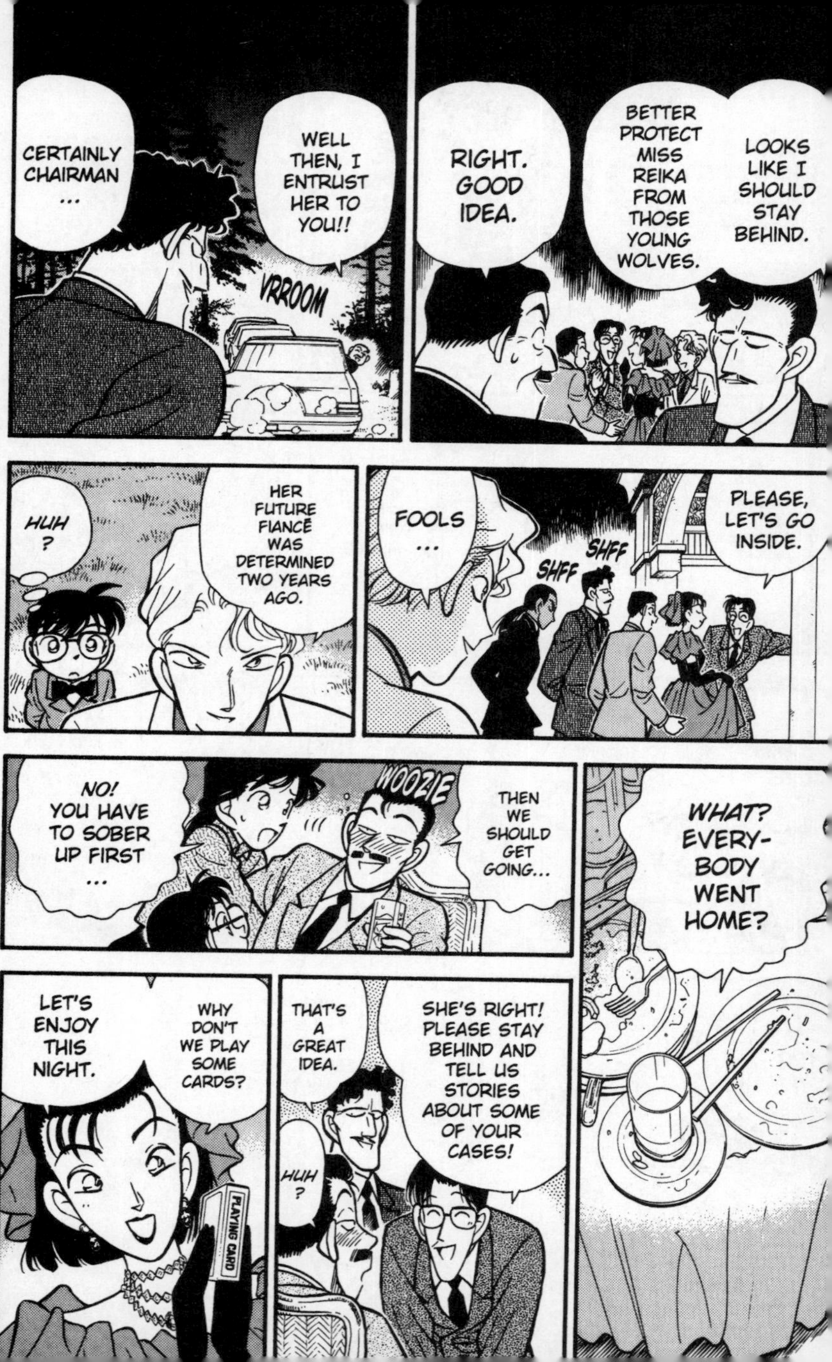
LOOKS LIKE I SHOULD STAY BEHIND.
BETTER PROTECT MISS REIKA FROM THOSE YOUNG WOLVES.
RIGHT. GOOD IDEA.
WELL THEN, I ENTRUST HER TO YOU!!
VRROOM
CERTAINLY CHAIRMAN ...
PLEASE, LET'S GO INSIDE.
SHFF
SHFF
FOOLS ...
HER FUTURE FIANCÉ WAS DETERMINED TWO YEARS AGO.
HUH ?
WHAT? EVERY-BODY WENT HOME?
WOOZIE
THEN WE SHOULD GET GOING...
NO! YOU HAVE TO SOBER UP FIRST ...
SHE'S RIGHT! PLEASE STAY BEHIND AND TELL US STORIES ABOUT SOME OF YOUR CASES!
THAT'S A GREAT IDEA.
HUH ?
WHY DON'T WE PLAY SOME CARDS?
LET'S ENJOY THIS NIGHT.
PLAYING CARD

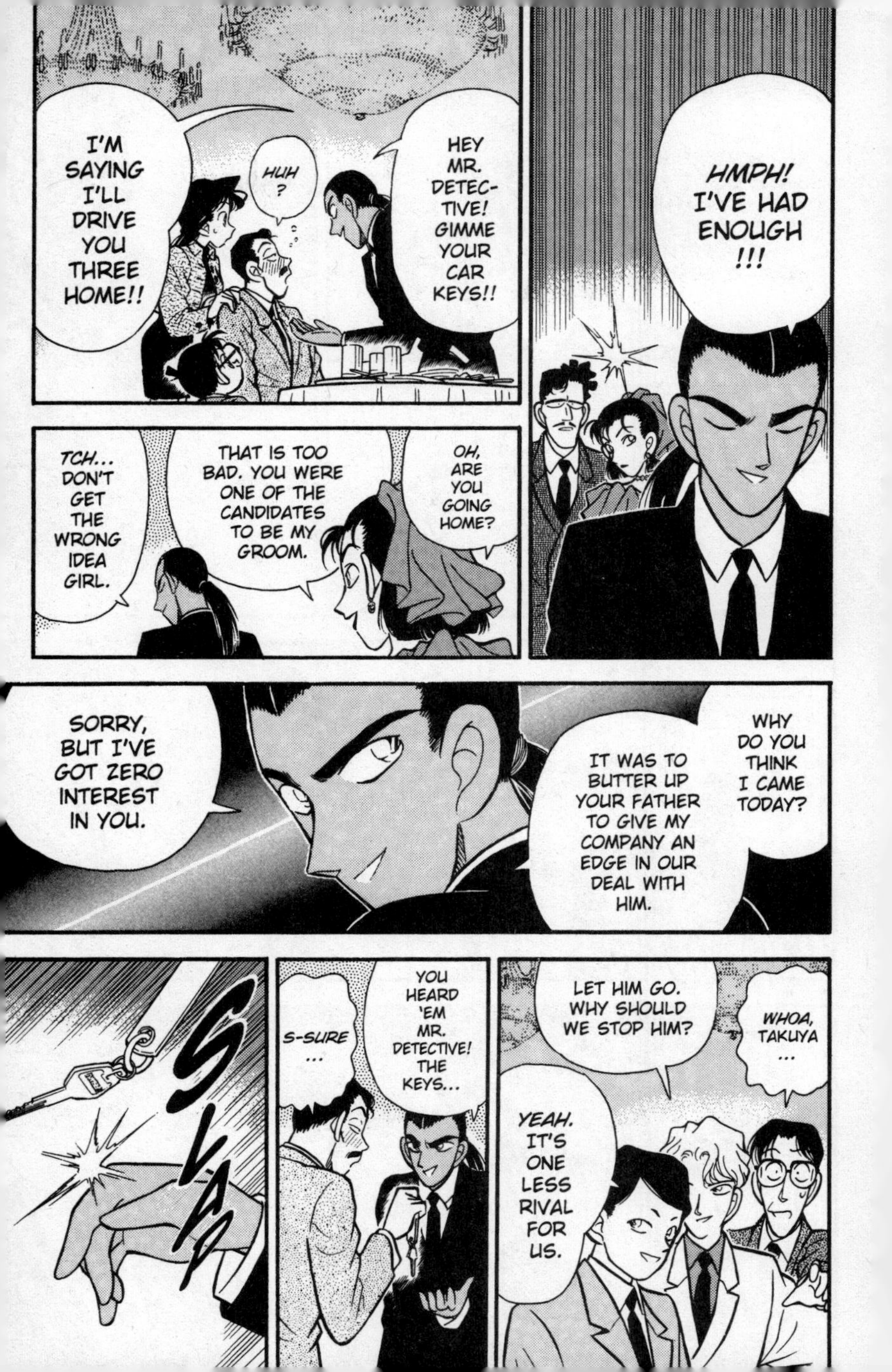
HMPH! I'VE HAD ENOUGH!!!
HEY MR. DETECTIVE! GIMME YOUR CAR KEYS!!
HUH?
I'M SAYING I'LL DRIVE YOU THREE HOME!!
OH, ARE YOU GOING HOME?
THAT IS TOO BAD. YOU WERE ONE OF THE CANDIDATES TO BE MY GROOM.
TCH... DON'T GET THE WRONG IDEA GIRL.
WHY DO YOU THINK I CAME TODAY?
IT WAS TO BUTTER UP YOUR FATHER TO GIVE MY COMPANY AN EDGE IN OUR DEAL WITH HIM.
SORRY, BUT I'VE GOT ZERO INTEREST IN YOU.
WHOA, TAKUYA...
LET HIM GO. WHY SHOULD WE STOP HIM?
YEAH. IT'S ONE LESS RIVAL FOR US.
YOU HEARD 'EM MR. DETECTIVE! THE KEYS...
S-SURE...
SWAP

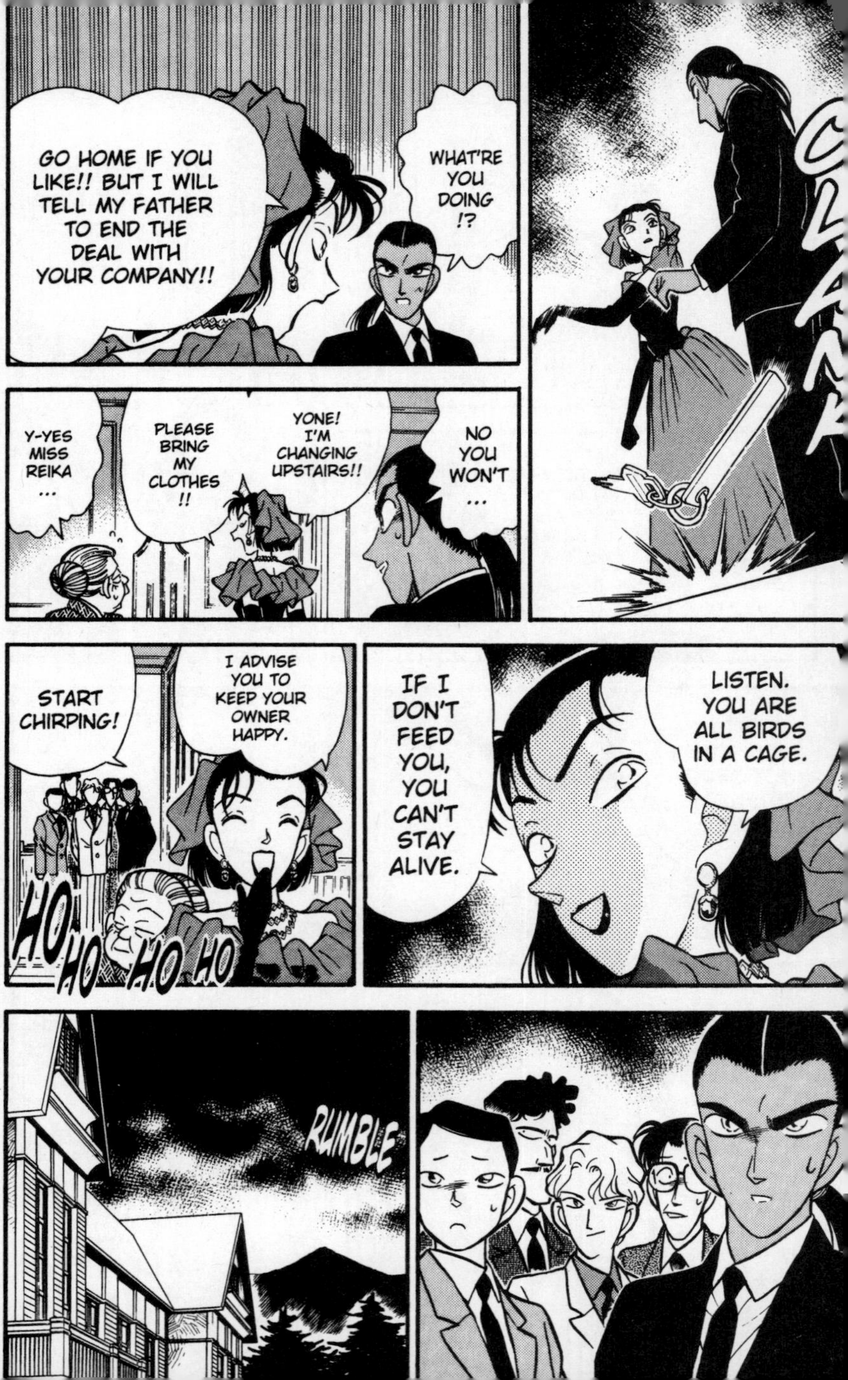
CLANK
WHAT'RE YOU DOING !?
GO HOME IF YOU LIKE!! BUT I WILL TELL MY FATHER TO END THE DEAL WITH YOUR COMPANY!!
NO YOU WON'T ...
YONE! I'M CHANGING UPSTAIRS!!
PLEASE BRING MY CLOTHES !!
Y-YES MISS REIKA ...
LISTEN. YOU ARE ALL BIRDS IN A CAGE.
IF I DON'T FEED YOU, YOU CAN'T STAY ALIVE.
I ADVISE YOU TO KEEP YOUR OWNER HAPPY.
START CHIRPING!
HO HO HO HO HO
RUMBLE

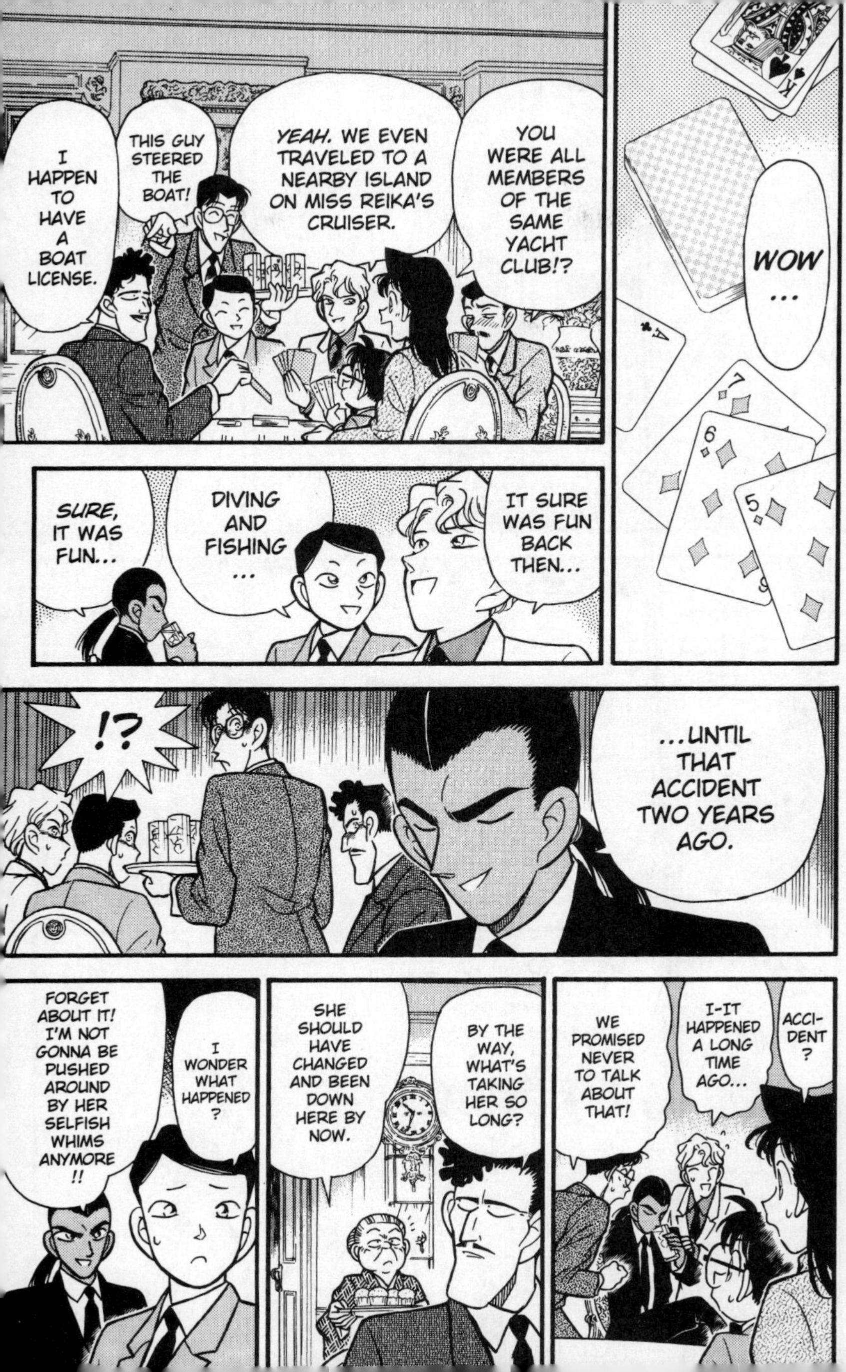
WOW ...
YOU WERE ALL MEMBERS OF THE SAME YACHT CLUB!?
YEAH. WE EVEN TRAVELED TO A NEARBY ISLAND ON MISS REIKA'S CRUISER.
THIS GUY STEERED THE BOAT!
I HAPPEN TO HAVE A BOAT LICENSE.
IT SURE WAS FUN BACK THEN...
DIVING AND FISHING ...
SURE, IT WAS FUN...
...UNTIL THAT ACCIDENT TWO YEARS AGO.
!?
ACCI-DENT?
I-IT HAPPENED A LONG TIME AGO...
WE PROMISED NEVER TO TALK ABOUT THAT!
BY THE WAY, WHAT'S TAKING HER SO LONG?
SHE SHOULD HAVE CHANGED AND BEEN DOWN HERE BY NOW.
I WONDER WHAT HAPPENED?
FORGET ABOUT IT! I'M NOT GONNA BE PUSHED AROUND BY HER SELFISH WHIMS ANYMORE!!

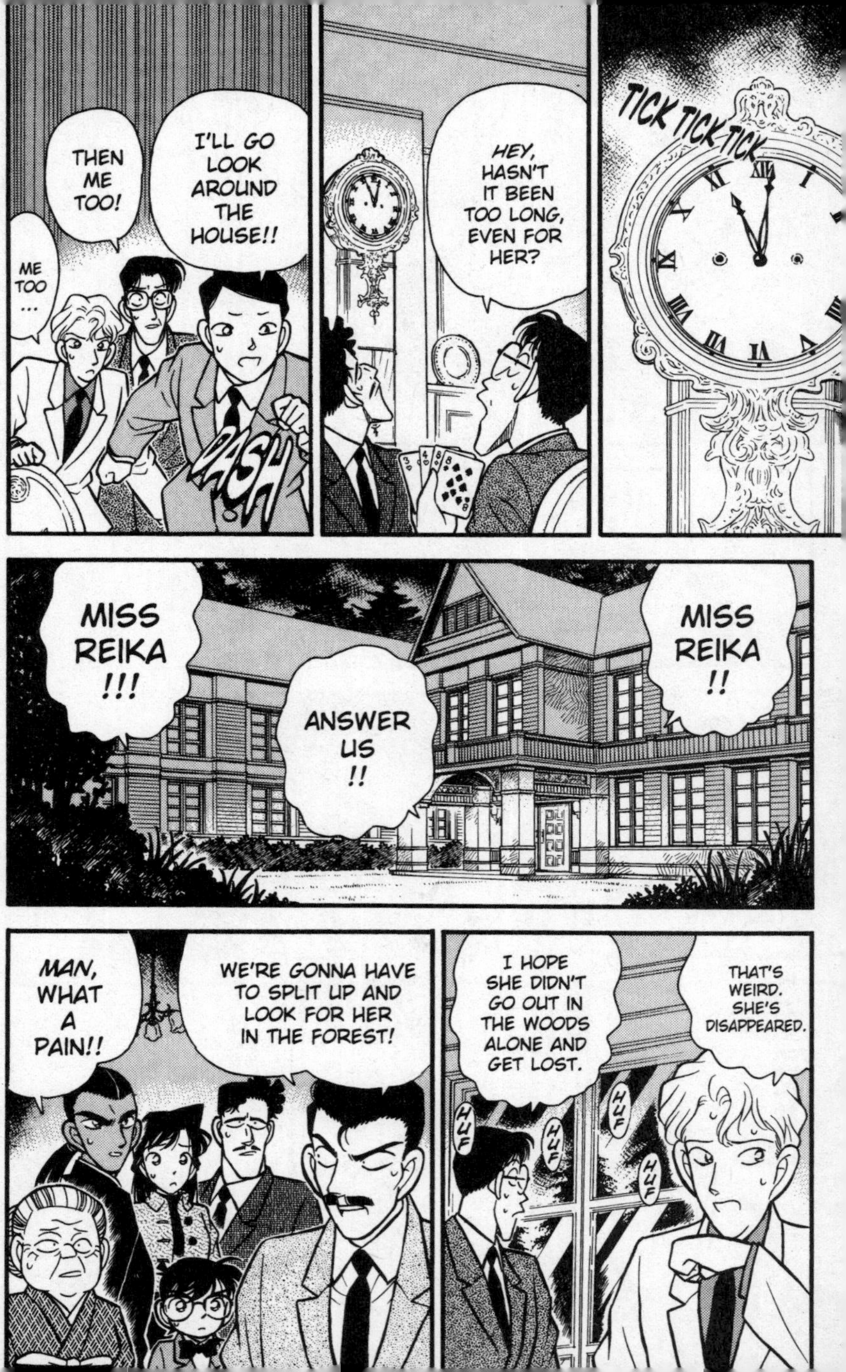
TICK TICK TICK
HEY, HASN'T IT BEEN TOO LONG, EVEN FOR HER?
I'LL GO LOOK AROUND THE HOUSE!!
THEN ME TOO!
ME TOO ...
DASH
MISS REIKA !!
ANSWER US !!
MISS REIKA !!!
THAT'S WEIRD. SHE'S DISAPPEARED.
HUF HUF HUF HUF
I HOPE SHE DIDN'T GO OUT IN THE WOODS ALONE AND GET LOST.
WE'RE GONNA HAVE TO SPLIT UP AND LOOK FOR HER IN THE FOREST!
MAN, WHAT A PAIN!!

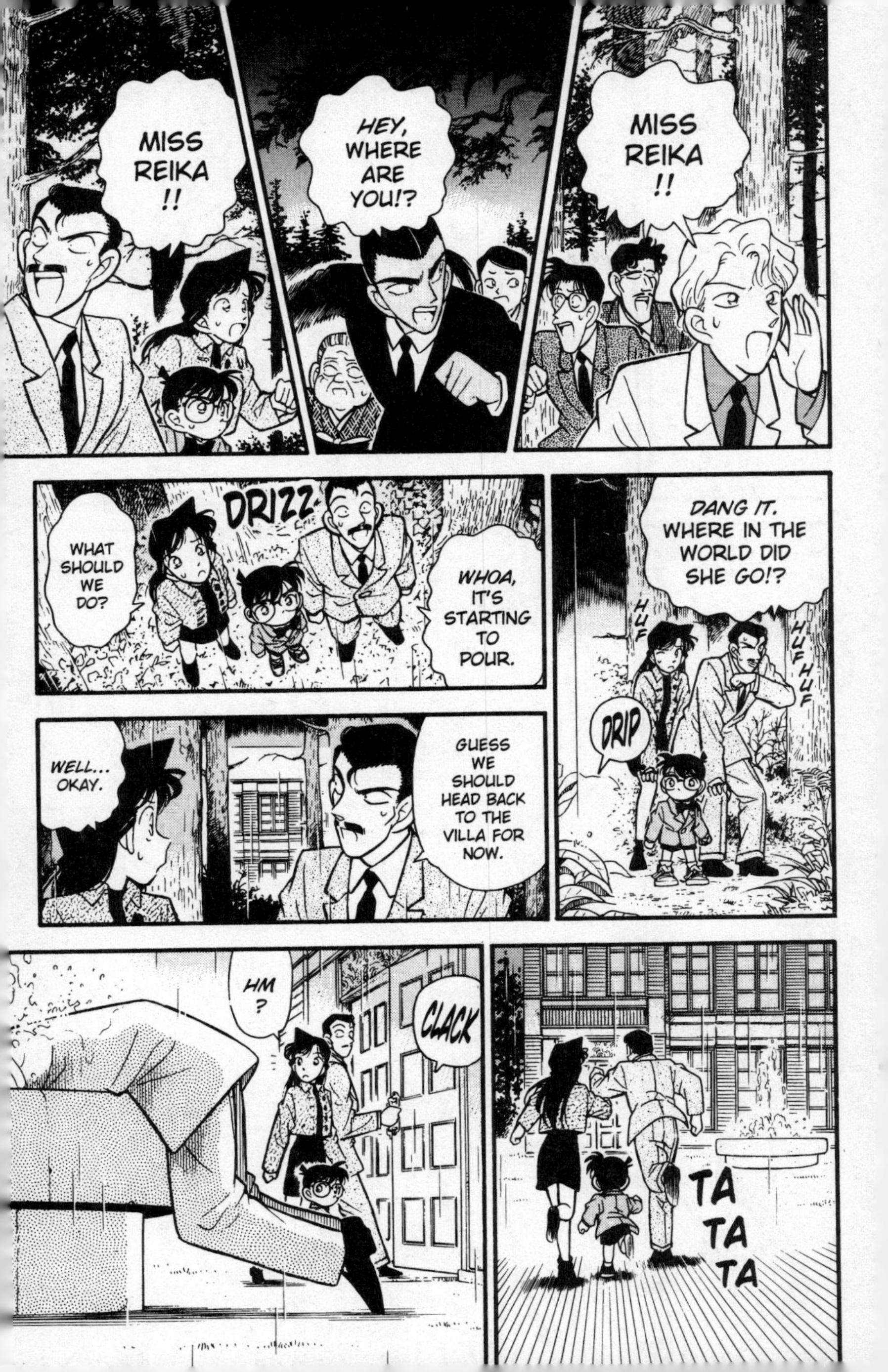
MISS REIKA !!
HEY, WHERE ARE YOU!?
MISS REIKA !!
DANG IT. WHERE IN THE WORLD DID SHE GO!?
HUF
HUF HUF
DRIP
WHOA, IT'S STARTING TO POUR.
DRIZZ
WHAT SHOULD WE DO?
GUESS WE SHOULD HEAD BACK TO THE VILLA FOR NOW.
WELL... OKAY.
TA TA TA
CLACK
HM ?

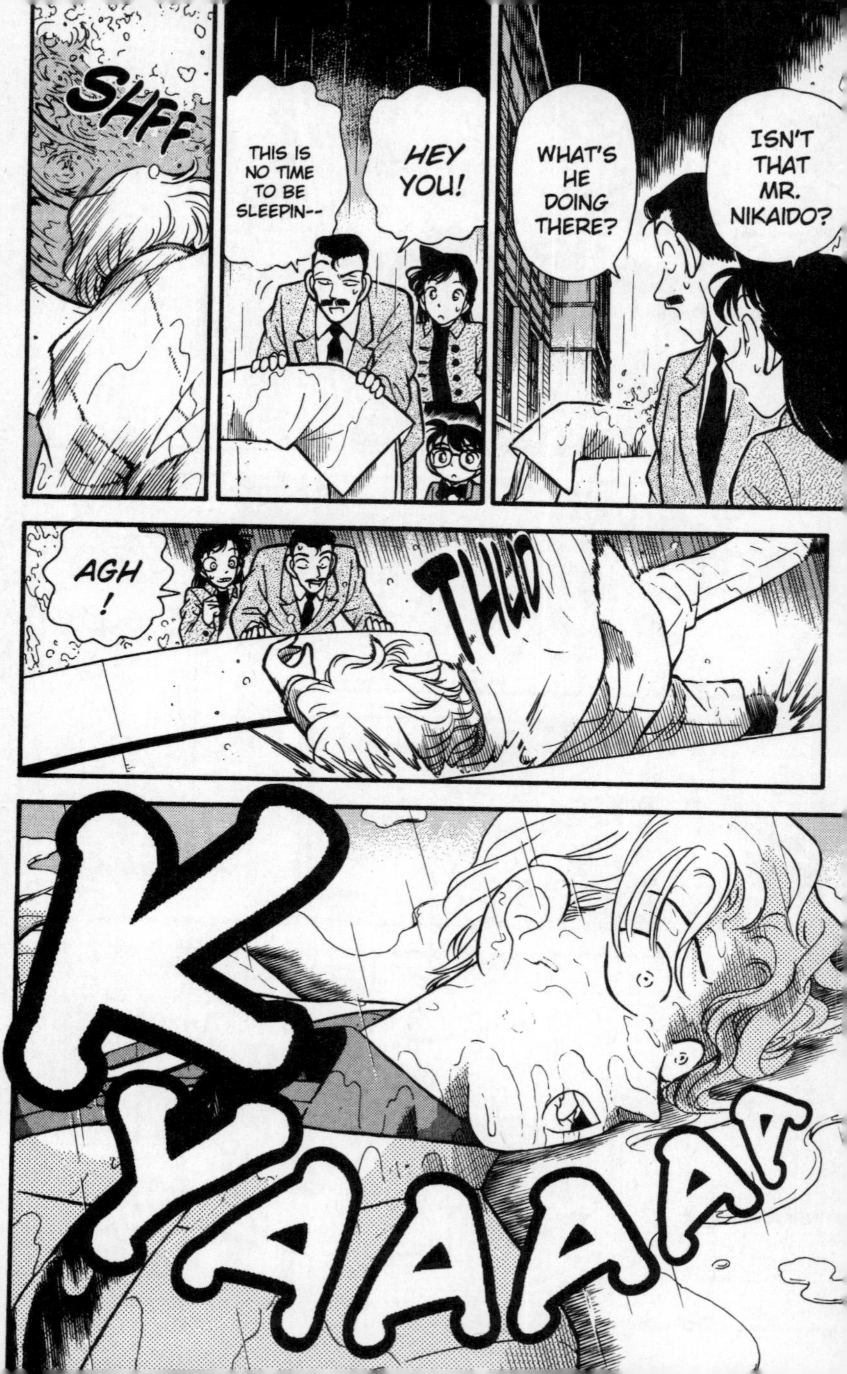
ISN'T THAT MR. NIKAIDO?
WHAT'S HE DOING THERE?
HEY YOU!
THIS IS NO TIME TO BE SLEEPIN--
SHFF
THUD
AGH!
KYAAAAA

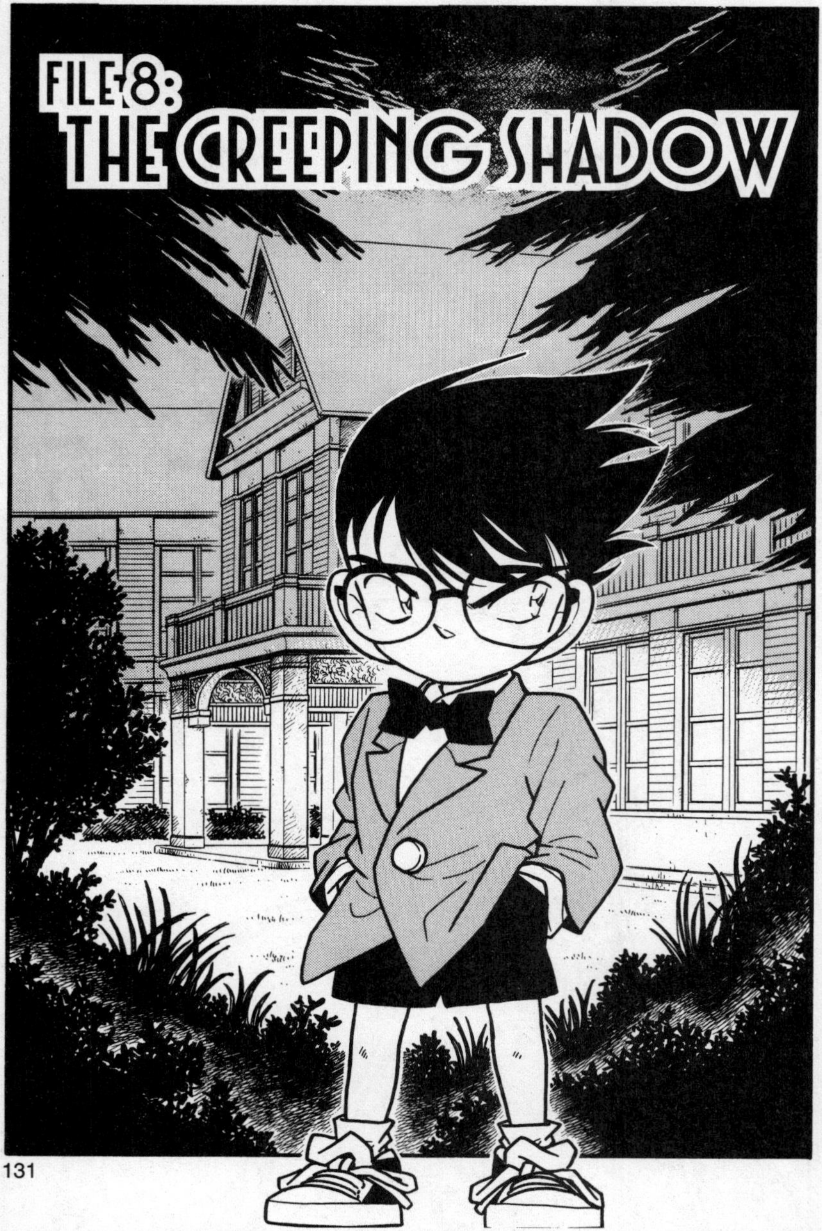
FILE 8:
THE CREEPING SHADOW

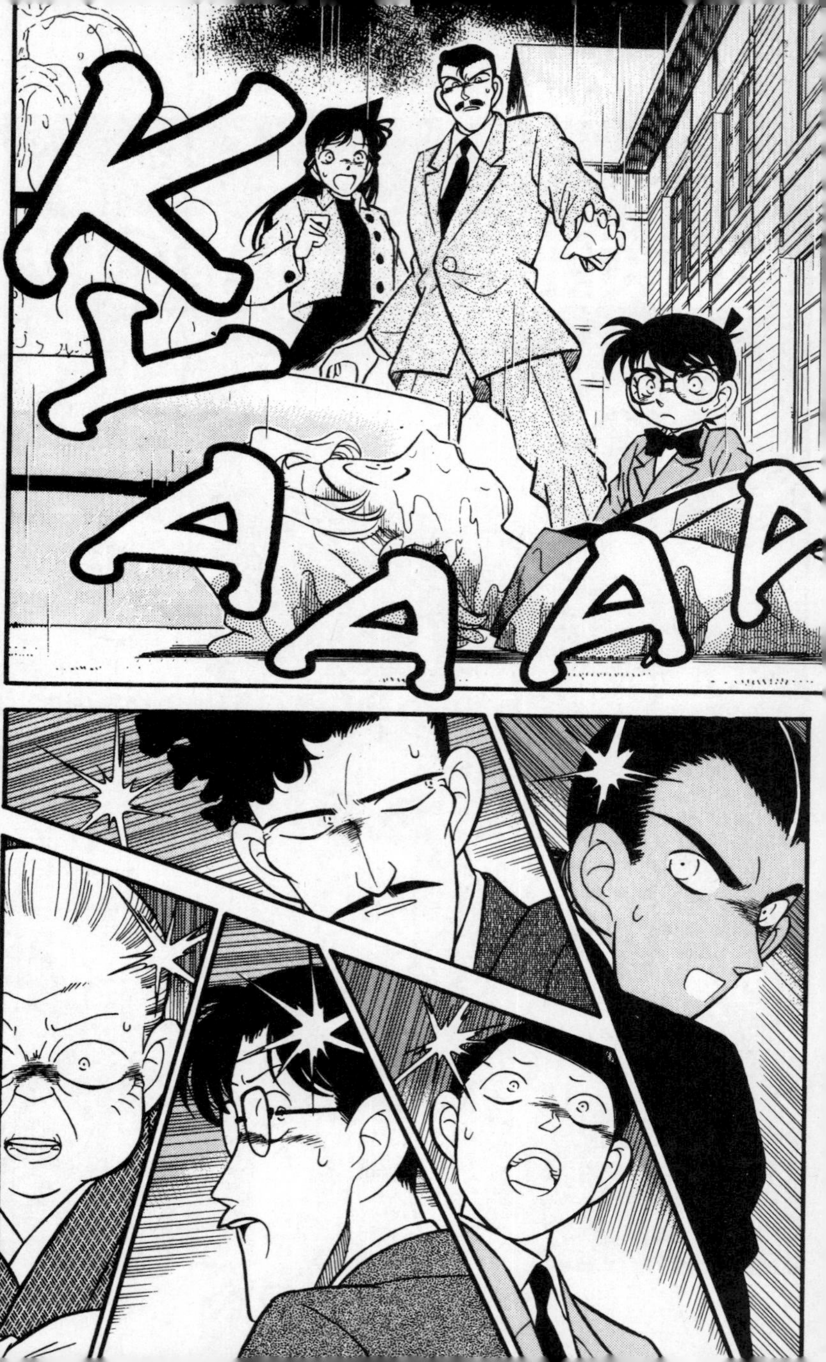
KYAAAA

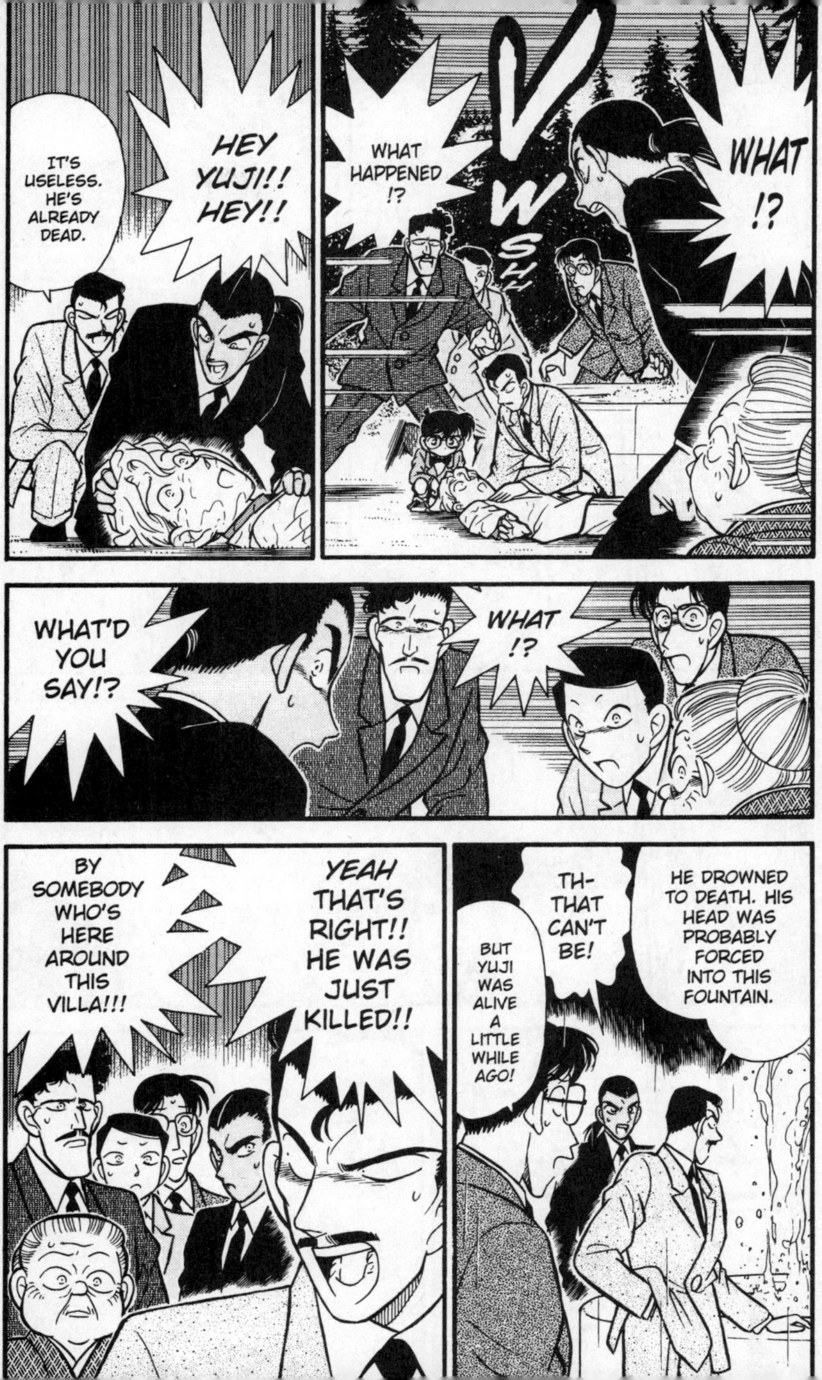
WHAT !?
WHAT HAPPENED !?
WSHH
HEY YUJI!! HEY!!
IT'S USELESS. HE'S ALREADY DEAD.
WHAT !?
WHAT'D YOU SAY!?
HE DROWNED TO DEATH. HIS HEAD WAS PROBABLY FORCED INTO THIS FOUNTAIN.
TH-THAT CAN'T BE!
BUT YUJI WAS ALIVE A LITTLE WHILE AGO!
YEAH THAT'S RIGHT!! HE WAS JUST KILLED!!
BY SOMEBODY WHO'S HERE AROUND THIS VILLA!!!

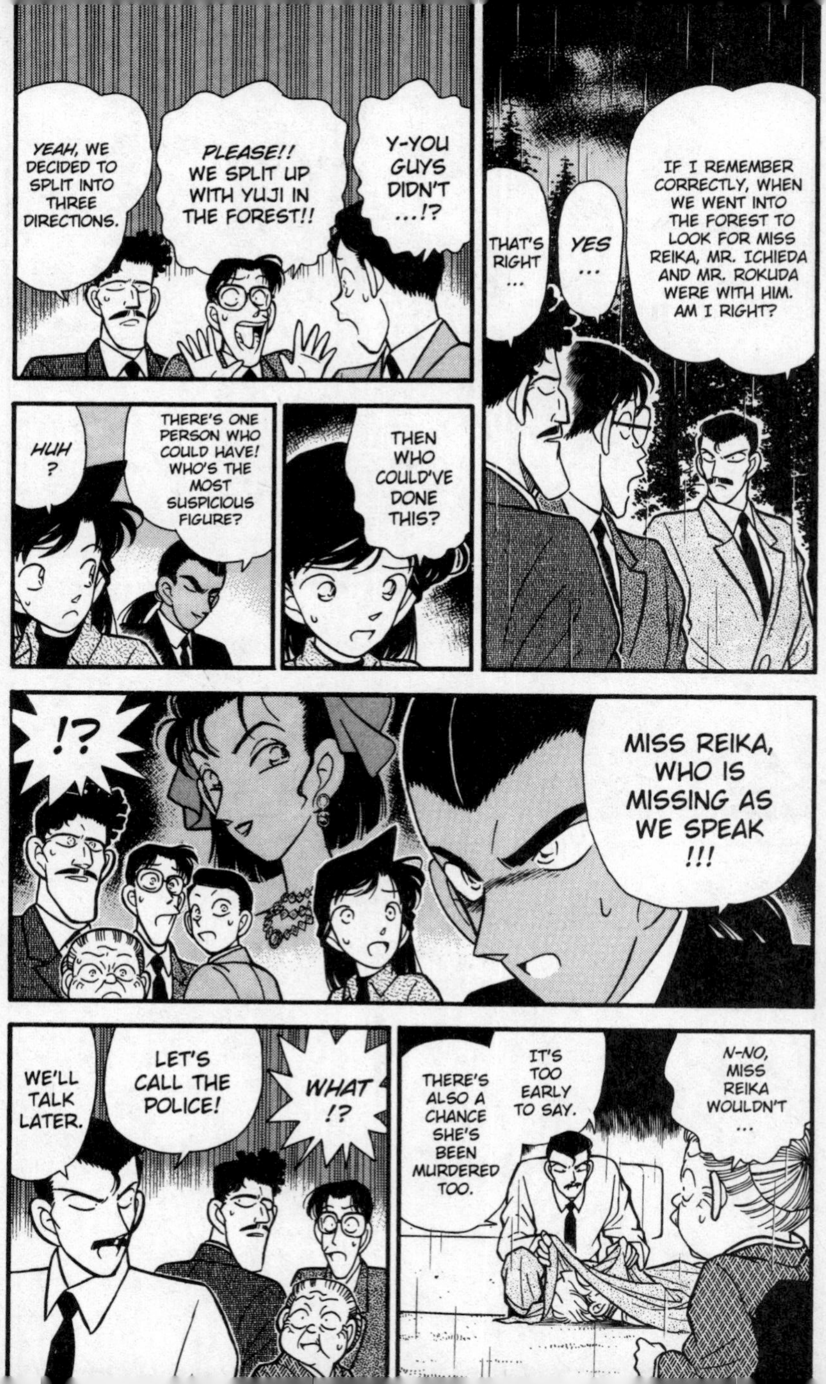
IF I REMEMBER CORRECTLY, WHEN WE WENT INTO THE FOREST TO LOOK FOR MISS REIKA, MR. ICHIEDA AND MR. ROKUDA WERE WITH HIM. AM I RIGHT?
YES ...
THAT'S RIGHT ...
Y-YOU GUYS DIDN'T ...!?
PLEASE!! WE SPLIT UP WITH YUJI IN THE FOREST!!
YEAH, WE DECIDED TO SPLIT INTO THREE DIRECTIONS.
THEN WHO COULD'VE DONE THIS?
THERE'S ONE PERSON WHO COULD HAVE! WHO'S THE MOST SUSPICIOUS FIGURE?
HUH ?
MISS REIKA, WHO IS MISSING AS WE SPEAK !!!
!?
N-NO, MISS REIKA WOULDN'T ...
IT'S TOO EARLY TO SAY.
THERE'S ALSO A CHANCE SHE'S BEEN MURDERED TOO.
WHAT !?
LET'S CALL THE POLICE!
WE'LL TALK LATER.

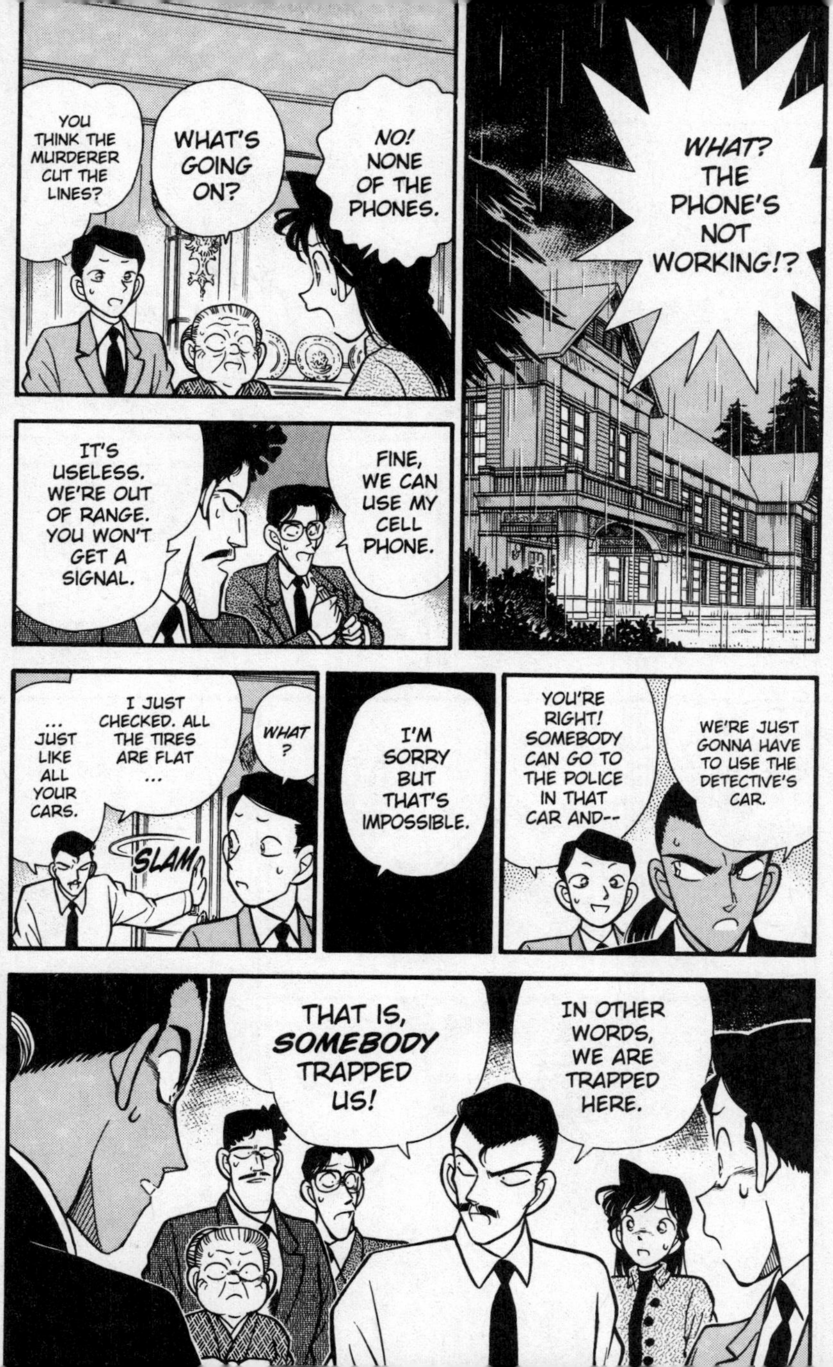
WHAT? THE PHONE'S NOT WORKING!?
NO! NONE OF THE PHONES.
WHAT'S GOING ON?
YOU THINK THE MURDERER CUT THE LINES?
FINE, WE CAN USE MY CELL PHONE.
IT'S USELESS. WE'RE OUT OF RANGE. YOU WON'T GET A SIGNAL.
WE'RE JUST GONNA HAVE TO USE THE DETECTIVE'S CAR.
YOU'RE RIGHT! SOMEBODY CAN GO TO THE POLICE IN THAT CAR AND--
I'M SORRY BUT THAT'S IMPOSSIBLE.
WHAT?
I JUST CHECKED. ALL THE TIRES ARE FLAT ...
... JUST LIKE ALL YOUR CARS.
SLAM
IN OTHER WORDS, WE ARE TRAPPED HERE.
THAT IS, SOMEBODY TRAPPED US!

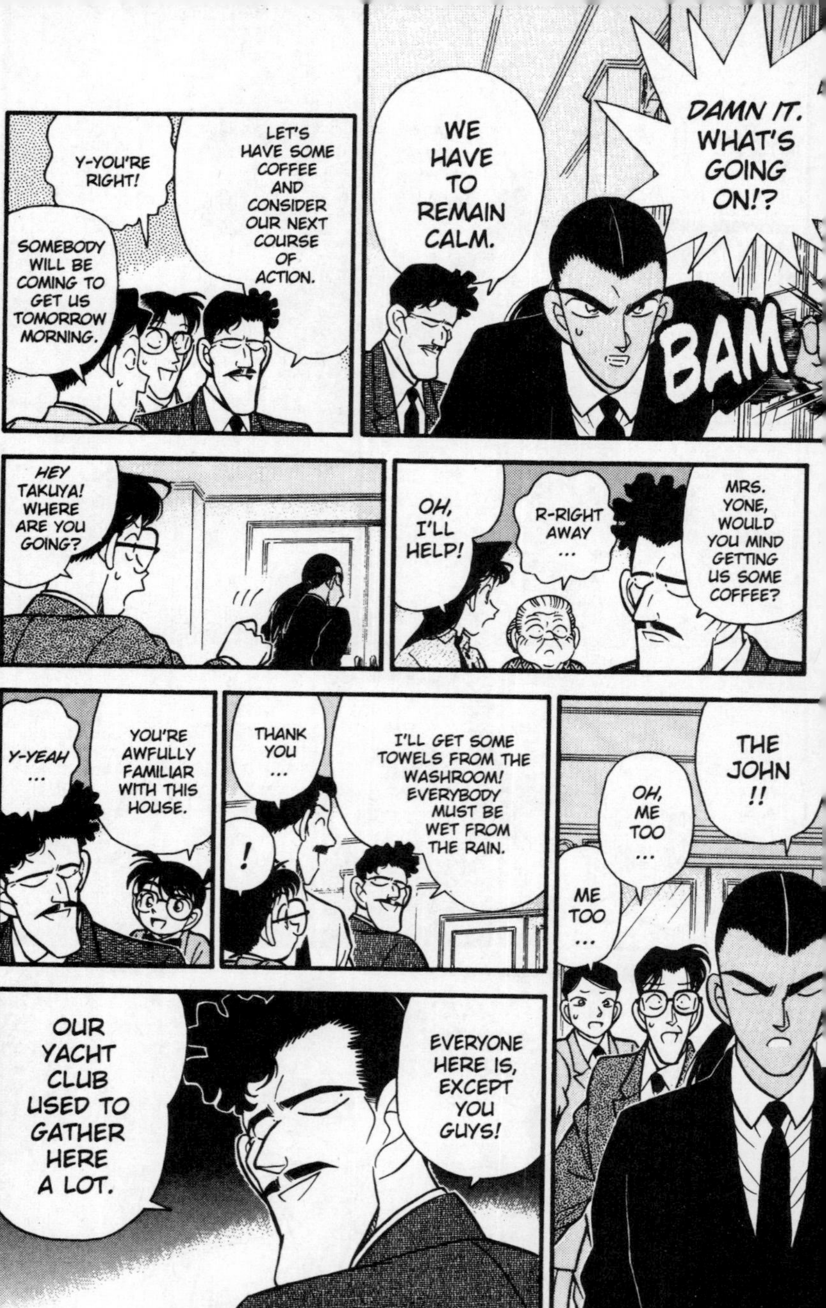
DAMN IT. WHAT'S GOING ON!?
WE HAVE TO REMAIN CALM.
BAM
LET'S HAVE SOME COFFEE AND CONSIDER OUR NEXT COURSE OF ACTION.
Y-YOU'RE RIGHT!
SOMEBODY WILL BE COMING TO GET US TOMORROW MORNING.
MRS. YONE, WOULD YOU MIND GETTING US SOME COFFEE?
R-RIGHT AWAY ...
OH, I'LL HELP!
HEY TAKUYA! WHERE ARE YOU GOING?
THE JOHN !!
OH, ME TOO ...
ME TOO ...
I'LL GET SOME TOWELS FROM THE WASHROOM! EVERYBODY MUST BE WET FROM THE RAIN.
THANK YOU ...
!
YOU'RE AWFULLY FAMILIAR WITH THIS HOUSE.
Y-YEAH ...
EVERYONE HERE IS, EXCEPT YOU GUYS!
OUR YACHT CLUB USED TO GATHER HERE A LOT.

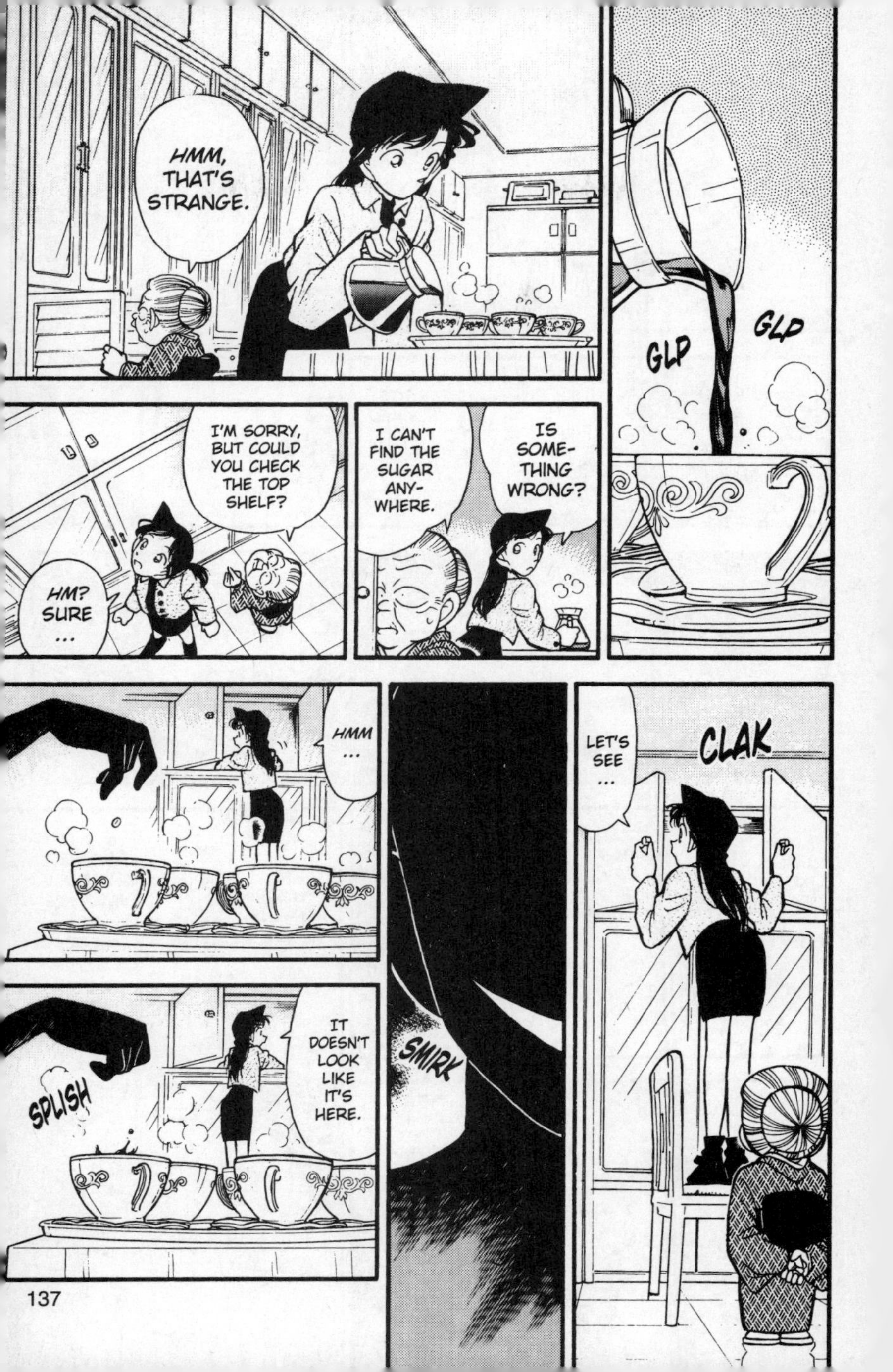
GLP
GLP
HMM, THAT'S STRANGE.
IS SOME-THING WRONG?
I CAN'T FIND THE SUGAR ANY-WHERE.
I'M SORRY, BUT COULD YOU CHECK THE TOP SHELF?
HM? SURE ...
LET'S SEE ...
CLAK
SMIRK
HMM ...
IT DOESN'T LOOK LIKE IT'S HERE.
SPLISH

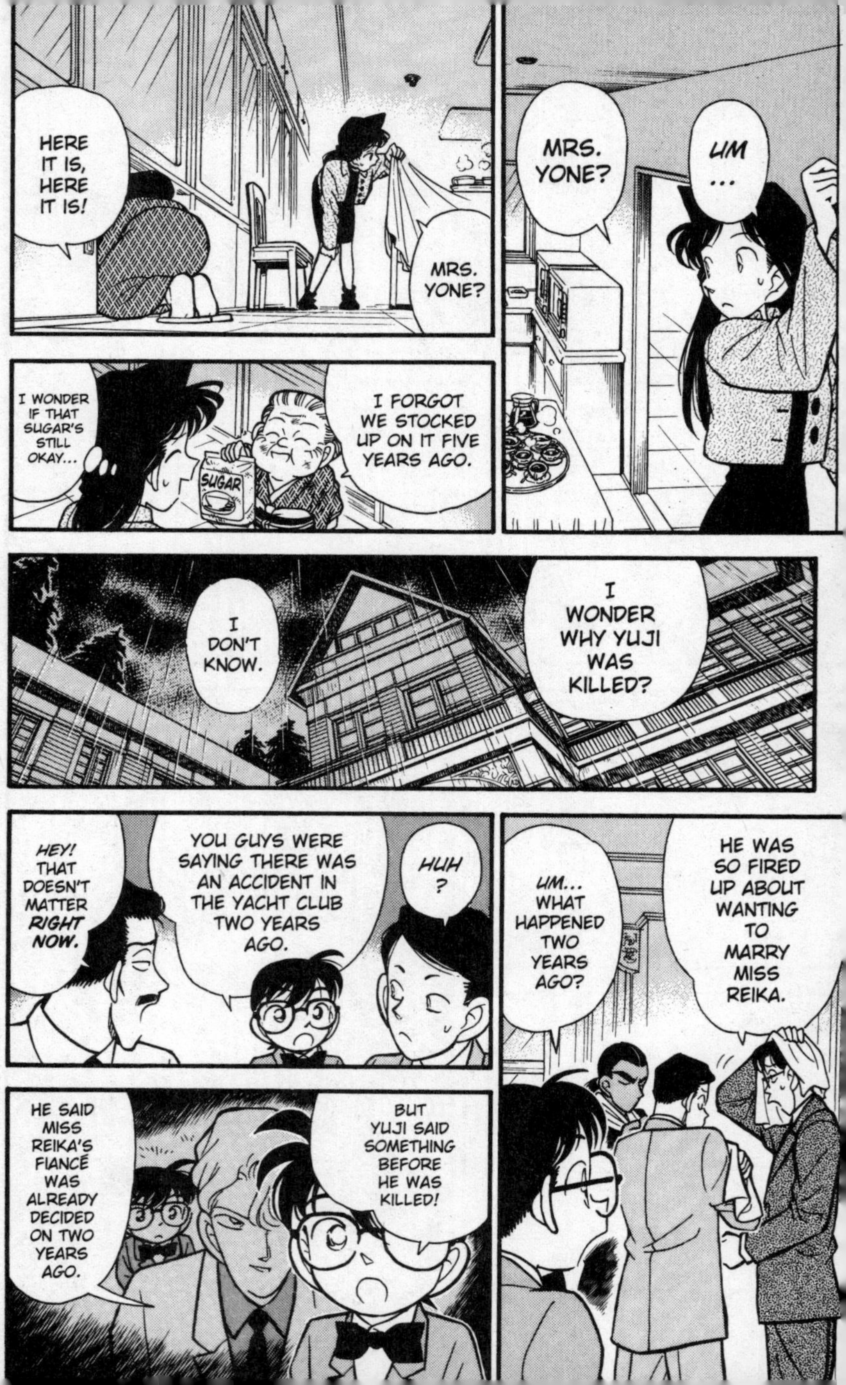
UM ...
MRS. YONE?
MRS. YONE?
HERE IT IS, HERE IT IS!
I FORGOT WE STOCKED UP ON IT FIVE YEARS AGO.
SUGAR
I WONDER IF THAT SUGAR'S STILL OKAY...
I WONDER WHY YUJI WAS KILLED?
I DON'T KNOW.
HE WAS SO FIRED UP ABOUT WANTING TO MARRY MISS REIKA.
UM... WHAT HAPPENED TWO YEARS AGO?
HUH?
YOU GUYS WERE SAYING THERE WAS AN ACCIDENT IN THE YACHT CLUB TWO YEARS AGO.
HEY! THAT DOESN'T MATTER RIGHT NOW.
BUT YUJI SAID SOMETHING BEFORE HE WAS KILLED!
HE SAID MISS REIKA'S FIANCÉ WAS ALREADY DECIDED ON TWO YEARS AGO.

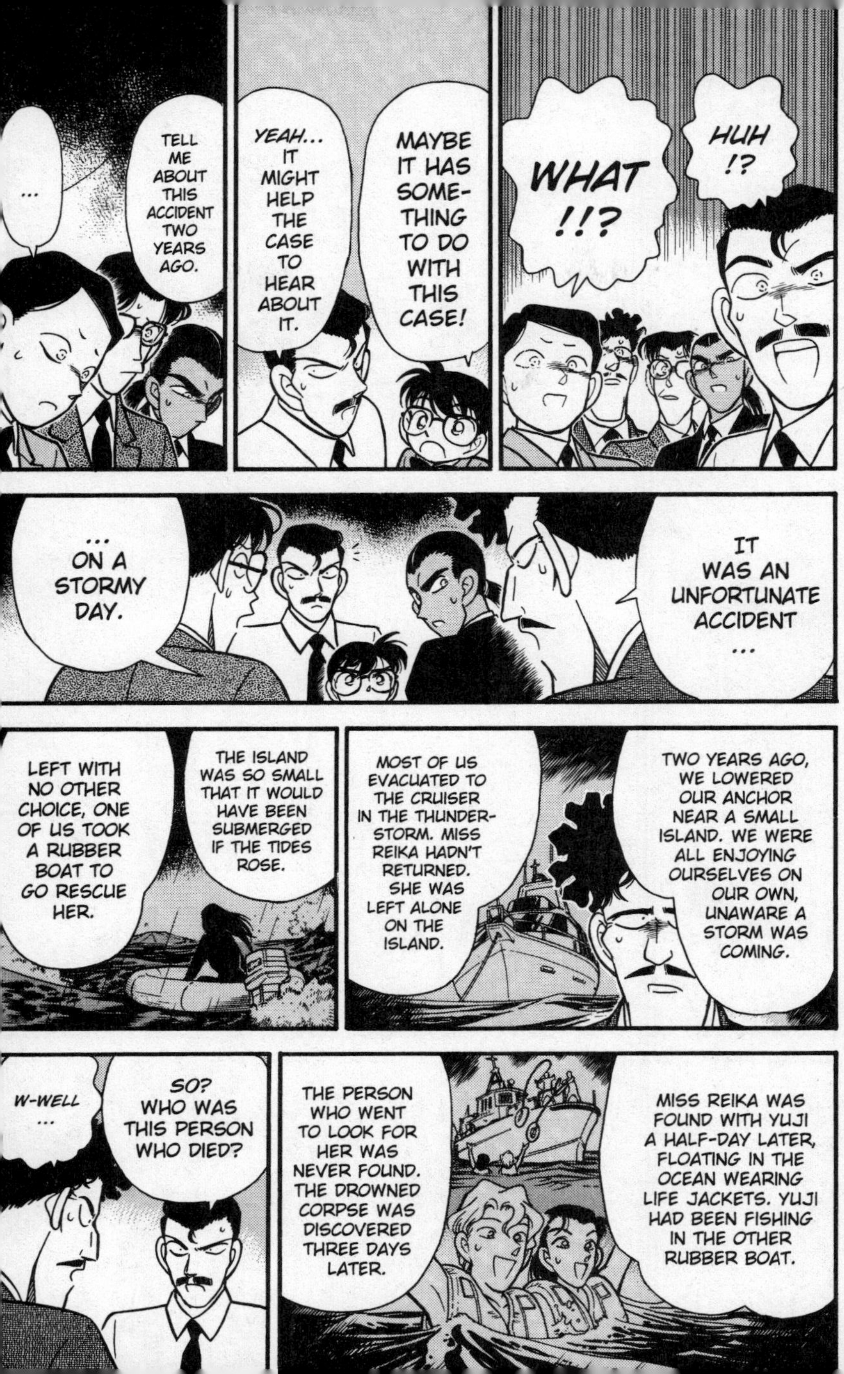
HUH !?
WHAT !!?
MAYBE IT HAS SOMETHING TO DO WITH THIS CASE!
YEAH... IT MIGHT HELP THE CASE TO HEAR ABOUT IT.
TELL ME ABOUT THIS ACCIDENT TWO YEARS AGO.
...
IT WAS AN UNFORTUNATE ACCIDENT ...
... ON A STORMY DAY.
TWO YEARS AGO, WE LOWERED OUR ANCHOR NEAR A SMALL ISLAND. WE WERE ALL ENJOYING OURSELVES ON OUR OWN, UNAWARE A STORM WAS COMING.
MOST OF US EVACUATED TO THE CRUISER IN THE THUNDERSTORM. MISS REIKA HADN'T RETURNED. SHE WAS LEFT ALONE ON THE ISLAND.
THE ISLAND WAS SO SMALL THAT IT WOULD HAVE BEEN SUBMERGED IF THE TIDES ROSE.
LEFT WITH NO OTHER CHOICE, ONE OF US TOOK A RUBBER BOAT TO GO RESCUE HER.
MISS REIKA WAS FOUND WITH YUJI A HALF-DAY LATER, FLOATING IN THE OCEAN WEARING LIFE JACKETS. YUJI HAD BEEN FISHING IN THE OTHER RUBBER BOAT.
THE PERSON WHO WENT TO LOOK FOR HER WAS NEVER FOUND. THE DROWNED CORPSE WAS DISCOVERED THREE DAYS LATER.
SO? WHO WAS THIS PERSON WHO DIED?
W-WELL ...

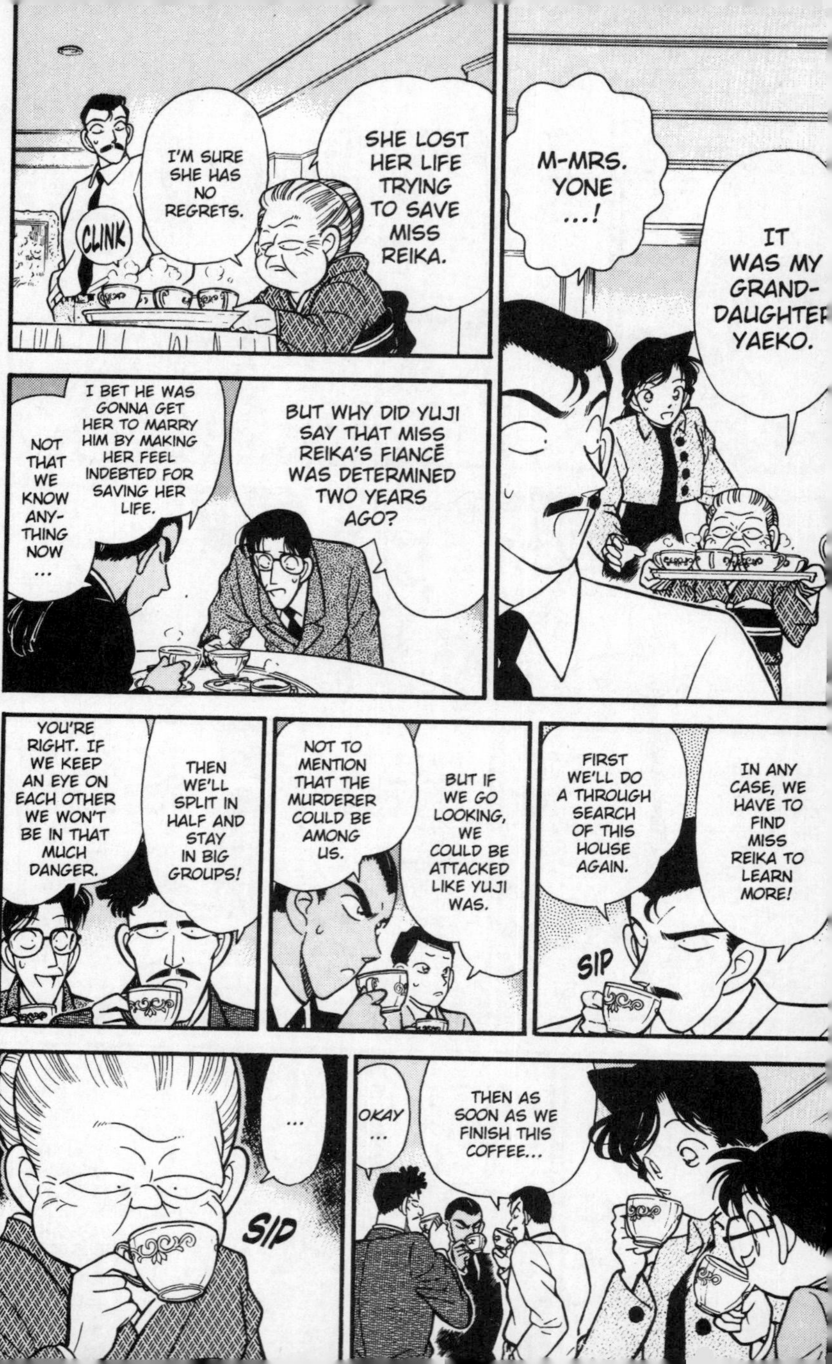
IT WAS MY GRAND-DAUGHTER YAEKO.
M-MRS. YONE ...!
SHE LOST HER LIFE TRYING TO SAVE MISS REIKA.
I'M SURE SHE HAS NO REGRETS.
CLINK
BUT WHY DID YUJI SAY THAT MISS REIKA'S FIANCÉ WAS DETERMINED TWO YEARS AGO?
I BET HE WAS GONNA GET HER TO MARRY HIM BY MAKING HER FEEL INDEBTED FOR SAVING HER LIFE.
NOT THAT WE KNOW ANY-THING NOW ...
IN ANY CASE, WE HAVE TO FIND MISS REIKA TO LEARN MORE!
FIRST WE'LL DO A THROUGH SEARCH OF THIS HOUSE AGAIN.
SIP
BUT IF WE GO LOOKING, WE COULD BE ATTACKED LIKE YUJI WAS.
NOT TO MENTION THAT THE MURDERER COULD BE AMONG US.
THEN WE'LL SPLIT IN HALF AND STAY IN BIG GROUPS!
YOU'RE RIGHT. IF WE KEEP AN EYE ON EACH OTHER WE WON'T BE IN THAT MUCH DANGER.
THEN AS SOON AS WE FINISH THIS COFFEE...
OKAY ...
...
SIP

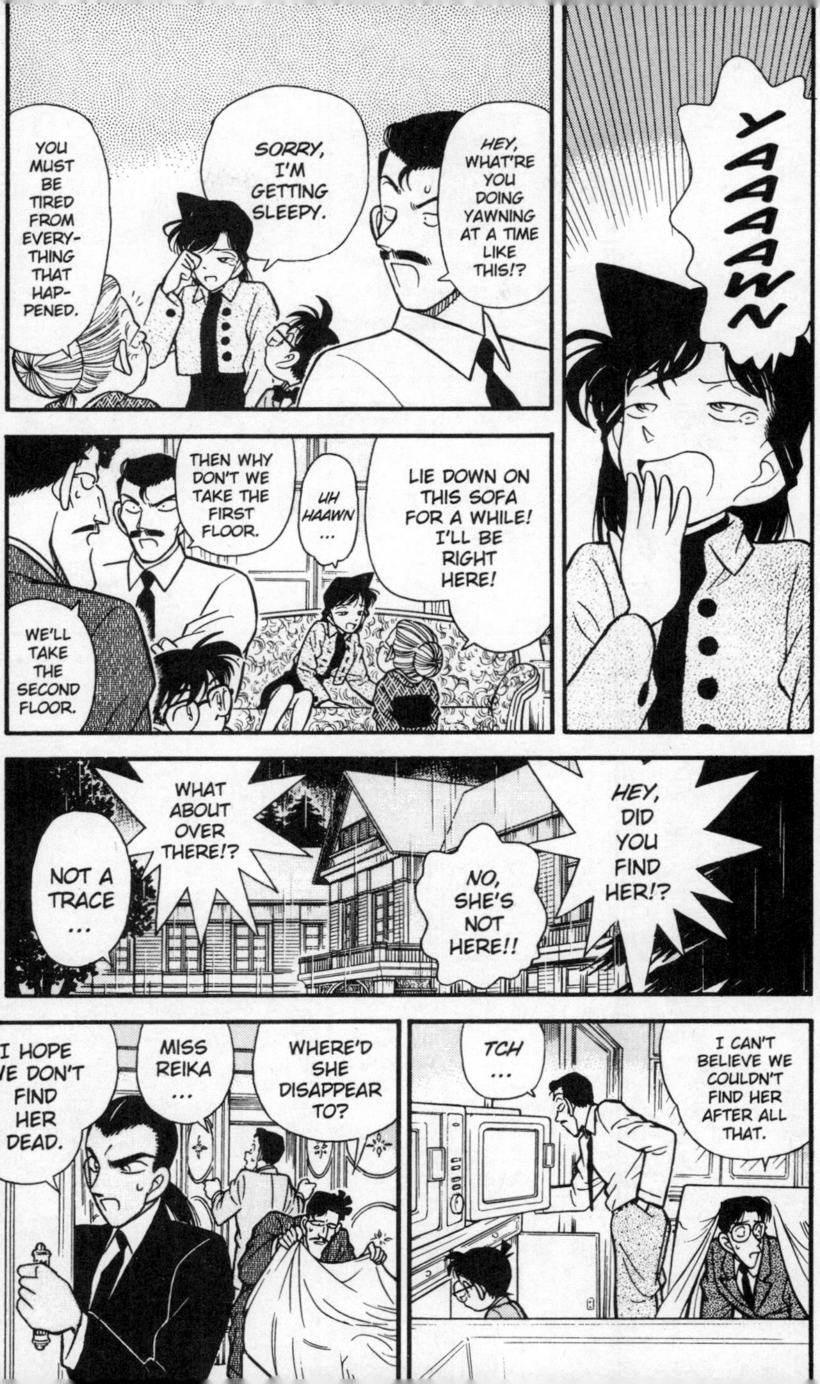
YAAAAWN
HEY, WHAT'RE YOU DOING YAWNING AT A TIME LIKE THIS!?
SORRY, I'M GETTING SLEEPY.
YOU MUST BE TIRED FROM EVERY-THING THAT HAP-PENED.
LIE DOWN ON THIS SOFA FOR A WHILE! I'LL BE RIGHT HERE!
UH HAAWN ...
THEN WHY DON'T WE TAKE THE FIRST FLOOR.
WE'LL TAKE THE SECOND FLOOR.
HEY, DID YOU FIND HER!?
NO, SHE'S NOT HERE!!
WHAT ABOUT OVER THERE!?
NOT A TRACE ...
I CAN'T BELIEVE WE COULDN'T FIND HER AFTER ALL THAT.
TCH ...
WHERE'D SHE DISAPPEAR TO?
MISS REIKA ...
I HOPE WE DON'T FIND HER DEAD.

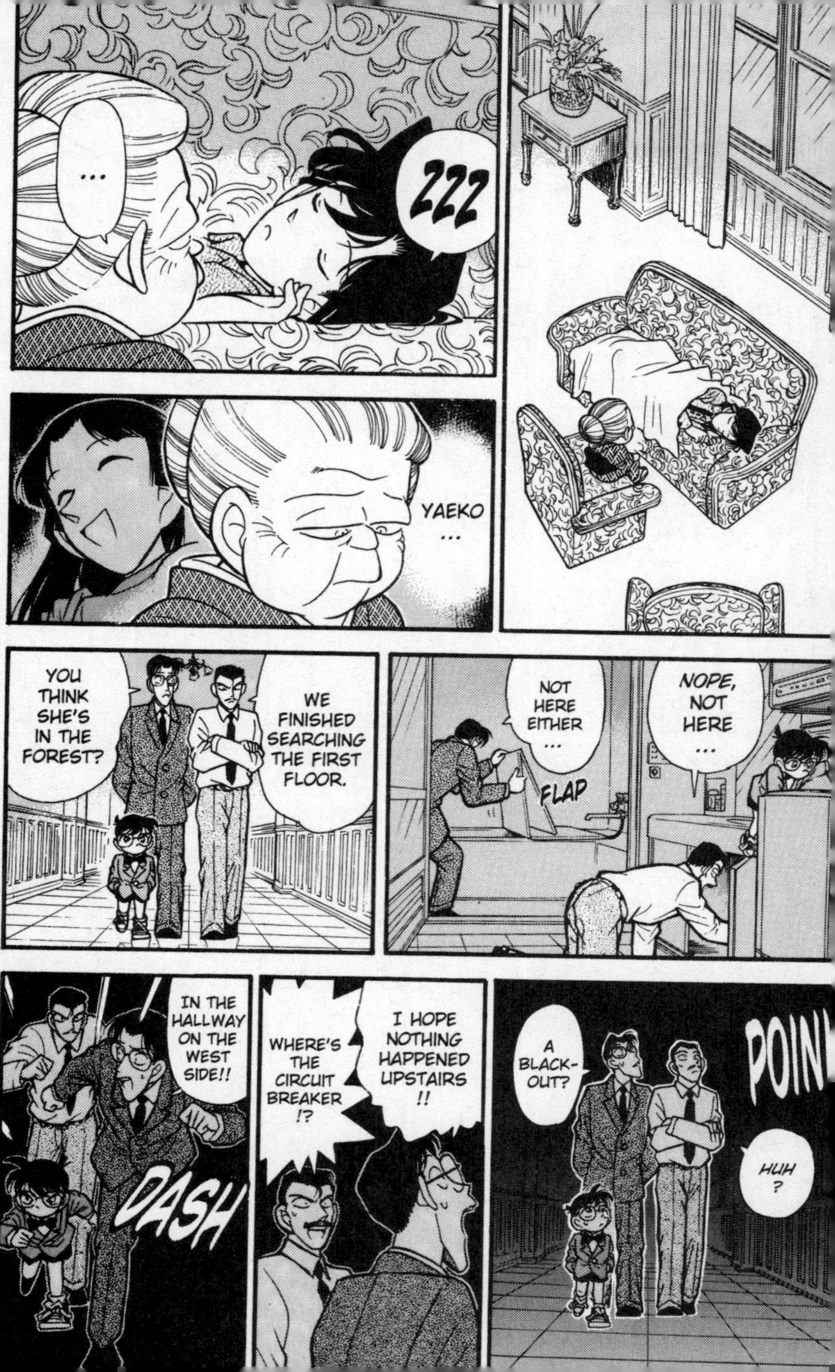
ZZZ
...
YAEKO ...
NOPE, NOT HERE ...
NOT HERE EITHER ...
FLAP
WE FINISHED SEARCHING THE FIRST FLOOR.
YOU THINK SHE'S IN THE FOREST?
POIN
A BLACK-OUT?
HUH ?
I HOPE NOTHING HAPPENED UPSTAIRS !!
WHERE'S THE CIRCUIT BREAKER !?
IN THE HALLWAY ON THE WEST SIDE!!
DASH

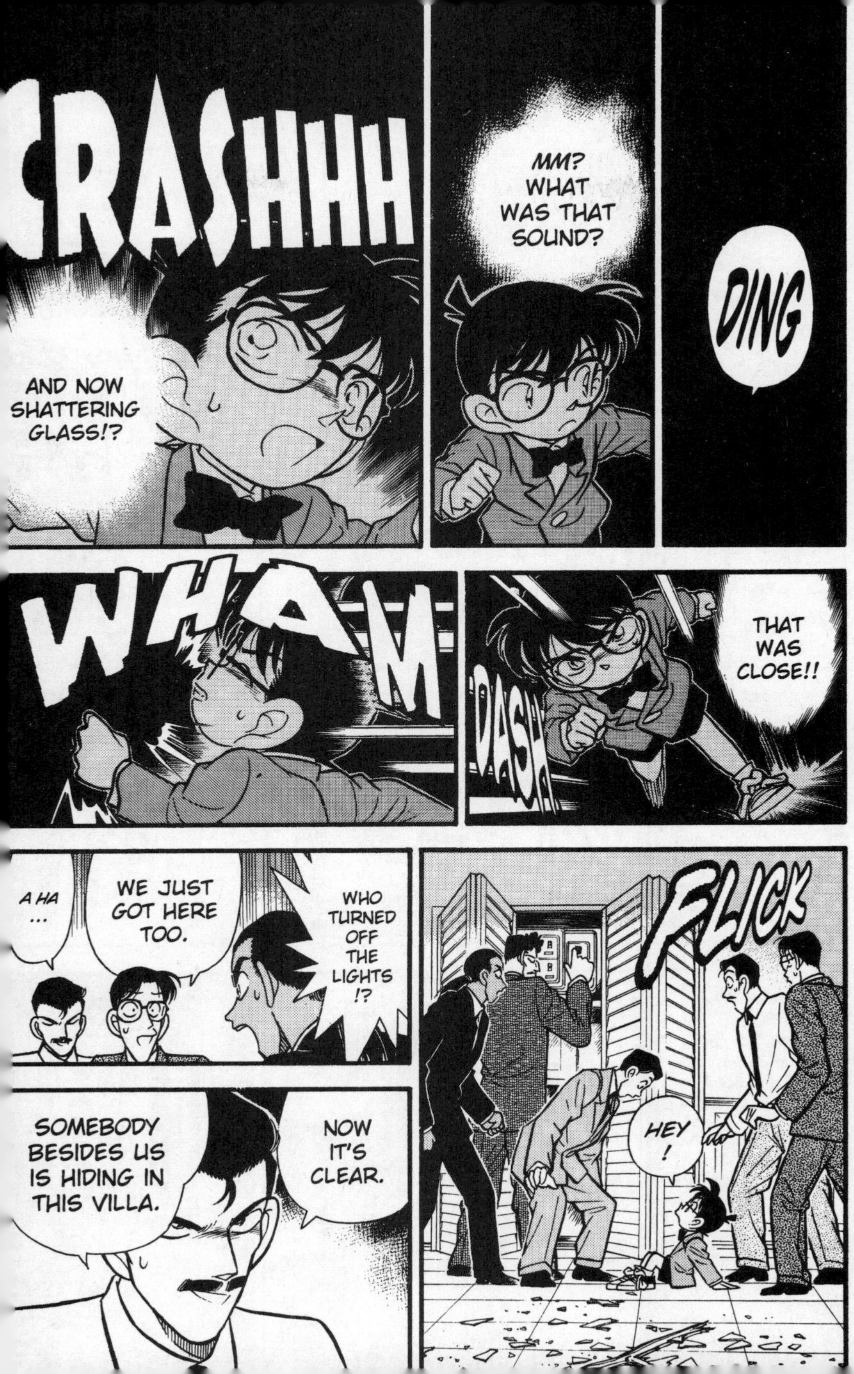
DING
MM? WHAT WAS THAT SOUND?
CRASHHH
AND NOW SHATTERING GLASS!?
THAT WAS CLOSE!!
DASH
WHAM
FLICK
HEY!
WHO TURNED OFF THE LIGHTS!?
WE JUST GOT HERE TOO.
A HA ...
NOW IT'S CLEAR.
SOMEBODY BESIDES US IS HIDING IN THIS VILLA.

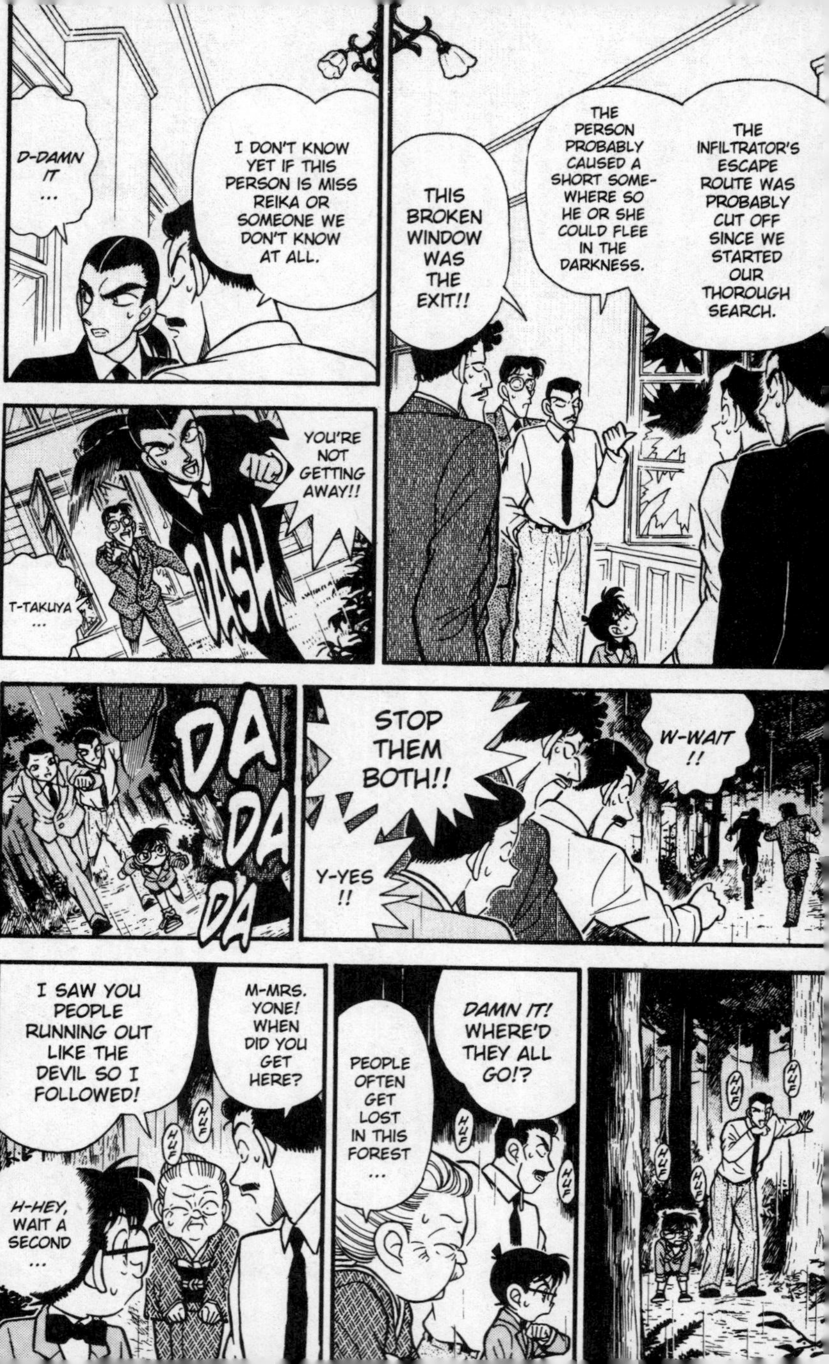
THE INFILTRATOR'S ESCAPE ROUTE WAS PROBABLY CUT OFF SINCE WE STARTED OUR THOROUGH SEARCH.
THE PERSON PROBABLY CAUSED A SHORT SOMEWHERE SO HE OR SHE COULD FLEE IN THE DARKNESS.
THIS BROKEN WINDOW WAS THE EXIT!!
I DON'T KNOW YET IF THIS PERSON IS MISS REIKA OR SOMEONE WE DON'T KNOW AT ALL.
D-DAMN IT ...
YOU'RE NOT GETTING AWAY!!
DASH
T-TAKUYA ...
W-WAIT !!
STOP THEM BOTH!!
Y-YES !!
DA DA DA
HUF
HUF
HUF
HUF
DAMN IT! WHERE'D THEY ALL GO!?
HUF
HUF
PEOPLE OFTEN GET LOST IN THIS FOREST ...
M-MRS. YONE! WHEN DID YOU GET HERE?
I SAW YOU PEOPLE RUNNING OUT LIKE THE DEVIL SO I FOLLOWED!
HUF
HUF
H-HEY, WAIT A SECOND ...

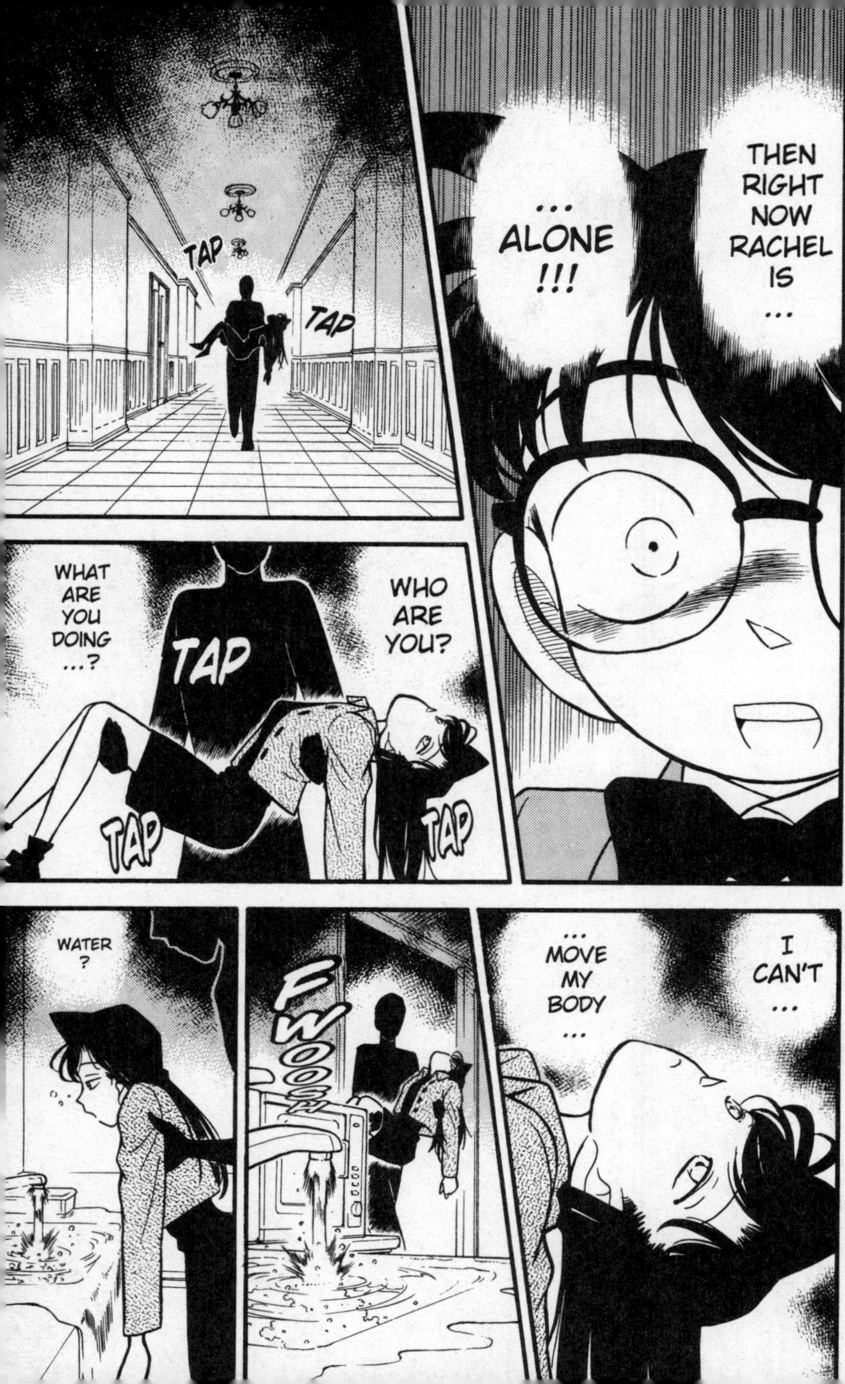
THEN RIGHT NOW RACHEL IS ...
... ALONE !!!
TAP
TAP
WHO ARE YOU?
WHAT ARE YOU DOING ...?
TAP
TAP
TAP
I CAN'T ...
... MOVE MY BODY ...
FWOOSH
WATER ?

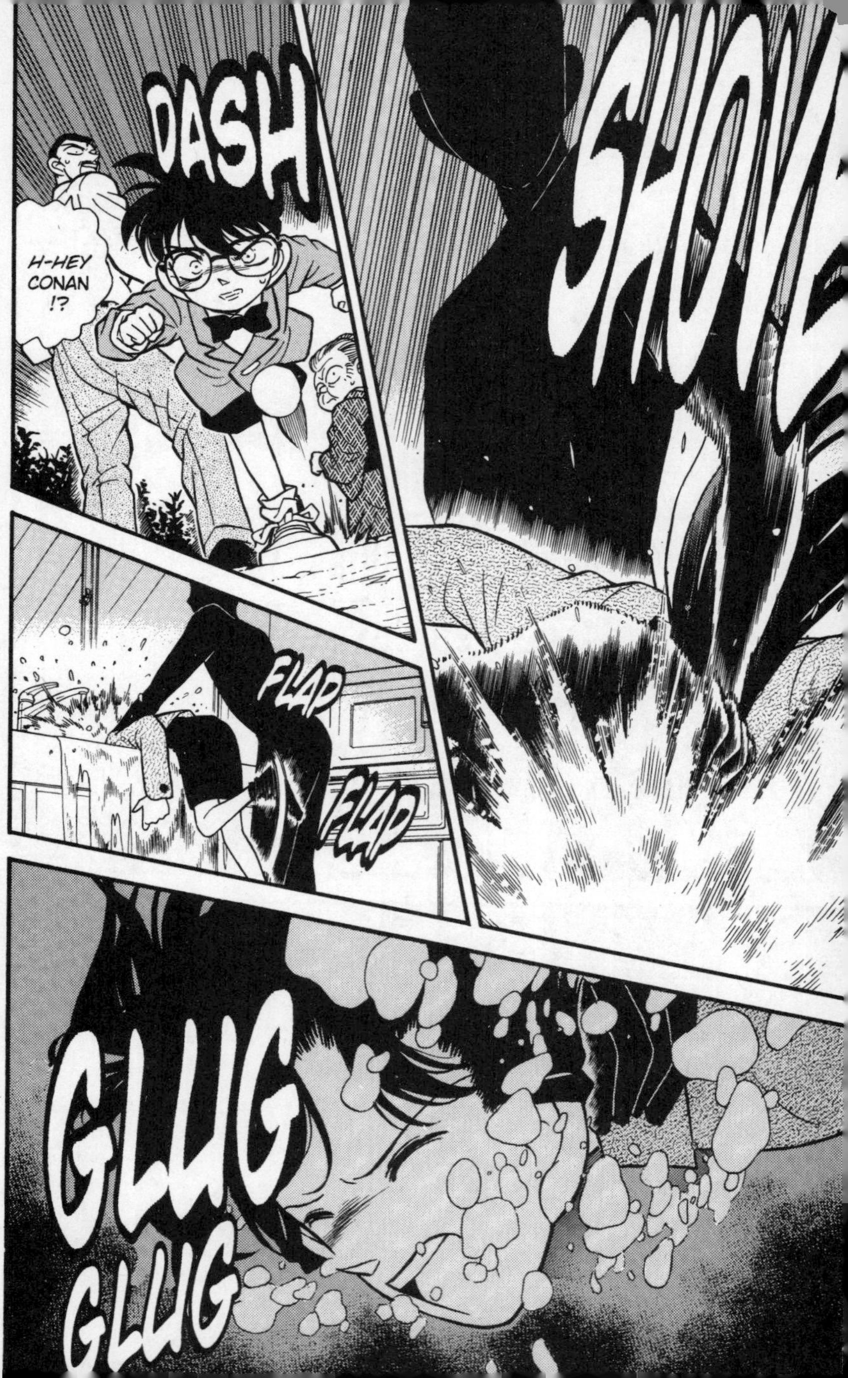
SHOV
DASH
H-HEY CONAN !?
FLAP
FLAP
GLUG
GLUG

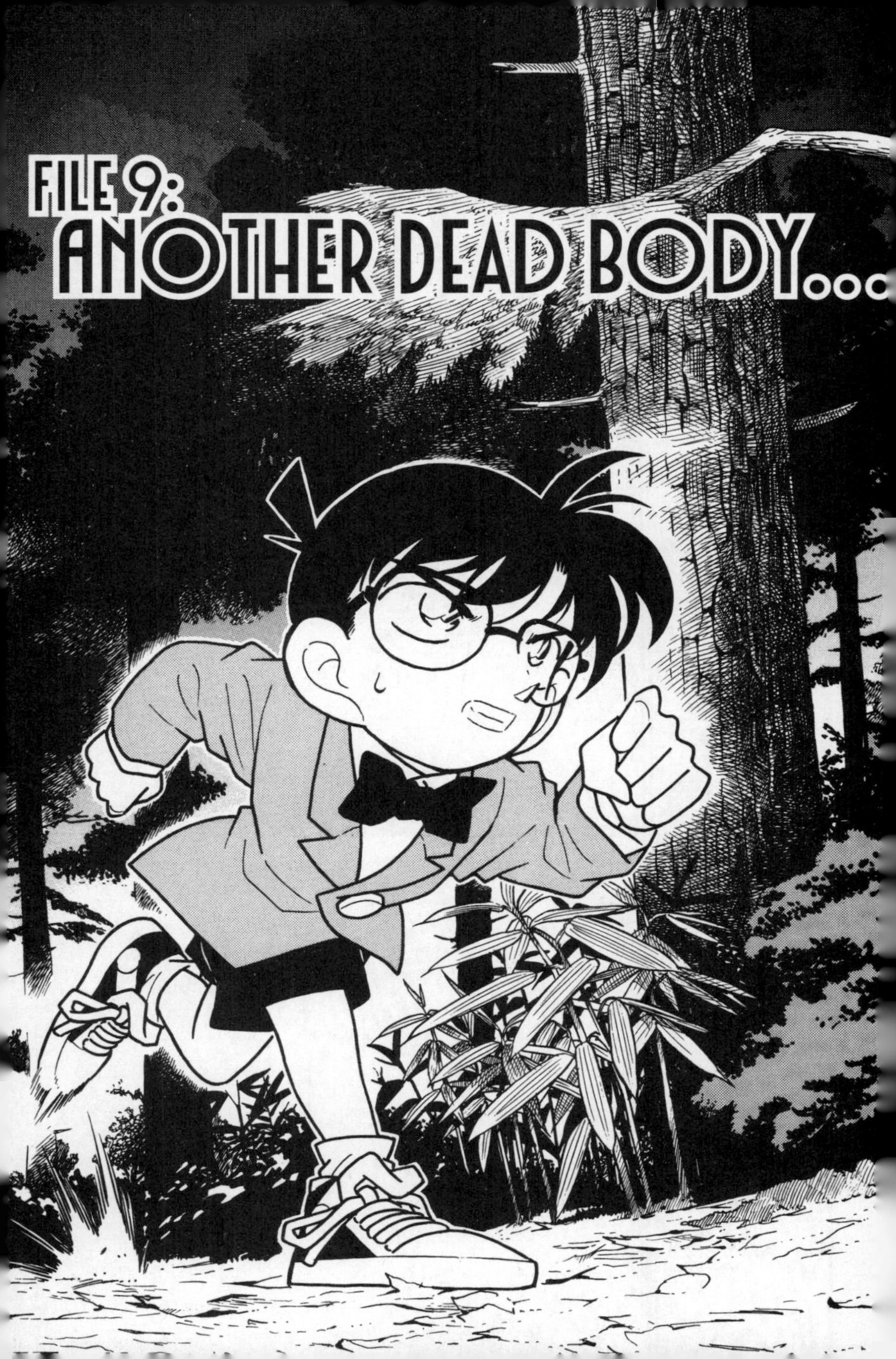
FILE 9:
ANOTHER DEAD BODY...

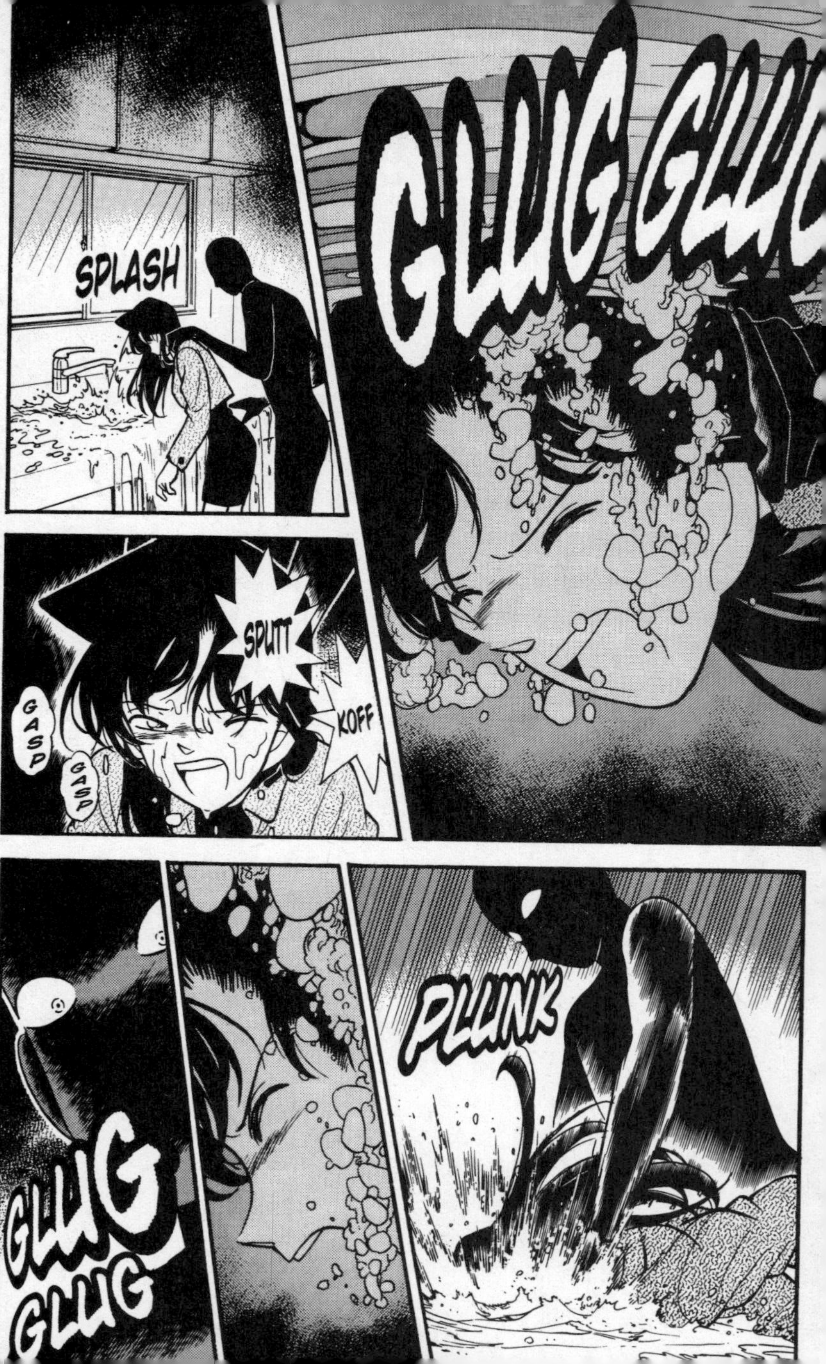
GLUG GLU
SPLASH
SPUTT
KOFF
GASP
GASP
PLLINK
GLUG
GLUG

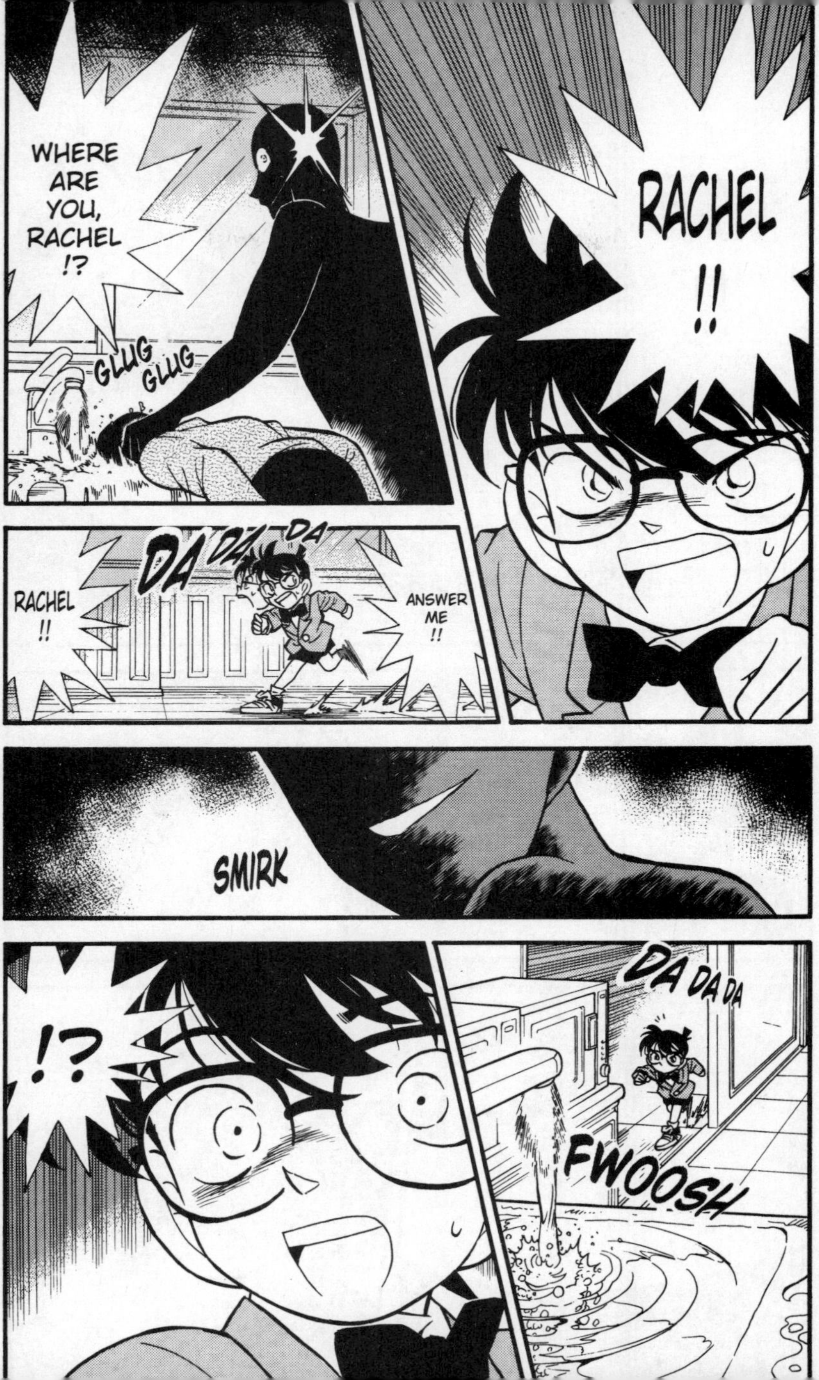
RACHEL !!
WHERE ARE YOU, RACHEL !?
GLUG GLUG
DA DA DA
ANSWER ME !!
RACHEL !!
SMIRK
DA DA DA
FWOOSH
!?

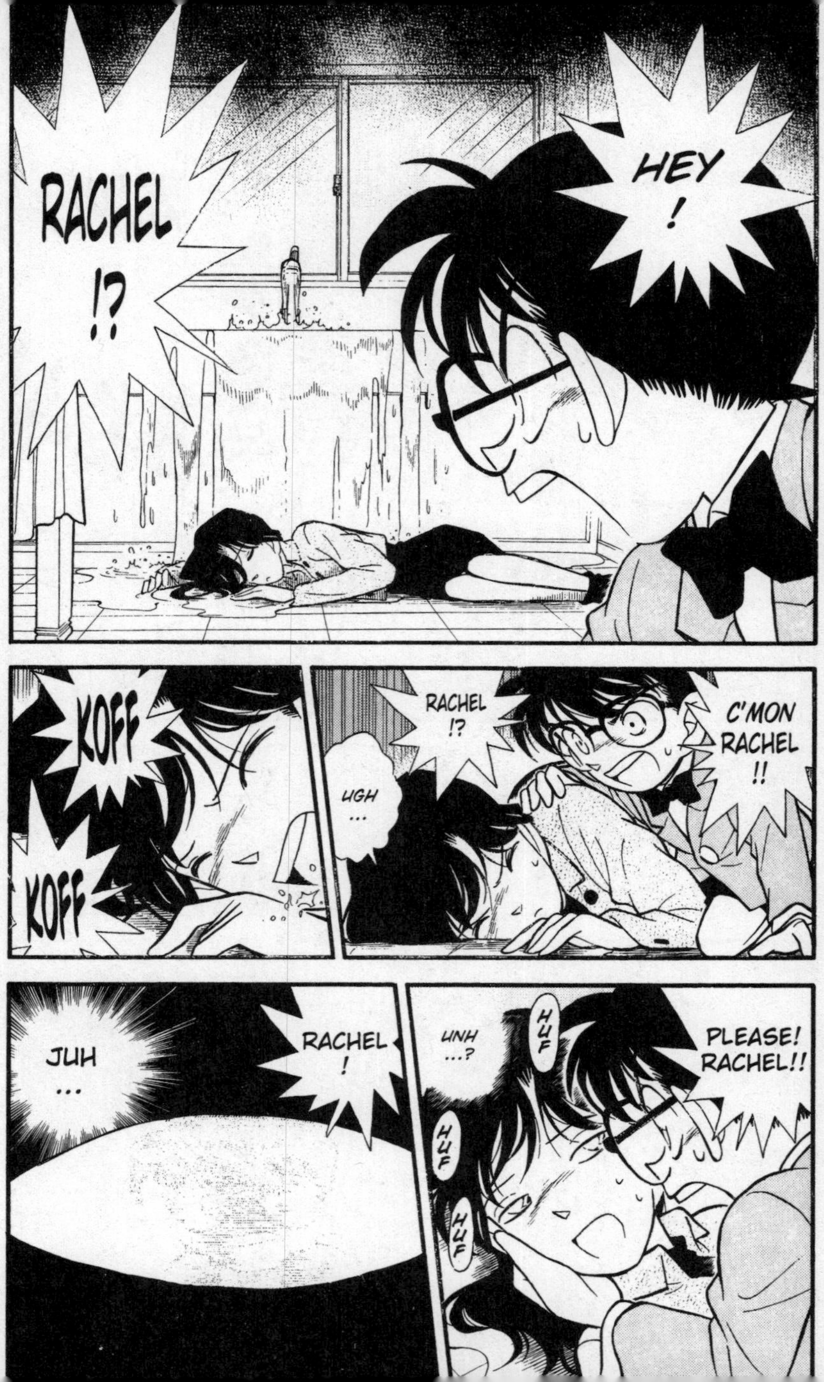
HEY!
RACHEL!?
C'MON RACHEL!!
RACHEL!?
UGH...
KOFF
KOFF
PLEASE! RACHEL!!
HUF
UNH...?
HUF
HUF
RACHEL!
JUH...

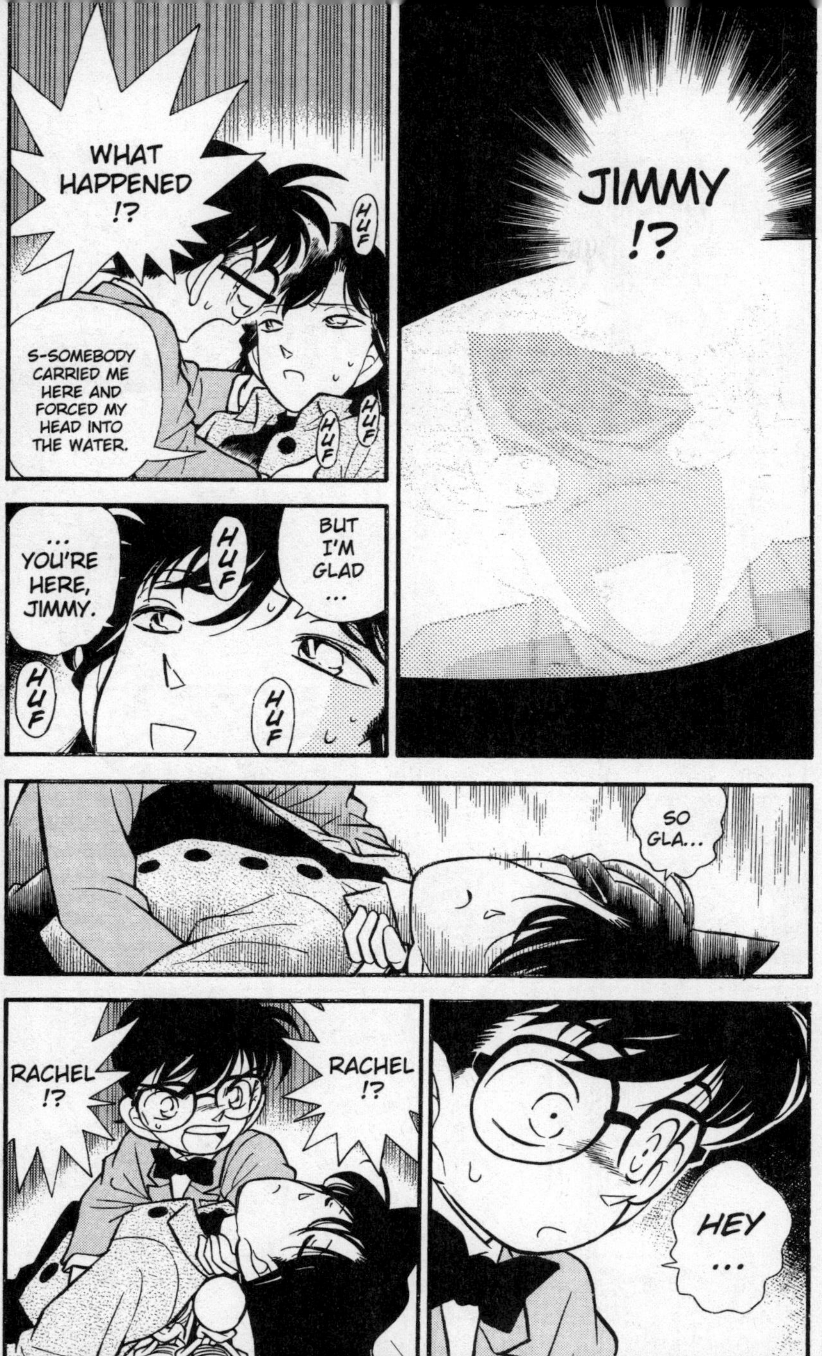
JIMMY !?
WHAT HAPPENED !?
HUF
HUF
HUF
S-SOMEBODY CARRIED ME HERE AND FORCED MY HEAD INTO THE WATER.
BUT I'M GLAD ...
HUF
... YOU'RE HERE, JIMMY.
HUF
HUF
SO GLA...
HEY ...
RACHEL !?
RACHEL !?

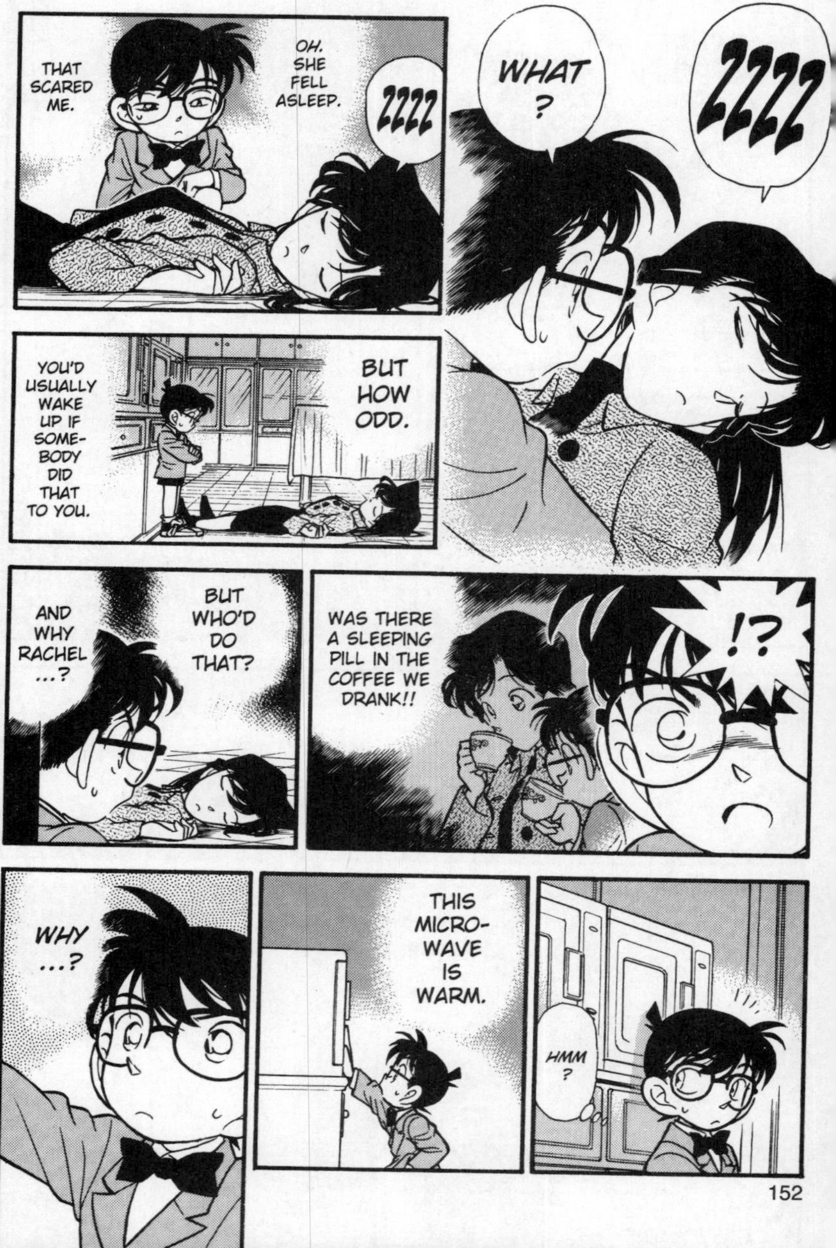
ZZZZ
WHAT ?
ZZZZ
OH. SHE FELL ASLEEP.
THAT SCARED ME.
BUT HOW ODD.
YOU'D USUALLY WAKE UP IF SOME-BODY DID THAT TO YOU.
!?
WAS THERE A SLEEPING PILL IN THE COFFEE WE DRANK!!
BUT WHO'D DO THAT?
AND WHY RACHEL ...?
HMM ?
THIS MICRO-WAVE IS WARM.
WHY ...?

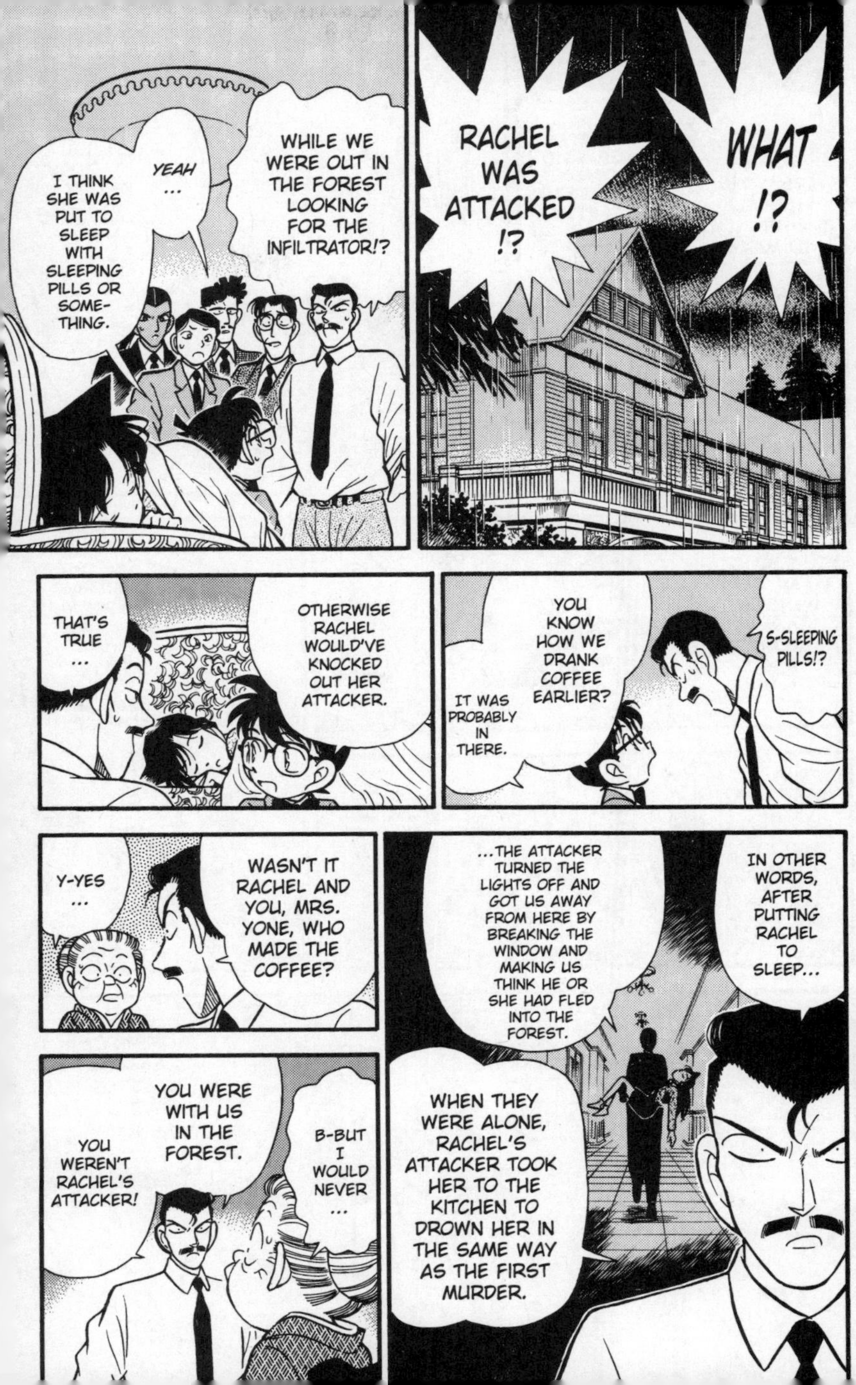
WHAT !?
RACHEL WAS ATTACKED !?
WHILE WE WERE OUT IN THE FOREST LOOKING FOR THE INFILTRATOR!?
YEAH ...
I THINK SHE WAS PUT TO SLEEP WITH SLEEPING PILLS OR SOME-THING.
S-SLEEPING PILLS!?
YOU KNOW HOW WE DRANK COFFEE EARLIER?
IT WAS PROBABLY IN THERE.
OTHERWISE RACHEL WOULD'VE KNOCKED OUT HER ATTACKER.
THAT'S TRUE ...
IN OTHER WORDS, AFTER PUTTING RACHEL TO SLEEP...
...THE ATTACKER TURNED THE LIGHTS OFF AND GOT US AWAY FROM HERE BY BREAKING THE WINDOW AND MAKING US THINK HE OR SHE HAD FLED INTO THE FOREST.
WHEN THEY WERE ALONE, RACHEL'S ATTACKER TOOK HER TO THE KITCHEN TO DROWN HER IN THE SAME WAY AS THE FIRST MURDER.
WASN'T IT RACHEL AND YOU, MRS. YONE, WHO MADE THE COFFEE?
Y-YES ...
B-BUT I WOULD NEVER ...
YOU WERE WITH US IN THE FOREST.
YOU WEREN'T RACHEL'S ATTACKER!

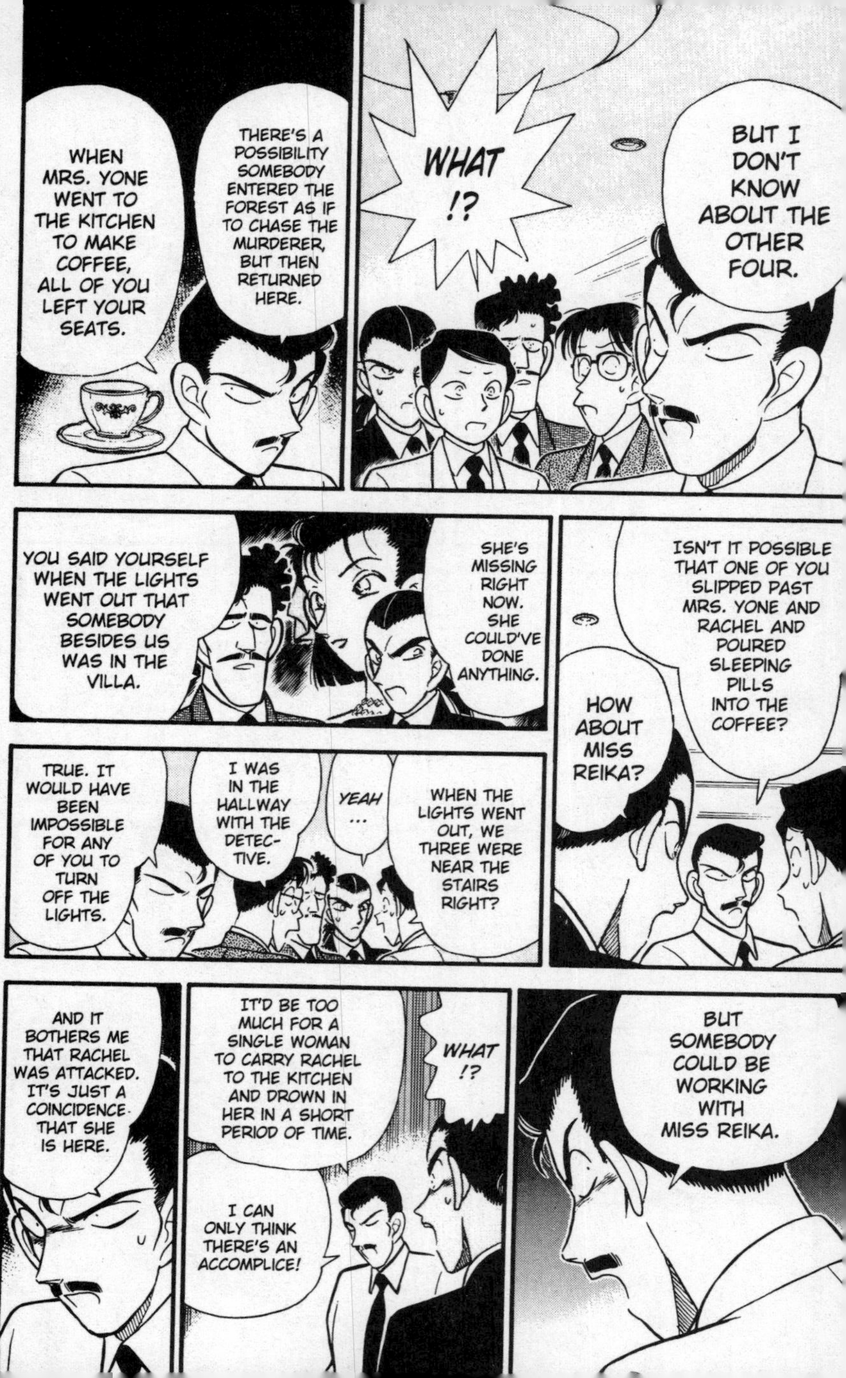
BUT I DON'T KNOW ABOUT THE OTHER FOUR.
WHAT !?
THERE'S A POSSIBILITY SOMEBODY ENTERED THE FOREST AS IF TO CHASE THE MURDERER, BUT THEN RETURNED HERE.
WHEN MRS. YONE WENT TO THE KITCHEN TO MAKE COFFEE, ALL OF YOU LEFT YOUR SEATS.
ISN'T IT POSSIBLE THAT ONE OF YOU SLIPPED PAST MRS. YONE AND RACHEL AND POURED SLEEPING PILLS INTO THE COFFEE?
HOW ABOUT MISS REIKA?
SHE'S MISSING RIGHT NOW. SHE COULD'VE DONE ANYTHING.
YOU SAID YOURSELF WHEN THE LIGHTS WENT OUT THAT SOMEBODY BESIDES US WAS IN THE VILLA.
WHEN THE LIGHTS WENT OUT, WE THREE WERE NEAR THE STAIRS RIGHT?
YEAH ...
I WAS IN THE HALLWAY WITH THE DETECTIVE.
TRUE. IT WOULD HAVE BEEN IMPOSSIBLE FOR ANY OF YOU TO TURN OFF THE LIGHTS.
BUT SOMEBODY COULD BE WORKING WITH MISS REIKA.
WHAT !?
IT'D BE TOO MUCH FOR A SINGLE WOMAN TO CARRY RACHEL TO THE KITCHEN AND DROWN IN HER IN A SHORT PERIOD OF TIME.
I CAN ONLY THINK THERE'S AN ACCOMPLICE!
AND IT BOTHERS ME THAT RACHEL WAS ATTACKED. IT'S JUST A COINCIDENCE THAT SHE IS HERE.

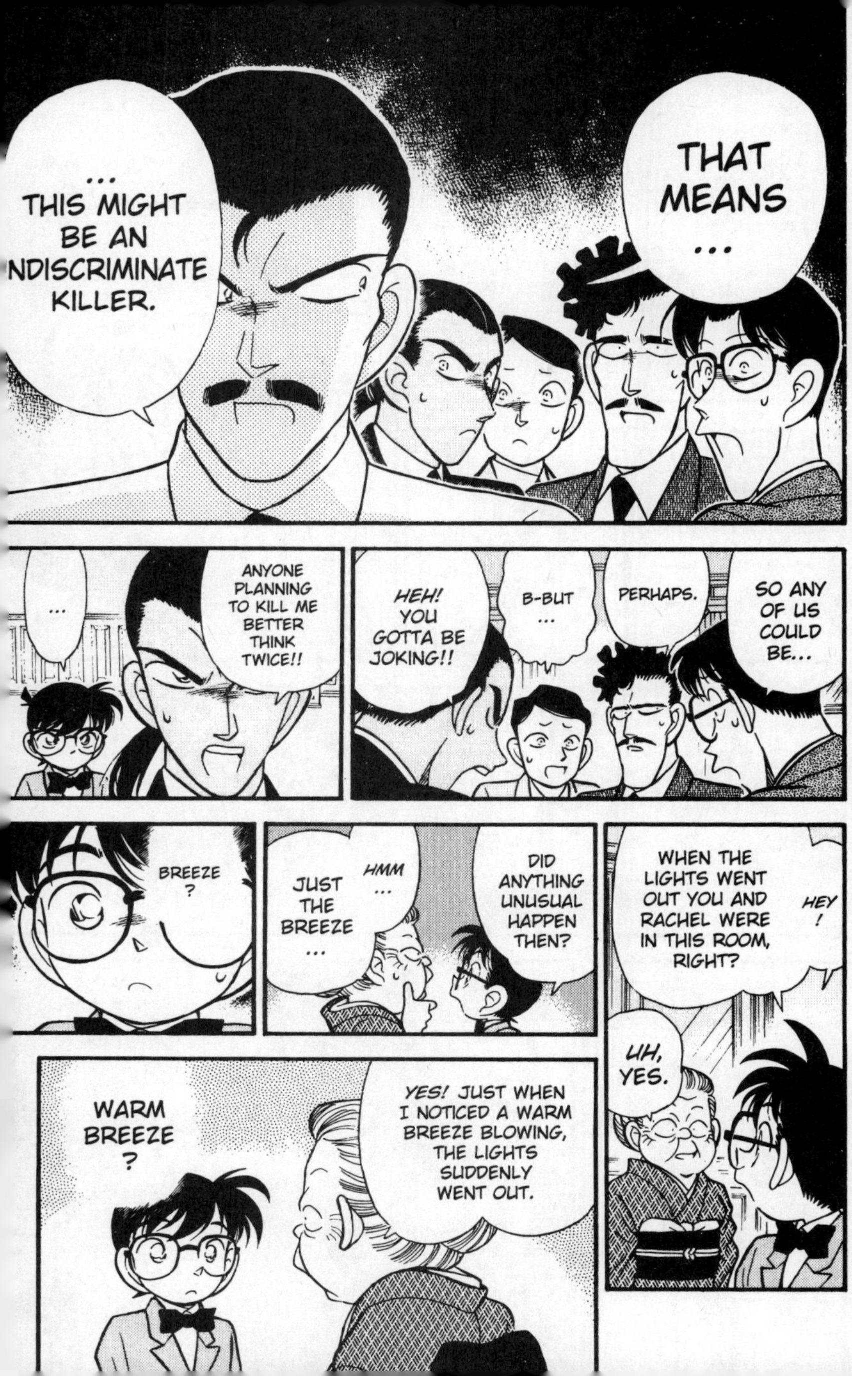

THAT MEANS ...
... THIS MIGHT BE AN NDISCRIMINATE KILLER.
SO ANY OF US COULD BE...
PERHAPS.
B-BUT ...
HEH! YOU GOTTA BE JOKING!!
ANYONE PLANNING TO KILL ME BETTER THINK TWICE!!
...
HEY !
WHEN THE LIGHTS WENT OUT YOU AND RACHEL WERE IN THIS ROOM, RIGHT?
UH, YES.
DID ANYTHING UNUSUAL HAPPEN THEN?
HMM ...
JUST THE BREEZE ...
BREEZE ?
YES! JUST WHEN I NOTICED A WARM BREEZE BLOWING, THE LIGHTS SUDDENLY WENT OUT.
WARM BREEZE ?

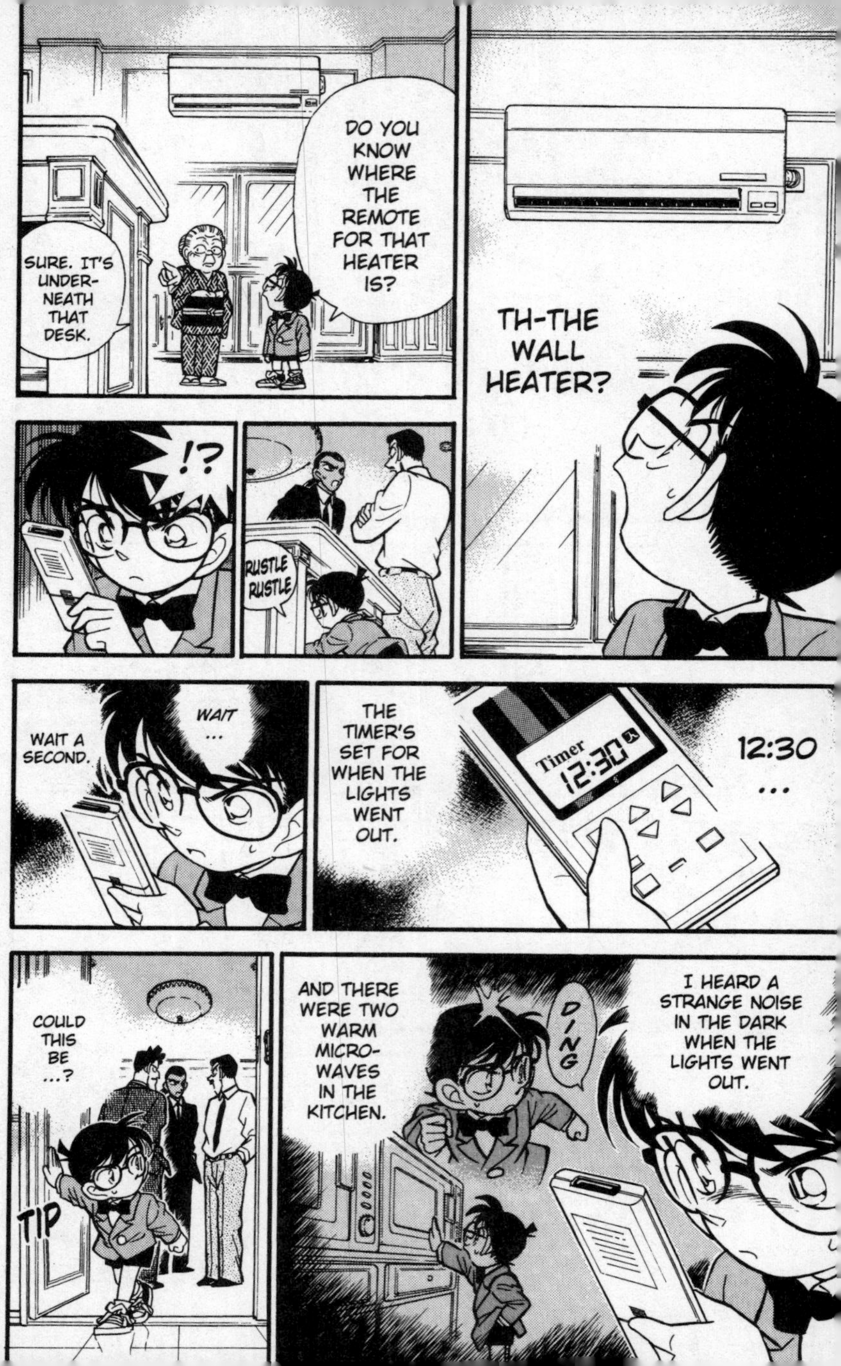
TH-THE WALL HEATER?
DO YOU KNOW WHERE THE REMOTE FOR THAT HEATER IS?
SURE. IT'S UNDER-NEATH THAT DESK.
RUSTLE RUSTLE
!?
12:30 ...
Timer 12:30
THE TIMER'S SET FOR WHEN THE LIGHTS WENT OUT.
WAIT ...
WAIT A SECOND.
I HEARD A STRANGE NOISE IN THE DARK WHEN THE LIGHTS WENT OUT.
DING
AND THERE WERE TWO WARM MICRO-WAVES IN THE KITCHEN.
COULD THIS BE ...?
TIP

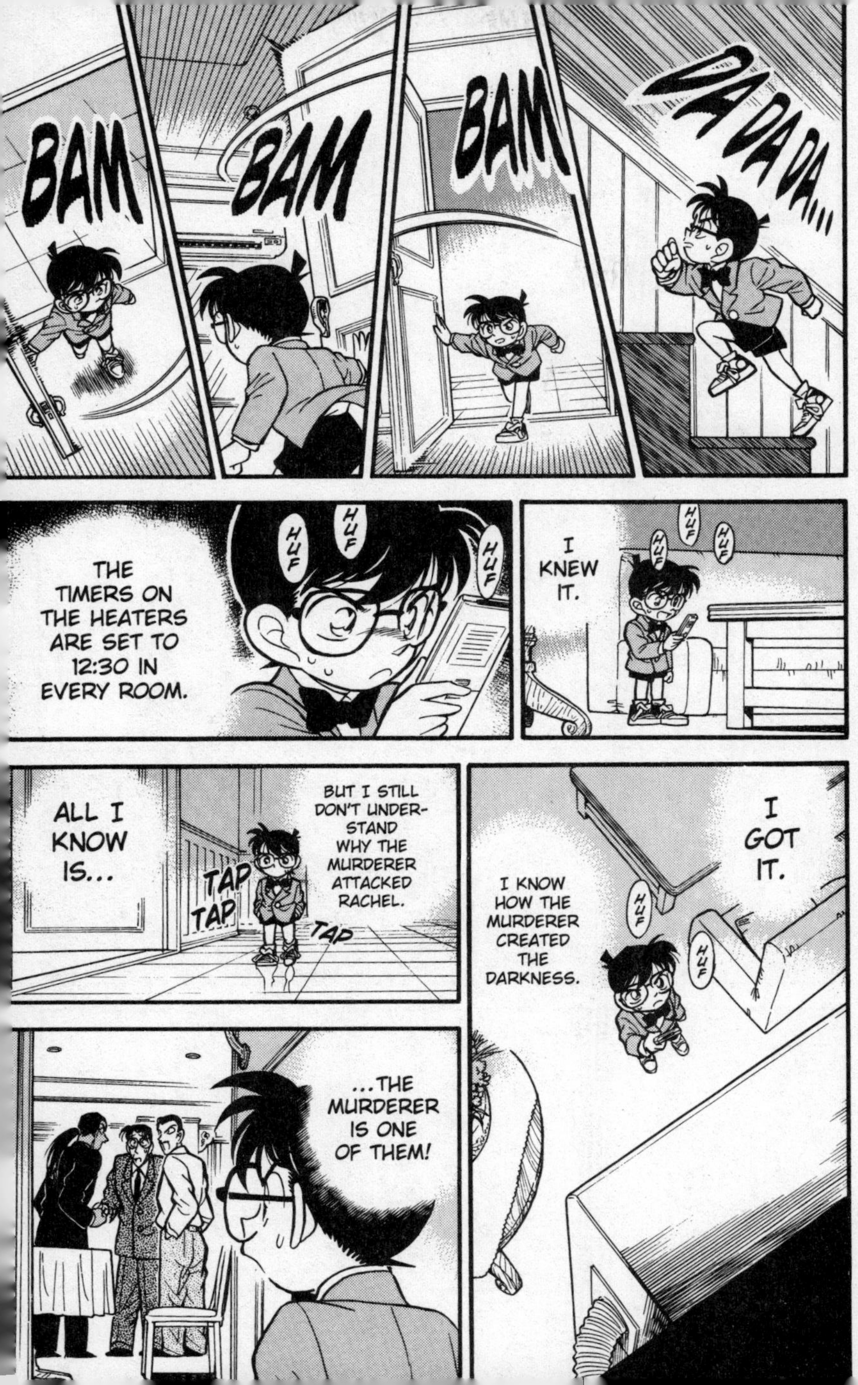
DA DA DA...
BAM
BAM
BAM
HUF
HUF
HUF
I KNEW IT.
HUF
HUF
HUF
THE TIMERS ON THE HEATERS ARE SET TO 12:30 IN EVERY ROOM.
I GOT IT.
I KNOW HOW THE MURDERER CREATED THE DARKNESS.
HUF
HUF
BUT I STILL DON'T UNDER-STAND WHY THE MURDERER ATTACKED RACHEL.
ALL I KNOW IS...
TAP
TAP
TAP
...THE MURDERER IS ONE OF THEM!

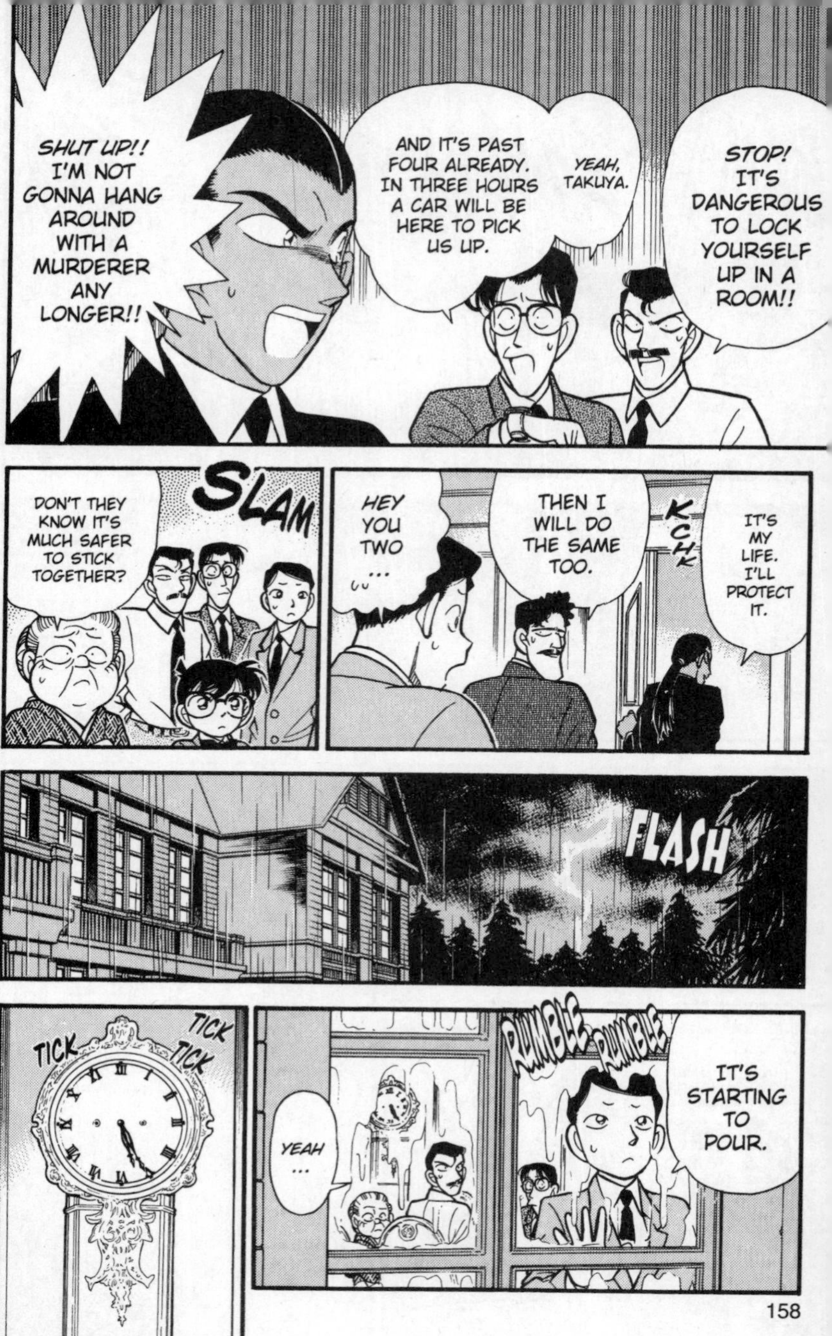
STOP! IT'S DANGEROUS TO LOCK YOURSELF UP IN A ROOM!!
YEAH, TAKUYA.
AND IT'S PAST FOUR ALREADY. IN THREE HOURS A CAR WILL BE HERE TO PICK US UP.
SHUT UP!! I'M NOT GONNA HANG AROUND WITH A MURDERER ANY LONGER!!
IT'S MY LIFE. I'LL PROTECT IT.
KCHK
THEN I WILL DO THE SAME TOO.
HEY YOU TWO ...
SLAM
DON'T THEY KNOW IT'S MUCH SAFER TO STICK TOGETHER?
FLASH
RUMBLE RUMBLE
IT'S STARTING TO POUR.
YEAH ...
TICK TICK
TICK

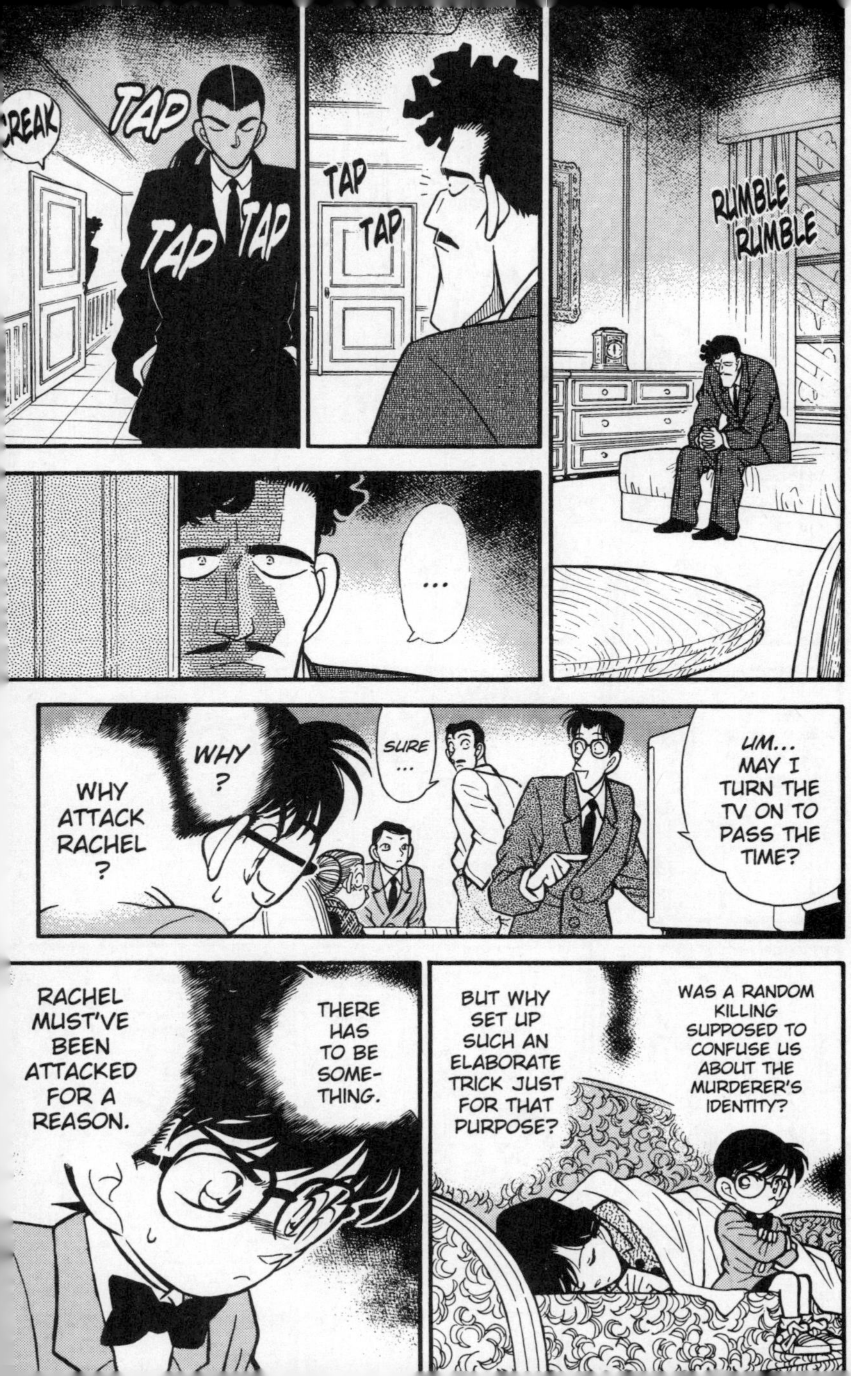
RUMBLE RUMBLE
TAP
TAP
CREAK
TAP
TAP
TAP
...
UM... MAY I TURN THE TV ON TO PASS THE TIME?
SURE...
WHY?
WHY ATTACK RACHEL?
WAS A RANDOM KILLING SUPPOSED TO CONFUSE US ABOUT THE MURDERER'S IDENTITY?
BUT WHY SET UP SUCH AN ELABORATE TRICK JUST FOR THAT PURPOSE?
THERE HAS TO BE SOME-THING.
RACHEL MUST'VE BEEN ATTACKED FOR A REASON.

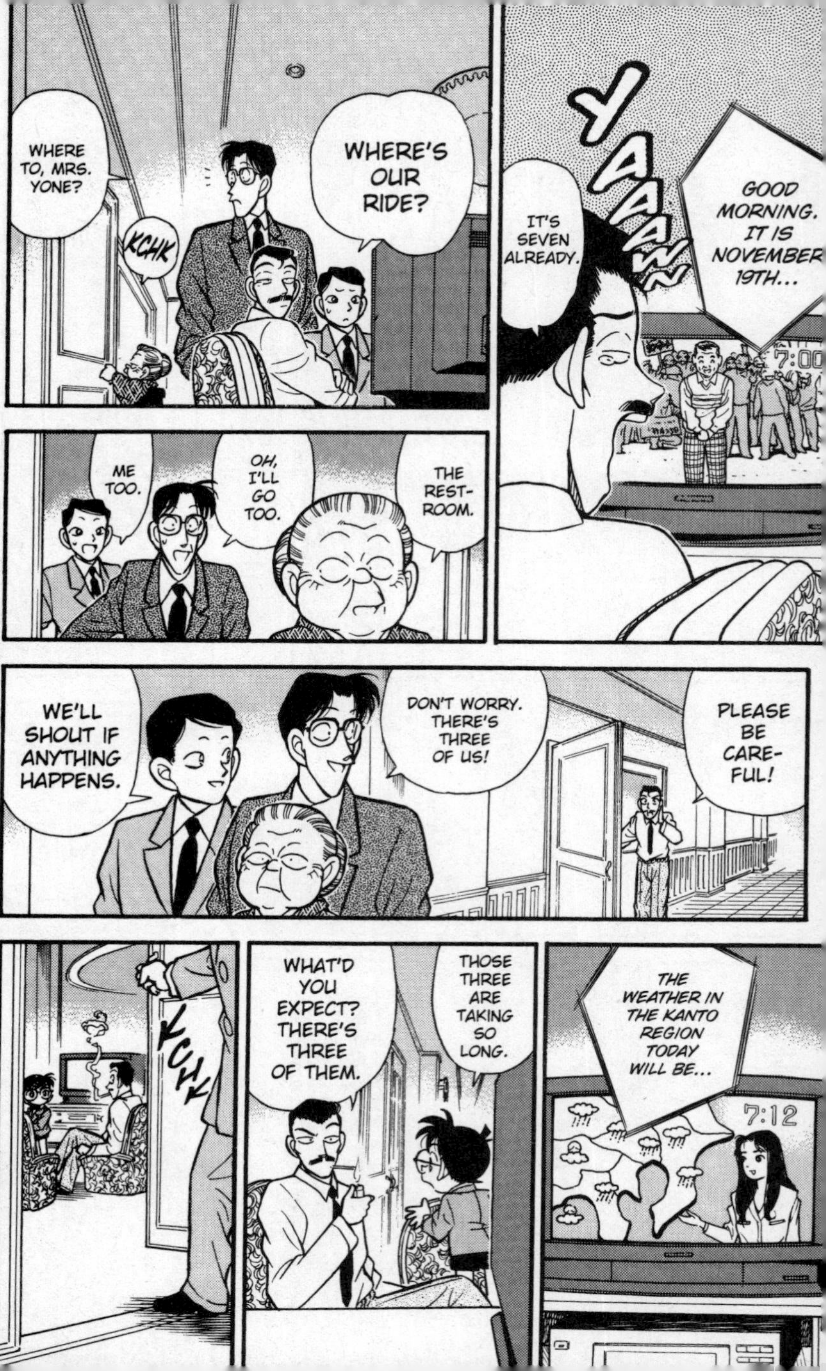
YAAAWN
GOOD MORNING. IT IS NOVEMBER 19TH...
IT'S SEVEN ALREADY.
WHERE'S OUR RIDE?
KCHK
WHERE TO, MRS. YONE?
THE REST-ROOM.
OH, I'LL GO TOO.
ME TOO.
PLEASE BE CARE-FUL!
DON'T WORRY. THERE'S THREE OF US!
WE'LL SHOUT IF ANYTHING HAPPENS.
THE WEATHER IN THE KANTO REGION TODAY WILL BE...
7:12
THOSE THREE ARE TAKING SO LONG.
WHAT'D YOU EXPECT? THERE'S THREE OF THEM.
KCHK

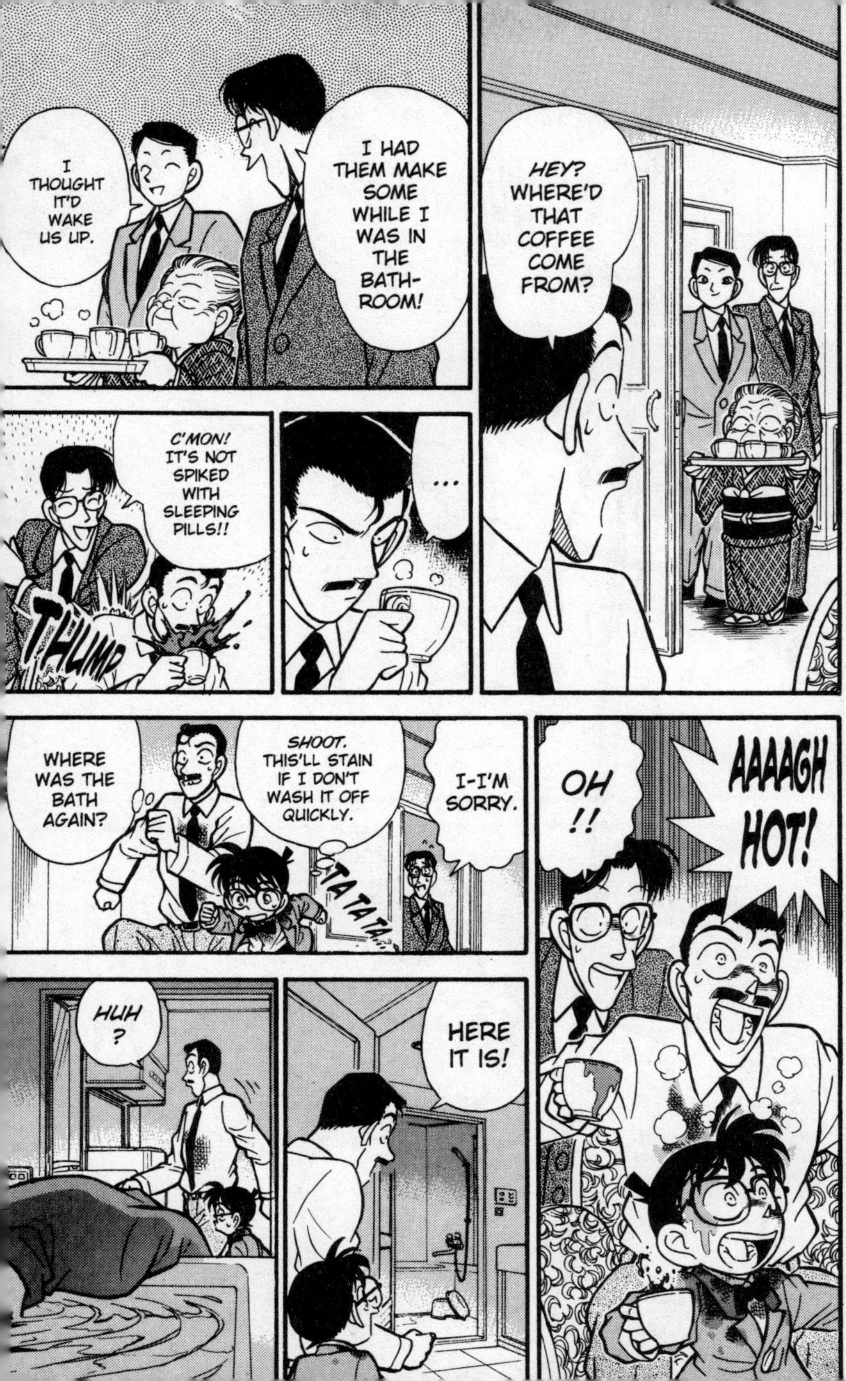
HEY? WHERE'D THAT COFFEE COME FROM?
I HAD THEM MAKE SOME WHILE I WAS IN THE BATH-ROOM!
I THOUGHT IT'D WAKE US UP.
...
C'MON! IT'S NOT SPIKED WITH SLEEPING PILLS!!
THUMP
AAAAGH HOT!
OH !!
I-I'M SORRY.
SHOOT. THIS'LL STAIN IF I DON'T WASH IT OFF QUICKLY.
WHERE WAS THE BATH AGAIN?
TA TA TA
HERE IT IS!
HUH ?

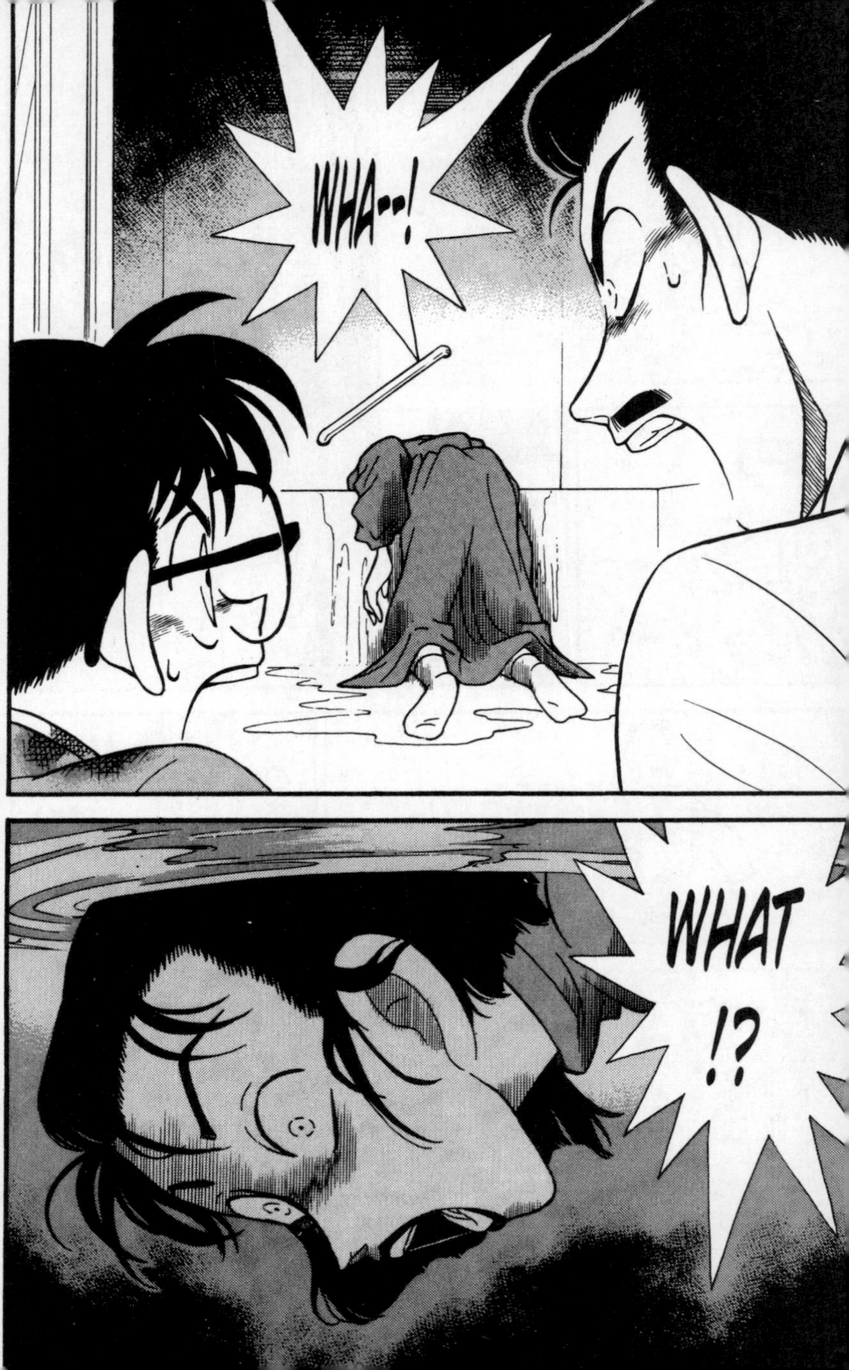
WHA--!
WHAT !?

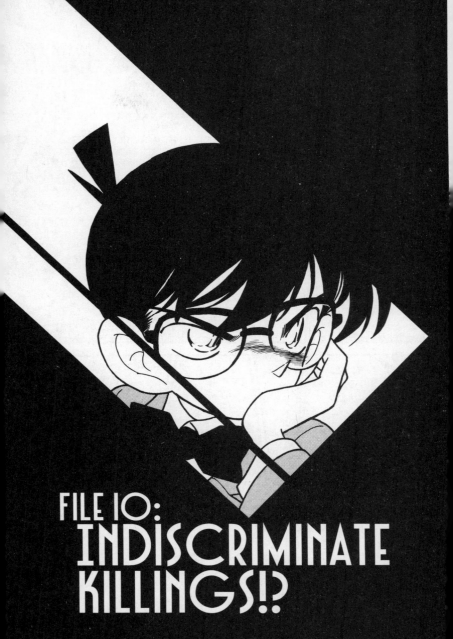

FILE 10:
INDISCRIMINATE
KILLINGS!?

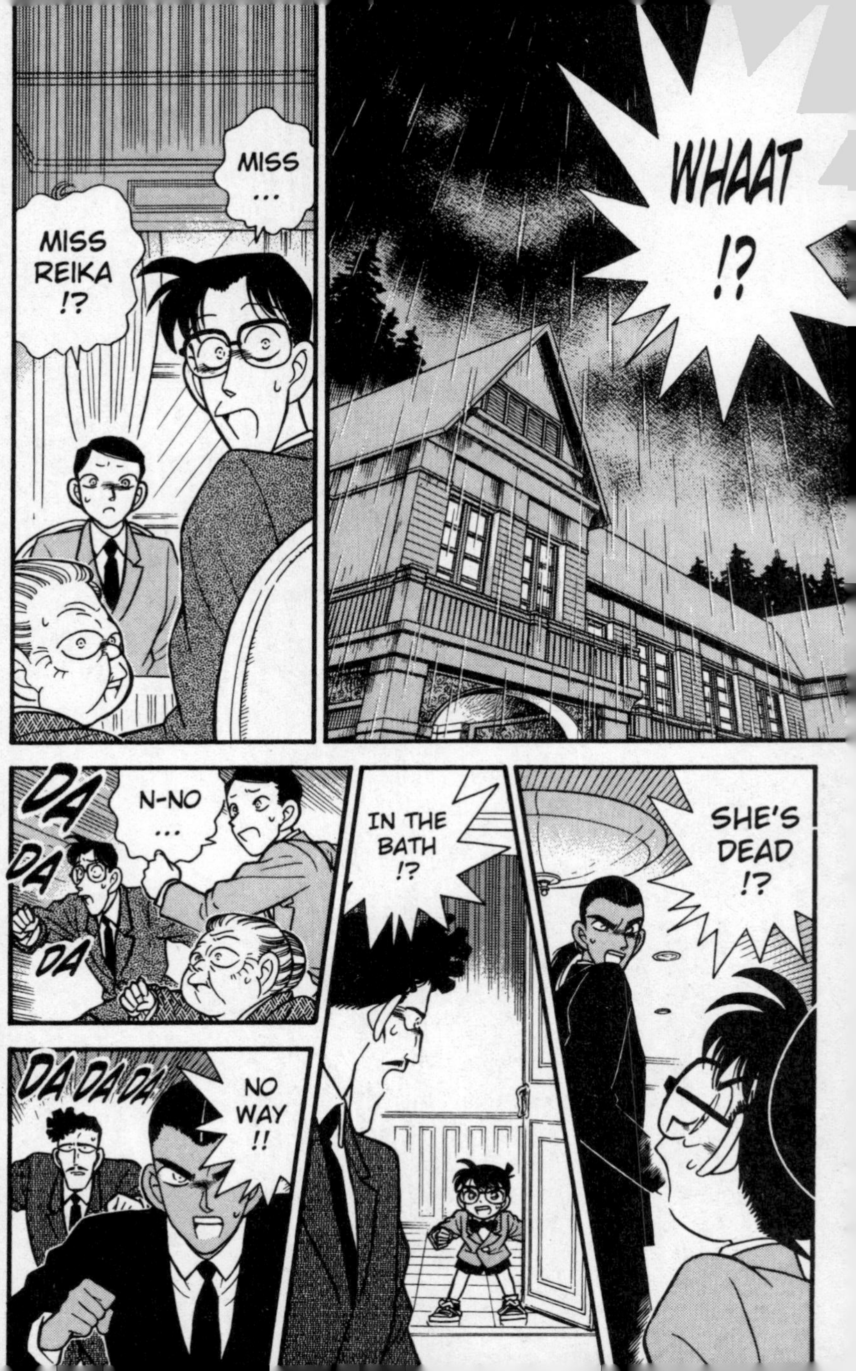
WHAAT !?
MISS ...
MISS REIKA !?
SHE'S DEAD !?
IN THE BATH !?
N-NO ...
DA DA DA
NO WAY !!
DA DA DA

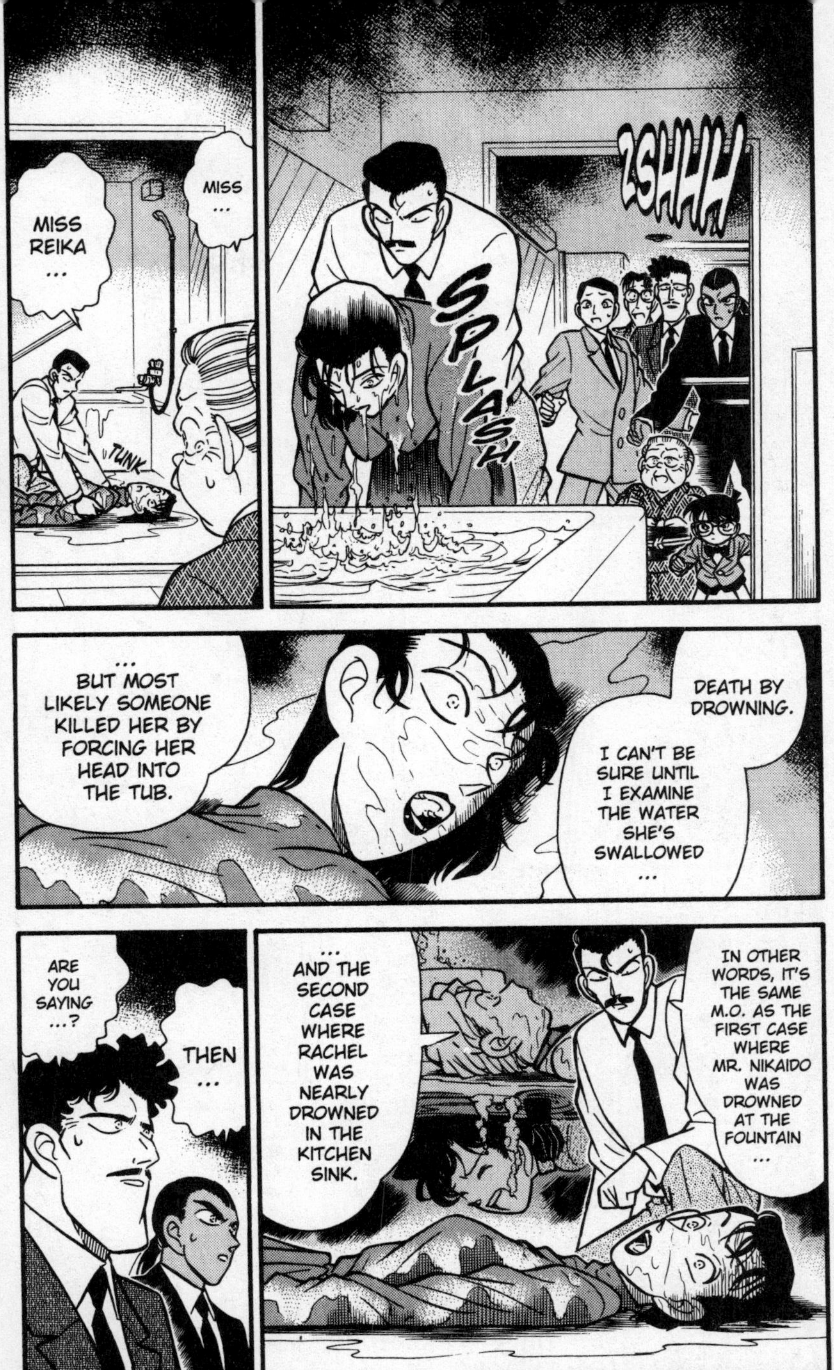
ZSHHH
SPLASH
MISS ...
MISS REIKA ...
TUNK
DEATH BY DROWNING.
I CAN'T BE SURE UNTIL I EXAMINE THE WATER SHE'S SWALLOWED ...
... BUT MOST LIKELY SOMEONE KILLED HER BY FORCING HER HEAD INTO THE TUB.
IN OTHER WORDS, IT'S THE SAME M.O. AS THE FIRST CASE WHERE MR. NIKAIDO WAS DROWNED AT THE FOUNTAIN ...
... AND THE SECOND CASE WHERE RACHEL WAS NEARLY DROWNED IN THE KITCHEN SINK.
THEN ...
ARE YOU SAYING ...?

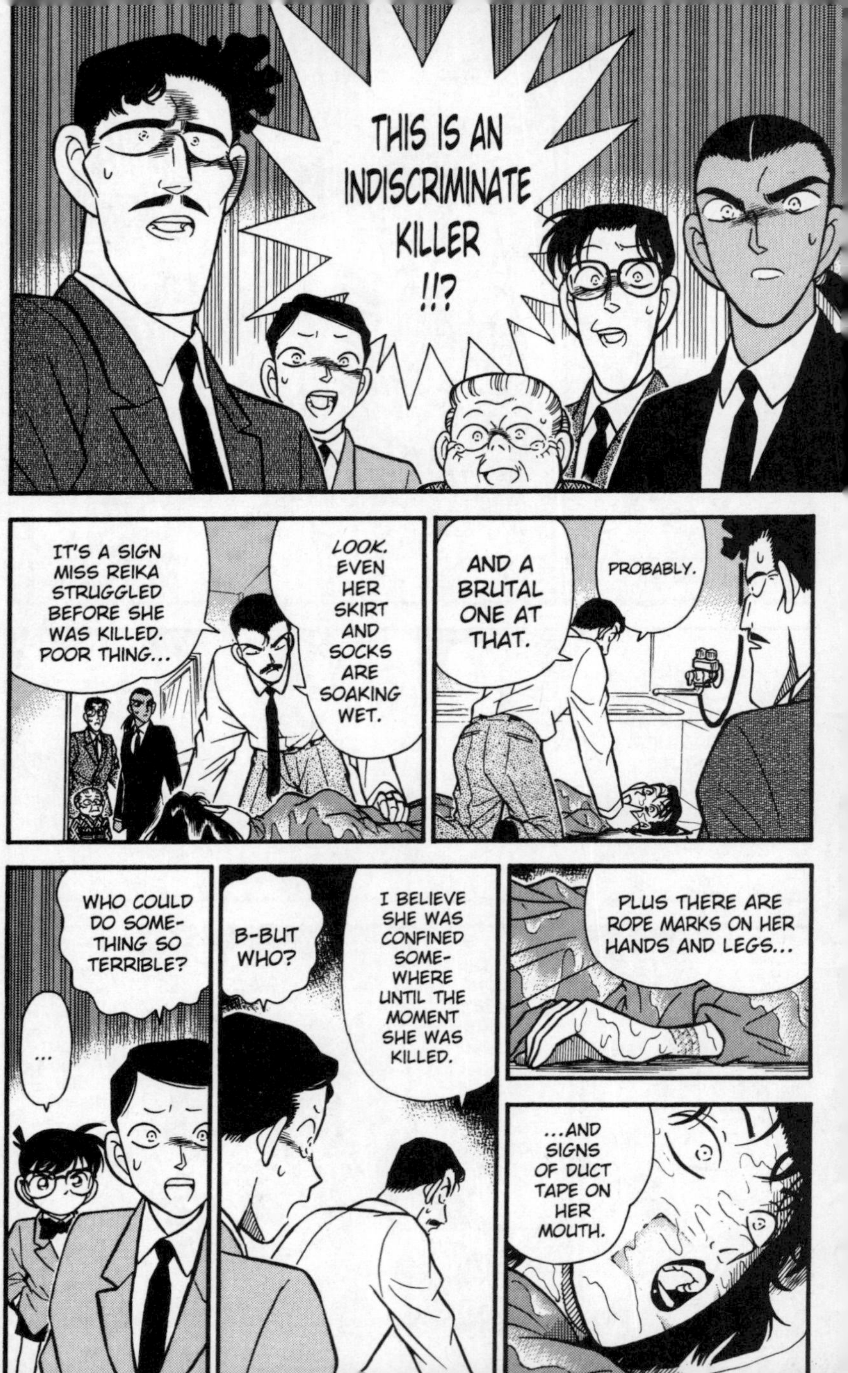
THIS IS AN INDISCRIMINATE KILLER !!?
PROBABLY.
AND A BRUTAL ONE AT THAT.
LOOK. EVEN HER SKIRT AND SOCKS ARE SOAKING WET.
IT'S A SIGN MISS REIKA STRUGGLED BEFORE SHE WAS KILLED. POOR THING...
PLUS THERE ARE ROPE MARKS ON HER HANDS AND LEGS...
...AND SIGNS OF DUCT TAPE ON HER MOUTH.
I BELIEVE SHE WAS CONFINED SOME-WHERE UNTIL THE MOMENT SHE WAS KILLED.
B-BUT WHO?
WHO COULD DO SOME-THING SO TERRIBLE?
...

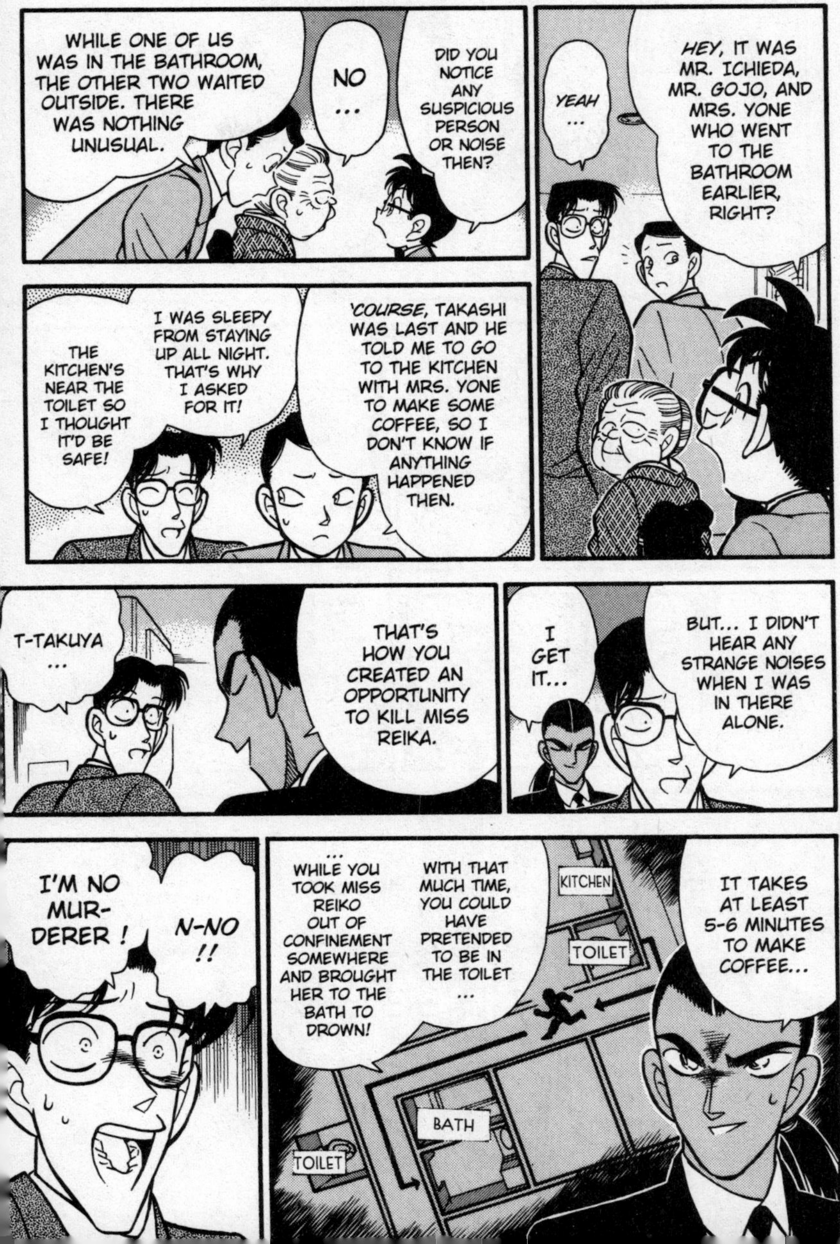
HEY, IT WAS MR. ICHIEDA, MR. GOJO, AND MRS. YONE WHO WENT TO THE BATHROOM EARLIER, RIGHT?
YEAH ...
DID YOU NOTICE ANY SUSPICIOUS PERSON OR NOISE THEN?
NO ...
WHILE ONE OF US WAS IN THE BATHROOM, THE OTHER TWO WAITED OUTSIDE. THERE WAS NOTHING UNUSUAL.
'COURSE, TAKASHI WAS LAST AND HE TOLD ME TO GO TO THE KITCHEN WITH MRS. YONE TO MAKE SOME COFFEE, SO I DON'T KNOW IF ANYTHING HAPPENED THEN.
I WAS SLEEPY FROM STAYING UP ALL NIGHT. THAT'S WHY I ASKED FOR IT!
THE KITCHEN'S NEAR THE TOILET SO I THOUGHT IT'D BE SAFE!
BUT... I DIDN'T HEAR ANY STRANGE NOISES WHEN I WAS IN THERE ALONE.
I GET IT...
THAT'S HOW YOU CREATED AN OPPORTUNITY TO KILL MISS REIKA.
T-TAKUYA ...
IT TAKES AT LEAST 5-6 MINUTES TO MAKE COFFEE...
KITCHEN
TOILET
WITH THAT MUCH TIME, YOU COULD HAVE PRETENDED TO BE IN THE TOILET ...
... WHILE YOU TOOK MISS REIKO OUT OF CONFINEMENT SOMEWHERE AND BROUGHT HER TO THE BATH TO DROWN!
BATH
TOILET
N-NO !!
I'M NO MUR-DERER !

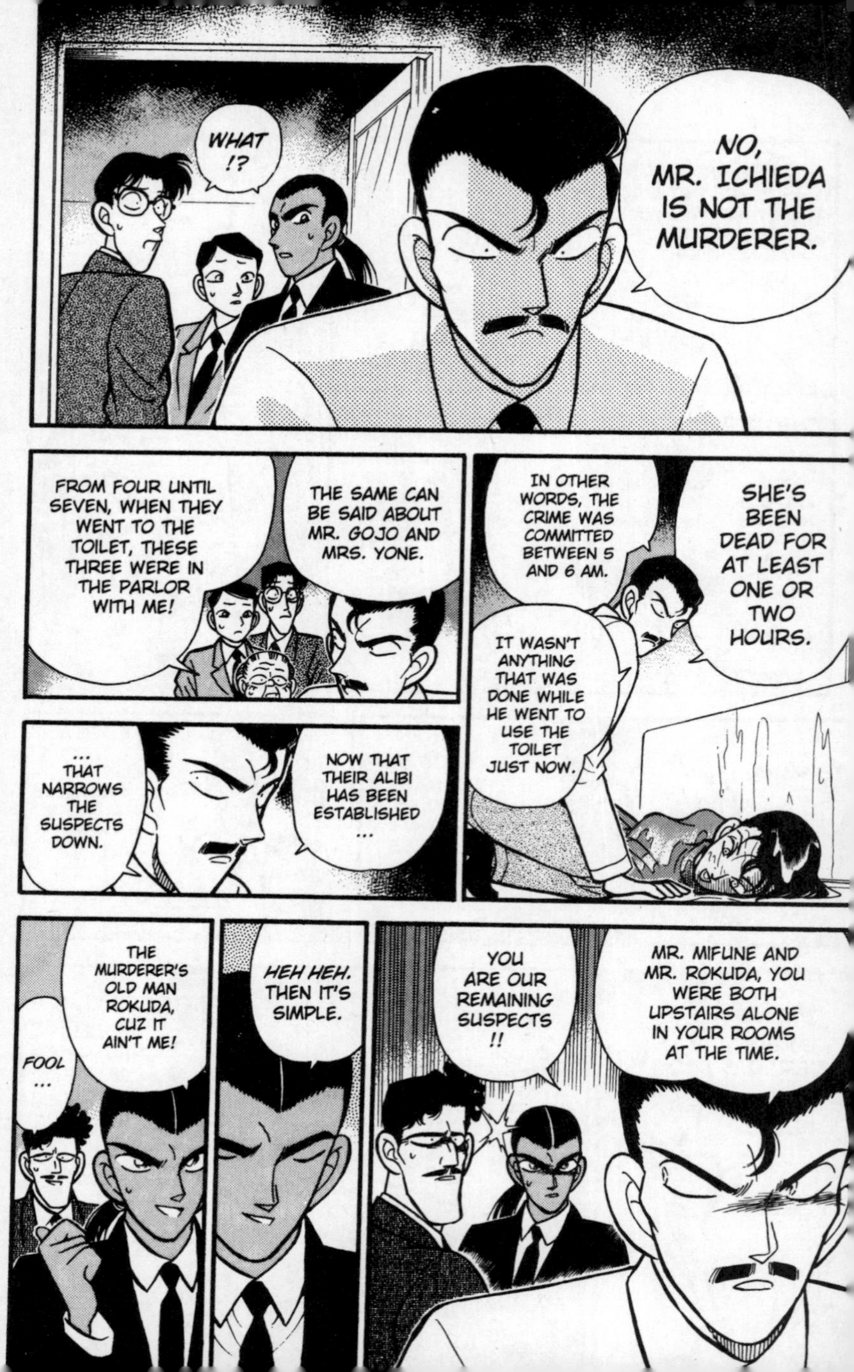
NO, MR. ICHIEDA IS NOT THE MURDERER.
WHAT !?
SHE'S BEEN DEAD FOR AT LEAST ONE OR TWO HOURS.
IN OTHER WORDS, THE CRIME WAS COMMITTED BETWEEN 5 AND 6 AM.
IT WASN'T ANYTHING THAT WAS DONE WHILE HE WENT TO USE THE TOILET JUST NOW.
THE SAME CAN BE SAID ABOUT MR. GOJO AND MRS. YONE.
FROM FOUR UNTIL SEVEN, WHEN THEY WENT TO THE TOILET, THESE THREE WERE IN THE PARLOR WITH ME!
NOW THAT THEIR ALIBI HAS BEEN ESTABLISHED ...
... THAT NARROWS THE SUSPECTS DOWN.
MR. MIFUNE AND MR. ROKUDA, YOU WERE BOTH UPSTAIRS ALONE IN YOUR ROOMS AT THE TIME.
YOU ARE OUR REMAINING SUSPECTS !!
HEH HEH. THEN IT'S SIMPLE.
THE MURDERER'S OLD MAN ROKUDA, CUZ IT AIN'T ME!
FOOL ...

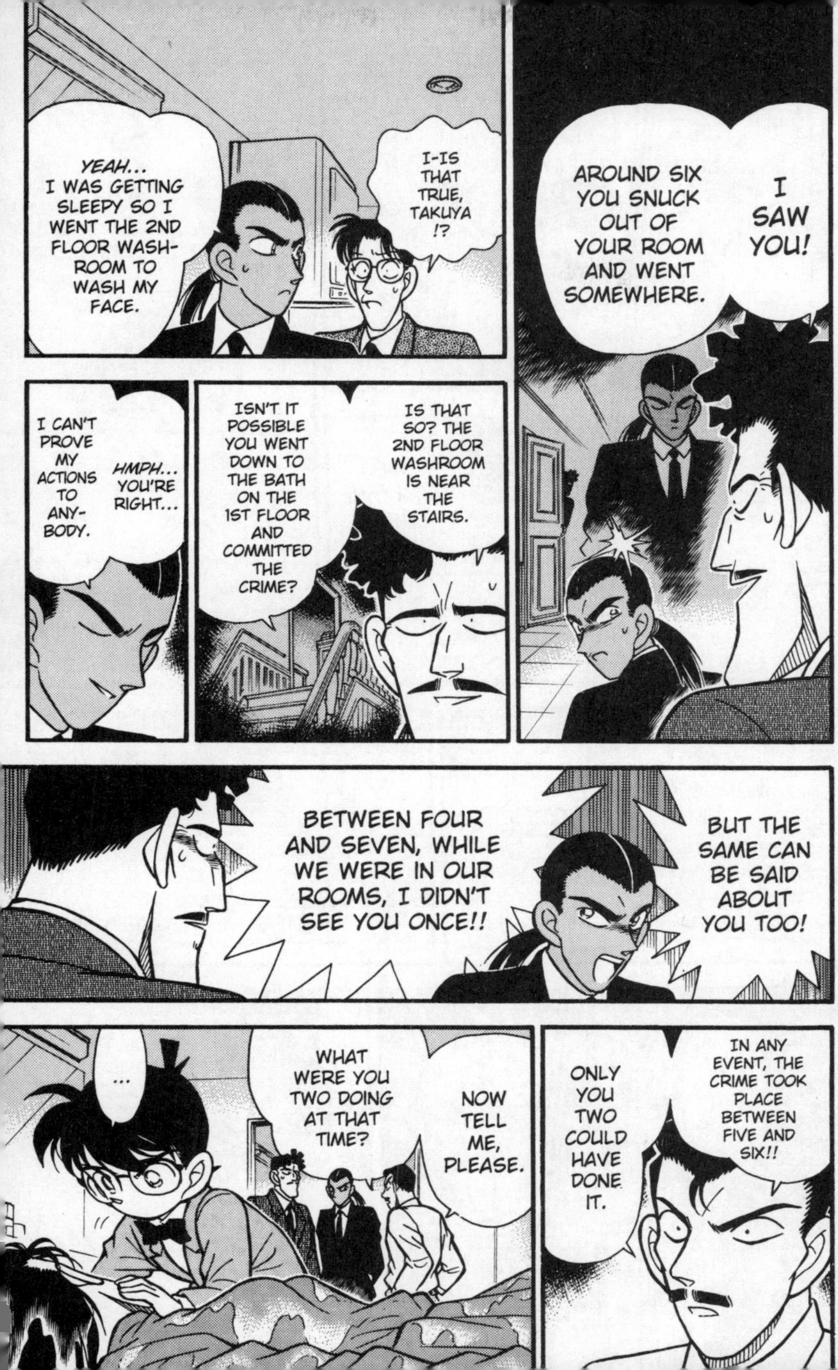
I SAW YOU!
AROUND SIX YOU SNUCK OUT OF YOUR ROOM AND WENT SOMEWHERE.
I-IS THAT TRUE, TAKUYA!?
YEAH... I WAS GETTING SLEEPY SO I WENT THE 2ND FLOOR WASH-ROOM TO WASH MY FACE.
IS THAT SO? THE 2ND FLOOR WASHROOM IS NEAR THE STAIRS.
ISN'T IT POSSIBLE YOU WENT DOWN TO THE BATH ON THE 1ST FLOOR AND COMMITTED THE CRIME?
HMPH... YOU'RE RIGHT...
I CAN'T PROVE MY ACTIONS TO ANY-BODY.
BUT THE SAME CAN BE SAID ABOUT YOU TOO!
BETWEEN FOUR AND SEVEN, WHILE WE WERE IN OUR ROOMS, I DIDN'T SEE YOU ONCE!!
IN ANY EVENT, THE CRIME TOOK PLACE BETWEEN FIVE AND SIX!!
ONLY YOU TWO COULD HAVE DONE IT.
NOW TELL ME, PLEASE.
WHAT WERE YOU TWO DOING AT THAT TIME?
...

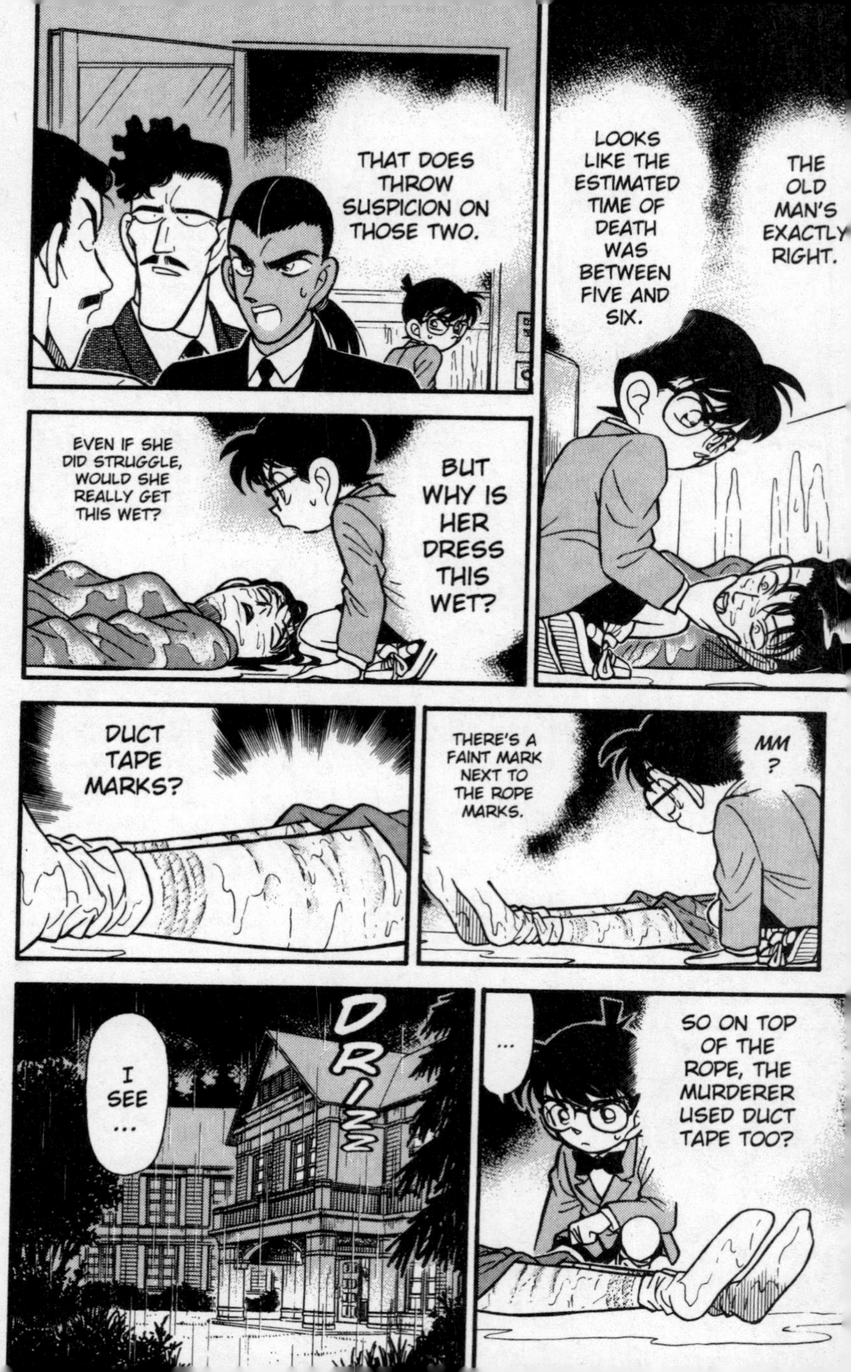
THE OLD MAN'S EXACTLY RIGHT.
LOOKS LIKE THE ESTIMATED TIME OF DEATH WAS BETWEEN FIVE AND SIX.
THAT DOES THROW SUSPICION ON THOSE TWO.
BUT WHY IS HER DRESS THIS WET?
EVEN IF SHE DID STRUGGLE, WOULD SHE REALLY GET THIS WET?
MM ?
THERE'S A FAINT MARK NEXT TO THE ROPE MARKS.
DUCT TAPE MARKS?
...
SO ON TOP OF THE ROPE, THE MURDERER USED DUCT TAPE TOO?
DRIZZ
I SEE ...

... | YEAH THAT'S RIGHT! | AND THE ONLY TIME YOU LEFT THE ROOM WAS TO WASH YOUR FACE, MR. MIFUNE...?

NO ... | THEN YOU DID NOT SET FOOT OUT OF YOUR ROOM BETWEEN FOUR AND SEVEN?

WE LOOKED EVERY-WHERE, BUT COULDN'T FIND HER. | ISN'T IT STRANGE!?

HUH? | BUT... WHERE WAS MISS REIKA CONFINED?

NO. THE TUB WAS EMPTY TOO. | WE SEARCHED FOR MISS REIKA AROUND TEN. WE WERE THE ONES TO SEARCH THE BATH AREA. YOU DIDN'T SEE ANYTHING, DID YOU?

NOT THE FOREST. IF IT WAS OUTSIDE, THERE WOULD HAVE BEEN A BETTER PLACE TO HIDE HER.

THEN WAS SHE OUTSIDE THE HOUSE... IN THE FOREST!? | BUT WE LOOKED ALL OVER.

NO. THERE'S A CHANCE SHE WAS TIED UP AND ASLEEP FROM THE PILLS. | AND MISS REIKA WAS STILL ALIVE THEN. WOULDN'T SHE HAVE MADE SOME NOISE IF WE WERE LOOKING CLOSE BY?

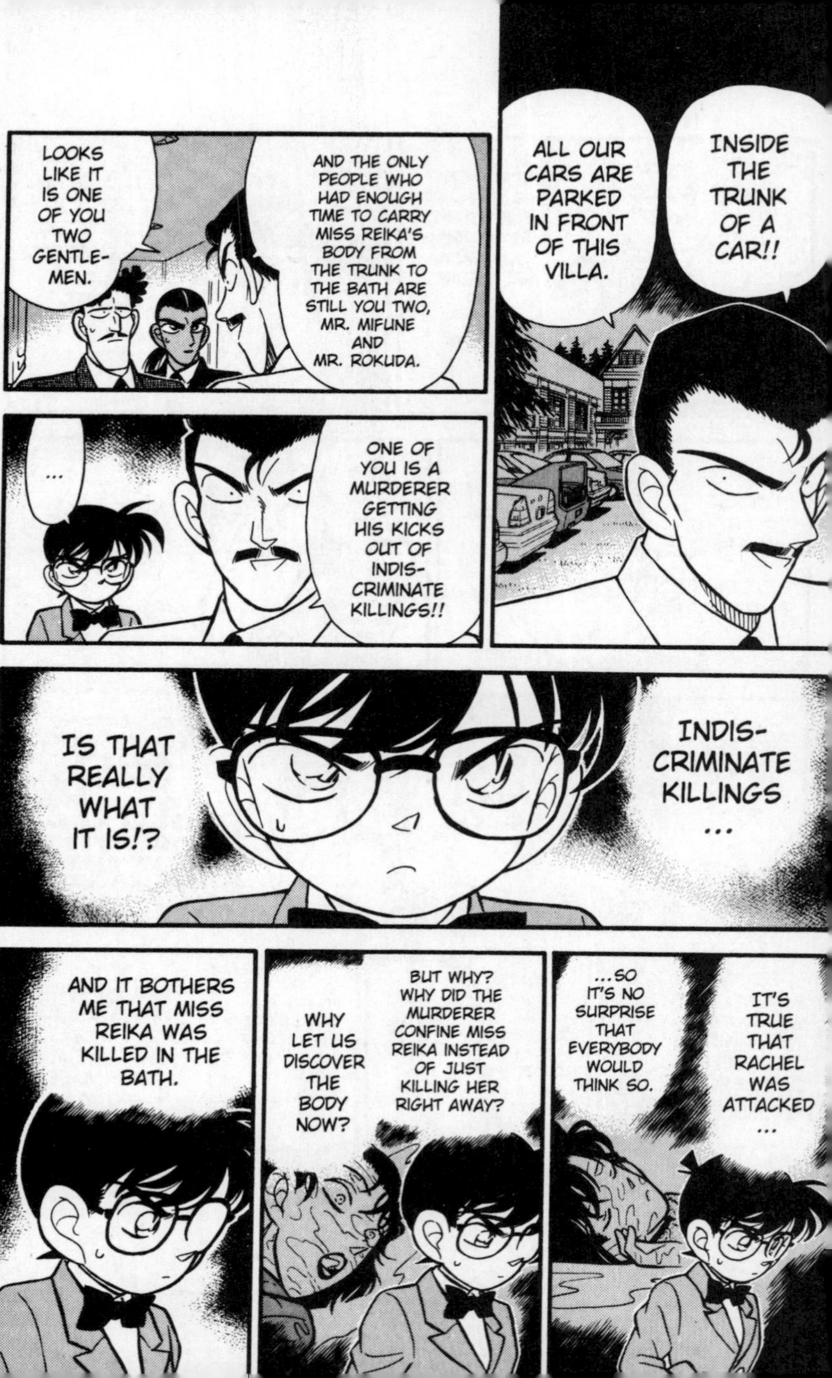
INSIDE THE TRUNK OF A CAR!!
ALL OUR CARS ARE PARKED IN FRONT OF THIS VILLA.
AND THE ONLY PEOPLE WHO HAD ENOUGH TIME TO CARRY MISS REIKA'S BODY FROM THE TRUNK TO THE BATH ARE STILL YOU TWO, MR. MIFUNE AND MR. ROKUDA.
LOOKS LIKE IT IS ONE OF YOU TWO GENTLE-MEN.
ONE OF YOU IS A MURDERER GETTING HIS KICKS OUT OF INDIS-CRIMINATE KILLINGS!!
...
INDIS-CRIMINATE KILLINGS ...
IS THAT REALLY WHAT IT IS!?
IT'S TRUE THAT RACHEL WAS ATTACKED ...
...SO IT'S NO SURPRISE THAT EVERYBODY WOULD THINK SO.
BUT WHY? WHY DID THE MURDERER CONFINE MISS REIKA INSTEAD OF JUST KILLING HER RIGHT AWAY?
WHY LET US DISCOVER THE BODY NOW?
AND IT BOTHERS ME THAT MISS REIKA WAS KILLED IN THE BATH.

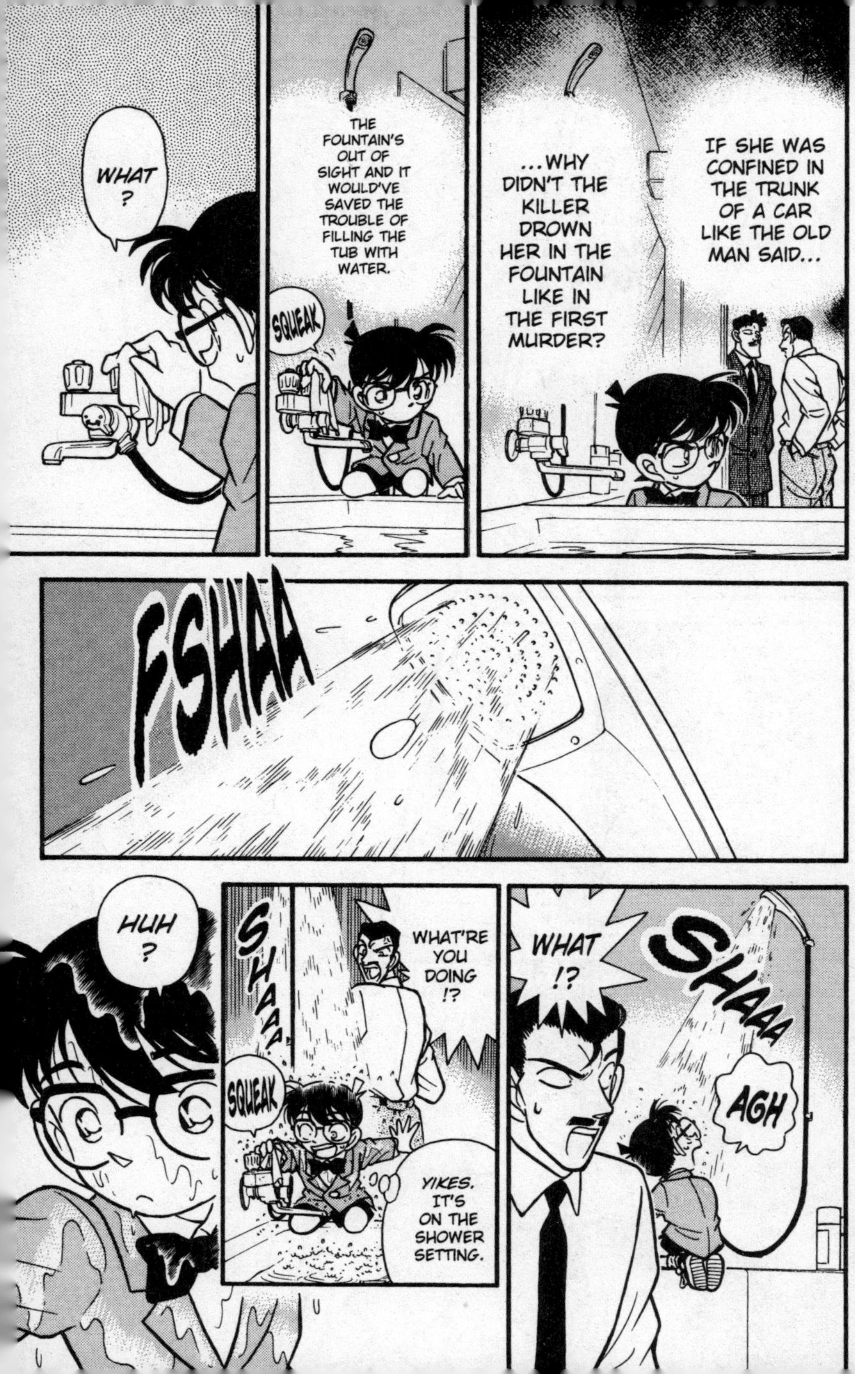
IF SHE WAS CONFINED IN THE TRUNK OF A CAR LIKE THE OLD MAN SAID...
...WHY DIDN'T THE KILLER DROWN HER IN THE FOUNTAIN LIKE IN THE FIRST MURDER?
THE FOUNTAIN'S OUT OF SIGHT AND IT WOULD'VE SAVED THE TROUBLE OF FILLING THE TUB WITH WATER.
SQUEAK
WHAT?
FSHAA
SHAAA
WHAT!?
AGH
WHAT'RE YOU DOING!?
SHAAA
SQUEAK
YIKES. IT'S ON THE SHOWER SETTING.
HUH?

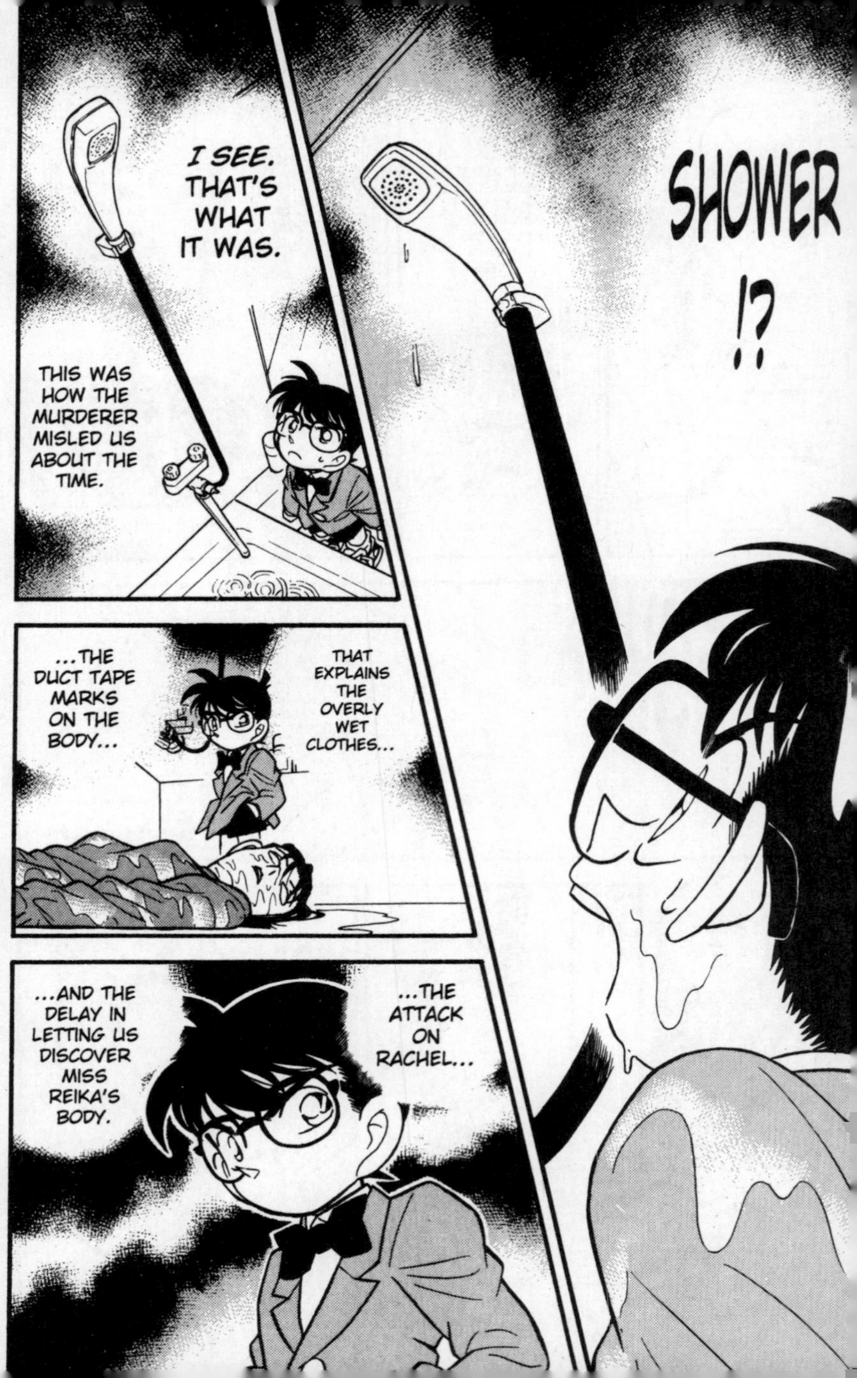
SHOWER !?
I SEE. THAT'S WHAT IT WAS.
THIS WAS HOW THE MURDERER MISLED US ABOUT THE TIME.
THAT EXPLAINS THE OVERLY WET CLOTHES...
...THE DUCT TAPE MARKS ON THE BODY...
...THE ATTACK ON RACHEL...
...AND THE DELAY IN LETTING US DISCOVER MISS REIKA'S BODY.

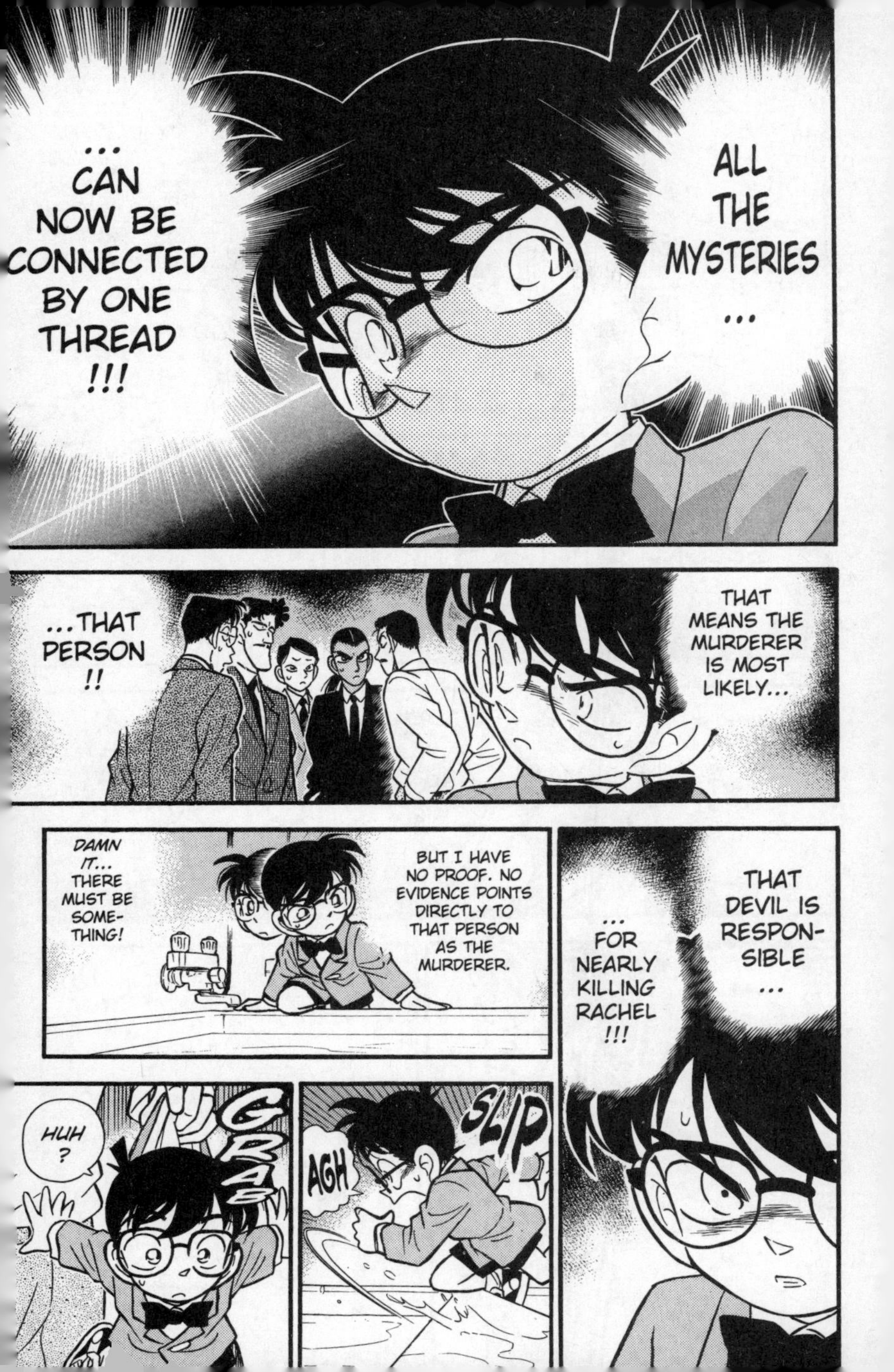
ALL THE MYSTERIES...
...CAN NOW BE CONNECTED BY ONE THREAD!!!
THAT MEANS THE MURDERER IS MOST LIKELY...
...THAT PERSON!!
THAT DEVIL IS RESPONSIBLE...
...FOR NEARLY KILLING RACHEL!!!
BUT I HAVE NO PROOF. NO EVIDENCE POINTS DIRECTLY TO THAT PERSON AS THE MURDERER.
DAMN IT... THERE MUST BE SOME-THING!
SLIP
AGH
GRAB
HUH?

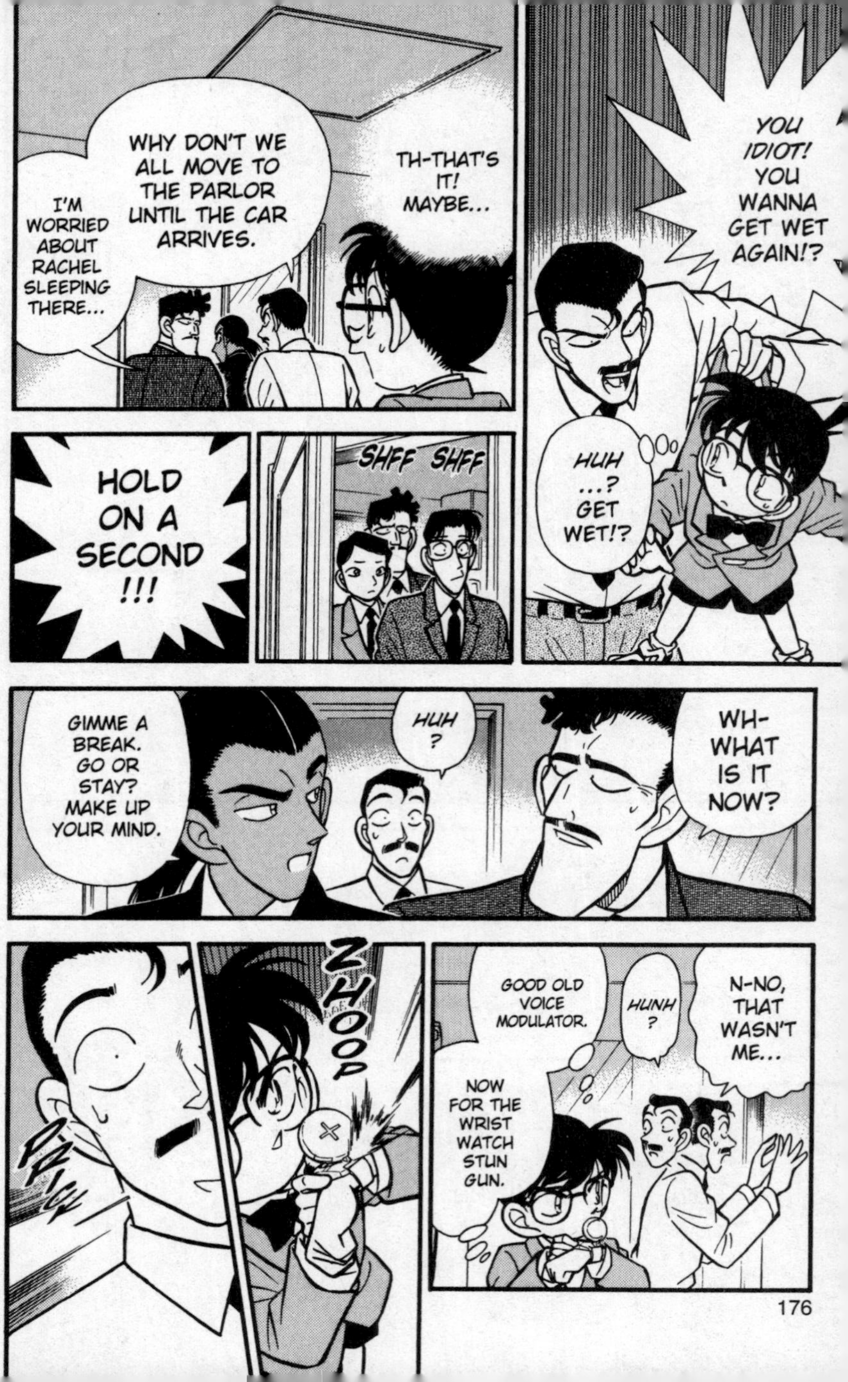
YOU IDIOT! YOU WANNA GET WET AGAIN!?
HUH ...? GET WET!?
TH-THAT'S IT! MAYBE...
WHY DON'T WE ALL MOVE TO THE PARLOR UNTIL THE CAR ARRIVES.
I'M WORRIED ABOUT RACHEL SLEEPING THERE...
SHFF SHFF
HOLD ON A SECOND !!!
WH-WHAT IS IT NOW?
HUH ?
GIMME A BREAK. GO OR STAY? MAKE UP YOUR MIND.
N-NO, THAT WASN'T ME...
HUNH ?
GOOD OLD VOICE MODULATOR.
NOW FOR THE WRIST WATCH STUN GUN.
ZHOOOP
PZICK

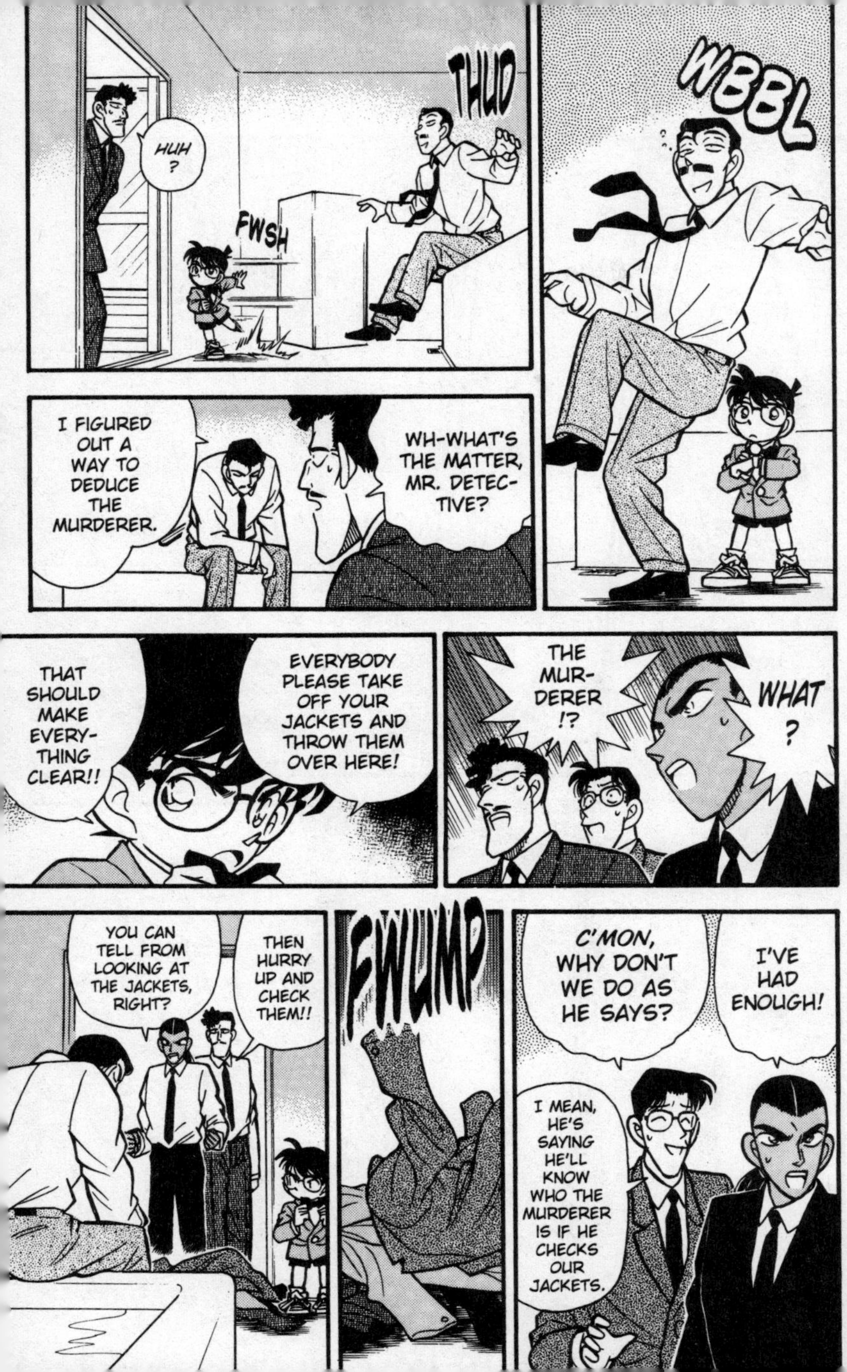
WBBL
THUD
HUH?
FWSH
WH-WHAT'S THE MATTER, MR. DETECTIVE?
I FIGURED OUT A WAY TO DEDUCE THE MURDERER.
WHAT?
THE MURDERER!?
EVERYBODY PLEASE TAKE OFF YOUR JACKETS AND THROW THEM OVER HERE!
THAT SHOULD MAKE EVERYTHING CLEAR!!
I'VE HAD ENOUGH!
C'MON, WHY DON'T WE DO AS HE SAYS?
I MEAN, HE'S SAYING HE'LL KNOW WHO THE MURDERER IS IF HE CHECKS OUR JACKETS.
FWUMP
THEN HURRY UP AND CHECK THEM!!
YOU CAN TELL FROM LOOKING AT THE JACKETS, RIGHT?

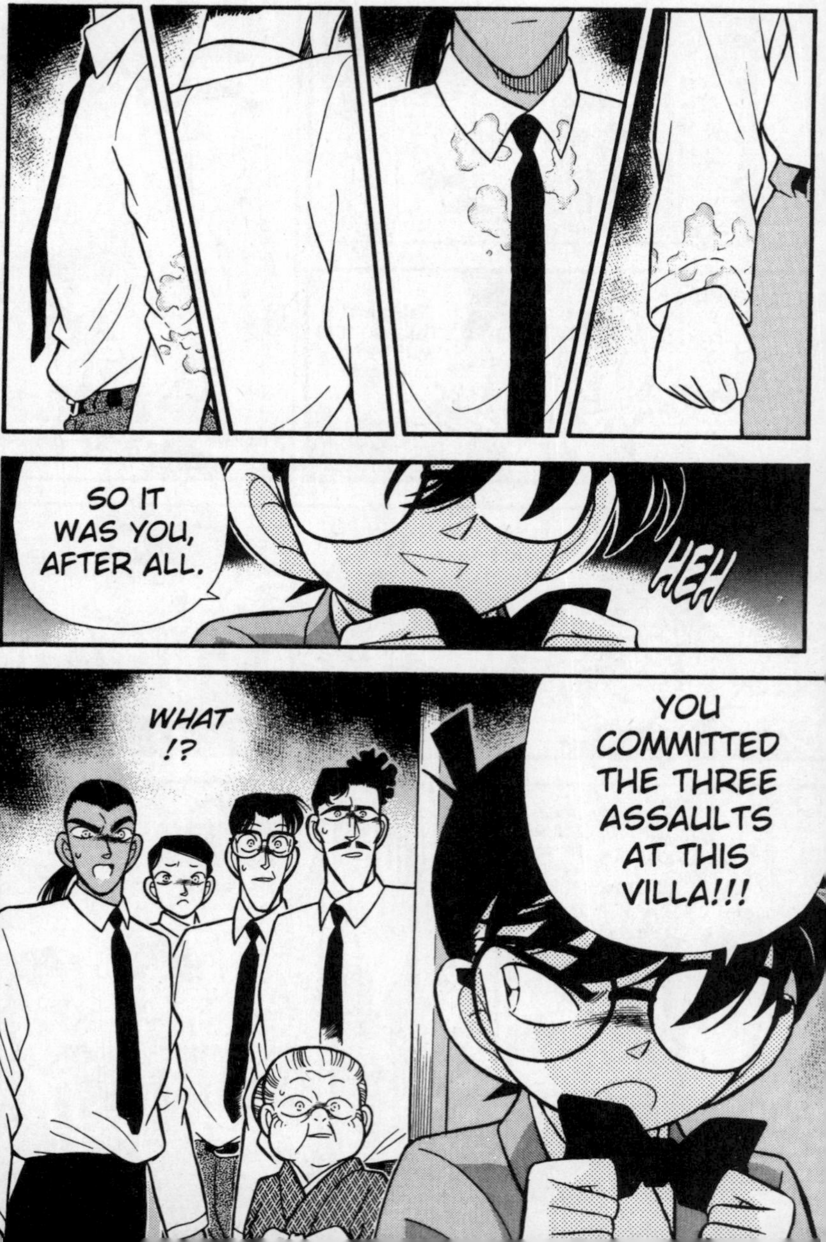
HEH
SO IT WAS YOU, AFTER ALL.
YOU COMMITTED THE THREE ASSAULTS AT THIS VILLA!!!
WHAT !?

Hello, Aoyama here.

The Case Closed anime is finally beginning! Whoa, he's moving! He's talking! A good song's playing! Woo hoo, I can't believe it!! I'd wanted to savor this excitement as I relaxed at a warm kotatsu table, but for some strange reason I have a G-pen in my right hand... (Skritch skritch skritch...)

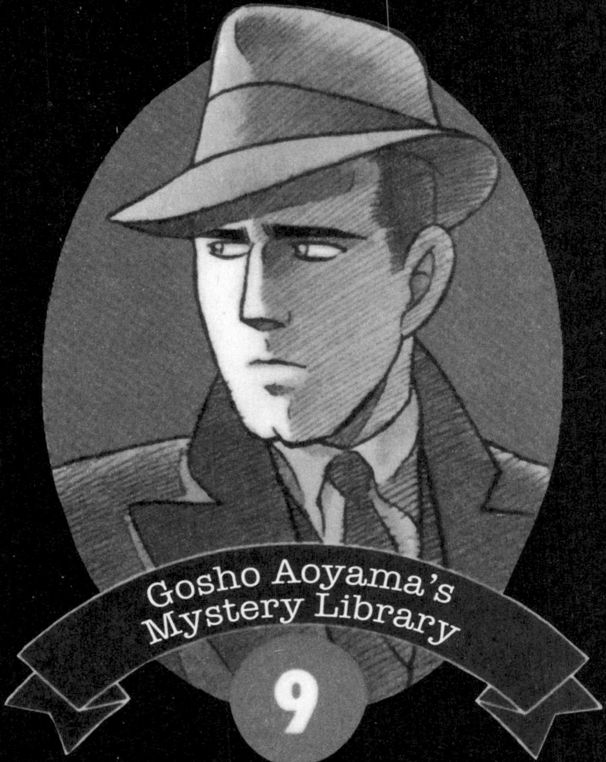
Gosho Aoyama's
Mystery Library
9

PHILIP MARLOWE

"I'm a private detective. It's a piddling hand-to-mouth job, but even I have pride. That's right...If I wasn't hard, I wouldn't be alive. If I wasn't gentle, I wouldn't deserve to be alive." The only man who can truly pull off such a hard-boiled line is Philip Marlowe, the private detective that Raymond Chandler created. A former police officer, he has an office for his detective agency in Hollywood. Fired for disobeying his boss, he boasted, "I test very high on insubordination." He is not the type to compromise on anything. Of course, as a handsome man with dark brown hair and dark brown eyes he has a steady stream of women coming on to him, but he never gets too involved with his clients. That's a point of pride for him as a private detective! He's a tough guy making it in a vast city, relying on no one but himself. I could never do that...(I recommend *The Long Goodbye*.)

EDITOR'S RECOMMENDATIONS

If you enjoyed this volume of **Case Closed** then here's some more manga you might be interested in:

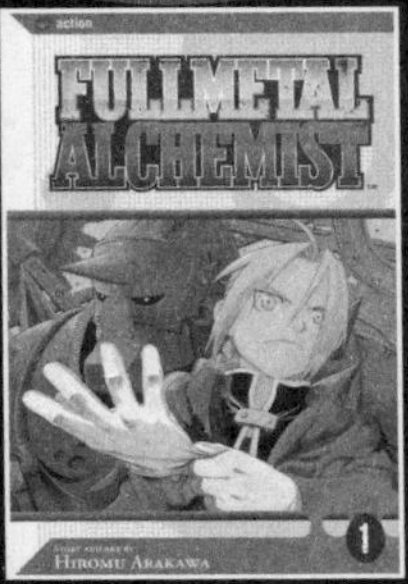
action
FULLMETAL ALCHEMIST
1
HIROMU ARAKAWA

Fullmetal Alchemist
Trapped in a world of magic, art and science, two brothers battle evil using the mysterious power of alchemy. You've seen the phenomenally popular TV show, now read the manga by Hiromu Arakawa.

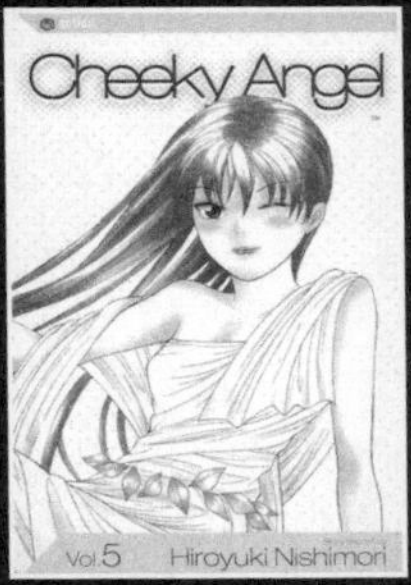
Cheeky Angel
Vol.5
Hiroyuki Nishimori

Cheeky Angel
Poor Megumi. One day he's the toughest guy in town, and the next day he's the most beautiful girl in school. Gender-bending comedy from the poison pen of Hiroyuki Nishimori.

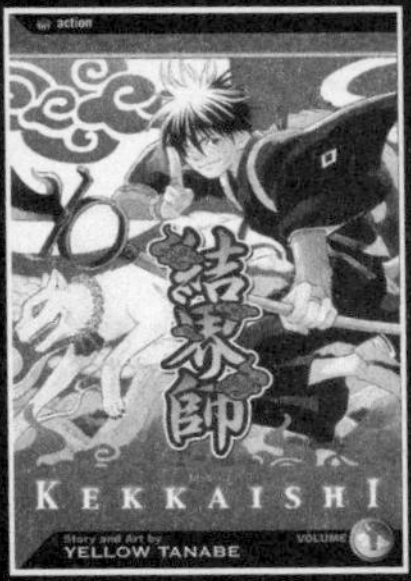
action
結界師
KEKKAISHI
Story and Art by
YELLOW TANABE
VOLUME 1

Kekkaishi
Fighting demons and baking pastries—it's all part of young Yoshimori's daily routine. And, oh yeah, there's a cute girl living next door. Ain't life grand? Creator Yellow Tanabe has created a wild mix of comedy and supernatural high jinks. Highly recommended!

Kidnapped by the Demon King and imprisoned in his castle, Princess Syalis is...bored.

SLEEPY PRINCESS IN THE DEMON CASTLE

Story & Art by
KAGIJI KUMANOMATA

Captured princess Syalis decides to while away her hours in the Demon Castle by sleeping, but getting a good night's rest turns out to be a lot of work! She begins by fashioning a DIY pillow out of the fur of her Teddy Demon guards and an "air mattress" from the magical Shield of the Wind. Things go from bad to worse—for her captors—when some of Princess Syalis's schemes end in her untimely—if temporary—demise and she chooses the Forbidden Grimoire for her bedtime reading...

Komi Can't Communicate

Story & Art by Tomohito Oda

The journey to a hundred friends begins with a single conversation.

Socially anxious high school student Shoko Komi's greatest dream is to make some friends, but everyone at school mistakes her crippling social anxiety for cool reserve. With the whole student body keeping its distance and Komi unable to utter a single word, friendship might be forever beyond her reach.

Reading in the Wrong Direction!

This is the **end** of this graphic novel!

To properly enjoy this VIZ graphic novel, please turn it around and begin reading from **right to left.** Unlike English, Japanese is read right to left, so Japanese comics are read in reverse order from the way English comics are typically read.

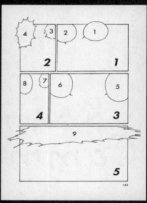

Follow the action this way

This book has been printed in the original Japanese format in order to preserve the orientation of the original artwork. Have fun with it!